# Lexical and Constructional Aspects of Linguistic Explanation

*Studies in Constraint-Based Lexicalism*

*A series edited by*
Andreas Kathol, *University of California, Berkeley*
Jean-Pierre Koenig, *State University of New York at Buffalo*
Sam Mchombo, *University of California, Berkeley*

The aim of this series is to make works in the various grammatical frameworks characterized as constraint-based lexicalism available to those working within the field.

Studies in
Constraint-Based Lexicalism

# Lexical and Constructional Aspects of Linguistic Explanation

edited by
## Gert Webelhuth
## Jean-Pierre Koenig
## Andreas Kathol

CSLI Publications
CENTER FOR THE STUDY OF
LANGUAGE AND INFORMATION
STANFORD, CALIFORNIA

Copyright © 1999
CSLI Publications
Center for the Study of Language and Information
Leland Stanford Junior University
Printed in the United States
03 02 01 00 99      5 4 3 2 1

Library of Congress Cataloging-in-Publication Data

Lexical and constructional aspects of linguistic explanation / edited by Gert
Webelhuth, Jean-Pierre Koenig & Andreas Kathol.
p.   cm.
Includes bibliographical references and index.
ISBN 1-57586-153-4 (hardcover : alk. paper).
ISBN 1-57586-152-6 (pbk. : alk. paper)

1. Head-driven phrase structure grammar. 2. Lexical grammar. 3. Grammar,
Comparative and general—Syntax. 4. Explanation (Linguistics)
I. Webelhuth, Gert. II. Koenig, Jean-Pierre. III. Kathol, Andreas, 1965–   .
P158.4.L49   1999
415—dc21   98-26881
CIP

The California poppies on the cover of the paperback edition of this book
were photographed by Maureen Burke. Cover design by Tony Gee.

∞ The acid-free paper used in this book meets the minimum requirements of
the American National Standard for Information Sciences—Permanence of
Paper for Printed Library Materials, ANSI Z39.48-1984.

CSLI was founded early in 1983 by researchers from Stanford University, SRI
International, and Xerox PARC to further research and development of integrated
theories of language, information, and computation. CSLI headquarters and CSLI
Publications are located on the campus of Stanford University.

CSLI Publications reports new developments in the study of language, information,
and computation. In addition to the books in this series, our publications include
lecture notes, monographs, working papers, revised dissertations, and conference
proceedings. Our aim is to make new results, ideas, and approaches available as
quickly as possible. Please visit our web site at
http://csli-www.stanford.edu/publications/
for comments on this and other titles, as well as for changes and corrections by the
author and publisher.

# Contents

# Contributors

ANNE ABEILLÉ is Associate Professor of Linguistics at the University of Paris VII (`Anne.Abeille@linguist.jussieu.fr`).

DAVID BAXTER is a PhD student in linguistics at the University of Illinois at Urbana-Champaign (`dbaxter@cogsci.uiuc.edu`).

EMILY BENDER is a PhD student in linguistics at Stanford University (`bender@csli.stanford.edu`).

ANTÓNIO BRANCO is is a PhD student in Computational Linguistics and a lecturer at the University of Lisbon, Portugal (`Antonio.Branco@di.fc.ul.pt`).

KEARSY CORMIER is a PhD student in linguistics at the University of Texas at Austin (`kearsy@mail.utexas.edu`).

KORDULA DE KUTHY is a PhD student at the Deutsche Forschungszentrum für Künstliche Intelligenz (DFKI), Saarbrücken, Germany (`kdk@dfki.de`).

MICHAEL DUKES is Lecturer in Linguistics at the University of Canterbury, New Zealand (`m.dukes@ling.canterbury.ac.nz`).

CHARLES FILLMORE is Professor of Linguistics at the University of California at Berkeley (`fillmore@icsi.berkeley.edu`).

DAN FLICKINGER is Senior Researcher at the Center for the Study of Language and Information (CSLI), Stanford University and Project Manager of Linguistic Grammars Online (LinGO) (`dan@csli.stanford.edu`).

DANIÈLE GODARD is Senior Researcher et the Centre National de la Recherche Scientifique (CNRS) in Lille, France (Godard@Univ-Lille3.fr).

THILO GÖTZ is a PhD student in Computational Linguistics at the University of Tübingen, Germany (tg@sfs.nphil.uni-tuebingen.de).

HOWARD GREGORY is a PhD student in Linguistics at the School of Oriental and African Studies in London (HG4@soas.ac.uk).

ANDREAS KATHOL is Assistant Professor of Linguistics at the University of California at Berkeley (kathol@socrates.berkeley.edu).

DIMITRA KOLLIAKOU is Lecturer in Linguistics at the University of Newcastle upon Tyne and a visiting lecturer at the Hebrew University in Jerusalem (msdmk@mscc.huji.ac.il).

JEAN-PIERRE KOENIG is Assistant Professor of Linguistics at the State University of New York at Buffalo (jpkoenig@acsu.buffalo.edu).

SHALOM LAPPIN is Professor of Linguistics at the School of Oriental and African Studies, London (SL3@soas.ac.uk).

ROBERT MALOUF is a postdoctoral fellow at the Center for the Study of Language and Information (CSLI) at Stanford University and a lecturer at the University of California at Berkeley (malouf@csli.stanford.edu).

CHRISTOPHER MANNING is Lecturer in Linguistics at the University of Sydney, Australia (cmanning@mail.usyd.edu.au).

PALMIRA MARRAFA is Professor for Computational Linguistics at the University of Lisbon, Portugal (Palmira.Marrafa@ip.pt).

RICHARD MEIER is Associate Professor of Linguistics at the University of Texas at Austin (rmeier@mail.utexas.edu).

DETMAR MEURERS is a PhD student and a lecturer at the Seminar für Sprachwissenschaft, University of Tübingen, Germany (dm@sfs.nphil.uni-tuebingen.de).

GUIDO MINNEN is a research fellow at the School of Cognitive and Computing Science, University of Sussex at Brighton, United Kingdom (guidomi@cogs.susx.ac.uk).

CARL POLLARD is Professor of Linguistics at The Ohio State University (pollard@ling.ohio-state.edu).

ADAM PRZEPIÓRKOWSKI is a PhD student at the University of Tübingen, Germany (adamp@sfs.nphil.uni-tuebingen.de).

IVAN SAG is Professor of Linguistics at Stanford University (sag@csli.stanford.edu).

JEFFREY SMITH is Associate Professor of Mathematics and Computer Science at San Jose State University (smithj@mathcs.sjsu.edu).

GERT WEBELHUTH is Associate Professor of Linguistics at the University of North Carolina at Chapel Hill (webelhut@mindspring.com).

STEPHEN WECHSLER is Associate Professor of Linguistics at the University of Texas at Austin (wechsler@mail.utexas.edu).

GRAHAM WILCOCK is Senior Research Scientist of Sharp Corporation and a visiting researcher at the University of Manchester Institute of Science and Technology (UMIST), United Kingdom and at the Nara Institute of Science and Technology (NAIST), Japan (graham@ccl.umist.ac.uk).

# 1

# Introduction

GERT WEBELHUTH, JEAN-PIERRE KOENIG, AND
ANDREAS KATHOL

## 1.1  Introduction

This volume constitutes the first in a series of books on work in constraint-based lexicalist theories of grammar published by CSLI Publications. The books in this series are intended to make available in easily obtainable and affordable form a broad range of linguistic, foundational, and computational work in constraint-based lexicalist (CBL) frameworks such as Head-Driven Phrase Structure Grammar (HPSG), Lexical-Functional Grammar (LFG), and related frameworks such as Construction Grammar. The papers in the present volume represent the revised versions of talks presented at conferences and workshops on HPSG (which were held annually between 1994 and 1997 in Copenhagen (Denmark), Tübingen (Germany), Marseilles (France), and Ithaca (United States)).

We would like to thank the many reviewers who participated in the reviewing processes for the initial presentation and the final selection for this volume. The resulting line-up of papers documents the unusual breadth of coverage and insight into linguistic structure that the framework of HPSG makes possible. Special thanks go to Dan Flickinger, Emily Bender, Tony Gee, Rob Malouf, and Susanne Riehemann for their most generous help with the preparation of the final manuscript.

We would also like to thank the authors of the papers for their enthusiasm and for the care they took in accommodating reviewers' criticisms and suggestions. As editors, we feel that the present volume faithfully represents the diverse research interests of linguists, logicians,

We would like to thank Ivan Sag for helpful comments on an earlier draft. The opinions expressed here are entirely those of the authors.

*Lexical and Constructional Aspects of Linguistic Explanation.*
Gert Webelhuth, Jean-Pierre Koenig, and Andreas Kathol.
Copyright © 1998, Stanford University.

and computer scientists working on HPSG (and the related framework of Construction Grammar), as well as the common core of ideas and methodological concerns that bind them together into a unified and mutually supportive research community.

## 1.2 HPSG as a Theory of Grammar

HPSG was created in a research collaboration between Carl Pollard and Ivan Sag that began in the 1980s and continues to this day (cf., in particular, Pollard and Sag 1987, Pollard and Sag 1994). The theory evolved directly from Generalized Phrase Structure Grammar (GPSG) as developed in the late 1970s and early to mid 1980s. Together with LFG, which emerged around the same time, GPSG provided one of the most well-known demonstrations that interesting grammatical phenomena can be adequately described in a *monostratal* framework, i.e., one that dispenses entirely with multiple levels (or stages) of syntactic representations and the transformations that mediate among them. But as much as HPSG is indebted to its predecessor for a great deal of the conceptual and formal foundations of the current theory, it is a mistake—a common one, it turns out—to think of HPSG as simply a variation on GPSG. For one thing there are strong influences from Categorial Grammar, LFG, and Government-Binding Theory that have reshaped the way that HPSG addresses many analytical issues. In addition, one of the chief features setting it apart from GPSG is the highly developed theory of lexical information, both in the form of lexical rules and multidimensional inheritance hierarchies. The latter is an especially powerful tool for expressing linguistically significant lexical generalizations as well as paradigmatic relationships among lexical items. Recent proposals to extend inheritance hierarchies to syntactic description (e.g., Sag 1997, Kathol 1995) have, moreover, opened a very fruitful exchange with Construction Grammar (Fillmore and Kay Forthcoming).

HPSG continues to attract scientists from diverse academic disciplines, reflecting the HPSG community's belief that language must be studied from several different perspectives simultaneously in order for a full theory of linguistic structures and their usage to emerge. One crucial decision that Pollard and Sag made early on and which continues to inform all present work, is that HPSG should be a scientific theory of observable language. That is, the object of study cannot be arbitrarily restricted (by removal of recalcitrant data) as is the case with Chomsky's Principles and Parameters (P&P) approach to syntax, which restricts its attention to structurally regularized and exceptionless objects dubbed 'core languages':

The systems called "languages" in common sense usage tolerate exceptions: irregular morphology, idioms, and so forth. These exceptions do not fall naturally under the principles-and-parameters conception of UG. (Chomsky 1986, 147)

... it is hardly to be expected that what are called "languages" or "dialects" or even "ideolects" will conform precisely or perhaps even very closely to the systems determined by fixing the parameters of UG ... (Chomsky 1981, 7)

HPSG's methodology insists upon accepting linguistic analyses as explanatory only when they can be shown to be compatible with a broad and representative database of facts from a given language. This is sometimes misunderstood as a lack of interest in linguistic explanation and a mere focus of the theory on description. But HPSG is as much interested in finding explanations for linguistic facts and the human language faculty as other grammatical frameworks. What sets HPSG (and other CBL frameworks with similar methodologies) apart from P&P is that its methodological underpinnings require a considerably more careful and complete demonstration of analytical success before one is entitled to the claim of having provided an explanatory analysis. This cultural difference between the work in HPSG and the dominant P&P framework can be documented in several ways.

First, as already mentioned, the HPSG community is very unforgiving about analyses with obvious counterexamples. References to the "non-core status" of counterexamples or suggestions that as yet undetected explanatory principles will someday account for obvious counterexamples do not suffice to overcome this community's belief that explanation entails broad description.

A second explanatory hurdle concerns the level of analytic precision. This ever-present concern can be seen in many of the contributions to this book, which are at pains to prove that the analytical tools they employ are mathematically and logically sound and computationally efficient. We conjecture that it is precisely this feature of the HPSG culture that attracts not only linguists but also a considerable number of logicians, mathematicians, and computer scientists to the framework. This arguably makes this linguistic research community very diverse in terms of the scientific and academic qualifications of its members. The formal expertise available in the community, as well as the demand for formal demonstrations of internal consistency and the empirical success of new linguistic proposals has spawned the creation of a considerable number of so-called *grammar development environments*, i.e., computer programs that allow the linguist to develop and test HPSG grammars (without any particular programming expertise). Each of these dozen or so environments allows the researcher to demonstrate the standards of precision and formality expected by the community. Many authors make the implementations of their theories available for public inspection on the Internet or through other demonstrations.

A third methodological restriction that enters into the concept of explanation in HPSG is the prohibition against the use of empirically and theoretically undermotivated analytical tools that P&P analyses systematically depend on for "explanation". Among others, HPSG does not permit its analyses to refer to:

- phonologically and morphologically abstract (i.e., non-observable) case distinctions (so-called "Cases");
- phonologically abstract affixes;
- phonologically inert functional heads;
- structure-destroying movement operations, especially "covert" movements (to "Logical Form") whose existence is not empirically observable.

For instance, Ackerman and Webelhuth (1998) list 21 different functional heads that have been proposed in various places in the P&P literature and which would be postulated to exist for every language—often in unobservable form—according to those versions of the P&P theory that attempt to reduce all natural languages to identical sentence structures.

It may first appear that the proliferation of functional heads in P&P is analogous to the rich inventory of features in HPSG; however this would constitute a serious misunderstanding of the role that features play within CBL theories.

While feature-based analyses are often viewed as inelegant or non-explanatory, the putative descriptive economy of many P&P analyses is obtained only because of the extraordinary fact that no actual theory of features has ever been articulated for that framework. Similarly, even though features are alluded to in much of the P&P work (cf., for instance, Chomsky's recent notion of movement as movement of features), the principles of their distribution within and across syntactic categories have never been developed in sufficient detail to evaluate their empirical consequences, and certainly not with the high degree of precision that is standard in HPSG. This is particularly apparent in the case of head and agreement features and there is no reason to believe that the use of functional categories would make a fully developed theory of P&P features more economical than its HPSG counterpart.

Furthermore, features in CBL theories are classificatory devices grounded in manifest distinctions in the languages under consideration.

This differs quite starkly from functional categories which, while occurring within a hypertrophy of tree-configurational relations, serve as curiously lexical reifications of certain constructional distinctions that are pervasive in natural language.

Another, particularly extreme example of explanation by assuming the unobservable is found in Baker's (1996) book on polysynthetic languages and brought out in the review of that work by Koenig and Michelson (1998, 135):

> Not only are all (nonincorporated) NP arguments in fact zero *pro's* in Mohawk, but there are also zero incorporated roots. Finally, in cases of three-place predicates such as *-u-* 'give', the goal argument is realized as a PP complement whose head is a null preposition and whose complement is a null *pro*!

Within HPSG's methodology, analyses would not count as explanatory, if in order to make the theory's principles applicable to observable data, the linguist must first postulate a multitude of affixes, words, and phrases that are neither audible nor visible, and for which there is no theory-independent motivation from the data under analysis.

In sum, there is less talk about explanation in works on HPSG, simply because explanation is a more substantive notion that is harder to achieve: Satisfying the explanatory prerequisites of the community simultaneously is very difficult, which means that progress typically is slow and cumulative rather than seemingly instantaneous.

On the other hand, progress gained by toil is not easily foiled. The stringent quality control imposed on HPSG analyses ensures that explanatory generalizations can almost always be ported to subsequent evolutions of the theory. In this way, the carefully maintained balance between explanation and description protects the theory from the regular cataclysmic changes that rock a theory like P&P. To illustrate, there was great hope in the 1980s—expressed in works such as Chomsky 1981 and in many syntax textbooks since—that the basic structure of natural language was understood well enough that the derivation of the syntactic forms of individual languages was merely a matter of systematically describing the set of parameters and their options.

Contrast this with the following recent evaluation of the conceptual underpinnings and the empirical success of the Minimalist Program of Chomsky 1995, the current version of the P&P theory:

> The overall character of the minimalist program is highly speculative, as Chomsky notes throughout MP. In a recent paper (Chomsky 1996) he is virtually categorical on this point 'There are minimalist questions, but no specific minimalist answers' ... Whatever answers

can be discovered will result from following the research agenda of the program. Unfortunately, how this is to be done is rather unclear ...

(Freidin 1997, 580)

A parallel reduction in empirical coverage of the current P&P theory is mentioned in Chomsky 1995, 242 "... many open questions remain, including some that are quite central to language." Chomsky's sentence ends in a footnote that reads "we still have no good phrase structure theory of such simple matters as attributive adjectives, relative clauses, and adjuncts of many different types."

HPSG sails a smoother course. At the present time the theory neither claims to have all the right answers nor even to know all the right questions to ask about the structure of natural language and the human language capacity. On the other hand, by proposing concrete, carefully worked out, and well motivated analyses based on a thorough inspection of a wide variety of empirically observable data, the theory has offered *many* answers to *many* questions that *any* linguistic theory will eventually have to answer. The papers that we have collected in the present book continue this tradition of making systematic progress through solid and reliable research.

## 1.3 An Overview of the Papers in this Volume

We now turn to a brief summary of each article. The diversity of the topics covered will give the reader some idea of the wide array of phenomena HPSG and Construction Grammar typically address.

### 1.3.1 Argument Structure

Several papers deal with argument structure, in particular, the relationship between the valence lists and the argument structure list (ARG-ST) introduced in recent HPSG (see, for instance, Dini and Balari 1997).

**Michael Dukes** shows how the ARG-ST list can be used to model phenomena that were assumed to argue for multistratality. Concentrating on Chamorro objects, Dukes demonstrates that the presence of an ARG-ST list on lexical entries allows us to account monostratally for instances where the order of combination of subcategorized for elements is dissociated from their relative obliqueness. The former is encoded in the various valence lists, while the latter is represented by the ordering of elements on the ARG-ST list.

**Chris Manning and Ivan Sag** make a similar point and argue on the basis of Russian and Austronesian languages that both valence and ARG-ST lists are needed. In particular, they show that the Austronesian 'voices' affect the valence lists, but not necessarily the ARG-ST list. Consequently, the surface structures of sentences in which alternate verbs appear may differ without the application of binding conditions being affected. They also suggest that argument structure lists are needed in the case of (Russian) passives to account for the existence of two possible ARG-ST subject binders of anaphors.

**Dimitra Kolliakou** extends the by now classic notion of argument composition (see, for instance Hinrichs and Nakazawa 1994) to NPs to account for Modern Greek possessive 'weak forms'. Such forms, which she argues to be affixes, can simply be composed with higher heads.

Finally, **Rob Malouf** discusses West Greenlandic deverbal nouns that are created through noun incorporation. He argues that such deverbal nouns are instances of a mixed category, like the English gerund, that is as a category that shares some properties of verbs and nouns. He thus demonstrates how a 'modular' grammar whose modules interact locally can account, despite apparent challenges, for mismatches between morphological and syntactic "modules".

### 1.3.2 Lexical and Constructional Issues

**Anne Abeillé and Danièle Godard**'s paper returns to the much discussed French floating quantifiers. They argue that these elements can be either adverbs that complement finite verbs or adjuncts to infinitival verbs. More importantly, they propose a lexical analysis of the phenomenon—in tune with its locality and lexical sensitivity—and argue for a single (lexical) rule for both subject and object floating quantifiers; the difference between the two stems from general binding principles rather than the rule itself.

**Kordula De Kuthy** discusses German pied-piping infinitives and asks whether they should be handled through a movement analysis or a linearization construction. She concludes that the movement analysis is superior, thus suggesting some ways to choose between the various analytical tools made available in recent HPSG.

**Charles Fillmore**'s paper illustrates the growing importance of Construction Inheritance in recent "unification-based" grammars. Assuming the existence of constructions as primitive building blocks, he shows how inheritance relations among constructions can lead to an economical and detailed analysis of the various forms of subject/auxiliary inversion in English.

**Detmar Meurers** adds to the rich literature on German VP Topicalization and suggests that an analysis of the phenomenon which uses (obligatory) argument composition is compatible with several constituent-structure and unbounded-dependency analyses: flat, right- or left- branching constituency for the verbal complex are equally possible, and so are trace and traceless approaches to long-distance dependencies. He thus reminds us to what extent linguistic structure and grammatical theories are underdetermined by our currently available data.

Finally, **Jeff Smith** illustrates the broad-coverage goal of HPSG by focusing on the often neglected complex English number names such as *two hundred twelve thousand and twenty two*. He suggests that such strings are phrases rather than complex lexical items and proposes an explicit analysis of such complex number name phrases, including a representation of their semantics using a Minimal Recursion Semantics representational scheme.

### 1.3.3 Binding Theory

Five papers deal with binding phenomena and provide new, challenging data.

First, **António Branco and Palmira Marrafa** discuss the Portuguese anaphor *el proprio*. They show, *contra* often held assumptions within a Principles and Parameters approach, that it is indeed a non-subject oriented long-distance anaphor, even though it is morphologically complex. They then suggest the existence of four universal binding principles which form a square of oppositions as well as propose a new non-linear ordering of elements on ARG-ST to reflect the special status of subjects with respect to the binding theory.

**Stephen Wechsler** compares Principles and Parameters and HPSG approaches to binding phenomena in his paper and shows on the basis of new data from Balinese, that ARG-ST-based and configurational approaches involving c-command to binding can be distinguished empirically and that the apparent correspondence between the two theories disappears when the Balinese facts are considered.

**Emily Bender and Dan Flickinger** argue that a look at the English peripheral tag question construction and the gender-neutral pronoun *they* can lead to new insights into agreement phenomena. In particular, they suggest that the two constructions demonstrate that two kinds of agreements are needed: the old INDEX agreement of Pollard and Sag 1994 and a new AGR. Although their values are often co-indexed, they need not be, and it is the latter which is relevant to verb-subject agreement.

**Kearsy Cormier, Stephen Wechsler and Richard Meier** discuss locus agreement in American Sign Language (ASL). They argue that ASL locus functions as a discourse marker. They thus show that agreement properties cannot be reduced to the typical $\phi$ features and provide an interesting confirmation of the index view of agreement, presented in PS94.

Finally, **Adam Przepiórkowski** presents a new theory of case assignment and strong evidence for the need to revise the argument/adjunct distinction. He proposes a non-configurational, obliqueness-based set of case assignment rules and also motivates a treatment of modifiers as complements which are present on the ARG-ST list. The argument is simple: to state (Finnish) case assignment rules in the most general fashion, all dependents of a head must be on the same list.

### 1.3.4 Implementation and Formalization

Several papers illustrate the healthy exchange, typical for HPSG, between linguistic analysis and issues arising from implementation and formalization.

**Thilo Goetz and Detmar Meurers**'s discuss three ways of computationally checking grammaticality with respect to an HPSG theory. They show how one of them, lazy evaluation, can be obtained as the result of an off-line compilation technique, and argue that such a processing strategy has advantages for efficiency of processing, the termination properties of HPSG grammars, and leads to more compact replies.

**Detmar Meurers and Guido Minnen** address similar efficiency processing issues. They show that it is possible (using constraint-propagation techniques) to automatically make a theory more specific where the use of underspecification in the linguistically best motivated analysis leads to processing inefficiencies.

**Jean-Pierre Koenig** and **Carl Pollard** discuss the relationship between the logical languages within which grammars are written and their model-theoretic interpretations. Pollard examines anew the relation between a grammar and the token utterances it licenses (predicts). He is particularly interested in the relationship between linguistic tokens and what they are tokens of as well as in providing a precise definition of the strong generative capacity of a grammar. Koenig illustrates the need to distinguish between the logical language within which grammars are written and the mathematical structures they denote, which serve as models of utterance types, by discussing phenomena which suggest a way to choose between logical languages underlying HPSG grammars without altering the denoted mathematical structures.

### 1.3.5 Semantics and Pragmatics

Finally, several papers discuss semantic and pragmatic issues.

**David Baxter** proposes that the semantic representations of verbal constituents consist of conjoined logical clauses on the basis of intersective adverbial modifiers. The difference between conjunctive and non-conjunctive semantics for modifiers then naturally models the difference between transparent and opaque modifiers.

**Andreas Kathol** advances a constructional analysis of the scope marking or partial *wh*-movement construction in German. He first shows that the idea of scoping via quantifier retrieval can be fruitfully applied to this phenomenon, obviating the need for Logical Form. Moreover, Kathol argues that contrary to first appearances, the scope marking construction differs semantically from ordinary long-distance extraction. At the same time however, there is evidence suggesting that its properties cannot be entirely derived from its semantics.

**Howard Gregory and Shalom Lappin** discuss antecedent contained ellipsis (hereafter ACE); they propose a syntactically-based *in situ* analysis of ACE that makes use of the traceless, head-driven account of extraction common in current HPSG. They then present briefly a computational implementation of ACE.

**Graham Wilcock** continues the push toward the lexicalization of grammatical processes (see Sag 1997 for lexicalization of SLASH amalgamation) and proposes that the amalgamation of contextual information occurs at the lexical level (simply put, the head amalgamates the contextual information of its dependents). He presents arguments from both (head-driven) generation, and register variation in the use of the English relative pronouns (*who* vs. *whom*) that such a lexicalization is needed.

## References

Ackerman, F., and G. Webelhuth. 1998. *A Theory of Predicates*. Stanford: CSLI Publications.

Baker, M. 1996. *The Polysynthesis Parameter*. New York and Oxford: Oxford University Press.

Chomsky, N. 1981. *Lectures on Government and Binding*. Dordrecht: Foris.

Chomsky, N. 1986. *Knowledge of Language: its Nature, Origin, and Use*. New York: Praeger.

Chomsky, N. 1995. *The Minimalist Program*. Current Studies in Linguistics. Cambridge: MIT Press.

Chomsky, N. 1996 Some Observations on Economy in Generative Grammar. Unpublished manuscript, MIT.

Dini, L., and S. Balari (ed.). 1997. *Romance in* HPSG. Stanford: CSLI Publications.

Fillmore, C., and P. Kay. Forthcoming. *Construction Grammar*. Stanford: CSLI Publications.

Freidin, R. 1997. Review Article of 'The Minimalist Program' by Noam Chomsky. *Language* 73.3:571–582.

Hinrichs, E., and T. Nakazawa. 1994. Linearizing Finite AUX in German Verbal Complexes. In *German in Head-Driven Phrase Structure Grammar*, ed. J. Nerbonne, K. Netter, and C. J. Pollard, 11–38. Stanford: CSLI Publications.

Kathol, A. 1995. *Linearization-Based German Syntax*. PhD thesis, Ohio State University.

Koenig, J.-P., and K. Michelson. 1998. Review of 'The Polysynthesis Parameter' by Mark Baker. *Language* 74(1):129–136.

Pollard, C. J., and I. A. Sag. 1987. *Information-based Syntax and Semantics*. Volume 1, CSLI Lecture Notes Series No. 13. CSLI Publications.

Pollard, C. J., and I. A. Sag. 1994. *Head-Driven Phrase Structure Grammar*. Chicago, IL: University of Chicago Press and Stanford: CSLI Publications.

Sag, I. A. 1997. English Relative Clause Constructions. *Journal of Linguistics* 33(2):431–484.

# Part I

## Lexical Argument Structure

**2**

# Kinds of Objecthood in Chamorro Grammar

MICHAEL DUKES

## 2.1 Introduction

Perlmutter (1982) and Gibson (1990), employing the framework of Relational Grammar (RG), discuss various grammatical phenomena which appear to require reference to grammatical relation (GRs) other than surface or 'final' GRs. Accordingly, they argue for the superiority of 'multistratal' theories, such as RG, which provide multiple formal representations of GRs over 'monostratal' theories, like Categorial Grammar and Head-Driven Phrase Structure Grammar, that do not. The 'surfacy' approach to GRs suffices to account for a range of agreement and other facts in a number of languages (as discussed in Dowty 1982). However, Gibson (1990) shows that Dowty's approach to GRs fails to account for a number of morphosyntactic generalizations in Chamorro, a Western Austronesian language, that are straightforwardly accounted for under an approach that recognizes the existence of nonfinal GRs.

In this paper I show how Gibson's Chamorro data might be accounted for within a version of HPSG that assumes the existence of an argument structure feature (ARG-ST), which arguably can be used to provide a representation analogous to RG's initial grammatical relations. The discussion focuses on the characterization of 'object' in Chamorro and on certain rules which target objects in Chamorro.

I would like to thank two anonymous reviewers for helpful comments on an earlier draft of this paper. Remaining errors are mine.

*Lexical and Constructional Aspects of Linguistic Explanation.*
Gert Webelhuth, Jean-Pierre Koenig, and Andreas Kathol.
Copyright © 1998, Stanford University.

## 2.2 Arguments for Underlying GRs in Relational Grammar

Relational Grammarians have over the years marshalled a number of important arguments supporting the view that grammatical theory must recognize the existence of grammatical relations that are not identical to those manifested on the surface in terms of case or agreement (see Bell 1983, Perlmutter 1982, 1984, Davies 1986, Gibson 1990 amongst many others). Some of these arguments have since been refuted but the majority have so far stood the test of time. It is incumbent on those who wish to dispute some aspect of such RG analyses to provide alternative treatments that do as well or better in accounting for the data.

While most of the analyses of grammatical phenomena referred to above are presented more or less independently of any previously stated theoretical position, Gibson (1990) discusses a body of data in Chamorro that is framed as a direct response to the categorial account of grammatical relations in Dowty 1982. Dowty shows that Categorial Grammar can provide an obliqueness-based theory of grammatical relations in which they are defined in terms of order of combination of arguments with the predicate (as also proposed in Keenan and Comrie 1977). This analysis also underlies the treatment of grammatical relations in versions of HPSG where the list order of SUBCAT reflects a scale of relative obliqueness. Dowty presents elegant analyses of passive, dative shift, causativization and various other processes affecting grammatical relations in a number of languages, thus illustrating the appeal of the 'surfacy' obliqueness-based approach. But Gibson's paper appears to demonstrate quite clearly that order of combination of arguments will not suffice to account for a number of robust morphosyntactic properties of valency-changing operations in Chamorro. In addition, since most recent discussion of grammatical relations and valency has focussed on how the notion 'subject' should be treated formally, there is considerable theoretical interest in the fact that the phenomena which Gibson examines seem to require reference to distinct notions of 'object'.

## 2.3 The Chamorro Data

Gibson's arguments for non-final GRs in Chamorro focus on the interaction of verbal morphology and the accessibility of certain nominals to such processes as dative shift, passive, wh-extraction and causativization. Gibson's arguments are briefly reviewed below. All data is from Gibson 1990 unless otherwise noted.

### 2.3.1 Passive and Dative Shift in Chamorro

Facts involving passive ('2-1 Advancement') and dative shift (which incorporates both '3-2 Advancement' and 'Oblique-2 Advancement') form the basis for much of the motivation for underlying GRs in Chamorro. Numerous examples and much discussion illustrating these phenomena can be found in Chung 1981, 1982 and Gibson 1990, 1992. I note briefly that Chamorro has a predominant VSO word order pattern with a fairly complex set of generalizations governing the appearance of agreement morphology on the verb (Chung 1981, Gibson 1992).

Passive in Chamorro advances an object to subject (both of which are straightforwardly characterizable in terms of case-marking, agreement, etc) and demotes the subject to oblique, as in English:

(1)   a.   I   famagu'un ma-dulalak si   Jose.
         the children   3Pl-follow   PN Jose

         'The children followed Jose.'

    b.   Ma-dulalak   si   Jose nu      i    famagu'un.
         Pas.Pl-follow PN Jose Obl.CN the children

         'Jose was followed by the children.'

    c.   Si   Juan ha-dulalak si   Jose.
         PN Juan 3Sg-follow   PN Jose

         'Juan followed Jose.'

    d.   D-in-ilalak     si   Jose as        Juan.
         Pas.Sg-follow PN Jose Obl.PN Juan

         'Jose was followed by Juan.'

         (examples from Gibson 1992, 32)

The operation of passive itself in Chamorro raises a potential problem for theories that lack some means of representing underlying GRs (although this is not one of the arguments presented by Gibson). This is because the passive morpheme in Chamorro agrees in number with the oblique *former* subject whenever it is specified. Thus, in (1b), the prefix *ma-* ('plural (or unspecified) agent') appears on the passivized verb because the demoted subject has a plural referent, while in (1d), the infix *-in-* ('singular agent') appears because the demoted subject is singular. The prefix *ma-* also appears when the underlying subject is not specified.

Dative shift in Chamorro, again, much as in English, promotes a range of obliques to object and demotes the original object to oblique:

(2)   a.   Hu-tugi' i    kätta pära i    che'lu-hu.
         1Sg-write the letter to    the sibling-my

         'I wrote the letter to my brother.'

    b.  Hu-tugi'-i     i   che'lu-hu  ni     kätta.
        1Sg-write-Dat the sibling-my Obl.CN letter
        'I wrote my brother the letter.'
        (examples from Gibson 1992, 34)

In (2b), the indirect object of *tugi'* 'write' is promoted to (direct) object and the original direct object becomes an oblique. The verb is marked with a suffix indicating that dative shift has occurred. The choice of oblique which can be promoted is generally governed by the particular verb. However Gibson (1992, 36) notes that advancement of benefactives is ungoverned and thus may apply quite generally with any predicate:

(3)    a.  Ha-punu' si  Miguel i    bäbui pära guahu.
         3Sg-kill   PN Miguel the pig    for   me
         'Miguel killed the pig for me.'
     b.  Ha-punu'-i yu' si  Miguel nu     i    bäbui.
         3Sg-kill-Dat 1Sg PN Miguel Obl.CN the pig
         'Miguel killed me the pig.'

    Gibson (1990, 251) provides examples showing that dative shift feeds passive (the derived object may become subject) but passive may not feed dative shift.

### 2.3.2  Wh-Extraction of Objects

Having introduced the basics of passive and dative shift in Chamorro we can examine some of Gibson's arguments in favour of multistratality in Chamorro.[1] Gibson (1990, 252–4) observes that the wh-extraction of object NPs in Chamorro proceeds differently depending on the derivational history of the NP concerned. Object NPs that are not derived (i.e. that are both 'initial' and 'final' objects) can be questioned by one of two strategies. They can either undergo 'chopping' (i.e. straightforward leftward wh-extraction leaving a gap) or they can be extracted out of a clause in which the verb has been nominalized:

(4)    a.  Ha-fahan si  Maria i    chetda gi   tenda.
         3Sg-buy  PN Maria the banana Loc store
         'Maria bought the bananas at the store.'
     b.  Hafa ha-fahan si  Maria gi   tenda?
         what 3Sg-buy  PN Maria Loc store
         'What did Maria buy at the store?'
     c.  Hafa f-in-ahan-ña si  Maria gi   tenda?
         what Nom-buy-her PN Maria Loc store
         'What did Maria buy at the store?'

---

[1] The data discussed here are also outlined by Chung (1982, 50).

Example (4b) illustrates the chopping strategy, (4c) illustrates the nominalization strategy. Examples such as these have been widely discussed under the rubric of 'Wh-agreement' (Chung 1982, 1994, Dukes 1993). It is important to note that Gibson's arguments do not hinge (though they may shed light) on the resolution of the controversy over wh-agreement. Whether wh-agreement is treated as the result of a relation-changing operation or as a mark of agreement between an extracted NP and a verb whose projection is crossed by the extractee, the same morphosyntactic subclasses of predicates must be formally characterizable.

When we turn to the extraction possibilities in clauses which have undergone dative shift, the facts are somewhat different. Underlying objects which have been demoted by dative shift can be extracted by exactly the same strategies as objects in non-dative-shifted clauses:

(5)  a.  Hafa un-tugi'-i    i    che'lu-mu?
          what 2Sg-write-Dat the sibling-your

          'What did you write to your brother?' (chopping)

    b.  Hafa t-in-igi'-i-nñiha      ni      che'lu-mu?
          what Nom-write-Dat-their Obl.CN sibling-your

          'What did they write to your brother?' (nominalization)

But NPs that are objects derived by dative shift can only extract via chopping:

(6)  a.  Hayi un-tugi'-i     nu     i    katta?
          who 2Sg-write-Dat Obl.CN the letter

          'Who did you write the letter to?' (chopping)

    b.  *Hayi t-in-igi'-i-nñiha      (ni     katta)?
          who Nom-write-Dat-their Obl.CN letter

          'Who did they write the letter to?' (nominalization)

As Gibson notes, there are two problems inherent in the above data for monostratal approaches like Dowty's. The first problem is to characterize object extraction so that initial objects subsequently demoted by dative shift may undergo extraction by nominalization with -*in*-. Note that initial objects promoted to subject may not undergo extraction by nominalization with -*in*- and neither can other obliques that have surface characteristics identical to demoted objects, including objects demoted to oblique by a rule of antipassivization (Gibson 1992, 181).[2] The second problem is to block extraction by nominalization of objects derived

---

[2]In fact, Gibson (1992, 181) notes that chômeurs created by antipassive cannot extract or undergo any subsequent grammatical processes at all. I do not consider the issue of accounting for the subtypes of Chamorro obliques in this paper.

by dative shift. In both cases, some notion of initial object seems to be required to account for the restrictions.

### 2.3.3 Chamorro Causatives Built on Transitive Roots

Alongside the facts involving dative shift and passive, Gibson presents data involving causatives that are somewhat paradoxical from a monostratal point of view.

Causatives in Chamorro are built by prefixing a causative morpheme *na'-* to a verb root. When a causative is built from a transitive root the resulting structure looks much like a clause derived by dative shift:

(7)    Ha-na'-balli    ham i    ma'estru nu    i    satgi.
       3Sg-Caus-sweep 1Pl  the teacher   Obl.CN the floor
       'The teacher made us sweep the floor.'

However, the wh-extraction facts differ somewhat from those observed with dative-shift. The initial object of the transitive root (which is realized above as an oblique) may be extracted either via chopping or via *-in-* nominalization, just like the initial object of a dative-shifted verb:

(8)   a.   Hafa ha-na'-balli    ham nu    i    ma'estra?
          what 3Sg-Caus-sweep 1Pl   Obl.CN the teacher
          'What did the teacher make us sweep?'
    b.   Hafa ni-na'-balle-nñiha       nu    hagu?
          what Nom-Caus-sweep-their Obl.Pn you
          'What did they make you sweep?'

But, contrary to what might have been expected in view of the dative shift facts, the derived object of the causative may also undergo both object extraction strategies:

(9)   a.   Hayi i    ma'estra ha-na'-balli     nu    i    satgi?
          who the teacher   3Sg-Caus-sweep Obl.CN the floor
          'Who did the teacher make sweep the floor?'
    b.   Hayi i    ma'estra ni-na'-balle-nña    nu    i    satgi?
          who the teacher Nom-Caus-sweep-her Obl.CN the floor
          'Who did the teacher make sweep the floor?'

These facts indicate that derived objects of transitive causative predicates must be distinguished from derived objects of dative-shifted predicates because they behave like underlying objects with respect to wh-extraction.[3]

---

[3] Two points about causatives built on intransitive roots in Chamorro add additional weight to the claim that multistratality is required to adequately describe Chamorro morphosyntax. Firstly, as in the case of causatives built on transitive roots, derived

## 2.4   Chamorro Grammatical Relations in HPSG

The facts discussed above are all straightforwardly dealt with in RG, which incorporates multistratality (see Gibson 1992 for details), but how are they to be accounted for in HPSG? Let us start with a version of HPSG in which GRs are represented by using a SUBCAT valence feature and no other list-based encoding of grammatical relations (aka 'HPSG2', as in Pollard and Sag 1992, 1994, Chs. 1–8). As we have seen, the following subclasses of 'object' can undergo extraction via -*in*-nominalization:

(10)   a.   non-derived surface objects (i.e. 'underlying' objects).
       b.   'former' objects demoted by dative shift (but not those demoted by antipassive or promoted by passive).
       c.   'former' objects demoted by causativization.
       d.   surface objects derived by causativization (but not those derived by dative shift).

What all these types of objects should have in common is that they fulfill the role of 'second least oblique element' on the SUBCAT list of some predicate. This generalization certainly seems to be correct; but not always with respect to the verb which is at the foot of a wh-dependency in Chamorro. Thus in all the cases of -*in*- nominalization involving former objects, the relevant SUBCAT list is not that of the verb which appears in the sentence that undergoes the extraction but rather another verb which is related by lexical rule (or possibly some other relation) to the verb which appears in the sentence. Furthermore, neither being a former object nor a surface object is sufficient in itself to guarantee that an NP can be extracted via -*in*- nominalization since it is also necessary to know how a surface object was derived or how a former object failed to become a surface object.

### 2.4.1   Possible Analyses Using a Monostratal HPSG

The version of HPSG assumed so far can deal with the above facts in one of three ways. One possibility is to simply list a set of distinct constraints correlating the appearance of -*in*- and wh-extraction for each of the different types of object listed above (some of which may be collapsable). Each different verb type can be assigned a distinct subsort to which a corresponding constraint can apply. Under this analysis, some of the cases of object extraction (i.e. those involving former objects) will

---

objects may extract by both object strategies. Secondly, such causatives display embedded *intransitive* subject agreement as well as the expected transitive agreement. Space precludes discussion of this data here. See Gibson 1992 for extensive discussion.

be analyzed as cases of oblique extraction which accidentally resemble object extraction. It will obviously miss numerous generalizations about objects in Chamorro and it will also fail to explain why no other cases of oblique extraction involve infixation of -*in*-.

A second possibility is to appeal to a more complex LOCAL representation for predicates derived by passivization, dative shift and/or causativization that allows access to multiple SUBCAT lists. Under this approach, derivational morphemes like passive, dative and causative can be viewed as higher predicates which embed the LOCAL information of the verb to which they apply, including the SUBCAT list of the modified verb (the 'initial' GRs). The complex predicate derived by this process will also be assigned a SUBCAT list representing the 'surface' GRs. Accounting for the object extraction possibilities in Chamorro would involve correlating the appearance of -*in*- with an object on one or other of the lists contained in the representation of the complex predicate.

This second analysis has considerable appeal, and indeed I believe something like it must be invoked in order to deal with the facts involving causatives in Chamorro, since causative derivation provides the only case in which a *derived* object may be extracted via -*in*- nominalization.[4] However, in contrast to the case of the causatives, the idea of treating passive and dative shift via morphologically-based embedding seems rather less appealing. While space precludes a detailed discussion of this issue, an embedding analysis of passive and dative shift seems to give rise to a considerable amount of unmotivated structure and fails to correlate with the available morphosyntactic evidence. The causee argument of a causative predicate arguably bears one thematic role with respect to the causative morpheme and another with respect to the embedded predicate. Furthermore, there are many languages in which causative sentences have an obvious biclausal structure, so that the diachronic and/or synchronic nature of the embedding relationship between the causative morpheme and the modified predicate can be easily seen. The extra structure resulting from causative embedding can thus be well motivated. But this is not the case with dative shift and passive. I am not aware of evidence in any language of a biclausal source for passive or dative shift nor of any evidence that arguments in passive clauses bear simultaneous but distinct thematic relations to the passive morpheme and to the verb stem.[5] In both of the embedding analyses cited above, the content of the passivized predicate is always structure-shared with

---

[4]Broadly similar analyses of passivization and causativization are outlined in Manning and Sag 1995 and Davis 1996 in which the feature STEM appears as an attribute of a derived verb and embeds the argument structure information of the verbal stem.

[5]Indeed, rather than being treated as higher predicates, passive morphemes have

the content of the verb stem, making it look like something of a coincidence that content is preserved. If the embedding analysis of passive and dative shift is not employed, there is no need to enforce structure sharing of CONTENT values, because there is only one content for each passive or dative shifted verb. The morphosyntactic distinctions observed in Chamorro between objects derived by dative-shift and those derived by causativization lend weight to the claim that only causativization involves embedding.

A third analysis utilizing only one valence feature would involve assuming that constraints on object extraction in Chamorro are partly governed by semantic considerations. More precisely, one might attempt to utilize relative prominence on a thematic hierarchy (Bresnan and Kanerva 1989, Alsina 1993) or alternatively, following Davis 1996, appeal to the quasi-semantic notion of 'undergoer' as a prototypical CONTENT role for objects in place of the notion 'initial object'. However, such an approach requires a reformulation of the structure of CONTENT and it is unclear whether it would provide enough structure to account for the data discussed above. Nevertheless, an analysis within Davis' framework might well be preferable to increasing the number of lists in CATEGORY.[6]

## 2.5   A 'Multistratal' Analysis within HPSG

The analysis of Chamorro objects presented here assumes the existence of a list-valued attribute of signs of sort *word* called ARG-ST, as proposed in Sag and Fodor 1994 and other works cited above.[7] ARG-ST elements are ordered according to a default order isomorphic to the ordering defined on SUBCAT by linking constraints in basic clauses un-

---

often been treated as 'absorbed' or 'suppressed' arguments of the main verb (e.g. Jaeggli 1986).

[6]In fact, the analyses of passive presented in Manning and Sag 1995 and Davis 1996 utilize almost all of the alternative types of formal machinery considered above. Such formalisms thus make available as many as five formally distinct characterizations of 'subject' and 'object'. Furthermore, the characterization of 'subject' becomes formally disjunctive since in some cases 'subject' is an obliqueness-based notion (e.g. 'a-subject' is the least oblique element on ARG-ST (Manning and Sag 1995)) while in others it is the value of a keyword feature (i.e. SUBJ). Whether grammatical theory needs to avail itself of so many potentially overlapping definitions for GRs is a question that deserves serious consideration.

[7]This attribute was called LEX in the original presentation of this paper. As used here, ARG-ST appears equivalent to the feature ROLES in Wechsler (1995, Ch. 4). Note that the use of ARG-ST here clearly contrasts with that in Manning and Sag 1995 (and related work) where ARG-ST is taken to be the locus for relation-changing operations.

modified by relation-changing morphology. Since ARG-ST is not an attribute of phrases it is not a true valence feature.[8]

The definition of 'object' and 'subject' assumed here is essentially the same as that found in Pollard and Sag 1994, Ch. 1–8, except that the definition can be applied equally to either SUBCAT or ARG-ST; a 'surface' subject is the least oblique element on the SUBCAT list of some predicate, an 'underlying' subject is the least oblique element on the ARG-ST list of the predicate. Corresponding objects are the second least oblique elements on each list.

### 2.5.1 Relation-Changing Operations

On the basis of this simple machinery we can attempt to state lexical rules to account for the relation-changing operations in Chamorro and for the extraction of wh-objects. Lexical rules for the two varieties of passive in Chamorro are given below in (11) and a rule for dative shift is given in (12).[9]

(11)  Chamorro Passive Lexical Rules
      a. For singular agents:

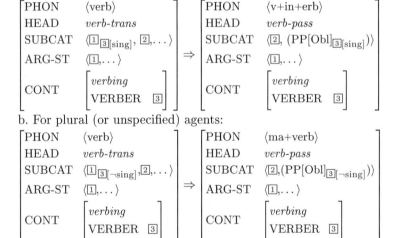

      b. For plural (or unspecified) agents:

The two rules given in (11) account for the number agreement observed in Chamorro between passive verbs and demoted agents by coindexing the agentive role in CONTENT with the subject demoted to oblique in the derived SUBCAT. The rules for passive do not specify any restric-

---

[8]See Davis 1996 for some discussion of constraints on the relationship between lexical semantics, ARG-ST and valence features, which I do not address here.

[9]Note that some intermediate nesting of information has been omitted in these representations to enhance readability.

tions on the semantic role of the object nor do they specify whether or not the surface object on the input must be an object on ARG-ST. This is because dative shift feeds passive in Chamorro and we therefore do not want passive restricted only to verbs whose object is underlying. However, since passive cannot reapply to its own output to demote a derived subject, it is necessary to restrict the application of the rule to initial (i.e. ARG-ST) subjects, as above.

I assume that Chamorro verbs are lexically sorted according to transitivity. Passive derives an intransitive verb of sort *verb-pass* from a transitive verb of sort *verb-trans*. Dative-shifted verbs will be treated as a subsort of transitive verbs called *verb-dat.*

The rule given in (12) derives a dative-shifted verb from a initially transitive verb, promoting an initial oblique to object and demoting the initial object to oblique.[10]

(12)   Chamorro Dative Shift Lexical Rule

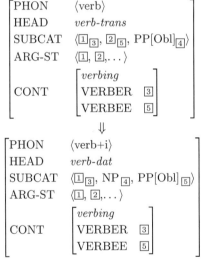

A rule corresponding to (12) is also required to derive dative-shifted verbs from initially intransitive verbs (Gibson 1992, 36), though since these forms lack demoted objects they are of no additional relevance to the discussion here. Note that, as in the case of passive, the ARG-ST

---

[10]Note that I follow Pollard and Sag 1994 in treating prepositions as case markers. Thus the indices of their complement NPs are accessible to the ARG-ST list of the verb.

value of the derived verb preserves the argument ordering observed in the ordinary active transitive verb categories.[11]

## 2.5.2 An Object Extraction Lexical Rule

The behaviour of object extraction by nominalization in Chamorro requires the statement of at least one lexical rule governing the appearance of verb morphology that correlates with the grammatical relation borne by the extracted element. The lexical rules governing object extraction will be the locus for capturing the role of surface and underlying grammatical relations in constraining extraction. Furthermore, the conditions on extraction must interact in the appropriate way with the relation-changing rules outlined in the previous section.[12]

Adopting the essentials of the traceless analysis of extraction presented in Pollard and Sag 1994, ch. 9, and Sag and Fodor 1995, it is necessary to provide lexical rules governing the appearance of *-in-* nominalization when Chamorro verbs have a nonempty SLASH value corresponding to a missing object of one of the types listed in (10). Obviously the goal is to provide as few such rules as possible without doing an injustice to the data.

It appears in fact that it is possible to account for all of the data presented above involving *-in-* nominalization (except the extraction of former objects demoted by causativization, which is discussed below) with just one lexical rule licensing object extraction. This rule is given in (13).

(13)    Chamorro Object Extraction Lexical Rule

$$
\begin{bmatrix}
\text{PHON} & \langle\text{verb}\rangle \\
\text{HEAD} & \textit{verb-trans} \\
\text{SUBCAT} & \langle\ldots, \boxed{2},\ldots\rangle \\
\text{ARG-ST} & \langle\boxed{1}, \boxed{2},\ldots\rangle \\
\text{SLASH} & \langle\,\rangle
\end{bmatrix}
\Rightarrow
\begin{bmatrix}
\text{PHON} & \langle\text{v+in+erb}\rangle \\
\text{HEAD} & \textit{noun} \\
\text{SUBCAT} & \langle\ldots, \ldots\rangle \\
\text{ARG-ST} & \langle\boxed{1}, \boxed{2},\ldots\rangle \\
\text{SLASH} & \langle\boxed{2}\rangle
\end{bmatrix}
$$

The rule in (13) accounts for the restrictions summarized in (10) in the following ways. Firstly, only underlying objects may trigger *-in-* nominalization because the slashed category must be structure-shared with the ARG-ST object. Secondly, underlying objects demoted by dative shift may trigger *-in-* nominalization because the SUBCAT description in the input of (13) places no restriction on the surface grammatical

---

[11]The Chamorro sources I have consulted do not indicate whether objects demoted by dative shift are optional or obligatory. The rule in (12) treats them as obligatory but could be easily modified if the facts are otherwise.

[12]Extraction by chopping may also involve some restrictions based on grammatical relations but these are not discussed here for reasons of space.

relation of the underlying object. Thirdly, underlying objects promoted by passive to subject cannot trigger *-in-* nominalization because (13) is restricted to transitive verbs. Passives in Chamorro are finally intransitive and so (13) cannot apply to the output of the passive lexical rule. The same restriction also applies correctly to block objects demoted by antipassivization from triggering *-in-* nominalization because antipassivized predicates are intransitive.

### 2.5.3 Chamorro Transitive Causativization

It remains to explain how the causative data presented earlier interacts with the lexical rules presented so far. As discussed in section 4.1, it seems reasonable to assume that a subject subcategorized by a verb that is subsequently causativized bears grammatical relations to both the verb stem and to the derived causative. Adopting the position that a causee is simultaneously an ARG-ST subject with respect to the verb stem and an ARG-ST object with respect to the derived causative straightforwardly explains the fact that the causee can undergo extraction via *-in-* nominalization. A lexical rule for transitive causativization is provided in (14).

(14)  Transitive Causativization

$$
\begin{bmatrix}
\text{PHON} & \langle \text{verb} \rangle \\
\text{HEAD} & \textit{verb-trans} \\
\text{SUBCAT} & \langle \boxed{1}, \boxed{2}, \ldots \rangle \\
\text{ARG-ST} & \langle \boxed{1}, \boxed{2}, \ldots \rangle
\end{bmatrix}
\Rightarrow
\begin{bmatrix}
\text{PHON} & \langle \text{na'+verb} \rangle \\
\text{HEAD} & \textit{verb-trans} \\
\text{STEM} & \begin{bmatrix} \text{ARG-ST} & \langle \boxed{1}, \boxed{2}_{\boxed{5}}, \ldots \rangle \end{bmatrix} \\
\text{SUBCAT} & \langle \boxed{3}, \boxed{1}, \text{PP[Obl]}_{\boxed{5}} \rangle \\
\text{ARG-ST} & \langle \boxed{3}, \boxed{1}, \boxed{2}_{\boxed{5}} \rangle
\end{bmatrix}
$$

The rule in (14) treats the causee as an ARG-ST object of a derived verb of type *verb-trans*. It is therefore eligible to undergo all the usual processes that apply to ARG-ST objects of transitive verbs including passivization, demotion by dative shift and extraction by *-in-* nominalization. No further wrinkles need to be added to account for the object properties of the causee since (13) can apply as expected to the output of (14) to allow *-in-* nominalization.

The properties of the STEM ARG-ST object do however require some additional discussion because it retains its object properties with respect to extraction even though it is *not* an ARG-ST object with respect to the derived causative verb. Going by the representation in (14), the likely reason that extraction of the oblique PP in a transitive causative can trigger *-in-* nominalization seems to be that it is *coindexed* with the ARG-ST object of the STEM. Thus, as it stands, the rule in (13) does not allow extraction by nominalization of the oblique in the output of (14), because the grammatical features of the surface PP are not structure-shared with the features of the STEM ARG-ST object.

Two possibilities suggest themselves as solutions to this problem. One approach, based on the hypothesis that the values of the elements on ARG-ST probably should not make reference to features determining 'surface' syntactic features like case and grammatical category, is to treat all case information in Chamorro (assuming again that prepositions are essentially a variety of case marker) as external to the NP itself and then allowing the remaining structure of NPs to be shared across ARG-ST and SUBCAT lists. Under this approach, no changes would be needed to the rules above except that we would now be able to stipulate structure-sharing of the STEM ARG-ST object value with the corresponding surface oblique in the SUBCAT list of the causative, despite the fact that one is an NP and the other a PP.[13] Rule (13) could then apply as required under the assumption that the structure-sharing of the value of the extracted element with an ARG-ST object is interpreted existentially (as in Manning and Sag's (1995) treatment of binding with causatives), requiring structure sharing with *at least one* ARG-ST object somewhere in the representation of the verb. Such an approach accords closely with the Relational Grammar approach to multistratality in which changes in surface features like case marking or the appearance of prepositions on demoted arguments play no role in constraining relationally based grammatical constraints.

An alternative approach is to suppose that it is not structure-sharing of grammatical category with an ARG-ST object but structure-sharing of indices with an ARG-ST object that is required to license extraction by *-in-* nominalization, again interpreting this requirement existentially.[14] Under this analysis, the lexical rule given in (13) would need to be reformulated to indicate that NPs extracted by *-in-* nominalization must be coindexed with at least one ARG-ST object somewhere in the representation of the verb. This analysis requires less tinkering with the formal machinery of HPSG but will potentially run into prob-

---

[13]This approach is already implicit in the extraction rule given in (13) where the slashed category structure-shares its features with some element on ARG-ST that is understood either to be an object NP or an oblique PP derived by demotion of the object.

[14]As a reviewer notes, the 'existential' interpretation of structure-sharing required to account for the cases of *-in-* nominalization licensed by embedded ARG-ST objects requires the grammar to 'ignore' the distinction between matrix and embedded structure. It is unclear to me at present to what extent this possibility should be allowed, if at all. However, the only apparent alternative to this analysis is to write another lexical rule specifically to deal with the embedded causative cases. This is not an appealing alternative.

lems in case where NPs are coindexed for other reasons (e.g. binding, control, etc). An analysis based on coindexation may incorrectly allow ungrammatical cases of -in- nominalization.

# References

Alsina, Alex. 1993. *Predicate Composition: A Theory of Syntactic Function Alternations.* Doctoral Dissertation, Stanford University.

Bell, Sarah. 1983. Advancements and Ascensions in Cebuano. In David Perlmutter (ed.), *Studies in Relational Grammar 1.* Chicago; University of Chicago Press.

Bresnan, Joan, and Jonni Kanerva. 1989. Locative Inversion in Chichewa: A Case Study of Factorization in Grammar. *Linguistic Inquiry* 20, 1–50.

Chung, Sandra. 1981. Transitivity and Surface Filters in Chamorro. In Jim Hollyman and Andrew Pawley (eds.), *Studies in Pacific Languages and Culture in Honour of Bruce Biggs.* Auckland; Linguistic Society of New Zealand.

Chung, Sandra. 1982. Unbounded Dependencies in Chamorro Grammar. *Linguistic Inquiry* 13, 39–77.

Chung, Sandra. 1994. Wh-Agreement and 'Referentiality' in Chamorro. *Linguistic Inquiry* 25, 1–44.

Davies, William. 1986. *Choctaw Verb Agreement and Universal Grammar.* Dordrecht; Reidel.

Davis, Anthony. 1996. *Linking and the Hierarchical Lexicon.* Doctoral Dissertation, Stanford University.

Dowty, David. 1982. Grammatical Relations and Montague Grammar. In Pauline Jacobson and Geoffrey K. Pullum (eds.), *The Nature of Syntactic Representation.* Dordrecht; Reidel.

Dukes, Michael. 1993. On the Status of Chamorro wh-Agreement. In Jonathan Mead, Murat Kural and Luc Moritz (eds.), *Proceedings of the Eleventh West Coast Conference on Formal Linguistics.* Stanford; CSLI.

Gibson, Jeanne. D. 1990. Categorial Grammatical Relations: the Chamorro Evidence. In Paul M. Postal and Brian D. Joseph (eds.), *Studies in Relational Grammar 3.* Chicago; University of Chicago Press.

Gibson, Jeanne. 1992. *Clause Union in Chamorro and in Universal Grammar.* New York; Garland Publishing.

Jaeggli, Osvaldo. 1986. Passive. *Linguistic Inquiry* 17, 587–622.

Keenan, Edward L., and Bernard Comrie. 1977. Noun Phrase Accessibility and Universal Grammar. *Linguistic Inquiry* 8, 63–99.

Manning, Christopher, and Ivan A. Sag. 1995. Dissociations between Argument Structure and Grammatical Relations. Ms, Stanford University.

Perlmutter, David. 1982. Syntactic Representation, Syntactic Levels and the Notion of Subject. In Pauline Jacobson and Geoffrey K. Pullum (eds.), *The Nature of Syntactic Representation.* Dordrecht; Reidel.

Perlmutter, David, 1984. The Inadequacy of some Monostratal Theories of Passive. In David Perlmutter and Carol Rosen (eds.), *Studies in Relational Grammar 2*. Chicago; University of Chicago Press.

Pollard, Carl, and Ivan A. Sag. 1992. Anaphors in English and the Scope of Binding Theory. *Linguistic Inquiry* 23, 261–303.

Pollard, Carl, and Ivan A. Sag. 1994. *Head-Driven Phrase Structure Grammar*. Chicago; University of Chicago Press.

Sag, Ivan A., and Janet Dean Fodor. 1995. Extraction Without Traces. In Raúl Aranovich et al (eds.), *Proceedings of the Thirteenth West Coast Conference on Formal Linguistics*. Stanford; CSLI.

Wechsler, Stephen. 1995. *The Semantic Basis of Argument Structure*. Stanford; CSLI.

# 3

# A Composition Approach to Modern Greek 'Weak Form' Possessives

Dimitra Kolliakou

## 3.1 Introduction

A long-standing problem in the literature on clitics has been the issue of whether they can be best analyzed as affixes or as syntactically autonomous words. According to one proposal, cf. e.g., Anderson 1992, all 'clitics' are phrasal affixes and should not be assigned the status of nodes in syntactic markers at all. Anderson discusses data from a number of languages and shows that there are very substantial similarities between the principles governing the placement of 'clitics' and those for the placement of affixes. An affixal approach to clitics will permit such generalizations to be expressed, and, moreover, dispense with, in his view, *ad hoc* syntactic categories such as *clitic* or *particle*. According to an alternative view, cf. e.g., Zwicky and Pullum 1983 and for a recent discussion Halpern 1995, it is essential to distinguish between (a) affixal clitics that are lexically attached, and (b) postlexical clitics (PLC) that have the syntax of phrases but prosodically are part of a *Clitic Group,* cf. Nespor and Vogel 1986. If the view represented by Anderson is right, then what remains to be done is to work out the specifics for each particular family of affixes. Otherwise, the issue of affix versus PLC status is a burning one. I start therefore by considering this issue with respect

Many thanks to Dora Alexopoulou, Jonathan Ginzburg, Aaron Halpern, Jack Hoeksema, Ineke Mennen, John Nerbonne, Ivan Sag, Ann Taylor, Jan-Wouter Zwart, two anonymous reviewers, and in particular Gosse Bouma, for comments and discussion. Due to space limitations, some rather significant parts of the evidence have been omitted. Readers wishing to inspect a fuller version are welcome to contact the author. The research reported here was supported by EU TMR grant No. ERB4001GT950989.

*Lexical and Constructional Aspects of Linguistic Explanation.*
Gert Webelhuth, Jean-Pierre Koenig, and Andreas Kathol.

to the Modern Greek 'weak form' possessive pronoun, henceforth, MG POSS (Sections 3.2 and 3.3). Given that I conclude that MG POSS *is* an affix, I do provide a detailed account of its morphosyntax. Thus, in Section 3.4 I show how a composition approach, in the spirit of previous work on pronominal affixation couched in the framework of Head-Driven Phrase Structure Grammar (HPSG), can be applied to MG POSS, despite apparent empirical and conceptual difficulties for extending to NP an approach originally intended for the placement of pronominal affixes in Romance VPs. The analysis proposed herein differs from the 'classical' composition approach in that it maintains hierarchical structuring, by permitting solely to affix members of complement lists to be composed by higher heads.

## 3.2 Basic Data and Previous Approaches

By way of introduction, I mention a number of essential and undisputed facts about MG POSS. First, MG POSS is an enclitic or suffix, as can be demonstrated by evidence from stress. It has often been observed that in MG lexical stress is allowed on any one of the last three syllables of a word but no further to the left (Stress Well-Formedness Condition (SWFC)). If a potential host for POSS is stressed on the antepenultimate, as e.g., *kalíteros* ('best'), once POSS is attached, a stress is added two syllables to the right, as in *kaliteros* in (1), to satisfy SWFC:

(1)  o    kalíterós MU      filos
     the  best      POSS.1sg friend
     'my best friend'

Second, POSS exhibits a 'floating' distribution: it can attach to a specifier (2a), any prenominal adjective (2b,c), or the noun (2d). However, multiple possessive marking, as e.g., in (2e) is not allowed.

(2)  a.  ola  TUS       ta-prosfata epistimonika arthra
         all  POSS.3pl  the-recent  scientific   papers
         'all their recent scientific papers'
     b.  ola ta-prosfata TUS epistimonika arthra
     c.  ola ta-prosfata epistimonika TUS arthra
     d.  ola ta-prosfata epistimonika arthra TUS
     e.  *ola TUS ta-prosfata epistimonika arthra TUS

To the best of my knowledge, no PLC analysis of MG POSS has been previously proposed. However, a prosodic approach to the Ancient Greek possessive enclitic (AG POSS) which assigns it PLC status is provided by Taylor (1996). I summarize this proposal and consider whether it can be extended to MG.

The following data (from texts dating back to 0–300 AD) demonstrate that AG POSS can appear in two positions: (a) the NP-initial position, henceforth, **1W** (first-word-position), as shown in (3a), and (b) in second-position, in fact, the position after the first word (position **2W** à la Halpern 1995), as shown in (3b,c).

(3)    a.    kai   peisthēsontai   [NP SOU      tais-rhēmasin]
             and   they-will-trust     POSS.2sg   the-D(AT) words-D
             'and they will trust your words'

      b.    aph'   hēs   [V elalēsas]   autois
             from   when      you-told   them-D

             [NP tas-entolas              MOU]
                the-A(CC) commandments-A   POSS.1sg

             'from the time when you told them my commandments'

      c.    metelabon    hoti   bareōs     douleuete
             I-understand   that   grudgingly   you-serve

             [NP tēn-kurian     HĒMŌN    mēteran]
                the-A lady-A   POSS.1pl   mother-A

             '. . . that you serve our lady mother grudgingly'

Following a tradition which assumes that **1W** and **2W** are related and derives the latter from the former in a 'post-syntactic' component of the grammar, Taylor provides a prosodic account of the **1W/2W** alternation: AG POSS is taken to be a *simple clitic* in the sense of Zwicky, which, however, is sensitive to phonological phrase (Φ) boundaries. As shown in (4a,b) below, AG POSS is syntactically left-adjoined to NP and prosodically attaches to a linearly preceding host outside its domain, due to its enclitic status, thus giving rise to syntax-phonology mismatches of the type discussed in Klavans 1985. In case a non-optional Φ boundary ('#') precedes the clitic, i.e., one that cannot be eliminated by Φ *restructuring* in the sense of Nespor and Vogel 1986, as e.g., in the case of (4c,d), *Prosodic Inversion* is triggered (cf. Halpern 1995, Taylor 1996), which essentially amounts to allowing the linear order of host and clitic inside the *Clitic Group* to be the reverse of their linear order in the syntax. ('=' marks prosodic attachment.)

(4)    a.    [VP [V peisthēsontai] [NP [CL SOU] [NP tais-rhēmasin]]]
      b.    (Φ peisthēsontai =SOU tais-rhēmasin)
      c.    [VP [V elalēsas] [NP autois] [NP [CL MOU] [NP tas-entolas]]]
      d.    ((Φ elalēsas) (Φ autois)# (Φ tas-entolas =MOU))

A crucial difference between AG and MG POSS is that the latter never attaches to a host outside its syntactic domain: (3a) is not an available option in MG. To start with, the fact that the MG counterpart of (3a) is ill-formed is more consistent with an affixal rather than a PLC analysis; as is shown in Halpern 1995, unlike PLCs, affixal clitics do not appear outside the projection of their licensing head. In addition, unless it could be shown that $\Phi$ boundaries are obligatory in MG in all contexts where Taylor takes them to be optional for AG, this distribution requires one to assume that the syntactic domain of MG POSS is never a maximal projection (NP), but rather the N'.[1] This would nonetheless go contrary to most of the literature which exclusively allows *maximal* categories to constitute the *syntactic domain* or *scope* of clitics. Let us for the moment ignore these two initial difficulties and assume that MG POSS is syntactically left-adjoined to N' and prosodically attaches to a linearly preceding host, due to its enclitic status. Such a proposal will account for examples (2a–c), which conform to the pattern [X [$_{N'}$ POSS [$_{N'}$ Y Z]]], i.e. they contain a clitic in N'-initial position.[2] Moreover, the requirement for left, as opposed to right adjunction will allow us to account for an additional fact, illustrated in (5), namely, that postnominal adjectives cannot host POSS:

(5)  a.  ena  arthro  TU           prosfato
         one  paper  POSS.3.masc/neut.sg  recent
         'a recent paper of his'
     b.  *ena arthro prosfato TU

Under Taylor's proposal, (2d), with *tou* in second position, would be derived from the structure [... [$_{N'}$ epistimonika [$_{N'}$ TUS [$_{N'}$ arthra]]]], by applying prosodic inversion. However, such an explanation would further require to assume that words may constitute (optional) phonological boundaries in MG NP—an assumption that has not previously been made. It can perhaps be argued that there are alternative ways for accounting for **1W/2W** alternations, e.g., by assuming that (2a–d) are all instances of discontinuous constituency, where a possessive clitic syntactically combines with an NP or N', is permitted to interleave with its daughters, and appears after the leftmost daughter in NP or N'—a specifier, adjective, or the noun. In the next section, I argue that the PLC approach to MG POSS, no matter whether prosodic or syntactic, will encounter a number of distributional problems.

---

[1]Besides, unless we take the N' as the domain, we cannot account for examples such as (2c) which are clearly not instances of second-position in NP, but rather instances of second-position (**2W**) in N'.

[2]In (2), *ola* is taken to be the specifier, whereas the proclitic or prefix definite article (*ta*) (which can appear repeatedly) is part of the N'.

## 3.3 Arguing for an Affixal Approach

A first problem for an analysis of MG POSS as a postlexical clitic is the existence of unexpected gaps in **1W** and **2W**. Along with the grammatical (6a) below, a prosodic or syntactic analysis along the lines of the one sketched above will allow for the ill-formed (6b), with MG POSS in **1W**, following the complement of a preceding adjective. (6b) cannot be excluded by appealing to an obligatory phonological phrase boundary to the left of *tu* since it is generally agreed that material inside the NP that precedes the noun plus the noun itself form a single phonological phrase.[3]

(6)  a.  ta   [AP gnosta   [se olus]]      kolpa TU
         the      familiar to everybody tricks POSS.3.m/n.sg
         'his tricks which are familiar to everybody'

    b.  *ta [AP gnosta [se olus]] TU kolpa

An approach à la Taylor would also permit the ill-formed (7b) below to be derived by prosodic inversion from (7a), where POSS is syntactically left-adjoined to the N′ whose first word is the adverbial *entelos*. Though a syntactic PLC approach could perhaps rule out (7b) by constraining MG POSS to exclusively interleave with the daughters of an N′/NP, rather than the daughters of an AP embedded inside that N′/NP, this latter type of approach would fail to allow for the grammatical (7c). In (7c), *tu* is again embedded inside an AP, but this time it is attached to the adjective, while the modifier occurs in post-head position. The contrast between (7b) and (7c) shows that APs cannot be homogeneously treated as syntactic boundaries for the purposes of clitic placement.

(7)  a.  orismenes TU
         certain    POSS.3.m/n.sg

         [N′ [AP entelos  katestramenes]  tixografies]
              totally  ruined            frescos

         'some of its totally ruined frescos'

    b.  *orismenes [AP entelos TU katestramenes] tixografies

    c.  [AP to   apagorevmeno TU        dia nomu] vivlio
            the forbidden      POSS.3m.sg by  law    book
         'his book which is forbidden by law'

---

[3] Neither could it be argued that MG POSS requires a strictly lexical host and resists a preceding phrase: not only does this assumption violate the spirit of the PLC approach, but it is also empirically refuted by the grammaticality of, for instance:

(i)    (ta) [AP para poli   gnosta] TU            kolpa
       the      very much familiar POSS.3.masc.sg tricks
       'his very familiar tricks'

The distribution patterns in (6) and (7) (as well as the example in footnote 3) can be straightforwardly accounted for if MG POSS is viewed as part of the morphology of nominal categories (determiners e.g., *orismenes*, adjectives e.g., *apagorevmeno*, and nouns e.g., *kolpa*). In terms of Miller 1992 and Halpern 1995, this amounts to treating POSS as 'extended' inflection that exhibits *head percolation,* that is, if it is to be located inside an AP daughter of N', it will be attached to the adjective head, if it is to be located inside the specifier, it will be attached to its determiner head, and so on; therefore, it cannot be found on the right or left edge of a daughter of N'/NP, as in the ungrammatical (6b) and (7b), respectively.[4]

A second problem for the PLC approach is the fixed order of POSS and NP-internal demonstratives—the latter must always follow the former inside NP, as shown in (8). It is commonly assumed that NP-internal demonstratives in MG have the syntactic status of adjectives. Given this, the PLC approach would predict that both (8a) and (8b) should be grammatical, in either case *tu* being syntactically left-adjoined to an N', and prosodically attached to a preceding adjective. An affixal approach on the other hand can circumvent this problem. Affixation is a lexical matter, therefore, there can be exceptions in a given morphological paradigm. NP-internal demonstratives can be treated as such an exception in that, unlike other adjectives, they do not participate in the morphological process of possessive affixation. Additional exceptions of this kind will be provided below.

(8)    a.    ta-kenuria  TU      afta    vivlia
               the-new   POSS.3sg these books
               'these new books of his'

        b.  *ta-kenuria afta   TU      vivlia
               the-new    these POSS.3sg books

Consider now some phonological evidence in favour of an affixal approach. In MG, two phonological rules can be identified whose domain of application is the word, where 'word' is to be interpreted either as

---

[4]A potential counterexample for the 'head percolation' generalization is the fact that POSS cannot intervene between an adjective and its phrasal complement, e.g., the string *ta gnosta TU se olous kolpa* is ill-formed—compare with the grammatical (6a). Notice, however, that this example would also be a problem for the prosodic inversion approach discussed above, and, moreover, for a syntactic approach assuming discontinuous constituency and which would provide the means for accounting for the grammatical (7c). Both types of account would allow for the 'surface' ordering [Y [AP Adj POSS XP] Z ... ], with 'XP' being the complement of the adjective. The composition-based proposal in Section 4 provides a tentative solution to this problem by assigning possessive morphology to adjectives which do not subcategorize for a thematic complement.

a plain inflectional form, or as an inflectional form plus possessive suffix combination. First, SWFC (see above) affects lexical stress in an entirely predictable way (a) in case of inflectional affixation, where the main stress moves one syllable to the right, as e.g., in *máthima* ('lesson-NOM/ACC.SG') → mathímatos ('lesson-GEN.SG'), and (b) in what has been traditionally referred to as *cliticization,* here analyzed as 'extended' or phrasal affixation. Though in (a) and (b) lexical stress is affected in two different ways—recall that in case of possessive affixation a new stress (main stress) is added two syllables to the right of the original lexical stress, whereas the latter weakens—this difference can be accommodated in the account proposed below which identifies two types of morphology for a given nominal word: *plain morphology,* which corresponds to inflected forms, and *clitic morphology,* which corresponds to inflected forms that also bear a possessive suffix, 'clitic' bearing no theoretical significance in this piece of terminology. The second rule is the voicing of a stop when it is preceded by a nasal. Stop Voicing (SV) applies inside a plain morphology word, as e.g., in case of αντίθεση ('antithesis') → [andithesi], and, moreover, inside a clitic morphology word, as e.g., in καθηγητών του (professors POSS-3.masc.sg; 'his professors') → [kathigiton du], but not across words; e.g., in καθηγητών τακτικών ('professors regural'; 'tenured professors'), the initial [t] of the postnominal adjective cannot be voiced: [kathigiton taktikon], but not *[kathigiton daktikon].

A further piece of evidence in favour of an affixal analysis is the existence of certain exceptions or 'arbitrary gaps' in the set of 'host'-POSS combinations, cf. Zwicky and Pullum 1983. For example, though POSS can occur inside indefinite NPs, as has been previously demonstrated in (5a), particular members of the determiner class appear to resist a possessive suffix. My consultants agree that there is a contrast between (9a) and (9b) below, despite the fact that *merikes* and *orismenes* do not appear to have different properties otherwise, e.g., they can both occur in the partitive construction (*merikes/orismenes apo tis fotografies* TU; 'some/certain of his pictures'), and neither of the two is licit inside definite NPs, unlike e.g., the cardinals (*i-tris/*i-merikes/*i-orismenes fotografies* 'the three/*the-some/*the-certain pictures').[5,6]

---

[5]POSS can function as 'object of comparison' for a number of comparative adjectives, which are not discussed here, due to space limitations. There too, the potential for possessive affixation is lexically determined given arbitrary contrasts such as *megaliteros ap'afton / megaliteros* TU ('older than him' / 'older POSS.3.masc.sg'), versus *spudeoteros ap'afton / *spudeoteros* TU (more important than him / *more important POSS.3.masc.sg).

[6]A few words about the coordination diagnostic are in order. Potential for wide

(9)  a.??merikes TU            fotografies
        some    POSS.3.m/n.sg  pictures
        (Intended:) 'some of his pictures'
     b.  orismenes TU           fotografies
        certain   POSS.3.m/n.sg pictures
        'certain of his pictures'

## 3.4  A Complement Composition Approach

This section reaches a conclusion that might at first sight appear rather surprising, namely, that an approach originally proposed for V pronominal affixes in Romance can be extended to account for the possessive suffix in Modern Greek. I start by discussing two problems for extending the 'classical' composition approach to possessive affixation. A first apparent problem is that composition requires all nominal categories in MG (determiners, adjectives and nouns) to be treated as heads of the phrase they occur in—an assumption that seems less obviously correct in case of adjectives, given the fact that they can iterate. A second more serious problem is that 'classical' composition would give rise to very flat NP structures which lack independent motivation. I show that a head approach to both determiners and adjectives—one which further assumes that adjectives and nouns in MG are subsumed within a supercategory *nominal*—is both consistent with previous proposals in diverse theoretical frameworks, and, moreover, is supported by independent evidence in

---

scope over a coordination of hosts is taken to support a PLC approach, and vice versa, cf. Miller 1992. E.g., the ill-formedness of *Pierre les voit et écoute*, as opposed to *Pierre les voit et les écoute* ('P. sees them and hears them') argues in favour of affix status for French V 'clitics' such as *les*. Unfortunately, the same test cannot provide conclusive evidence in case of MG POSS, since the latter, unlike V pronominal affixes, is not mandatory. Though for some speakers *o-kathigitis ke i-sinaderfos* MU ('the-professor-MASC and the-colleague-FEM POSS.1sg') can be assigned either of the readings 'the professor and my colleague' (preferred reading) and 'my professor and my colleague', this does not unambiguously indicate that POSS can take wide scope. Rather, usage of an NP that does not contain a possessive (e.g., *o kathigitis*) can often imply the existence of a 'possessor' (in this case, student of the professor), even outside coordination contexts with the rightmost conjunct bearing POSS. Even if we were to assume that the reading 'my professor and my colleague' can only be due to the possessive suffix's taking wide scope, that still wouldn't commit us to the PLC analysis: as Miller has shown, the credibility of the coordination test varies considerably, and 'it cannot be argued that an item is necessarily *not* an affix because it can have wide scope' (1992, 157). To this effect, Miller provides examples where elements for which he claims affix status appear to exhibit wide scope in coordination e.g., the definite and indefinite article in French (*le/un collegue et ami de mon père*; 'the/a friend and collegue of my father'), and shows that this is also true for elements whose affixhood is undisputed and is also reflected in the orthographic tradition, as e.g., *anti-* in *C'est un juge anti-dommage et intérêts* ('He is an anti-compensation judge').

MG. I present a composition approach whose innovative feature is that it maintains a hierarchical NP structure, by permitting solely to affix members of complement lists to be 'inherited' by 'composition' heads.

Previous HPSG accounts of pronominal affixation (cf. e.g., Sag and Miller 1997 and Abeillé et al. forthcoming for French) rely on *composition,* a notion reminiscent of *division categories* in categorial grammar, originally incorporated into HPSG by Hinrichs and Nakazawa. By composition, a functor (e.g., an auxiliary verb such as *avoir* 'have') can combine with an unsaturated argument (e.g., a participle such as *donné* 'given') whose valence requirements have not been satisfied, and also, *directly,* with the arguments of that participle (e.g., *le livre* 'the book' and *à Marie* 'to Mary'). Alternatively, the arguments the auxiliary 'inherits' from the participle can be realized as affixes, which allows to account for various instances of the phenomenon traditionally known as *clitic climbing,* such as e.g., in **le-lui**-*avons donné* ('(we) have given it to her/him').

In the last decade, most work on the syntax of determiners proposes their being treated as the head of the phrase they occur in. Such accounts for instance include the work of Abney (1987) and within the HPSG framework the proposal of Netter (1994). Assuming a head treatment of determiners à la Netter 1994 (and unlike Pollard and Sag 1994), and applying the 'classical' composition approach, a 'composition' determiner will be assigned the argument structure shown in (10), by which it can select for a lexical noun and 'inherit' the arguments of that noun. $\oplus$ stands for **append**.

(10)   Determiner (preliminary version)

$$\left[ \text{CAT} \begin{bmatrix} \text{HEAD} & det \\ \text{ARG-ST} & \langle \text{N[ARG-ST } \boxed{1}] \rangle \oplus \boxed{1} \end{bmatrix} \right]$$

The argument structure in (10) allows for two possibilities: (a) the determiner combines with its arguments 'in the syntax', as shown in (11a), where both arguments of *tria* ('three') are typed *canon(ical)* (*canon* is a subtype of *synsem* and signals that $\boxed{1}$ and $\boxed{2}$ are to be syntactically realized because *signs* (which are specified with a phonological value) are constrained to have canonical *synsem* values, cf. Sag and Miller 1997, Abeillé et al. forthcoming); (b) the determiner realizes the inherited possessive argument as an affix—*aff(ix)* also being a subtype of *synsem* which, however, is never associated with a PHON attribute, to constitute a word or phrase; this is shown in (11b) where the determiner's morphology consists of the inflected form *tria* ('three') and the possessive suffix *tu* (POSS.3.SG).

(11) a. [$_{DP}$ [$_{Det}$ tria ('three'); [ARG-ST ⟨ $\boxed{1}$*canon*, $\boxed{2}$*canon* ⟩]]
[$_{N}$ arthra ('papers'); $\boxed{1}$[ARG-ST ⟨ $\boxed{2}$*canon* ⟩]]
[$_{DP}$ tu Ilia ('of Ilias's'); $\boxed{2}$]]]

   b. [$_{DP}$ [$_{Det}$ tria-tu ('three-POSS.3sg');
   [ARG-ST ⟨ $\boxed{1}$*canon*, $\boxed{2}$*aff* ⟩]]
   [$_{N}$ arthra ('papers'); $\boxed{1}$[ARG-ST ⟨ $\boxed{2}$*aff* ⟩]]]]

However, with ARG-ST being an HPSG feature of lexical heads that does not propagate onto phrases, this type of composition approach gives rise to very flat structures like (11a), which lack independent motivation in Modern Greek. It is worth mentioning that all existing analyses assume a hierarchical structure for MG NPs with the determiner combining with a single constituent that contains both the N head and its complement(s). (For a literature review, see e.g., Kolliakou 1995.) Following authors who propose that partitives such as (12a) and 'simple' indefinites such as the one in (12b) are syntactically and semantically identical (cf. e.g., Matheson 1990), it can be argued that evidence from pronominalization is incompatible with the flat structure, but rather provides support for the hierarchical structure: the partitive *tus* can replace a single NP constituent that includes the noun's complement *tu Ilia*, as in (12c), rather than a lexical N complement of the determiner (see ill-formed (12d)).

(12) a. [tris [apo tus filous [tu Ilia]]] ('three of the friends of Ilias')
   b. [tris [fili [tu Ilia]]] ('three friends of Ilias')
   c. tris tus ('three of-them')
   d. *tris tus tu Ilia (lit. 'three of-them of Ilias')

Let us for the moment leave aside the problem concerning flat structuring, to which we will return below, and consider whether an argument composition approach can be extended to adjectives. This would require adjectives to be treated as heads, rather than adjuncts, when combining with N's, and AP mothers to 'dominate' noun heads and their complements. A treatment of adjectives as heads of nominal projections is not novel in the literature: it is familiar from categorial grammar where adjectives are assigned the type NP/NP, i.e. they are treated as functors that take an NP argument and yield another NP. In addition, it is commonly assumed in GB accounts, following Abney's proposal for English. In HPSG terms, this effect can be achieved (a) by modelling the types *adjective* and *noun*, which in Pollard and Sag 1994 constitute appropriate values of the feature HEAD, as subtypes of a supertype *nominal*, also meant to constitute an appropriate value of HEAD; and (b) by assuming that phrases consisting of an adjective and an N' (see below) are of type *hd-comp-ph (head-complement-phrase)*, cf. Sag 1997, or in terms of earlier HPSG work, they satisfy the head-complement ID-schema.

A variety of arguments for treating adjectives and nouns in MG as partly unified categories are provided in Kolliakou 1995. To briefly mention just a few, MG adjectives and nouns fall under the same morphological paradigms and both categories are morphologically marked for case and person/number/gender agreement. From a syntactic point of view, both adjectives/APs and nouns/NPs can 'host' a definite article in the MG multiple definite marking construction. No matter whether MG definite articles are to be treated as prefixes or proclitics (PLC), the supertype *nominal* allows us to generalize over their suitable 'hosts'. In addition, both adjectives and nouns can function as complements of higher heads (e.g., verbs and quantifier determiners) in 'canonical' and 'elliptical' contexts—the MG nominal system being quite different from the English one and allowing for both 'determinerless' and 'nounless' maximal nominal categories, as shown in (13) below. Modelling adjectives and nouns as subtypes of *nominal* will enable a unified account of the syntax of 'canonical' and 'elliptical' constructions to be provided, one that does not posit phonologically null noun heads and is in the spirit of semantic approaches to ellipsis resolution that do not assume reconstruction in the syntax.

(13)  a.  Exasa  to vivlio mu      ki    agorasa  [NomP kenurio].
          lost    the book POSS.1.sg  and  bought            new
          'I lost my book and bought a new one.'

      b.  I times      ton isitirion    pikilun.
          the prices  of the tickets  vary

          Kita  na  vris   kanena [NomP ftino].
          try        get   any            cheap

          'The prices of the tickets vary. Try to get a cheap one.'

(14) illustrates the proposed hierarchy of parts-of-speech (*p-o-s*) which includes *nom(inal)*.

(14)

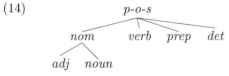

The feature description in (15) below with a preliminary ARG-ST value illustrates an adjective selecting for an N′ complement, N′ being an abbreviation for objects specified [HEAD *nominal*], and whose valence features do not contain any canonical elements, i.e. their subcategorization requirements have already been satisfied (but see below).

(15) Adjective as head (with preliminary version of ARG-ST value):

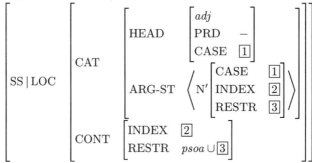

(15) will permit phrases containing no, one, or more adjectives, the noun, and the noun's phrasal complements (if any) to syntactically combine with an adjective head which will in turn head a Nominal Phrase. Thus, we generate 'binary structures' necessitating a hierarchical structure for NPs, and which have been uniformly adopted in previous work on MG.[7] Case concord and agreement in person/number/gender between the adjective head and its N' complement is straightforwardly accounted for by structure-sharing (1 and 2, respectively.) The RESTR value of the adjective is specified exactly as in the adjunct approach to adjectives of Pollard and Sag 1994, by lexically unioning the set of psoas contributed by the N' (3) with the adjective's own psoa.

Having shown that a head treatment of determiners and adjectives in MG is consistent with previous proposals in diverse theoretical frameworks and supported by independent evidence, I return to the issue of how to maintain an overall hierarchical structure for NP. I present a composition approach which (a) is similar to the one proposed for French causative constructions by Abeillé et al. (forthcoming) in that the 'composed' elements are members of COMPS rather than ARG-ST, and (b)

---

[7] This proposal as it currently stands will allow for 'elliptical' nominals with recursive adjectives, as in (i), which are not considered to be grammatical by all speakers.

(i)    ??Agorases    [DP kenena [NomP kenurio [NomP ftino]]]?
         bought-2.SG       any            new              cheap
         (Intended:) 'Did you buy any new cheap one?'

One way for eliminating such nominals could be by distinguishing between adjectives and nouns, the latter being specified [N+] in all instances, whereas the former being [N−] as a default, but [N+] when combining with an NP complement—their complement's specification overriding their own default when the two are put together. Assuming that adjective heads select for [N+] nominal complements, elliptical examples with recursive adjectives will thus be ruled out. A shortcoming of this proposal is however that it appeals to a notion of default which has not hitherto been commonly assumed in HPSG work, but see *order independent default unification*. Thanks to Ivan Sag for pointing this out as an issue.

differs from the 'classical' composition approach to pronominal affixation in Romance in that only affix members of COMPS and not phrases can be 'inherited' by 'composition' heads.

Following Sag and Miller 1997 and Abeillé et al. forthcoming for verbs in Romance, I assume two types of nominals: *plain-nominal-word (pl-nom-wd)* and *clitic-nominal-word (cl-nom-wd)*. The phonology value of *pl-nom-wd* is the basic inflected form that does not bear a possessive suffix. I assume that it will be computed by an inflectional function ($F_M$) which will take into account the root value specified in the lexeme type as well as information specified inside the index. On the other hand, the phonology value of *cl-nom-wd* in addition incorporates a possessive suffix. It is computed by a two argument function—a simpler version of Sag and Miller's $F_{PRAF}$—its first argument $\boxed{1}$ being the PHON value provided by $F_M$, and its second argument $\boxed{2}$ the word's ARG-ST value.

(16)

a.
$$\begin{bmatrix} lexeme \\ \text{PHON} & \boxed{1} \\ \text{ARG-ST} & \boxed{2} \end{bmatrix}$$
b.
$$\begin{bmatrix} pl\text{-}nom\text{-}wd \\ \text{PHON} & \langle F_M(\boxed{1}) \rangle \\ \text{ARG-ST} & \boxed{2} \end{bmatrix}$$
c.
$$\begin{bmatrix} cl\text{-}nom\text{-}wd \\ \text{PHON} & \langle F_{PRAF}(\boxed{1}, \boxed{2}) \rangle \\ \text{ARG-ST} & \boxed{2} \end{bmatrix}$$

Plain nominal forms are defined as having their argument structure list correspond to the concatenation of their valence features[8] plus a possibly empty list of gaps, in case some argument is being extracted. The list value of COMPS is unconstrained, thus allowing for plain morphology adjectives and nouns that contain an affix element in their COMPS list (and by unification in their ARG-ST list too). This is crucial for the type of composition approach proposed, one which is compatible with hierarchical NP structures. "$\bigcirc$" stands for the *shuffle* operation.

(17)
$$\begin{bmatrix} pl\text{-}nom\text{-}wd \\ \text{COMPS} & \boxed{1} \\ \text{ARG-ST} & \boxed{1} \bigcirc list(gap) \end{bmatrix}$$

For clitic morphology nominal forms, on the other hand, ARG-ST comprises (potentially empty) list of at most one affix in addition to the valence features (and a potentially empty list of gaps). It should be mentioned here that the only type of noun complement that can be realized in the morphology as an affix is one that is realized in the syntax as a genitive NP. A noun head in MG can take at most one phrasal genitive or affix argument, a fact which can be formulated as a constraint on ARG-ST lists of MG nouns. An argument typed *gen*, to

---

[8]For simplicity, SPR and SUBJ are omitted from ARG-ST: the SPR list of most nominal examples considered in this paper is empty—SPR being reserved for selecting certain adverbials and degree words modifying adjectives (cf. Pollard and Sag 1994); the SUBJ list of [PRED −] nominals is empty as well.

be realized as a phrase or affix, is also the leftmost argument inside the noun's ARG-ST. Note that the COMPS list of *cl-nom-wd* is constrained to exclusively contain canonical elements. As will become clear below, this is crucial for preventing the multiple realization of a given possessive in the same NP.

$$(18) \quad \begin{bmatrix} \textit{cl-nom-wd} \\ \text{COMPS} \quad \boxed{1}(\textit{canon}) \\ \text{ARG-ST} \quad \langle \textit{aff, gen} \rangle \oplus \boxed{1} \bigcirc \textit{list}(\textit{gap}) \end{bmatrix}$$

Consider now the (revised) ARG-ST list of the MG adjective:

(19)   Argument structure of MG adjective (final version):

$$\begin{bmatrix} \text{ARG-ST} \quad \boxed{1}[\textit{aff, gen}] \oplus \langle \text{N}'[\text{COMPS} \ \boxed{1}] \rangle \end{bmatrix}$$

The ARG-ST value in (19) is intended to replace the preliminary ARG-ST value specified in (15) above. The second slot is occupied by an N' element whose CASE, INDEX and RESTR, omitted here for simplicity, relate with the CASE, INDEX and RESTR of the adjective's exactly as was shown in (15). The crucial innovation is that N' is specified with a potentially nonempty COMPS list which is 'inherited' by the adjective and is constrained to contain elements of type *affix* (as it turns out, at most one). In case the 'inherited' affix list is nonempty, two possibilities exist: (a) the affix is not present in the adjective's own COMPS list, rather it is morphologically realized, in other words, the adjective is an instantiation of *cl-nom-wd*; and (b) the affix is a member of both ARG-ST and COMPS of the adjective head and will be 'inherited' by a higher head, the adjective thus being an instantiation of *pl-nom-adj*. These two options are illustrated in the tree-diagram in (21) on page 45 below.

The head-complement phrases represented in terms of branching nodes inherit the *head-complement-phrase* (*hd-comp-ph*) constraint:

(20)   *hd-comp-ph* →

$$\begin{bmatrix} \text{COMPS} & \boxed{0} \\ \text{HD-DTR} & \begin{bmatrix} \text{COMPS} & \boxed{0} \oplus \langle \boxed{1} \dots \boxed{n} \rangle \end{bmatrix} \\ \text{NON-HD-DTR} & \langle [\text{SS } \boxed{1}] \dots [\text{SS } \boxed{n}] \rangle \end{bmatrix}$$

(20) is in the spirit of type-specific constraints on phrasal types, as in Sag 1997. This formulation enables the first affixal element $\boxed{0}$ in the COMPS list of a given nominal to propagate to its mother's COMPS list from where it can be inherited by complement composition, the phrasal complements $\boxed{1} \dots \boxed{n}$ being cancelled off in the syntax. $\boxed{0}$ can alternatively be the empty list.

(21)  (see (2b))

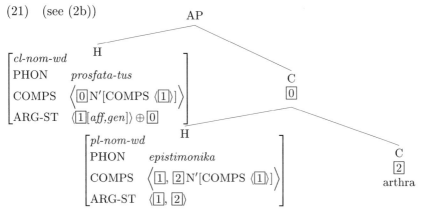

We can now apply the same to determiner heads and ensure that they combine with a single phrasal complement in the syntax, thus giving rise to hierarchical structures. The (revised) determiner's argument structure shown in (22) is the same as that of the adjective. I also assume a plain and a clitic morphology determiner type, analogous to those provided for nominals in (16b,c) above.

(22)  Argument structure of determiner (final version):

$$\left[\text{ARG-ST}\quad \boxed{1}[\textit{aff, gen}] \oplus \langle \text{N}'[\text{COMPS } \boxed{1}]\rangle\right]$$

Consider finally one remaining issue, namely, the requirement that post-nominal adjectives should not bear a possessive suffix, as was shown in (5) above. Postnominal adjectives with clitic morphology can be simply ruled out by the *Left Triggering Linear Precedence (LP) Constraint* in (23) which orders adjectives of this type to the left of their nominal syntactic sister[9]:

(23)  Left Triggering LP Constraint: [*cl-nom-wd, adj*] ≺ [*nom*]

## 3.5  Conclusion

In this paper I have presented evidence in support of an affix analysis of the MG 'weak form' possessive pronoun and discussed problems for a PLC approach in terms of *prosodic inversion*. I have proposed a *complement composition* account that is reminiscent of previous HPSG work in French, but differs from such accounts in that it maintains hierarchical structuring in NP by permitting solely to affix members of

---

[9] An alternative and probably more interesting option, which will not be explored here due to space limitations, is to follow Stavrou 1996 in assuming that post-nominal adjectives are quite different from pre-nominal ones—in the current system, the former could thus be construed as modifiers rather than heads, therefore explaining their inability to 'inherit' an affix complement.

complement lists to be composed by higher heads. This approach presupposes an analysis of both determiners and adjectives in MG as heads of the phrase they occur in—a hypothesis which has been entertained in diverse theoretical frameworks (GB and Categorial Grammar), and, in addition, is independently motivated in MG.

# References

Abeillé, Anne, Danièle Godard, and Ivan A. Sag. Forthcoming. Two Kinds of Composition in French Complex Predicates. In *Complex Predicates in Nonderivational Syntax*, ed. Erhard Hinrichs, Andreas Kathol, and Tsuneko Nakazawa. New York: Academic Press.

Abney, Steven. 1987. *The English Noun Phrase in its Sentential Aspect*. Cambridge, MA: MIT Press.

Anderson, Stephen. 1992. *A-Morphous Morphology*. Cambridge: CUP.

Halpern, Aaron. 1995. *On the Placement and Morphology of Clitics*. Stanford: CSLI Publications.

Klavans, Judith. 1985. The Independence of Syntax and Phonology in Cliticization. *Language* 61.1:95–120.

Kolliakou, Dimitra. 1995. *Definites and Possessives in Modern Greek: An HPSG Syntax for Noun Phrases*. University of Edinburgh: PhD thesis.

Matheson, Colin. 1990. *Syntax and Semantics of English Partitive Noun Phrases: A Phrase Structure Account*. University of Edinburgh: PhD thesis.

Miller, Philip. 1992. *Clitics and Constituents in Phrase Structure Grammar*. New York: Garland.

Nespor, Marina, and Irene Vogel. 1986. *Prosodic Phonology*. Dordrecht, The Netherlands: Foris Publications Holland.

Netter, Klaus. 1994. Towards a Theory of Functional Heads: German Nominal Phrases. In *German in Head-Driven Phrase Structure Grammar*, ed. John Nerbonne, Klaus Netter, and Carl Pollard. Stanford: CSLI Publications.

Pollard, Carl, and Ivan A. Sag. 1994. *Head-Driven Phrase Structure Grammar*. Chicago: University of Chicago Press.

Sag, Ivan A. 1997. English Relative Clause Constructions. *Journal of Linguistics* 33:431–484.

Sag, Ivan A., and Philip Miller. 1997. French Clitic Movement Without Clitics or Movement. *NLLT*.

Stavrou, Melita. 1996. Adjectives in Modern Greek: An Instance of Predication or an Old Issue Revisited. *Journal of Linguistics* 32:79–112.

Taylor, Ann. 1996. A Prosodic Account of Clitic Position in Ancient Greek. In *Second Position Clitics and Related Phenomena*, ed. Aaron Halpern and Arnold M. Zwicky. Stanford: CSLI Publications.

Zwicky, Arnold, and Geoffrey Pullum. 1983. Cliticization vs. Inflection: English n't. *Language* 59.3.

# 4

# West Greenlandic Noun Incorporation in a Monohierarchical Theory of Grammar

ROBERT MALOUF

## 4.1 Introduction

West Greenlandic noun incorporation (NI) is a highly productive category changing morphological operation that converts a noun into a verb by the addition of one of a set of bound verbalizing suffixes:

(1)    a. Kami-lisaar-puq.
          kamik-have.on-3SG.INDIC

          'He has kamiks on.'                          (Fortescue 1984, 322)
        b. Hansi      ino-ror-poq.
          Hans(ABS) man-develop.into-3SG.INDIC

          'Hans grew up.'                             (Sadock 1985, 402)

The resulting denominal verb (DV) has the full syntactic and morphological distribution of any verb in West Greenlandic. It also retains some of the properties of the incorporated nominal, which has led some researchers to analyze this construction as a kind of NI. However, as Sapir (1911), Mithun (1986) and others have argued, it has little in common with NI constructions in languages like Mohawk or Southern Tiwa. In this paper, I will explore an alternative HPSG analysis of these DVs as a

Versions of this paper were presented at the 1997 Meeting of the Linguistic Society of America and at the 1997 Conference on Head-driven Phrase Structure Grammar. I would like to thank Chris Manning, Ivan Sag, and an anonymous reviewer for helpful comments on earlier drafts.

*Lexical and Constructional Aspects of Linguistic Explanation.*
Gert Webelhuth, Jean-Pierre Koenig, and Andreas Kathol.
Copyright © 1998, Stanford University.

kind of mixed category construction that shares some of the properties of both verbs and nouns.

## 4.2  Properties of Denominal Verbs

A DV can head a clause like any other verb can. West Greenlandic is an ergative language, so a verb can govern an absolutive argument and, if transitive, an ergative argument. A DV also has all the morphological properties of a verb, and can even be nominalized and re-denominalized:

(2)    Apeqqutissa-qar-to-qar-poq.
       question-have-NOM-have-3SG.INDIC

  'There is someone with a question.'  (Sadock 1991, 85)

Unlike a verb, though, a DV can also occur with dependents that are characteristic of nouns. For example, nouns can take a possessor in the ergative case:

(3)  a. Kaalip  illua
    Karl-ERG house-ABS.3SG

    'Karl's house'    (Sadock 1985, 394

  b. piniartup  qajaa
   hunter-ERG kayak-ABS.3SG

   'the hunter's kayak'  (Fortescue 1984, 216)

As we see in (4), DVs can, like nouns, also take an ergative possessor.

(4)    Kunngi-p panip-passua-qar-poq.
       king-ERG daughter-many-have-3SG.INDIC

  'There are many king's daughters (i.e., princesses).'

      (Sadock 1991, 96)

Note that intransitive verbs cannot normally occur with an ergative argument.[1]

Even more strikingly, in some cases when the DV is itself transitive it can occur with two ergative NPs, the subject of the verb and the possessor of the incorporated nominal:

(5)    Hansi-p  qimmi-p ame-qar-tip-paa.
       Hans-ERG dog-ERG skin-have-CAUS-3SG.INDIC

  'Hans let him have (i.e., gave him) a dog's skin.'

      (Sadock 1991, 97)

---

[1]Van Geenhoven (1997) discusses a type of NI in West Greenlandic in which the possessor of the incorporated nominal appears in the absolutive or instrumental case. This construction could be derived under the present approach via a lexical rule which combines the *argument structures* of the noun stem and the verbal base rather than their *valences*. However, a complete discussion is beyond the scope of this paper.

Verbs in West Greenlandic do not otherwise take two ergative arguments, and examples like (5) are, as Sadock (1991, 97) points out, "not even grossly like anything that occurs independently of noun incorporation". If the possessor is actually associated with the incorporated noun root, though, then (5) is syntactically no different from any other clause with a transitive verb and a possessed noun.

In addition to taking an ergative possessor, nouns can occur with nominal modifiers, which must agree with the head noun in case and number:

(6)    a. Kaalip    illuanut
         Karl-ERG house-ALL.3SG

         'to Karl's house'                             (Sadock 1985, 394)

       b. Kaalip    illuanut        mikisumut
         Karl-ERG house-ALL.3SG small-ALL.SG

         'to Karl's small house'                       (Sadock 1985, 394)

And, as with possessors, modifiers can occur with DVs:

(7)    a. Kissartu-mik kavvi-sur-put.
         hot-INST        coffee-drink-3PL.INDIC

         'They drank hot coffee.'               (Fortescue 1984, 83)

       b. Nutaa-mik piili-siur-punga.
         new-INST    car-look.for-1SG.INDIC

         'I am looking for a new car.'          (Fortescue 1984, 83)

## 4.3   A Problem

A possible source of confusion here is that the examples in (7) look superficially like the 'half-transitive' or 'antipassive' case-marking pattern, shown in (8b), that is available for many semantically transitive verb roots.

(8)    a. Tuttu        taku-aa.
         caribou(ABS) see-3SG.3SG.INDIC

         'He saw the caribou.'                  (Fortescue 1984, 86)

       b. Tuttu-mik    taku-vuq.
         caribou-INST see-3SG.INDIC

         'He saw a caribou.'                    (Fortescue 1984, 86)

The agent (if expressed) appears in the absolutive case and the patient appears in the instrumental case. Since nominal modifiers are formally nouns, one might be tempted to explain the examples in (7) as antipassives and not as stranding. This is the essence of Rosen's (1989) lexicalist analysis of NI in languages like Mohawk. She argues that apparently 'stranded' modifiers are actually headless arguments, and that the in-corporated noun root's function is to semantically restrict the reference of the verb's direct object. However, Sadock provides several convincing pieces of evidence that such an analysis cannot be maintained for West Greenlandic DVs.

First, nominal modifiers differ from head nouns in that they cannot be marked for possession, as demonstrated in (9).

(9)    a. qatannguti-n-nik
         sibling-1SG-INST

         'my sibling (INST)'                          (Sadock 1991, 91)

       b. qatanngutinnik   arna-mik
          sibling-1SG-INST female-INST

          'my sister (INST)'                          (Sadock 1991, 91)

       c.*qatanngutinnik   arna-n-nik
          sibling-1SG-INST female-1SG-INST

          'my sister (INST)'                          (Sadock 1991, 91)

In this respect, modifiers occurring with DVs behave as if they were modifiers of the incorporated nominal and not as head nouns:

(10)   a. Arna-mik    qatanngu-seri-voq.
          female-INST sibling-be.occupied.with-3SG.INDIC

          'He is occupied with (someone's) sister.'

                                                      (Sadock 1991, 91)

       b.*Arna-n-nik       qatanngu-seri-voq.
          female-1SG-INST sibling-be.occupied.with-3SG.INDIC

          'He is occupied with my sister.'            (Sadock 1991, 91)

A second piece of evidence comes from agreement. A handful of nouns in West Greenlandic are semantically singular but formally plural. For example, the noun *qamutit* 'sled' is historically related to a root meaning 'sled runner' and is syntactically plural, though it denotes a single sled. Since nominal modifiers must agree with the noun they modify in number, *qamutit* triggers plural agreement on its modifiers. This is true even when it is incorporated into a DV:

(11)   a. Hansi       ataatsi-nik qamute-qar-poq.
          Hans(ABS) one-INST.PL sled-have-3SG.INDIC

          'Hans has one sled.'                        (Sadock 1985, 402)

       b.*Ataatsi-mik qamute-qar-poq.
          one-INST.SG sled(PL)-have-3SG.INDIC

          'He has one sled.'                          (Sadock 1991, 92)

While verbs in West Greenlandic can select for semantically plural NPs, they do not otherwise place purely formal agreement constraints on their arguments. So, the facts in (11) can be most simply explained if the nominal modifier is actually modifying the incorporated noun root.

Finally, Sadock observes that DVs with stranded non-intersective modifiers have the interpretation that would be expected if the modifiers are associated directly with the incorporated noun.

(12) peqquserluuti-nik aningaas-ior-toq
     false-INST.PL      money(PL)-make-NOM

     'one who makes false money, a counterfeiter'     (Sadock 1991, 95)

It is difficult to see how the incorporated noun root *aningaasaq* 'money' in (12) could be restricting the reference of the object: 'false money' is not stuff that is false and money. In fact, it is not money at all. The meaning of (12) follows, however, if the modifier takes scope over the noun root directly.

## 4.4 A Solution: Autolexical Grammar

These facts create a problem: incorporated nominals in West Greenlandic seem to select specifiers and modifiers as if they were independent heads of full NPs, yet they are clearly not independent words in the morphology. To resolve this paradox, Sadock (1985, 1991) has proposed a theory of grammatical information (Autolexical Grammar) that takes syntax and morphology as two independent levels of linguistic structure. 'Lexical' morphemes have associated representations in both projections, while inflectional morphemes only appear in the morphological structure and correspond to morphosyntactic features in the syntactic projection. If syntax and morphology are allowed to diverge, then West Greenlandic NI does not create a paradox; it simply is an example of a mismatch between the two levels of representation.

Sadock takes the behavior West Greenlandic NI to be evidence that morphology and syntax are in principle independent. Typically, though, the morphological structure matches the syntactic structure very closely. And, there seem to be strict limits on how much the two levels can diverge: it would be surprising indeed to find a language in which, say, the morphological structure was always the mirror image of the syntactic structure. So, Sadock (1991) proposes a set of universal **homomorphism constraints** on the association between syntactic and morphological representations that restrict the kinds of possible mismatches. Two of these constraints are given in (13).

(13)  a. Linearity Constraint (lc)
      The associated elements of the morphological and syntactic representations must occur in the same order. (Sadock 1991, 103)

   b. Constructional Integrity Constraint (cic)
      If a lexeme combines with a phrase P in the syntax and with a host in the morphology, then the morphological host must be associated with the head of the syntactic phrase P. (Sadock 1991, 103)

The purpose of the LC is pretty straightforward, but the CIC is perhaps a little more opaque. In (11a) the verbalizing suffix *qar* 'have' combines in the syntax with its direct object, the entire NP *ataatsinik qamut* 'one sled'. In principle, this suffix should be able to combine morphologically with either lexical word in the NP. In this kind of DV construction, though, the verbal morpheme always combines with the head noun, stranding modifiers, and not with a modifier, stranding the head noun.[2] This is what the CIC ensures.

Not all constructions will satisfy both of these constraints. The balance between these two constraints limits the range of possible mismatches: a structure can only violate one constraint to the extent that it satisfies the other. In particular, NI produces structures that violate the LC but satisfy the CIC. This is expressed in the construction-specific constraint in (14).

(14)  Incorporation Principle
      If a lexeme combines with a stem in the morphology and with a phrase in the syntax, its morphosyntactic association will conform to the CIC. (Sadock 1991, 105)

Since the CIC and the LC are complementary, a corollary of (14) is that NI is not subject to the LC.

## 4.5   A Better Solution: Mixed Categories

Sadock's arguments for a polyhierarchical analysis rest on the assumption that if a word has some of the properties of more than one syntactic category then it must at some level be represented as more than one word. Also, in defense of a lexical view of NI, Mithun (1986) has pointed out that NI in West Greenlandic has little in common with incorporation processes in other languages. In particular, true NI involves the morphological combination of a noun and a verb. West Greenlandic

---

[2]The exceptions to this generalization involve incorporation of a fully inflected word rather than a stem, and are probably better analyzed as the combination of an entire phrase with a verbalizing clitic (Manning 1996, 121).

DVs however are formed by the additional of a verbalizing suffix to a noun. These verbalizing suffixes are morphologically unrelated to the free form of the verb:

(15)    a.  Marlun-nik ammassat-tor-punga.
          two-INST.PL sardine-eat-1SG.INDIC

          'I ate two sardines.'                      (Sadock 1991, 94)

    b.  Ammassan-nik marlun-nik neri-vunga.
          sardine-INST.PL two-INST.PL eat-1SG.INDIC

          'I ate two sardines.'                      (Sadock 1991, 94)

West Greenlandic verbalizing suffixes are bound forms which by themselves have none of the morphosyntactic properties of true verbs.

In the remainder of this paper, I will show how the West Greenlandic DV can be seen as a kind of mixed category construction, parallel to the English verbal gerund. Under this view, the possessor and modifiers that occur with a DVs are not stranded by incorporation, nor do they bear a relation to the incorporated nominal directly. Instead, the DV inherits its subcategorization requirements from both the verbalizing suffix and the incorporated nominal. This is exactly parallel to mixed category constructions in other languages. For example, the English verbal gerund, like *devouring* in *Pat's devouring the pancakes,* occurs with both a genitive specifier, like nouns do, and an accusative direct object, like verbs do (Malouf 1996).

For concreteness, I will assume that all verbal elements in West Greenlandic (including verbal bases) are subtypes of one or more of the valence patterns in (16).

(16)    a.  *verbal-valence* → *transitive* ∨ *intransitive* ∨ *half-transitive*

    b.  *transitive* →

$$\begin{bmatrix} \text{SUBJ} & \langle \boxed{1} \rangle \\ \text{COMPS} & (\boxed{2} \oplus \boxed{3}) - list(noncanon) \\ \text{ARG-ST} & \langle \boxed{2}\text{NP}[erg], \boxed{1}\text{NP}[abs]\rangle \oplus \boxed{3}\, list(oblique) \end{bmatrix}$$

    c.  *intransitive* →

$$\begin{bmatrix} \text{SUBJ} & \langle \boxed{1} \rangle \\ \text{COMPS} & \boxed{3} - list(noncanon) \\ \text{ARG-ST} & \langle \boxed{1}\text{NP}[abs]\rangle \oplus \boxed{3}\, list(oblique) \end{bmatrix}$$

    d.  *half-transitive* →

$$\begin{bmatrix} \text{SUBJ} & \langle \boxed{1} \rangle \\ \text{COMPS} & (\boxed{2} \oplus \boxed{3}) - list(noncanon) \\ \text{ARG-ST} & \langle \boxed{1}\text{NP}[abs], \boxed{2}\text{NP}[inst]\rangle \oplus \boxed{3}\, list(oblique) \end{bmatrix}$$

The three types in (16) correspond to the transitive, intransitive, and half-transitive valence patterns. Some verbs may occur in any of these valence patterns, while other verbs are lexically specified as occurring in only one. Following Manning (1996), in each case the absolutive argument is identified as the subject, even when it is not the initial element on the ARG-ST list. The COMPS list consists of all non-absolutive canonical arguments. Any arguments that are not realized directly as dependents of the verb are **non-canonical** and so are not included in the verb's valence features. Types of non-canonical arguments proposed in the literature include the gaps associated with fillers in unbounded dependency constructions (Sag 1997, Bouma et al. 1998) and pronominal affixes (Miller and Sag 1997). Incorporated noun stems also must be included as a type of non-canonical argument:

(17)

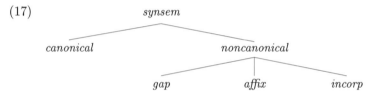

One thing to note is that none of the constraints in (16) is specific to DVs. These types reflect general constraints on case assignment and on the linking of argument positions to grammatical relations in West Greenlandic.

Given this theoretical background, intransitive verbalizing suffixes in West Greenlandic can be accounted for by the lexical rule in Figure 1.[3] This is a binary lexical rule that combines a verbal base with a nominal stem to form a DV. The resulting DV will combine with an absolutive subject, by virtue of its being a verb, and it will project a phrase that is like any other verbal projection following general principles of argument saturation. But, the derived verb also inherits the incorporated nominal's selection for an optional ergative possessor and complements, so any constraints which the noun stem places on its specifier and complements will be inherited by the DV. This accounts for the fact that the external specifier has the properties it would have had if it had appeared with the incorporated nominal alone.

To see how this analysis works, it will be helpful to go through an example in detail. First, consider the lexical entry for a noun root:

---

[3]The formulation of Figure 1 as a binary lexical rule is due to a suggestion by Carl Pollard.

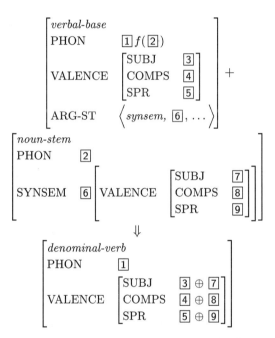

FIGURE 1  Noun incorporation lexical rule

(18)
$$\begin{bmatrix} noun\text{-}stem \\ \text{PHON} \quad \langle ammassak \rangle \\ \text{HEAD} \quad noun \\ \text{VALENCE} \begin{bmatrix} \text{SUBJ} \quad \langle \, \rangle \\ \text{COMPS} \quad \langle \, \rangle \\ \text{SPR} \quad \langle \text{NP}[erg] \rangle \end{bmatrix} \\ \text{CONTENT} \quad sardine\_rel \end{bmatrix}$$

Of course, some of the information in (18), such as the selection for an optional ergative specifier, will be inherited from a more general type. Similarly, much of the information in the entry for a verbal base in (19) will also be inherited from higher types:

(19)
$$\begin{bmatrix} verbal\text{-}base \\ \text{PHON} \quad f_{\text{tor}}(\_\_) \\ \text{HEAD} \quad verb \\ \text{VALENCE} \begin{bmatrix} \text{SUBJ} \quad \langle \boxed{1} \rangle \\ \text{COMPS} \quad \langle \, \rangle \\ \text{SPR} \quad \langle \, \rangle \end{bmatrix} \\ \text{ARG-ST} \quad \langle \boxed{1}\text{NP}[abs]\text{:}\boxed{2}, \; incorp \; \& \; \text{NP}[inst]\text{:}\boxed{3} \rangle \\ \text{CONTENT} \begin{bmatrix} eat\_rel \\ \text{ACTOR} \qquad \boxed{2} \\ \text{UNDERGOER} \quad \boxed{3} \end{bmatrix} \end{bmatrix}$$

As a verbal base, -tor has no status as an independent verb. It carries some verbal features, but by itself a verbal base is simply an affix. A verbal base also obligatorily incorporates its second argument. Thus, the second member of the ARG-ST in (19) is lexically specified as being of type incorp.

Given the lexical entries in (18) and (19), the lexical rule in Figure 1 produces the deverbal noun in (20), which selects for and can potentially combine with two dependents: an absolutive subject and an ergative possessor.

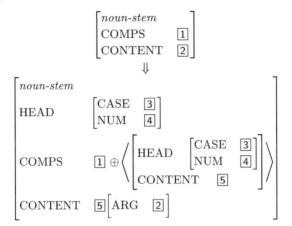

FIGURE 2  Adjunct lexical rule

(20)
$$\begin{bmatrix} \text{PHON} & \langle ammassattor \rangle \\ \text{HEAD} & verb \\ \text{VALENCE} & \begin{bmatrix} \text{SUBJ} & \langle\boxed{1}\rangle \\ \text{COMPS} & \langle\ \rangle \\ \text{SPR} & \langle \text{NP}[erg]\rangle \end{bmatrix} \\ \text{ARG-ST} & \langle\boxed{1}\text{NP}[abs]{:}\boxed{2},\ \text{NP}[inst]{:}\boxed{3}\rangle \\ \text{CONTENT} & \begin{bmatrix} eat\_rel \\ \text{ACTOR} & \boxed{2} \\ \text{UNDERGOER} & \boxed{3}\,sardine\_rel \end{bmatrix} \end{bmatrix}$$

The modification facts can also be explained by the lexical rule in Figure 1. I assume that nominal modifiers are actually non-thematic oblique complements introduced by the Adjunct Lexical Rule in Figure 2.[4] This rule adds a nominal modifier to the ARG-ST list of a noun stem. The modifier must agree in case and number with the head noun. Since the content of the modifier has scope over the content of the head noun, modifiers introduced by Figure 2 behave semantically like adjuncts.

---

[4]Here I am drawing on work on Japanese causatives by Manning et al. (to appear). Also, similar type-shifting rules have been proposed for modifiers in French, Dutch, and English. The present analysis is also compatible with alternative formulations of the Adjunct Lexical Rule, such as the constraint based approach proposed by van Noord and Bouma (1994).

When a noun stem which this rule has applied to occurs as the free-standing head of an NP, the result is a structure like that in Figure 3. If, on the other hand, the noun stem is incorporated into a DV, the result is a structure like that in Figure 4. In Figure 4, the modifier is selected by the DV, and the incorporated nominal has no independent syntactic existence. But, the valence requirement for the modifier (marked [2]) is introduced by Figure 2 on the incorporated nominal and inherited by the DV. Since, the modifier is selected in exactly the same way a modifier of an independent head noun would be, It has all the properties of a regular nominal modifier.

Finally, observe that Sadock's homomorphism constraints follow directly as theorems of a rule like Figure 1. First, since 'stranded' elements are licensed by the valence potential of the DV inherited from the incorporated nominal, incorporation structures must satisfy the CIC. Only the head noun can contribute the valence requirements needed to license stranded possessors or modifiers. If a verbalizing suffix were to combine with something other than the head, the resulting DV would not inherit any valence values that would license a stranded head noun. So, it follows directly from a mixed category analysis that it must be the head noun that gets incorporated. The CIC need not be stipulated as an additional constraint.

The word order properties of NI constructions also follow immediately from the present analysis. In West Greenlandic, constituent order within sentences is fairly free but tends to be Subject – Object – Verb (Fortescue 1984, 93). Within the noun phrase, the possessor must precede the head noun and any modifiers must follow it (Fortescue 1984, 117). Under Sadock's analysis, examples like (7), where a nominal modifier precedes an incorporated nominal, violate the linear precedence constraints for noun phrases. Under the analysis presented here, on the other hand, the word order seen in (7) is exactly what one would expect. The verb (which happens to be a DV) is preceded by its single complement (which happens to be inherited from an incorporated nominal). Because the incorporated nominal has no independent existence in the syntax, it is naturally exempt from word order constraints. There is no need to relax the LC for NI constructions since they satisfy all word order constraints.

## 4.6 Conclusion

The analysis I have sketched here can account for the behavior of West Greenlandic DVs with no reference to syntactic word formation or multiple hierarchical structures. This analysis does involve a limited kind

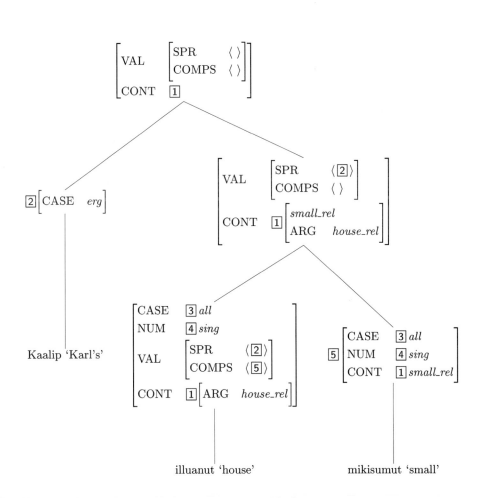

FIGURE 3  Structure of (6b)

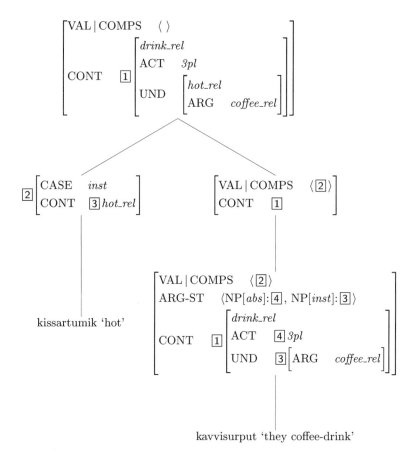

FIGURE 4  Structure of (7a)

of mismatch: a DV projects a VP but also has some noun-like valence requirements. However, the unusual properties of DVs are restricted to the lexicon and HPSG's independently motivated theory of lexical information places strong restrictions on the kinds of mismatches that can be induced. So, there is no need for additional stipulations limiting the degree of mismatch between syntax and morphology.

AG and HPSG have much in common. Both are non-derivational, essentially lexicalist (see Manning 1996, 108ff) theories of grammar that represent linguistic expressions as complex 'modular' bundles of syntactic, semantic, and discourse functional information. The most important difference is in how these information modules interact. In HPSG, the interaction is highly constrained. The parts of the sign are built up in parallel through a single recursive operation, and lexical and phrasal constructions impose constraints on all feature values simultaneously. In AG, on the other hand, each dimension of grammatical information is independent, with its own atoms and its own rules for recursive combination. These independent representations are only related to each other by very general interface conditions.

Each approach has its limitations. In AG, it is difficult to account for complex and idiosyncratic transmodular constraints, such as those associated with the kinds of phrasal constructions which have received so much attention in the Construction Grammar literature (e.g., Fillmore and Kay in press). In HPSG, it has been argued, it is difficult to account for constructions involving radical mismatches between the modules. I have shown here how West Greenlandic NI, one of the most radical of these constructions, can be given a natural account in HPSG.

## References

Bouma, Gosse, Robert Malouf, and Ivan A. Sag. 1998. Satisfying Constraints on Extraction and Adjunction. Paper presented at the 1998 LSA meeting.

Fillmore, Charles, and Paul Kay. in press. *Construction Grammar*. Stanford: CSLI Publications.

Fortescue, Michael. 1984. *West Greenlandic*. London: Croom Helm.

Malouf, Robert. 1996. A Constructional Approach to English Verbal Gerunds. In *Proceedings of the Berkeley Linguistics Society*, 255–266.

Manning, Christopher D. 1996. *Ergativity: Argument Structure and Grammatical Relations*. Stanford: CSLI Publications.

Manning, Christopher D., Ivan A. Sag, and Masayo Iida. to appear. The Lexical Integrity of Japanese Causatives. In *Readings in Modern Phrase Structure Grammar*, ed. Robert Levine and Georgia Green. Cambridge University Press.

Miller, Philip, and Ivan A. Sag. 1997. French Clitic Movement without Clitics or Movement. *Natural Language and Linguistic Theory* 15:573–639.

Mithun, Marianne. 1986. On the Nature of Noun Incorporation. *Language* 61:32–37.

van Noord, Gertjan, and Gosse Bouma. 1994. Adjuncts and the Processing of Lexical Rules. In *Proceedings of the Fifteenth International Conference on Computational Linguistics (COLING '94)*. Kyoto, Japan.

Rosen, Sara Thomas. 1989. Two Types of Noun Incorporation: A Lexical Analysis. *Language* 65:294–317.

Sadock, Jerrold M. 1985. Autolexical Syntax: A Proposal for the Treatment of Noun Incorporation and Similar Phenomena. *Natural Language and Linguistic Theory* 3:379–439.

Sadock, Jerrold M. 1991. *Autolexical Syntax*. Chicago: University of Chicago Press.

Sag, Ivan A. 1997. English Relative Clause Constructions. *Journal of Linguistics* 33:431–484.

Sapir, Edward. 1911. The Problem of Noun Incorporation in American Indian Languages. *American Anthropologist* 13:250–282.

van Geenhoven, Veerle. 1997. A Semantic Analysis of External Possessors in West Greenlandic Noun Incorporating Constructions. Paper presented at the Conference on External Possession, University of Oregon, September 9.

# 5

# Dissociations Between Argument Structure and Grammatical Relations

CHRISTOPHER D. MANNING AND IVAN A. SAG

In Pollard and Sag 1987 and Pollard and Sag 1994, Chs. 1–8, the subcategorized arguments of a head are stored on a single ordered list, the SUBCAT list. However, Borsley (1989) argues that there are various deficiencies in this approach, and suggests that the unified list should be split into separate lists for subjects, complements, and specifiers. This proposal has been widely adopted in what is colloquially known as HPSG3 (Pollard and Sag 1994, Ch. 9 and other recent work in HPSG). Such a move provides in HPSG an analog of the external/internal argument distinction generally adopted in GB, solves certain technical problems such as allowing prepositions to take complements rather than things identical in SUBCAT list position to subjects, and allows recognition of the special features of subjects which have been noted in the LFG literature, where keyword grammatical relations are used. In HPSG3, it is these *valence features* SUBJ, COMPS and SPR whose values are 'cancelled off' (in a Categorial Grammar-like manner) as a head projects a phrase. A lexical head combines with its complements and subject or specifier (if any) according to the lexically inherited specification, as in (1).

---

This paper is based on part of a talk given at the Tübingen HPSG workshop in June 1995, and distributed as Manning and Sag 1995. However, it excludes much material presented there, which will now appear in other places (Manning et al. in press, Manning and Sag submitted, Sag and Manning forthcoming). The paper also has an updated analysis—one consistent with that of Manning et al. in press—which we believe avoids the flaws attributed to the analysis of Manning and Sag

*Lexical and Constructional Aspects of Linguistic Explanation.*
Gert Webelhuth, Jean-Pierre Koenig, and Andreas Kathol.
Copyright © 1998, Stanford University.

(1)

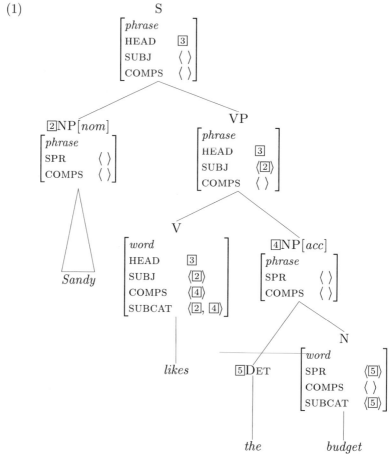

When Borsley (1989) suggested dividing the SUBCAT list into multiple valence lists, we believe that he intended that they would replace the SUBCAT list, but this is not in fact what happened. In Pollard and Sag 1994, Ch. 9, the SUBCAT list is kept as an attribute of lexical signs. Its value is the append of the SUBJ, SPR and COMPS lists. As presented there, this move seems more an expediency than a necessity: it allows the HPSG binding theory to be retained unchanged, rather than having to redefine it over the new valence lists. But the SUBCAT list merely summarizes the valence of a lexical sign, without

1995 by Webelhuth (forthcoming). However, because of space limitations, causatives are no longer discussed here and the reader interested in this topic should see the other papers just mentioned. We thank the audience at Tübingen, and, particularly, Georgia Green and Stephen Wechsler for helpful comments.

having any independent life of its own. It remains unaffected in the construction of syntactic phrases, except that, in virtue of the various identities between SUBCAT list members and members of valence lists, the SUBCAT list's members become fully specified as the valence list values are identified with actual subjects, complements and specifiers. Once a complete phrase is constructed, the lexical head's SUBCAT list is fully specified, as indicated in (1), and may be used as the locus of binding theory.

This redundancy has been broken in recent work. The *canonical* relationship between the SUBCAT list and the valence lists is still an append relationship, but various other possibilities have been explored. To begin with a simple example, many languages allow arguments to not be realized, in what is sometimes known as "free pro-drop", as in the Japanese sentence (2a):

(2) a. Naoki-ga mi-ta.
Naoki-NOM see-PAST
'Naoki saw (it).'

b.
$$
\begin{bmatrix}
\text{SUBJ} & \langle \boxed{1}\text{NP}[nom] \rangle \\
\text{COMPS} & \langle\,\rangle \\
\text{SUBCAT} & \langle \boxed{1}_i,\ \text{NP}[pro]_j \rangle \\
\text{CONT} & \begin{bmatrix} seeing \\ \text{SEER} & i \\ \text{SEEN} & j \end{bmatrix}
\end{bmatrix}
$$

In this sentence, there is only one surface argument. Recent work has argued that the supposition of traces or other empty elements is unnecessary to explain *wanna* 'contraction' (Pullum 1997), and stands in the way of understanding a host of other phenomena thought to legitimate inaudibilia (Sag and Fodor 1994, Sag 1998), and so we would not want to postulate an empty 'pro' element as an independent sign. But nevertheless one wants to capture how in some sense *mi-* 'see' takes two arguments. For example, these two arguments need to appear in an analysis of binding, when discussing interpretations of this sentence. One can do this by proposing an 'object pro-drop' lexical entry for the verb as shown in (2b), and maintaining the approach that binding theory operates on the SUBCAT list, not the valence lists.

In this model, the SUBCAT list no longer captures surface subcategorization, but is an attribute of only lexical signs, used to explain phenomena such as binding, linking, and 'deep' subcategorization, and hence it has become similar to certain notions of *argument structure*. Thus, in recent work the SUBCAT list has been renamed as ARG-ST, and we will use this name henceforth. But it should be emphasized that the ARG-ST list is a syntactic representation, just like its predecessor the SUBCAT list, and is not to be viewed as a partial semantic representation or some sort of substitute for one.

Pro-drop is one of a class of cases, together with unbounded dependencies and pronominal affixes, where arguments do not appear on a valence list (Sag and Fodor 1994, Sag and Godard 1994, Miller and Sag 1997, Bouma et al. 1998). Other recent work has focussed on the analysis of data that involves somewhat more interesting dissociations between valency and argument structure than just the valence lists being a subset of the ARG-ST list (Manning 1996, Manning et al. in press, Abeillé et al. to appear). The ability to dissociate argument structure from valence in this way takes HPSG a certain distance from the monolevel, monostratal roots of GPSG and early HPSG. The purpose of this paper is to better motivate the existence of two independent syntactic notions of valency and argument structure and to examine the kinds of dissociations that can occur, with reference to passives, binding and ergative languages. While doing that, we will suggest some argument structure representations that differ from those presented previously, and for which there is interesting empirical support.

## 5.1 Binding Theory and Passives

The HPSG binding theory is based on hierarchical argument structure rather than constituent structure (as also in Johnson 1977). As Pollard and Sag (1992, 1994) demonstrate, this approach to binding provides an immediate solution to a variety of dilemmas facing any account of English binding stated in terms of constituency-based notions such as c-command. It maintains three binding principles, analogous to those of GB; they are given informally in (3):[1]

(3) HPSG Binding Theory:

    Principle A. A locally a-commanded anaphor must be locally a-bound.

    Principle B. A personal pronoun must be locally a-free.

    Principle C. A non-pronoun must be a-free.

These principles require an anaphor to be coindexed with a less oblique ARG-ST member, if there *is* such a less oblique coargument. Otherwise, anaphors are free (subject to various discourse and processing considerations) to be bound by appropriate elements in the discourse context.

---

[1] A-command, a-bound, and a-free are the same notions as o-command, o-bound, and o-free from Pollard and Sag 1994, now defined on ARG-ST, but the new names are meant to evoke the argument structure based theory of binding we employ.

This binding theory is adequate for English, but crosslinguistic coverage of binding phenomena requires more parametric options (Dalrymple 1993). In many languages, reflexives cannot be bound by just any less oblique (local) NP, but rather their antecedence is restricted to what we might loosely call "subjects". At least to a first approximation this is true of languages such as Japanese, Russian, Inuit, and Sanskrit. Given that the binding theory in HPSG is defined on ARG-ST (an assumption that we will later actively argue for), the natural explanation for such data is to suggest that in these languages, reflexives must be bound by the first element on some ARG-ST list. We will formalize such a notion with the definition and principle in (4), drawn from Manning 1996.

(4)  a. An **a-subject** is an entity that is first on some ARG-ST list.

   b. A-subject-oriented anaphors must be a-bound by an a-subject.

This allows us to explain why *Kaali* is not a possible binder in the Inuit example (5):

(5) Juuna-p    Kaali     immi-nik uqaluttuup-p-a-a.
    Juuna-ERG Kaali.ABS self-MOD tell-IND-TR-3SG.3SG
    'Juuna$_i$ told Kaali$_j$ about self$_{i/*j}$.'

A second parametrization of the binding theory is that while classical reflexives are clause bounded, many languages allow long distance reflexives. For example, both the Inuit reflexive *immi* and the Japanese reflexive *zibun* can be bound by any a-commanding a-subject. Such long distance anaphors might be said to obey Principle Z (Xue et al. 1994):

(6) Principle Z.
    A locally a-commanded long distance anaphor must be a-bound.

Now consider the interaction of passive and subject-oriented reflexives. If our theory of passive was that drawn from HPSG1—a lexical rule that cyclically permuted the SUBCAT, now ARG-ST, list as in (7):[2]

$$(7) \quad \begin{bmatrix} active\text{-}verb \\ \text{ARG-ST} \quad \langle \boxed{1}_i, \boxed{2}, \ldots \rangle \\ \text{CONT} \qquad \boxed{3} \end{bmatrix} \Rightarrow \begin{bmatrix} passive\text{-}verb \\ \text{ARG-ST} \quad \langle \boxed{2}, \ldots \rangle \; ( \; \oplus \langle \text{PP}[by]_i \rangle \; ) \\ \text{CONT} \qquad \boxed{3} \end{bmatrix}$$

then our prediction is clear: the only possible binder of subject-oriented reflexives, the a-subject, is now the NP that is the subject of the passive ($\boxed{2}$). However, in many languages, this is not in fact the case. Perlmutter (1984) observed this for the case of Russian. While in (8a), the reflexive *sebe* must be bound by the subject, in the passive (8b), the antecedent

---

[2] We use $\oplus$ to indicate list concatenation or **append**, and round brackets to indicate optionality.

can be either the surface subject or the agent argument (sometimes known as the logical subject, following Jespersen (1924)).

(8) a. Boris      mne      rasskazal anekdot o      sebe.
     Boris.NOM me.DAT told      joke      about self
     'Boris$_i$ told me a joke about himself$_i$.'

     b. Èta kniga      byla kuplena Borisom      dlja sebja.
     this book.NOM was bought Boris.INSTR for      self
     'This book was bought by Boris$_i$ for himself$_i$.'

Perlmutter argued from these data that the passive must have a complex representation of some sort. In particular, Perlmutter used these examples to argue within Relational Grammar (RG) that both the logical subject and the surface subject of a passive must be a 1 at some level: the logical subject is the initial 1, while the surface subject is the final 1.

In essence we accept this argument, and suggest that we want a representation for passives (at least in languages like Russian) where both the surface subject and the logical subject qualify as a-subjects. However, we argue that such an analysis does not require multiple strata of grammatical relations, as in RG, but can more restrictively be captured by suggesting that passive lexemes possess a nested argument structure, which has the immediate result that passive clauses have two a-subjects.[3] Indeed, below we will present arguments from ergative languages that such an alternative analysis in terms of argument structure rather than grammatical relations is not only possible but necessary.

Various ways have been suggested within HPSG for licensing derived types, such as the passive lexemes that we are dealing with here. While any of them could be used to produce an analysis similar to the one presented here, we will develop our account in terms of a theory of derivational types, which specify a declarative relationship between a SOURCE stem and a RESULT stem (which is morphologically 'derived' from it). Such an approach is closely related to what Copestake (1992) proposes (see also Meurers 1995). It has the advantages of allowing inheritance within the hierarchical lexicon of HPSG to extend over both stem and word types and derivational types (as in the approach of Riehemann 1993) while preserving the locality of information and lexical integrity of words within the syntax that is well-captured within the lexical rules approach. Thus we will suppose that the universal characterization of passive is as in (9):[4]

---

[3] For a similar argument, cf. Grimshaw 1990, 167–173.

[4] This passive is intrinsically promotional; some have argued that the universal rule of passive should only mention subject demotion, to account for passive-like struc-

(9)
$$
\begin{bmatrix}
\textit{passive-drv} \\
\text{RESULT} \quad
\begin{bmatrix}
\textit{pass-v-lxm} \\
\text{ARG-ST} \quad \langle \boxed{2}_j, \langle \boxed{1}, \text{PRO}_j \rangle \oplus \boxed{3} \rangle \\
\text{CONT} \quad \boxed{4}
\end{bmatrix} \\
\text{SOURCE} \quad
\begin{bmatrix}
\textit{trans-v-lxm} \\
\text{ARG-ST} \quad \langle \boxed{1}, \boxed{2} \rangle \oplus \boxed{3} \\
\text{CONT} \quad \boxed{4}
\end{bmatrix}
\end{bmatrix}
$$

Such a derivational type is to be read as saying that basic and other derived lexemes of the SOURCE type license additional lexemes of the RESULT type. We propose that the passive lexeme's ARG-ST value is a list consisting of the second (undergoer) argument of the source lexeme followed by a list that is the same as the ARG-ST value of the source, except that the second element has been replaced by a PRO placeholder. These placeholder elements in ARG-ST lists are used to mark positions coindexed with an element higher in the ARG-ST, and are needed for binding, as we will see below. The passive's ARG-ST value is thus a 'nested' list (a list that contains another list as a member), a fact that will play a crucial role in our account of constraints on binding.

The passive verb of (8b) will then be:

(10)
$$
\begin{bmatrix}
\textit{pass-v-lxm} \\
\text{ARG-ST} \quad \langle \boxed{2}\text{NP}[\textit{nom}]_j, \langle \boxed{1}\text{NP}[\textit{instr}]_i, \text{PRO}_j, \boxed{5}\text{PP}_k \rangle \rangle \\
\text{CONT} \quad
\begin{bmatrix}
\textit{buying} \\
\text{BUYER} \quad i \\
\text{BOUGHT} \quad j \\
\text{BENEFICIARY} \quad k
\end{bmatrix}
\end{bmatrix}
$$

In (10), the reflexive beneficiary $\boxed{5}$ is inside the nested ARG-ST list, and therefore it is a-bound by two a-subjects. This means that if the beneficiary $\boxed{5}$ is a long distance a-subject-oriented anaphor, then Principle Z and the a-subject principle can be satisfied by $\boxed{5}$ being coindexed with either $\boxed{1}$ or $\boxed{2}$, both of which are a-commanders and a-subjects. This is exactly the result we want to explain the Russian data above. Note that our theory predicts that the surface subject is another possible binder of the anaphor in (8b), but this is being ruled out due to its being an inanimate NP. Similar data that support this analysis occur in many languages; (11) shows a passive from the syntactically ergative language

---

tures where nothing is promoted, such as in Lithuanian, but we would provide a different (though related) type for such cases.

West Greenlandic Inuit.[5] Examples from Sanskrit, Hindi, and Japanese are discussed by Manning (1996, 57,124–127), and Shibatani (1988).

(11) Naja      Tobiasi-mit uqaluttuun-niqar-p-u-q  taa-ssu-ma
     Naja.ABS Tobias-ABL tell-PASS-IND-INTR-3SG [DEM-SG-ERG
     itigartis-sima-ga-a-ni.
     turn.down-PRF-PRT.TR-3SG-4SG]
     'Naja$_j$ was told by Tobias$_i$ that he$_k$ had turned self$_{i/j}$ down.'

Thus the data from passives that we have examined argues for three things: (i) that there must be a new more articulated argument structure for passives along the lines that we have proposed; (ii) that passive must be stated so as to realign argument structure, not valence lists; and (iii) that binding possibilities are sensitive to this argument structure, and not to surface phrase structure or surface valence patterns.

## 5.2   Syntactically Ergative Constructions

In cases of dissociations between argument structure and surface valency, the HPSG architecture predicts that binding possibilities and related phenomena should depend solely on the argument structure and be independent of valency. This prediction is startlingly confirmed by the behavior of syntactically ergative and Western Austronesian languages. This is examined in more detail in Manning 1996, Wechsler and Arka to appear, and Wechsler this volume, but will be illustrated briefly here, with an eye to the development of an HPSG analysis.

Western Austronesian languages allow various relationships between argument structure and valence list configuration, mediated by so-called voice morphology. The best known case of this is Tagalog (Schachter 1976, Kroeger 1993), but here we will present some evidence from Toba Batak (Schachter 1984), which has a more rigid configurational surface structure than Tagalog, and hence demonstrates some points more clearly. In particular, it clearly shows the independence of binding from surface structure command relationships. Toba Batak has a distinction between active voice (*mang-*) and objective voice (*di-*) forms of verbs:

(12) a. Mang-ida si  Ria si  Torus.     b. Di-ida si  Torus si  Ria.
        AV-see      PM Ria PM Torus        OV-see PM Torus PM Ria
        'Torus sees/saw Ria.'              'Torus sees/saw Ria.'

The active voice (12a) has the logical subject of the clause in the clause final subject position, while the objective voice (12b), which tends to

---

[5] As well as lexical reflexives, Inuit has a reflexive pronominal agreement marker, here glossed as '4th person', its traditional name. See Manning 1996 for justification of the syntactic ergativity of Inuit.

be used in unmarked contexts, has what we might term the Undergoer (Foley and Van Valin 1984) in subject position. Schachter (1984) provides evidence that both arguments in both voices in (12) are core roles (as opposed to obliques and adjuncts); see also the more extensive arguments in Kroeger 1993 for Tagalog. Thus the correct analysis is not to view one of (12a) or (12b) as a passive or antipassive (as has often been done in the generative literature), but rather as both exhibiting different relationships between argument structure and surface valence. There is strong evidence that a verb and the following NP of a transitive clause form a constituent, which we will call a VP, regardless of the verbal voice chosen. These VPs can be coordinated regardless of their voice:

(13)  a.  Man-uhor baoang jala  mang-olompa mangga   halak an.
         [AV-buy    onions] and [AV-cook        mangoes] man
         'The man buys onions and cooks mangoes.'

     b.  Di-tuhor si  Ore jala di-lompa si  Ruli mangga.
         [OV-buy   PM Ore] and [OV-cook PM Ruli] mangoes
         'Ore buys and Ruli cooks mangoes.'

Other arguments are that an adverb cannot appear in the middle of the VP between the verb and the NP, though adverbs can generally occur between other major constituents, and that the pitch accent of a sentence occurs on the last stressed syllable of this VP, in both voices, including on the verb of an intransitive sentence (Emmorey 1984). Thus the first NP of transitive clauses will be analyzed as being on the COMPS list and will combine with the verb to form a head-complement phrase.

Conversely, the final NP in the examples above will be analyzed as a VP-external subject. This NP behaves similarly to the *ang*-marked NP in Tagalog. It may optionally be fronted before the verb in questions or as a topic, while the VP-internal NP may not be. Further, as in Tagalog, relativization is restricted to this NP, and following the Keenan-Comrie (1977) hierarchy, if only one NP can be relativized on, then that NP is the subject. Moreover it is this VP-external subject NP that must be the controllee, regardless of the verbal voice:

(14)  a.  Mang-elek   si  Bill si  John [man-uhor biang __].
         AV-persuade PM Bill PM John AV-buy      dog
         'John is persuading Bill to buy a dog.'

     b.  Mang-elek   si  Bill si  John [di-pareso   doktor __].
         AV-persuade PM Bill PM John OV-examine doctor
         'John is persuading Bill to have a doctor examine him.'

This suggests an analysis of (12b) as in (15), and lexical entries for the verbs in (12a) and (12b) as in (16a) and (16b), respectively.

(15)

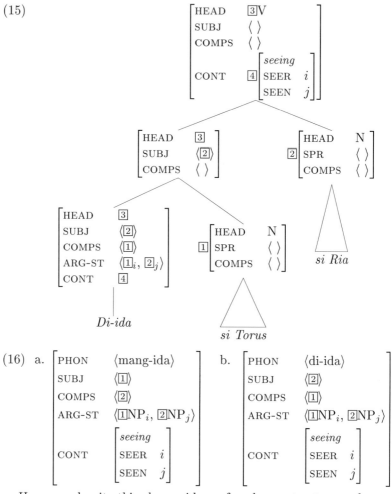

(16) a.
$$\begin{bmatrix} \text{PHON} & \langle \text{mang-ida} \rangle \\ \text{SUBJ} & \langle \boxed{1} \rangle \\ \text{COMPS} & \langle \boxed{2} \rangle \\ \text{ARG-ST} & \langle \boxed{1}\text{NP}_i, \boxed{2}\text{NP}_j \rangle \\ \text{CONT} & \begin{bmatrix} seeing \\ \text{SEER} & i \\ \text{SEEN} & j \end{bmatrix} \end{bmatrix}$$
b.
$$\begin{bmatrix} \text{PHON} & \langle \text{di-ida} \rangle \\ \text{SUBJ} & \langle \boxed{2} \rangle \\ \text{COMPS} & \langle \boxed{1} \rangle \\ \text{ARG-ST} & \langle \boxed{1}\text{NP}_i, \boxed{2}\text{NP}_j \rangle \\ \text{CONT} & \begin{bmatrix} seeing \\ \text{SEER} & i \\ \text{SEEN} & j \end{bmatrix} \end{bmatrix}$$

However, despite this clear evidence for phrase structure and grammatical relations, reflexive binding is insensitive to this structure. Reflexivization shows that an a-subject can bind a non-a-subject (and not vice versa) regardless of the verbal voice of the sentence (Sugamoto 1984):

(17) a. [Mang-ida diri-na] si John.
     AV-saw    self-his PM John
     'John$_i$ saw himself$_i$.'

b. *[Mang-ida si  John] diri-na.
     AV-saw    PM John self-his
     *'Himself$_i$ saw John$_i$.'

(18) a. *[Di-ida diri-na] si John.
     OV-saw self-his PM John
     *'Himself$_i$ saw John$_i$.'

b. [Di-ida si  John] diri-na.
     OV-saw PM John self-his
     'John$_i$ saw himself$_i$.'

To account for these reflexivization patterns using a surface structure based notion of command would mean suggesting that the phrase structures of the sentences in (17) and (18) are radically different. But all available evidence indicates that the phrase structure is the same despite the changing verbal voice. On the other hand, these facts just fall out of the HPSG theory of binding. For instance, although the NP *si John* does not c-command the reflexive in (18b), it nevertheless a-commands the reflexive—the structure of this example is identical to (15). Thus these data provide startling support for defining binding theory on a level of argument structure that is distinct from both surface phrase structure and valence lists.[6]

## 5.3 Generating Different Linking Patterns

Finally we will discuss briefly how the various different patterns of mapping between argument structure and the valence lists can be licensed. We can seek to explain both the commonality of types like intransitive verbs and transitive verbs across all languages and the systematic linking differences between syntactically ergative and accusative languages through the use of multiple inheritance within a hierarchical lexicon (Pollard and Sag 1987, Riehemann 1993). That is, in a syntactically accusative language, a transitive verb will say both that it is transitive, and that it obeys an accusative linking pattern, and so on. A partial presentation of some necessary types is presented in (19). Note in particular that types like *intrans-v-lxm* and *trans-v-lxm* only specify the ARG-ST list of their type, and say nothing about the valence lists.[7]

(19)  a. *verb-lxm*: $\begin{bmatrix} \text{CAT} & \text{V} \\ \text{SPR} & \langle \, \rangle \end{bmatrix}$

   b. *subj-v-lxm*: *verb-lxm* $\wedge \begin{bmatrix} \text{SUBJ} & \langle \, [ \, ] \, \rangle \end{bmatrix}$

   c. *intrans-v-lxm* : *subj-v-lxm* $\wedge \begin{bmatrix} \text{ARG-ST} & \langle \text{NP}[\textit{core}] \rangle \oplus \textit{list}(\textit{obl-np}) \end{bmatrix}$

---

[6]See further Manning 1996 and Wechsler and Arka to appear for arguments and evidence that these binding facts cannot be explained simply by reference to a thematic hierarchy, as is argued for in Schachter 1984 and Sugamoto 1984. See also Davis 1996 and Davis and Koenig 1996 for general evidence against the use of thematic hierarchies.

[7]We assume a division among the arguments of a verb into *core* and *oblique* arguments (Manning 1996). In most languages, all verbs have a subject, and so the language would make all verbs *subj-v-lxm*, but we allow for subjectless verbs in the initial verb type. The disjunction in (19f) appears necessary. In syntactically ergative languages, with intransitive verbs, the first argument on the ARG-ST list becomes the subject, whereas with transitive verbs, it is the second argument on the ARG-ST list that becomes the subject.

d. $trans\text{-}v\text{-}lxm$ : $subj\text{-}v\text{-}lxm$ $\wedge$ $\left[\text{ARG-ST} \quad \langle \text{NP}[core], \text{NP}[core], \ldots \rangle\right]$

e. $acc\text{-}canon\text{-}lxm$: $\begin{bmatrix} \text{SUBJ} & \boxed{1} \\ \text{COMPS} & \text{compression}(\boxed{2}) \\ \text{ARG-ST} & \boxed{1} \oplus \boxed{2} \end{bmatrix}$

f. $erg\text{-}canon\text{-}lxm$: $erg\text{-}canon\text{-}intrans\text{-}lxm$ $\vee$ $erg\text{-}canon\text{-}trans\text{-}lxm$

g. $erg\text{-}canon\text{-}intrans\text{-}lxm$: $\begin{bmatrix} intrans\text{-}v\text{-}lxm \\ \text{SUBJ} & \boxed{1} \\ \text{COMPS} & \text{compression}(\boxed{2}) \\ \text{ARG-ST} & \boxed{1} \oplus \boxed{2} \end{bmatrix}$

h. $erg\text{-}canon\text{-}trans\text{-}lxm$: $\begin{bmatrix} trans\text{-}v\text{-}lxm \\ \text{SUBJ} & \boxed{1} \\ \text{COMPS} & \text{compression}(\langle \boxed{4} \rangle \oplus \boxed{2}) \\ \text{ARG-ST} & \langle \boxed{4} \rangle \oplus \boxed{1} \oplus \boxed{2} \end{bmatrix}$

Before, we suggested that a *canonical* lexeme is one where the valence lists 'add up' to the ARG-ST. We wish to maintain this intuition, but also to allow for recent work on the treatment of causatives and light verbs, and on the handling of syntactically ergative and Western Austronesian languages. In (19e–h), we therefore introduce a generalization of this notion, whereby the SUBJ and COMPS lists are allowed to add up in certain constrained ways to a list that is the compression of the argument structure, that is, what it 'flattens out' to once we promote the members of its embedded lists to be on a par with the other list members, eliminating embedded PROs in the process. See Manning et al. in press for further discussion and exemplification.[8]

Not all languages consistently maintain the relationship whereby the ARG-ST list is the append of the SUBJ, SPR, and COMPS lists, *in that order*. Rather, in Western Austronesian languages, another ordering is possible, and indeed is unmarked. In this pattern, it is the second core argument of the ARG-ST of a transitive verb that becomes the SUBJ. In syntactically ergative languages, the unmarked relationship in Philippine languages is the only relationship possible for expressing transitive verbs (Dixon 1994, Manning 1996). These languages, and

---

[8]compression can be defined as follows ('←' designates 'only if'):

(i) compression($\langle \, \rangle$) = $\langle \, \rangle$.

(ii) compression($\langle PRO|Y \rangle$) = $Z$ ← compression($Y$) = $Z$.

(iii) compression($\langle X|Y \rangle$) = $\langle X|Z \rangle$ ← $X$ is a *synsem*, compression($Y$) = $Z$.

(iv) compression($\langle X|Y \rangle$) = $Z$ ← $X$ is a *list*, compression($X$) = $X'$,
compression($Y$) = $Y'$, append($X', Y'$) = $Z$.

the Western Austronesian languages, provide strong support for two independent syntactic levels, realized in HPSG3 by the valence lists and ARG-ST, and provide crucial evidence for the argument structure based theory of binding that HPSG provides.

The relation between argument structure and the valence lists is handled by separate types (19e,f), which cross-classify with the arity or polyadicity types. A verb in a particular language will then inherit its subcategorization type, and one of the types in (19e,f). For an accusative language like English, a transitive verb has a type like (20a), for a syntactically ergative language like Inuit, there is a transitive verb type like (20b), while a Western Austronesian language like Toba Batak allows both these constructions via a transitive verb type like (20c). The type in (20c) (along with verb-particular information) will then license the two Toba Batak signs that were shown in (16).

(20)   a.  *eng-trans-v-lxm*: *trans-v-lxm* ∧ *acc-canon-lxm*

       b.  *inuit-trans-v-lxm*: *trans-v-lxm* ∧ *erg-canon-lxm*

       c.  *toba-trans-v-lxm*: *trans-v-lxm* ∧

                                       (*acc-canon-lxm* ∨ *erg-canon-lxm*)

## 5.4   Conclusion

We have argued that HPSG must draw a fundamental distinction between argument structure and the valence features which Borsley proposed, which distinguish grammatical relations. We have examined, unfortunately superficially, data from a range of languages to try to show that one can use this ARGUMENT-STRUCTURE list to considerable linguistic advantage. This in turn seems to alter the character of HPSG, by providing an important second kind of organization on the dependents of lexical heads. In particular, we have discussed how theories of grammar that define binding on surface phrase structure configurations or surface valence lists are unable to satisfactorily account for binding patterns seen in Austronesian and ergative languages, or the binding patterns of 'subject-oriented' reflexives when they occur with passive or causative verbs. Following the reasoning laid out in slightly different terms in Manning 1996, we have argued that it is possible to give a universal characterization of binding in terms of our notion of argument structure that generalizes nicely over accusative and ergative languages, and that correctly predicts binding patterns with passive—and causative—verbs.

In the process of developing this account, we have been led to a number of more specific proposals about the nature of passives and argument realization or linking. A perspicuous way of formulating these proposals seems to be in terms of a small set of universally available types and constraints associated with them (also universal, we might hope). Although the ideas sketched here are preliminary, we hope that they can serve as a basis for subsequent HPSG research that will try to distill generalizations from seemingly diverse cross-linguistic patterns like these and to organize them into a tight system of universally available types and simple constraints. The recognition of argument structure as an independent dimension of grammatical organization seems to be an important first step to take in the realization of this goal.

## References

Abeillé, Anne, Danièle Godard, and Ivan A. Sag. to appear. Two Kinds of Composition in French Complex Predicates. In *Complex Predicates in Non-Derivational Syntax*, ed. Andreas Kathol, Erhard Hinrichs, and Tsuneko Nakazawa. New York: Academic Press.

Borsley, Robert. 1989. Phrase-Structure Grammar and the *Barriers* Conception of Clause Structure. *Linguistics* 27:843–863.

Bouma, Gosse, Robert Malouf, and Ivan A. Sag. 1998. Satisfying Constraints on Extraction and Adjunction. MS, Groningen University and Stanford University.

Copestake, Ann. 1992. The Representation of Lexical Semantic Information. Doctoral dissertation, University of Sussex. Cognitive Science Research Paper, CSRP 280.

Dalrymple, Mary. 1993. *The Syntax of Anaphoric Binding*. Stanford, CA: CSLI.

Davis, Anthony. 1996. *Linking and the Hierarchical Lexicon*. Doctoral dissertation, Stanford.

Davis, Anthony, and Jean-Pierre Koenig. 1996. Lexical Semantics and Linking Constraints in the Hierarchical Lexicon. Paper presented at the 3rd International Conference on HPSG, Marseille.

Dixon, Robert M. W. 1994. *Ergativity*. Cambridge: Cambridge University Press.

Emmorey, Karen. 1984. The Intonation System of Toba Batak. In *Studies in the Structure of Toba Batak*, ed. Paul Schachter. 37–58. UCLA Occasional Papers in Linguistics, Number 5.

Foley, William A., and Robert D. Van Valin, Jr. 1984. *Functional Syntax and Universal Grammar*. Cambridge: Cambridge University Press.

Grimshaw, Jane. 1990. *Argument Structure*. Cambridge, MA: MIT Press.

Jespersen, Otto. 1924. *Philosophy of Grammar*. London: George Allen and Unwin.

Johnson, David Edward. 1977. On Relational Constraints on Grammars. In *Syntax and Semantics Volume 8: Grammatical Relations*, ed. Peter Cole and Jerrold M. Sadock. New York: Academic Press.

Keenan, Edward L., and Bernard Comrie. 1977. Noun Phrase Accessibility and Universal Grammar. *Linguistic Inquiry* 8:63–99.

Kroeger, Paul. 1993. *Phrase Structure and Grammatical Relations in Tagalog.* Stanford, CA: CSLI Publications.

Manning, Christopher D. 1996. *Ergativity: Argument Structure and Grammatical Relations.* Stanford, CA: CSLI Publications.

Manning, Christopher D., and Ivan A. Sag. 1995. Dissociations between Argument Structure and Grammatical Relations. Tübingen HPSG workshop,

Manning, Christopher D., and Ivan A. Sag. To appear. Argument Structure in HPSG: Modeling Valency Alternations and Binding. *Nordic Journal of Linguistics.*

Manning, Christopher David, Ivan A. Sag, and Masayo Iida. in press. The Lexical Integrity of Japanese Causatives. In *Readings in Modern Phrase Structure Grammar*, ed. Robert Levine and Georgia Green. Cambridge: Cambridge University Press.

Meurers, Detmar. 1995. Towards a Semantics for Lexical Rules as Used in HPSG. Paper presented at the Conference on Formal Grammar, Barcelona, Spain.

Miller, Philip H., and Ivan A. Sag. 1997. French Clitic Movement without Clitics or Movement. *Natural Language and Linguistic Theory* 15:573–639.

Perlmutter, David M. 1984. The Inadequacy of Some Monostratal Theories of Passive. In *Studies in Relational Grammar*, ed. David M. Perlmutter and Carol G. Rosen. 3–37. Chicago, IL: University of Chicago Press.

Pollard, Carl, and Ivan A. Sag. 1987. *Information-Based Syntax and Semantics.* Stanford, CA: Center for the Study of Language and Information.

Pollard, Carl, and Ivan A. Sag. 1992. Anaphors in English and the Scope of Binding Theory. *Linguistic Inquiry* 23:261–303.

Pollard, Carl, and Ivan A. Sag. 1994. *Head-Driven Phrase Structure Grammar.* Chicago, IL: University of Chicago Press.

Pullum, Geoffrey K. 1997. The Morpholexical Nature of English *to*-Contraction. *Language* 73:79–102.

Riehemann, Susanne. 1993. Word Formation in Lexical Type Hierarchies: A Case Study of *bar*-Adjectives in German. Master's thesis, Tübingen.

Sag, Ivan A. 1998. Explaining the Conjunct Constraint. Paper presented at the annual meetings of the Linguistic Society of America. New York.

Sag, Ivan A., and Janet D. Fodor. 1994. Extraction Without Traces. In *Proceedings of the Thirteenth West Coast Conference on Formal Linguistics*, 365–384. Stanford Linguistics Association.

Sag, Ivan A., and Danièle Godard. 1994. Extraction of *De*-Phrases from the French NP. In *Proceedings of the North Eastern Linguistics Society, 24*, ed. Mercè Gonzàlez, 519–541.

Sag, Ivan A., and Christopher D. Manning. forthcoming. Lexicalizing Quantifier Scope: A Response to Pollard and Yoo. MS, Stanford University and The University of Sydney.

Schachter, Paul. 1976. The Subject in Philippine Languages: Topic, Actor, Actor-Topic or None of the Above. In *Subject and Topic*, ed. Charles N. Li. 491–518. New York: Academic Press.

Schachter, Paul. 1984. Semantic-Role-Based Syntax in Toba Batak. In *Studies in the Structure of Toba Batak*, ed. Paul Schachter. 122–149. UCLA Occasional Papers in Linguistics, Number 5.

Shibatani, Masayoshi. 1988. Voice in Philippine languages. In *Passive and Voice*, ed. Masayoshi Shibatani. 85–142. Amsterdam: John Benjamins.

Sugamoto, Nobuko. 1984. Reflexives in Toba Batak. In *Studies in the Structure of Toba Batak*, ed. Paul Schachter. 150 171. UCLA Occasional Papers in Linguistics, Number 5.

Webelhuth, Gert. forthcoming. Causatives and the Nature of Argument Structure. In *Complex Predicates in Non-Derivational Syntax*, ed. Andreas Kathol, Erhard Hinrichs, and Tsuneko Nakazawa. New York: Academic Press.

Wechsler, Stephen. this volume.

Wechsler, Stephen, and I Wayan Arka. to appear. Syntactic Ergativity in Balinese: An Argument Structure Based Theory. *Natural Language and Linguistic Theory*.

Xue, Ping, Carl Pollard, and Ivan A. Sag. 1994. A New Perspective on Chinese *ziji*. In *Proceedings of the Thirteenth West Coast Conference on Formal Linguistics*, 432–447. Stanford, CA. CSLI Publications.

# Part II

## Lexical and Syntactic Constructions

# 6

# A Lexical Approach to Quantifier Floating in French

ANNE ABEILLÉ AND DANIÈLE GODARD

## 6.1   Introduction

Broadly construed, quantifier floating denotes a phenomenon characterized by a mismatch between the syntax and the semantics of the quantifier (Q). Thus, in the French example (1b), the Q is syntactically disjoint from the subject NP whose content is its semantic restriction, while it is a syntactic part of this NP in its usual position in (1a):

(1)   a.   Tous les enfants font la sieste. ('All the children take a nap.')
      b.   Les enfants font tous la sieste. ('The children all take a nap.')

Given the parallelism between the two sentences of (1) and the semantic dependency between the Q and the NP to which it is 'bound' in (1b), this phenomenon has been seen as a paradigmatic case of transformation (e.g. Kayne 1975, Sportiche 1988). However, there are difficulties with transformational approaches to Q floating, noted in Dowty and Brodie 1984 for English: there doesn't always exist a well-formed NP source, and there are meaning differences between the two sentences. The lexical treatment we propose here for French avoids these pitfalls; in particular, it accounts appropriately for the lexical restrictions and scopal properties of Q climbing. Although we cannot do justice to the interesting semantics of floating Qs, we sketch an analysis which relies on the co-indexation of the Q and the NP, and a storage mechanism.

Q floating comes in several varieties in French, involving two factors: the Q either is bound to a subject or object NP (as in (1b), (2b), (2c), (3b)) or is itself an object, as in (2a); it occurs either to the right or to the left of the verb, often in unusual positions for complements: it

*Lexical and Constructional Aspects of Linguistic Explanation.*
Gert Webelhuth, Jean-Pierre Koenig, and Andreas Kathol.
Copyright © 1998, Stanford University.

precedes the participle in (2a,b), and occurs to the left of the infinitival in (3):

(2)  a.  Marie a tout mangé. ('Marie has eaten everything.')
     b.  Marie les a tous mangés. ('Marie has eaten them all.')
     c.  Marie les lit tous. ('Marie reads them all.')

(3)  a.  Marie veut [tout lire]. ('Marie wants to read everything.')
     b.  Marie veut [tous les manger]. ('Marie wants to eat them all.')

We propose that floating Qs, both bound and non-bound, can have two functions: they are either adjuncts or complements.[1] Their positional properties follow the general pattern of elements which we call 'lite' (Abeillé and Godard 1997). Cases of long-distance association between Q and the V (or the NP it quantifies semantically) are handled by the argument composition approach that allows a predicate to inherit some of the complements subcategorized for by its VP (or S) complement.[2]

## 6.2  Two Syntactic Structures with Floating Qs

Drawing on similar analyses proposed for negative adverbs by Abeillé and Godard (1996) and Kim and Sag (1995), we analyze floating quantifiers as complements to the right of the V (4a) and as adjuncts to the left of V[$inf$] (4b):[3]

(4)  a. Paul dira tout à Marie.     b. Paul veut tout dire à Marie.

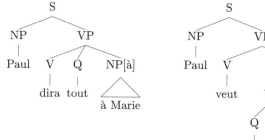

### 6.2.1  Adjunction to the Infinitival Lexical V

Accepting the general constraint that complements cannot precede the head, we give several arguments supporting the analysis that *tout* and

---

[1]Qs can also be adjoined to non-verbal constituents, a construction which we leave aside. For reasons of space, we also leave aside *chacun, tous les deux/ trois* etc. ('both of them, all three of them'), concentrating here on *tous, tout, rien*.

[2]For an early proposal, see Hinrichs and Nakazawa 1994.

[3]Our distinction is not co-extensive with rightward vs. leftward movement in Kayne 1975. Thus, there is no movement in (2c), but it is a floating Q for us.

*tous* in (3) are adjoined to the lexical infinitival V rather than to the VP. They systematically pattern like the class of V-adverbs, whose sole site of adjunction is the lexical V (Abeillé and Godard 1996). First, they must follow the negation and adverbs such as *heureusement, probablement,* which adjoin to the infinitival VP and can have wide scope over VP coordination:

(5)   a.   Il avait commencé à ne plus tout accepter/*à tout ne plus accepter.
           'He had begun to no more accept everything.'
      b.   Il avait commencé à ne plus tous les lire/*à tous ne plus les lire.
           'Paul had begun to no more read them all.'

(6)   Ils se réjouissaient d'heureusement tous pouvoir partir/*de tous heureusement pouvoir partir.
      'They rejoiced of fortunately all/*all unfortunately going away.'

Second, *tout* and *tous* in this structure cannot have wide scope over a coordination of VPs; (7a) is unacceptable, because the second V lacks a complement; although (7b) is acceptable, *tous* doesn't quantify over the complement of *expliquer*, only over that of *lire*:

(7)   a.   *Il veut [tout [$_{VP}$ lire attentivement et expliquer aux étudiants]].
           (intended) 'He wants to read everything attentively and explain everything to the students.'
      b.   Il avouait ne pas tous les lire attentivement et les expliquer cependant aux étudiants.
           'He admitted not to read them all attentively and still explain them to the students.'

Third, the Q cannot be shared by a conjunction of lexical Vs; this is a general property of adverbs (such as *bien, mal, beaucoup...*) which left-adjoin to a lexical category. Thus, (8a) is unacceptable, because *traduire* lacks an object, and (8b) fails to convey that Paul hoped for better drinking:

(8)   a.   *Paul essaiera de tout lire et traduire pour demain.
           'Paul will-try to read and translate everything for tomorrow.'
      b.   Paul espérait mieux manger et boire.
           'Paul hoped (for) better eating and (for) drinking.'

Finally, a coordination of Q+V[*inf*] behaves in the same way as a coordination of lexical V[*inf*] with respect to *de* marking. It is a property of *de* marking that it must be repeated on conjoined VPs, while it is optional on conjoined lexical Vs. The data in (9c) follow if the bare Q is left-adjoined to the lexical V[*inf*], and the whole structure counts as a head with respect to this marking.[4]

(9)   a.   Paul essayait de lire ces livres et *(de) travailler davantage.
           'Paul was trying to read these books and work more.'
      b.   Paul va essayer de lire et (de) traduire ces livres.
           'Paul will try to read and translate these books.'
      c.   Paul va essayer de tout lire et (de) tout traduire pour demain.
           'Paul will try to read and translate everything for tomorrow.'

### 6.2.2   Q as a Complement

The properties of bare Qs to the right of the head V contrast with those of adjunct Qs. Thus, they can be shared by a conjunction of lexical Vs, like ordinary complements (or adjuncts) to the right of the head:[5]

(10)  a.   Paul lit et comprend tout.
           'Paul reads and understands everything.'
      b.   Paul les a tous lus et expliqués à ses étudiants.
           'Paul has read and explained them all to his students.'
           (lit: 'them-has all read and explained to his students.')

We analyze tense auxiliaries as having a flat complementation structure, where the past participle does not form a constituent with the complements which it subcategorizes for, but is itself a lexical complement (Abeillé and Godard 1994). Pronominal clitics are affixes (Miller and Sag 1997). Under these assumptions, there are three possible structures for the VP in (10b), of which only the first gives the right result:

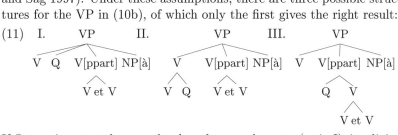

If Q *tous* is not at the same level as the complements (as in I), it adjoins either to the head (the auxiliary *a*) as in II or to the participle as in III. Structure III is excluded, since, as we have seen in (8a), a left-adjoined Q cannot have wide scope over a conjunction of lexical categories. Structure II raises difficulty, because the auxiliary can be separated from Q by adverbs:

---

[4]In our terms, the distinction is between lite and non-lite constituents, cf. Section 6.4.

[5]Note that the contrast between (8a) and (10a) would be strange if Qs to the left of the V[*inf*] were complements which can precede the head.

(12)   a.   Paul ne les a volontairement pas tous lus.
            'Paul has voluntarily not read all of them.'
       b.   Paul ne les a pas volontairement tous lus.
            'Paul ne-them-has not voluntarily read all of them.'

If *tous* is adjoined to the head *a,* then *volontairement* and *pas* must also
be so adjoined; this creates a problem with adverb scoping: *volontairement* is syntactically lower but has wider scope than the negation in
(12a), and the reverse is true of (12b), a situation which is unexpected
if they are adjoined to the lexical V, given the usual hypothesis that an
operator has at least scope over the constituents dominated by the head
daughter (Abeillé and Godard 1996). On the other hand, if both adverbs are sisters, then scoping can depend on their linear ordering (Horn
1972). We conclude that Q is at the same level as other complements,
as in (10b), for example.

   Qs to the right of the V also contrast with those to the left in being
unordered with respect to other adverbs, both S-adverbs (*heureusement*)
or VP-manner-adverbs (*attentivement*):

(13)   a.   Ils ont heureusement tous/tous heureusement parlé au pro-
            fesseur.
            'They fortunately all spoke to the teacher.'
       b.   Les élèves ont attentivement tout lu/ont tout attentivement
            lu.
            'The students have all read attentively.'

This is expected again if both the adverb and *tous* occur at the same
level as the complements: most adverbs are unordered with respect to
the complements in the French VP:

(14)   Paul a lu attentivement ce texte/a lu ce texte attentivement.
       'Paul has attentively read this text.'

Finally, while the bare Q is positionally restricted in the VP, it permutes
freely with the other constituents when it is modified (Blinkenberg 1928,
Kayne 1975):

(15)   a.   Paul dira [tout ou presque tout] à son fils/à son fils [tout ou
            presque tout].
            'Paul will-say everything or almost everything to his son.'
       b.   Paul ne dit à son fils [rien d'important]/[rien d'important] à
            son fils.
            'Paul does not say anything important to his son.'
       c.   Paul les a donnés [quasiment tous] à son fils/à son fils quasi-
            ment tous.
            'Paul gave nearly all of them to his son.'

This follows if the Q occurs at the same level as the other constituents in the VP; the restrictions on bare Q pertain to word order rather than hierarchical structure (see Section 6.5).

The above properties show that Qs occur as sisters of complements, but they are compatible with an analysis of Qs as adjuncts since we allow adjuncts and complements at the same level in the VP. However, it is more difficult to account for Q 'climbing' (see Section 6.5) if they are adjuncts rather than complements.

## 6.3 A Description in IIPSG

### 6.3.1 Types of Phrases for French VPs

Depending on its function, the floating quantifier is licensed by different descriptions, which we give as constraints on phrases, following Sag (in press). Headed phrases subdivide into head-nexus and head-adjunct phrases, the latter being characterized by the fact that they inherit their content and non-local features from the non-head daughter, while the others inherit them from the head daughter. Since we allow adjuncts and complements at the same level, we have a *head-comp-adj-ph* rather than a *head-comp-ph*.[6]

(16)  *hd-adj-ph* →

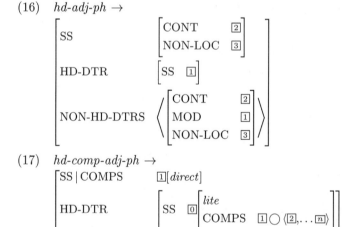

(17)  *hd-comp-adj-ph* →

$$
\begin{bmatrix}
\text{SS} \mid \text{COMPS} & \boxed{1}[direct] \\
\text{HD-DTR} & \left[\text{SS} \ \boxed{0}\begin{bmatrix} lite \\ \text{COMPS} \ \boxed{1} \bigcirc \langle \boxed{2}, \dots \boxed{n} \rangle \end{bmatrix}\right] \\
\text{NON-HD-DTRS} & \text{nelist}\langle[\text{SS} \ \boxed{2}], \dots, [\text{SS} \ \boxed{n}]\rangle \bigcirc \text{list}([\text{MOD} \ \boxed{0}])
\end{bmatrix}
$$

---

[6]The hd-adj-comp-ph can be considered as a type of *head-nexus-ph* if the handels of the adjuncts are stored in the content of the head in a Minimal Recursion Semantics (MRS) approach (Copestake et al. 1997). This description requires that there be at least one complement (Abeillé and Godard 1997), and allows the phrase to remain unsaturated for a complement with direct case (see Section 6.3.2), a possibility which LRs (38) and (39) exploit (see Section 6.5).

Thus, the VP in examples (1), (2) or (12), (14) corresponds to the *hd-comp-adj-ph*, and the sequence of Q + V in (3) to the *hd-adj-ph*.

## 6.3.2 Complement Q

The category Q abbreviates the (schematic) description in (18), where the content is represented as in 'Minimal Recursion Semantics (Copestake et al. 1997); handels, which label the content of expressions, specify scoping paths, and can be stored in the content of the syntactic head:[7]

$$(18) \quad \begin{bmatrix} \text{HEAD} & \begin{bmatrix} noun \\ \text{ADV} \quad + \end{bmatrix} \\ \\ \text{CONT} & \begin{bmatrix} pronominal\text{-}obj \\ \text{HANDEL} \quad \boxed{1} \\ \text{INDEX} \quad \boxed{2} \\ \text{LISZT} \quad \langle [quant\text{-}rel] \rangle \end{bmatrix} \end{bmatrix}$$

Qs are nouns, because they occur in nominal positions (see (10), (15)), but they also have a positive value for the syntactic boolean feature [ADV±]; this allows us to represent the common properties of Qs and adverbs with respect to word order, and is useful to note certain specific restrictions on their occurrence as complements. Accordingly, Qs have an index. Being underspecified as pronominal (like strong pronouns in French), they can behave as anaphors, as in the case of bound Qs introduced by LR (21), or as pronouns, as in the case of *tout, rien, non-bound tous* (26a) or Q climbing (Section 6.5).

While singular Qs *tout, rien* are ordinary subcategorized nominal arguments, bound Qs are added to the argument list of the V by a Lexical Rule. Any type of plural (definite) subject, but only non-canonical objects (pronominal affixes, gaps or PRO) can bind a floating Q (Kayne 1975); the complement is either accusative or dative ([à]), although a floating Q is unnatural with a dative gap:

(19)  a.  *Paul a tous lu ces livres. ('Paul has all read those books.')
      b.  Paul les a tous lus ('Paul has read them all.')
      c.  Ces livres que Paul a tous lus en une semaine.
          'Those books which Paul has all read in one week.'

(20)  a.  Paul leur a tous parlé/leur a parlé à tous.
          'Paul has spoken to them all.'

---

[7]As in the standard generalized quantifier theory, quantifier relations have three arguments, a bound-variable, whose value is identified with the index, a restriction and a scope.

  b. ?Les enfants auxquels Paul a tous parlé.
    'The children to all of whom Paul has spoken.'

A single LR, supplemented by the constraint in (21b), accounts for all the cases of bound floating Qs:

(21) a.

$$
\begin{bmatrix}
verb \\
\text{ARG-ST} \quad \boxed{1}\left(\left\langle \text{NP}_i \begin{bmatrix} \text{CASE } nom \vee acc \vee \boxed{3}[\text{à}] \\ \text{NUM} \qquad\qquad\qquad pl \end{bmatrix} \right\rangle \circ \boxed{2}\right)
\end{bmatrix}
$$

$$
\Rightarrow
\begin{bmatrix}
lexeme\text{-}with\text{-}bound\text{-}q \\
\text{ARG-ST} \quad \boxed{1} \oplus \left\langle Q_i \begin{bmatrix} \text{CASE} & intern \vee \boxed{3} \\ \text{HANDEL} & \boxed{4} \end{bmatrix} \right\rangle \\
\text{CONT} \quad \begin{bmatrix} \text{H-STORE} & \{\boxed{4}\} \end{bmatrix}
\end{bmatrix}
$$

  b. A non-pronominal NP cannot be co-indexed with a pronomi-
    nal which precedes and c-commands it.

 Syntactically, the LR adds a bare Q to the ARG-ST of a V. Thus, the ARG-ST of *font* in (1b), with a subject bound Q, and of auxiliary *a* in (2b) with an object-bound Q are as follows:

(22) a. *font*: ARG-ST $\langle \text{NP}[mpl]_i, \text{NP}[acc], \text{Q}[intern]_i \rangle$
   b. *a*: ARG-ST $\langle \text{NP}, \text{V}[ppart], \text{NP}[pro\text{-}aff, acc, mpl]_i, \text{Q}[intern]_i \rangle$

The new case 'intern(al)' which we introduce here is a direct case, like nominative and accusative (as opposed to oblique cases like [à]). It is independently justified: while nom(inative) and acc(usative) are acquired by the NP via unification with the requirements of Vs, intern(al) is the default case value for NPs (as complements of Prepositions, left-dislocated NPs, locative NPs). The bound Q either has the same case as the ([à]) argument NP or is [CASE *intern*]. The two possibilities are illustrated in (20a).

 Semantically, bound floating Qs denote a quantification relation, which we cannot investigate here. Co-indexation of the Q and the argument NP ensures that the Q quantifies over the entities which are in the NP denotation. As expected in the MRS' system (as well as in Pollard and Sag 1994, Pollard and Yoo 1996), the V puts the HANDEL value of the Q in its H(ANDEL)-STORE.

 Generalization (21b) is a restatement of the well-known constraint on backwards anaphora (e.g. Wasow 1979). Thus, while pronominals obey Binding Principles stated on the ARG-ST, we side with those who think that the constraint on lexical NPs is of a different nature and should be stated in configurational terms.[8] This position is supported by the behavior of Q. First, while the contrast between subject and object binding of floating Q, illustrated in (1b) vs. (19a), cannot be stated as a constraint on the argument list, it makes perfect sense using c-command: Q c-commands the NP in (19a), not in (1b). Second, as has often been noted, the floating Q has a low acceptability if the subject is inverted. Finally, the subject cannot be a lexical NP, if the Q "climbs". Thus, (23a,b) contrast with (1b):

(23)   a.??C'est un film qu'ont tous aimé les étudiants.
         'It is a movie which all the students have liked.'
       b.   Il faut tous que *les enfants/ils viennent.
         'It is necessary that the children/they come all of them.'

### 6.3.3   Specific Constraints

Complement Qs obey further minute constraints. *Tout* and *rien* can be accusative complements of finite verbs, not of infinitivals, unless they are modified or stressed. We note this quirky behavior as a constraint on the ARG-ST of V[*inf*], excluding 'lite' accusatives (see Section 6.4):

(24)   a.   Paul lit tout./ ??Paul veut lire tout (unstressed).
         'Paul reads everything.'/ 'Paul wants to read everything.'
       b.   Paul veut lire absolument tout.
         'Paul wants to read absolutely everything.'

(25)   V[*inf*] → [ARG-ST list([ADV −] ∨ [¬*acc*] ∨ [*non-lite*])]

*Tous,* if not bound, shares with most Qs the inability to be accusative:

(26)   a.   *Je recevrai tous./ *Je recevrai quasiment tous./ Tous vien-
            dront./ Je parlerai à tous./ Je ne peux compter sur tous.
         'I will receive (nearly) all (of them).'/ 'All will come.'/
         'I will talk to all (of them).'/ 'I can't count on all (of them).'
       b.   Je les recevrai tous/ Je promets de les recevoir tous.
         'I will receive them all'/ 'I promise to receive them all.'

We assume that the lexical description of Qs says which cases are available: *tous* can be nominative or internal, not accusative. In (26a), the sentence *Je recevrai tous* is bad, because *recevoir* wants an accusative complement, which *tous* cannot be; the sentence *Je les recevrai tous* is good, because *recevoir* has an accusative clitic, and *tous* has internal case. *Je ne peux compter sur tous* is good because prepositions want a complement with internal case.

---

[8]Pollard and Sag (1994, 254) mention an observation by K.P. Mohanan. See also Milner 1986.

### 6.3.4 Q as Adjunct to Infinitival V

Adjunct Qs are the same lexical item as argument or bound Qs: in addition to the features in (18), they also contain a MOD feature, which is taken into account by the constraint on *hd-adj-ph*, but is simply irrelevant when the Q is not an adjunct. The MOD feature value here formalizes the observation that adjunct Qs alternate with a complement; thus unbound *tous* is not an adjunct, because it is not a possible accusative complement (*Je veux tous lire/*Je veux lire tous* vs. *Je veux tous les lire/Je veux les lire tous* 'I want to read (them) all'). Roughly, Q adjoins to the V of which it could have been a complement, and acts as if it saturated the valence requirement. To obtain that effect, we say that Q adjoins to a V with a gap Q complement, which it binds.

(27)    Schematic lexical description of Q

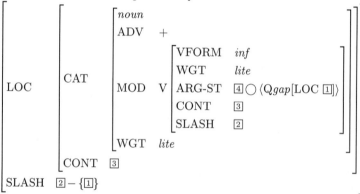

The infinitival V to which the Q adjoins is not saturated for any complement (it is 'lexical' or, in our terms, lite). Although one of its arguments is a gapped Q, it is not the bottom of a long-distance dependency because the adjunct fails to transmit the corresponding SLASH to the phrase (remember that SLASH inheritance goes through the adjunct daughter, cf. (17)). Note that the LOC values are not shared between the gap and the adjunct. Rather, the correspondence between complement and adjunct Qs is ensured by the sharing of contents between the V and the adjunct Q. Since the adjunct, which also transmits the content value to the phrase, doesn't add anything to the content of the V, the gap and the adjunct Q are constrained to have exactly the same semantic import (which is as in (18)). The description in (27) allows for a crucial weight difference between the gap and the adjunct: while adjunct Qs are lite, gaps in French are non-lite. Thus, the gap, eschewing constraint (25), can correspond to accusative *tout, rien,* which is not acceptable as a complement of V[*inf*]. The gap is either accusative (*Tout lire,* 'To read everything') or internal (*Tous les lire,* 'To read them all').[9]

## 6.4 Positions of Qs and Word Order

Regarding word order, we account for the position of adjunct Q (to the left of the V) and complement Q (to its right), as well as the different behavior of bare vs. modified or conjoined Qs in terms of a feature WEIGHT.

Bare Qs (except for [à]), bound or unbound, occur before phrasal complements; moreover, they occur before the past participle (which is also a bare complement):

(28)  *Paul ne dit à son fils rien/*OK:* rien à son fils.
      'Paul does not say anything to his son.'

(29)  Paul n'a rien lu/*n'a lu rien.
      'Paul has read nothing.'

Similar constraints are found with other bare complements, such as bare Ns in light verb constructions, which must occur before the other complements (but after the participle); the constraint disappears if they are phrasal or conjoined (Abeillé and Godard 1996, 1997):

(30)  a.  Ce livre fait plaisir à Marie/*à Marie plaisir.
          'This book gives pleasure to Marie.'
      b.  Ça fait le plaisir de sa vie à Marie/à Marie le plaisir de sa vie.
          'This gives the pleasure of her life to Marie.'

We propose that a feature WEIGHT is appropriate both for lexical items and phrases, with two possible values *lite* and *non-lite*.[10] Most Ns are specified as lite in the lexicon; on the other hand, most phrases are non-lite, although some phrases may be either lite or non-lite: those which are made of two lite constituents, either as conjuncts or adjunct and head.

(31)  Phrasal Constraints on Weight
      (i)   *phrase* → [WGT / *non-lite*]

      (ii)  $\begin{bmatrix} hd\text{-}adj\text{-}ph \\ \text{HD-DTR [WGT } lite\text{ ]} \\ \text{NON-HD-DTRS } \langle[\text{WGT } lite\text{ ]}\rangle \end{bmatrix}$ → [([WGT *lite* ])]

      (iii) $\begin{bmatrix} coord\text{-}ph \\ \text{NON-HD-DTRS list([WGT } lite\text{ ])} \end{bmatrix}$ → [([WGT *lite* ])]

---

[9][à]-adjuncts are excluded (**A tous leur parler* vs. *leur parler à tous/ Tous leur parler* 'To talk to them all') because *à tous* is non-lite, see fn. 11.

[10]The more complex phenomenon of 'heaviness' is not taken into account here.

Constraint (i) says that all phrases are non-lite by default (notated as "/"). For *hd-adj-phrases* and *coord-phrases*, if the daughters are all lite, the phrase can also be (optionally) of the same weight (for example lite). Constraints (ii) and (iii) may thus overcome the default in (i).

Bare Qs are lite in the lexicon (see (27)). They are non-lite, if they are modified by a non-lite adjunct (such as *de*+Adj), in which case they must not occur before the participle; if they are modified by a lite adjunct (such as *presque*) or conjoined to another lite Q, they are either lite or non-lite, and accordingly may occur either before or after the participle:

(32) a. Il n'a lu rien d'important./ *Il n'a rien d'important lu.
       'He has read nothing of importance.'
     b. Il les a presque tous lus./ Il les a lus presque tous.
       'He has read practically all (of them).'

To the left of the V[*inf*], Qs must be lite: they can only be modified by a lite adjunct, or conjoined to an equally lite Q; they behave, in this respect, like other adjuncts to the lexical V[*inf*], the class of *bien* adverbs (Abeillé and Godard 1997):

(33) a. Il avouait ne rien (*d'important) lire.
       'He confessed to read(ing) nothing (of importance).'
     b. Il est nécessaire de tout ou presque tout lire avant votre départ.
       'It is necessary to read everything or almost everything before you leave.'

*Tout* and *rien* are not allowed to the right of the V[*inf*], cf. (24a): they are ruled out as complements by constraint (25); they are also ruled out as adjuncts if lite adjuncts always occur to the left of the head. Bound *tous* is allowed to the right of V as an internal complement (see (21)), and to the left of V[*inf*] as a lite adjunct.

The Linear Precedence Rules relevant for the fragment of French studied here are given in (34), as constraints on types of phrases, where non-head daughters are noted NON-HD:

(34) Linear Precedence Rules
     a. *hd-subj-ph* → NON-HD < HEAD
     b. *hd-adj-ph*
        → NON-HD[*lite*] < HEAD[*lite*] < NON-HD[*non-lite*]
     c. *hd-comp-adj-ph* → HEAD < NON-HD
     d. *hd-comp-adj-ph* → [COMPS ⟨①⟩] < ①[ADV −]
     e. *hd-comp-adj-ph* → NON-HD[*lite*, ADV+]
        < NON-HD[*lite*, ADV−] < NON-HD[*non-lite*, ADV−]

(34b) orders lite adjuncts before the lite head and non-lite adjuncts after the lite head (33a), but the latter are found freely among the complements, since no other LP rule refers to them (13,14). (34c) orders the head before complements and adjuncts. (34d) orders all complements after the predicate which subcategorizes for them, except for those which are [ADV+]; this is relevant for non-head predicates, like participles complements of tense auxiliaries. Following (34e), lite Qs being [ADV+] occur before the (lite) past participle as in (29). In addition, lite constituents, whether adjuncts or complements, occur before the non-lite (non-adverbial) ones as in (28), (32a).[11]

## 6.5   Q 'Climbing'

A few Vs allow 'climbing' of bare (bound or non-bound) Qs creating a 'middle distance dependency'. The phenomenon is lexically controlled (Kayne 1975), and also the locus of variation. To do justice to the complexity of the data, we distinguish between two cases, differing both syntactically and sociolinguistically. In the first, the three Qs studied here (*tout, rien, tous*) can 'climb' out of a VP[*inf*] complement, and the 'raised' Q either is adjoined to a V[*inf*] or appears between the tense auxiliary and the participle:

(35)   a.   Il veut [tous pouvoir [les lire]].
           'He wants to be able to read them all.'
           (lit: 'all be-able them-read')
       b.   Paul a tous voulu [les lire].
           'Paul wanted to read them all.'
           (lit: 'has all wanted (to) then-read')

In the second case, only *tous* can be raised, but the class of matrix Vs is larger (including Vs with a subjunctive complement, *falloir*), and the Q may follow a finite Q-raising V:

(36)   a.   Paul commence tous [à les lire]./ *Paul commence tout [à lire].
           'Paul begins to read them all.' (lit: 'begins all to them-read')/
           'Paul begins to read everything.'
       b.   Il faut tous [qu'ils viennent].
           'It is necessary that they all come.' (lit: 'all that they come')

Interestingly, the syntactic raising of the Q correlates with wide scope: the Q must take scope in the S where it occurs, a fact which would be unexpected if the structure were due to movement. The difference in scope between a raised and a non-raised Q is illustrated by the following pair:

---

[11]The position of a Q bound by a dative clitic depends on its case: internal *tous* is lite, while *à tous* is non-lite; this indicates that *à tous* is a phrase, with *à* a marker or a preposition, rather than an affix.

(37)  a.  Il a refusé de les voir tous. ('He refused to see them all.')
      b.  Il a tous refusé de les voir. ('For all of them, he refused to see them.')

We propose two LRs, applying to different classes of Vs (although they may overlap) which inherit a Q from their VP[*inf*] or S[*subj*] complement, both schematized here as a VP complement. The semantic part of the rule is the same in both cases: the Q has scope over the V of which it is a complement, as indicated by the inheritance of the H-store.

(38)
$$
\begin{bmatrix} verb \\ \text{VFORM} \quad non\text{-}finite \\ \text{ARG-ST} \quad \boxed{1}\bigcirc \langle \text{VP}inf[\text{COMPS} \langle \ \rangle]\rangle \end{bmatrix} \Rightarrow
$$
$$
\begin{bmatrix} \text{ARG-ST} \quad \left( \boxed{1}\bigcirc \left\langle \text{VP}\begin{bmatrix} \text{COMPS} \ \langle \boxed{2}Q_i \,|\, \text{HANDEL} \ \boxed{3}\rangle \\ \text{CONT}\,|\,\text{H-STORE} \ \{\boxed{3}\} \end{bmatrix} \right\rangle \right) \oplus \langle \boxed{2}\rangle \\ \text{CONT}\,|\,\text{H-STORE} \quad \{\boxed{3}\} \end{bmatrix}
$$

(39)
$$
\begin{bmatrix} verb \\ \text{ARG-ST} \quad \boxed{1}\bigcirc \langle \text{VP}inf \vee subj[\text{COMPS} \langle \ \rangle]\rangle \end{bmatrix} \Rightarrow
$$
$$
\begin{bmatrix} \text{ARG-ST} \quad \boxed{1}\bigcirc \left\langle \text{VP}[\text{COMPS} \ \langle \boxed{2}Q_i[pl]]\rangle \right\rangle \oplus \langle \boxed{2}\rangle \end{bmatrix}
$$

LR (38) describes the first case, where a non-finite V (*inf* or *past part*) inherits a Q complement from its unsaturated infinitival VP complement (see description (17) for partially saturated phrases); the tense auxiliary then inherits it from the participle as in (35b). Accordingly, speakers who only have that rule have the following contrast (provided *commencer* is a Q-raising V for them):

(40)  *Paul commence tous à les lire./ Paul a tous commencé à les lire.
      'Paul begins to read them all.' (lit: 'begins all to them-read')/
      'Paul has begun to read them all.'
      (lit: 'has all begun to them-read')

LR (39) allows a verb taking an infinitival VP or subjunctive S complement to inherit a plural Q complement from its unsaturated verbal complement. For speakers who have both rules (38) and (39), some sequences may receive two analyses (*Je veux tous [les lire]/ Je veux [tous les lire]* 'I want to read them all'), and there are also variants such as in (41), with *tous* either adjoined to a V[*inf*] or complement of the finite Q-raising V:

(41)  Paul essaiera [de tous les lire]./ Paul essaiera tous [de les lire].
      'Paul will try to read them all.'

Thus, our lexical account is better adapted to the phenomenon than any version of movement: it accounts for the fact that it is lexically driven, and not a long-distance dependency; it also accounts for a complex variation in acceptability, and, crucially, for the scope of the Q, which is interpreted in the S in which it occurs.

## 6.6 Conclusion

In this paper we analyze the syntax of Q floating in a way compatible with a larger HPSG grammar for French, integrating the properties which they share with other categories. Like some adverbs, they lead a double life as complements of finite verbs and adjuncts to infinitival verbs, and, if bare, they behave like other lite elements with respect to word order. Q floating in a general way is a local phenomenon, a property which we do justice to by having a lexical treatment. Contrary to transformational approaches which need two different rules for leftward and rightward movement, we only have one lexical rule for subject- and object-bound Q, the difference between the two cases being handled via more general binding principles. Q climbing is lexically controlled, the consequence of a lexical process inducing argument composition.

## References

Abeillé, Anne, and Danièle Godard. 1994. The Complementation of Tense Auxiliaries in French. *WCCFL* 13.157–172. Stanford: CSLI Publ.

Abeillé, Anne, and Danièle Godard. 1996. The Syntax of French Negative Adverbs. in D. Forget, P. Hirschbühler, F. Martineau and A-M. di Sciullo, eds, *Negation and Polarity*, 1–27. Amsterdam: J. Benjamins.

Abeillé, Anne, and Danièle Godard. 1997. French Word Order and Lexical Weight. ms. University Paris 7.

Blinkenberg, Andreas. 1928. *L'ordre des mots en français moderne*. Kopenhagen: Bianco Lunos Bogtrykkeri, Historik-filologiske Meddelelser XVII:1 et XX:1.

Copestake, Ann, Dan Flickinger, and Ivan A. Sag. 1997. Minimal Recursion Semantics: An Introduction. ms. Stanford University.

Dowty, David, and Belinda Brodie. 1984. The Semantics of Floated Quantifiers in a Transformationless Grammar. *WCCFL* 3, 75–90. Stanford: CSLI Publications.

Hinrichs, Erhard, and Tsuneko Nakazawa. 1994. Linearizing AUX in German Verbal Complexes. In J. Nerbonne et al., eds, *German Grammar in HPSG*, 11–37. Stanford: CSLI Publications.

Horn, Lawrence. 1972. *On the Semantic Properties of Logical Operators in English*. PhD Dissertation. Distributed by IULC, 1976.

Kayne, Richard. 1975. *French Syntax: The Transformational Cycle*. Cambridge: MIT Press.

Kim, Jong-Bok, and Ivan A. Sag. 1995. The Parametric Variation of French and English Negation. *WCCFL 14,* 303–317. Los Angeles. Stanford: CSLI Publ.

Miller, Philip, and Ivan A. Sag. 1997. French Clitic Movement without Clitics or Movement. *Natural Language and Linguistic Theory* 15:573–639.

Milner, Jean-Claude. 1986. Coréference et coïndiciation: remarques à propos de l'axiome C. in Ronat, M. and D. Couquaux, eds, *La Grammaire modulaire,* 149–165. Paris: éd. de Minuit.

Pollard, Carl, and Ivan A. Sag. 1994. *Head-Driven Phrase Structure Grammar.* Chicago: UCP and Stanford: CSLI Publications.

Pollard, Carl, and Eun Jung Yoo. 1996. Quantifiers, Wh-phrases and a Theory of Argument Selection. To appear in *Journal of Linguistics.*

Sag, Ivan A. English Relative Clauses. In press. *Journal of Linguistics.*

Sportiche Dominique. 1988. A Theory of Floating Quantifiers and its Corollaries for Constituent Structure. *Linguistic Inquiry* 19:3.425–449.

Wasow, Thomas. 1979. *Anaphora in Generative Grammar.* Ghent: E-STORY-SCIENTIA.

# 7

## Linearization versus Movement: Evidence from German Pied-Piped Infinitives

KORDULA DE KUTHY

### 7.1 Introduction

In the last couple of years, several theories employing a powerful linearization component in the HPSG architecture have been proposed, e.g., in Reape 1994, Kathol 1995, Müller 1998. In these theories many phenomena previously analyzed as unbounded dependency constructions ('movement')[1]— such as verb-second, scrambling, or extraposition —are dealt with as linearization phenomena employing an ordering domain often larger than a local tree. With two mechanisms at hand, linearization and movement, an empirically motivated discussion when/why to prefer one or the other is of increasing importance.

In this paper we want to contribute to this discussion by taking a look at a phenomenon in German: the 'pied-piping' of infinitives in relative clauses. This construction is an interesting test case since the question whether the construction should be licensed by movement or a linearization-like mechanism is a much discussed topic in the GB literature. Riemsdijk (1985) and Trissler (1991) argue for a movement account of the pied-piping construction. Haider (1985) and Grewendorf (1986)

---

I would like to thank Tilman Höhle, Detmar Meurers, Frank Richter and Manfred Sailer for discussion and valuable suggestions, and Stefan Müller and the anonymous reviewers for their comments on an earlier version of this paper.

[1]We will use the term 'movement' also in the setting of the HPSG architecture to refer to all kinds of unbounded dependency constructions, be it traceless or with traces.

*Lexical and Constructional Aspects of Linguistic Explanation.*
Gert Webelhuth, Jean-Pierre Koenig, and Andreas Kathol.
Copyright © 1998, Stanford University.

propose a treatment employing scrambling or adjunction operations as a linearization-like mechanism.

We will argue that a linearization account of the pied-piping construction fails to capture empirical generalizations which automatically follow from a movement account. Two ways to formalize a movement analysis of the pied-piping construction in the HPSG architecture are presented.

## 7.2 The Data

The term 'pied-piping' goes back to Ross (1967), who introduced it to describe the well known cases of movement where the *wh*-word is not fronted alone, but together with the whole category dominating it. In this paper we discuss a construction involving the fronting of infinitives in relative clauses which, because of its topological similarity to Ross's cases, has also been referred to as pied-piping in the literature (cf., e.g., Riemsdijk 1985, Haider 1985, Grewendorf 1986). Infinitives in German relative clauses show the following topological pattern:

(1)   a.   die  Ratten,  *die*    er  *zu fangen*  versucht hat
               the   rats      which  he  to  catch   tried has
               'the rats which he tried to catch'
     b.   die Ratten, *die* er versucht hat *zu fangen*
     c.   die Ratten, *die zu fangen* er versucht hat

*Versuchen* ('try') is a subject-control verb which takes the non-finite transitive verb *zu fangen* ('catch') as its complement. The object of *zu fangen* is the relative pronoun *die* which has to occur as the leftmost constituent of the relative clause. Example (1a) shows the infinitive in its canonical position, to the left of its governor. In example (1b), the infinitive has been extraposed. Finally, example (1c) shows the pied-piping construction in which the infinitive occurs immediately following the relative pronoun. Whether an infinitive can occur in all three topological patterns depends on the class of its governor.

### 7.2.1  Coherence versus Incoherence

Following Bech (1955), verbs selecting a verbal complement can be divided into two classes: coherently constructing verbs and incoherently constructing ones. The pied-piping construction can only occur with incoherently constructing verbs. Such incoherently constructing verbs always govern a *zu*-infinitive and include raising verbs such as *anfangen* ('begin'), subject control verbs such as *versuchen* ('try'), *beabsichtigen* ('intend') and object control verbs such as *überreden* ('persuade'). A precise characterization of this class of verbs is beyond the scope of this paper[2] and plays no role for the argumentation.

Verbs selecting a bare infinitive or a past participle in German always belong to the coherently constructing verbs and thus do not allow the pied-piping construction. Example (2b) shows an ungrammatical pied-piping construction with the modal verb *mußte* which governs a bare infinitive. The same ungrammatical pattern occurs in example (3b) with the auxiliary verb *hat* selecting a past participle.

(2)  a.  die Ratten, die      er schon wieder *fangen*    mußte
         the rats      which he again          to catch   had
         'the rats which he had to catch again'
     b.  *die Ratten, die *fangen* er schon wieder mußte

(3)  a.  die Ratten, die      er schon      *gefangen* hat
         the rats      which he already    caught     has
     b.  *die Ratten, die *gefangen* er schon hat

Finally, example (4) shows that not all verbs governing a *zu*-infinitive can construct incoherently and thus they cannot occur in a pied-piping construction. *Pflegen* ('used to') is a raising verb which only constructs coherently and thus does not allow a pied-piping construction:

(4)  a.  die Ratten, *die*    er *zu fangen* pflegte
         the rats      which he to catch    used
         'the rats which he used to catch'
     b.  *die Ratten, *die zu fangen* er pflegte

In the rest of the paper we will only be concerned with the special properties of the pied-piping construction and thus only the incoherently constructing verbs will play a role.

## 7.3    Linearization versus Movement

### 7.3.1    The Theoretical Issue

It is generally assumed that relative clauses involve an extraction phenomenon which is responsible for the occurrence of the relative pronoun at the left edge of the relative clause. For a relative clause like (1b) one would, for example, get the following structure where the relative pronoun has been extracted from the embedded infinitive:

(5)    die Ratten, die$_i$ er versucht hat [$t_i$ zu fangen]

In the pied-piping construction not only the relative pronoun, but the entire infinitive occurs at the left edge of the relative clause. The ques-

---

[2] A discussion of these two verb classes can, for example, be found in Bech 1955 or Kiss 1995.

tion we are interested in is whether the infinitive is linearized to that position as sketched in example (6), or whether it is extracted together with the relative pronoun as shown in example (7).

(6)    die Ratten, die$_i$ [$t_i$ zu fangen] er versucht hat

(7)    die Ratten, [die zu fangen]$_i$ er $t_i$ versucht hat

We will refer to the analysis sketched in (6) as the linearization analysis of the pied-piping construction and to (7) as the movement analysis.

### 7.3.2 Linearization

For Haider (1985), the initial motivation for a linearization analysis of the pied-piping construction is the observation that the word order of subjects, complements and adjuncts in German is rather unrestricted. Nominal and verbal complements or adjuncts may, for example, precede the subject in a sentence. Therefore, not only a pied-piping construction like the one in (1c) allows an infinitive to be fronted, but ordinary embedded verb-final sentences like the one in (8) do too.

(8)    weil      die Ratten  zu fangen  Hubert  sich        vornahm
       because  the rats     to catch   Hubert  for himself  planned
       'because Hubert planned to catch the rats'

To formalize a linearization account one employs restrictions on possible linearizations, some kind of word order principles[3] that allow for the infinitive to occur in its canonical position, extraposed or fronted. Such a word order principle then licenses the fronted infinitive in sentences like (8) and in the pied-piping construction as in (1c). The structure of a linearization analysis for the pied-piping construction (1c) is shown in Figure 1.

Under this analysis, only the relative pronoun *die* is extracted from the whole relative clause, leaving a gap inside the infinitive *zu fangen*. Word order principles linearize the complement daughters of the relative sentence so that one gets the linear order shown in Figure 1 with the fronted infinitive preceding the subject. For relative clauses like (1a) and (1b), with the verbal complement directly preceding or following the main verb, one obtains the same tree structure as shown in Figure 1, but with a different linear order of the complement daughters.

---

[3]In GB, this is usually done via special transformations like adjunction, whereas in HPSG one can encode word order principles as constraints on the linear order among daughters or the phonology of elements in a certain domain.

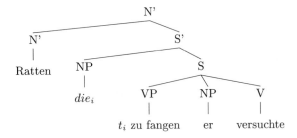

FIGURE 1  Example tree for a linearization of the infinitive

### 7.3.2.1  Problems of Linearization Approaches

Linearization approaches like the one sketched out can account for the basic data shown in (1). But there are two kinds of examples which are problematic for these theories. First of all, they fail to explain why in examples with subject or adjunct infinitives only the pied-piping construction is grammatical. The example in (9) shows the pattern with a subject infinitive, (10) with an adjunct infinitive.

(9)  a. *der Freund,  *dem*  ihn  *zu helfen* ruiniert  hat
        the friend   whom  him  to  help   ruined   has
        'the friend whom to help has ruined him'

     b. *der Freund, *dem* ihn ruiniert hat *zu helfen*

     c.  der Freund, *dem zu helfen* ihn ruiniert hat

(10) a. *eine Sache, *welcher* er  sich    *anzunehmen*   genügend
        a     thing   which   he  himself  to take care of  enough
        Zeit  hatte
        time  had
        'the matter which he had enough time to take care of'

     b. *die Sache, *welcher* er genügend Zeit hatte *sich anzunehmen*

     c.  die Sache, *welcher sich anzunehmen* er genügend Zeit hatte

In (9), the infinitive *zu helfen* ('help') is the subject of the object control verb *ruinieren* ('ruin'). In (10) the support verb construction *Zeit haben* ('have time') is modified by the infinitive *sich anzunehmen* ('take care of') and the relative pronoun *welcher* is the genitive object of this infinitive. Since under a linearization account there is no difference in the syntactic structures of the sentences in (9) and (10), it is unclear how it can be explained that the (a) and (b) examples are ungrammatical in contrast to the (c) examples.

The second kind of examples that are problematic for linearization approaches, as already observed in Grewendorf 1986, are those where the fronted infinitive belongs to a more deeply embedded clause within the relative clause. The following example, originally from Grewendorf 1986, p. 105, shows such a pied-piping construction, where the fronted infinitive belongs to an extraposed infinitive embedded by the main verb of the relative clause.

(11)  eine Tat,  *die*    *begangen zu haben*  Hans  sich     weigerte
      an action  which  committed to have  Hans  himself  refused
      [dem Richter   zu gestehen]
      to the judge    to confess
      'a crime which Hans refused to confess to having committed before the judge'

The fronted infinitive *begangen zu haben* ('having committed') is the verbal complement of the extraposed infinitive *zu gestehen* ('confess') which itself is the complement of the main verb of the relative clause, the subject control verb *weigern* ('refuse').

The only way to analyze this kind of example under a linearization approach would be to assume that any arbitrarily deeply embedded infinitive can be linearized to the position after the relative pronoun.

### 7.3.3   Movement

An alternative approach to analyzing the pied-piping construction is to move the infinitive together with its relative complement instead of moving only the relative constituent and linearizing the infinitive. Such a theory can explain the basic facts we saw in (1). It also predicts the existence of examples like the one in (11) where the fronted infinitive has been extracted from an embedded clause. Finally, such an extraction analysis provides an explanation for the subject and adjunct cases shown in (9) and (10) above, where only the pied-piping cases were grammatical. It has often been observed that adjuncts are strong extraction islands in German (e.g. Lutz 1993), i.e., no constituent can be moved/extracted from adjuncts and that subjects are weak islands, i.e. they may contain a gap only under certain circumstances. However, the extraction of the *entire* subject or adjunct is usually grammatical. Independent of the analysis of pied-piping constructions, a UDC theory for German will have to provide an explanation for these island constraints. One possibility for formulating a restriction to that effect in HPSG is to express an implicational constraint allowing extraction only in certain configurations. For adjuncts one could formulate such a constraint in the following way:

ADJUNCT ISLAND CONSTRAINT
If an adjunct daughter of a phrase has a nonempty SLASH value then the *local* object on its SLASH list must be identical to the LOCAL value of the adjunct daughter.

Once the appropriate constraints are formulated, the ungrammaticality of the examples in (9) and (10) automatically follows, since in these cases the relative constituent has been moved from the infinitive. The pied-piping constructions in (9c) and (10c), however, are grammatical because the relative pronoun and the infinitive have been fronted together, i.e. nothing has to be extracted from the adjunct or the subject.

Before we turn to a more complex set of data, we should draw attention to the fact that spurious ambiguities arise under any movement analysis for the pied-piping construction containing an object infinitive. In contrast to adjunct and subject infinitives, we need to allow extraction from object infinitives in any case, as objects never behave like extraction islands in German. In our case this is supported by the fact that with relative clauses containing an object infinitive not only the pied-piping construction is grammatical but also extraposition of the infinitive or the infinitive remaining in its canonical position. This pattern was shown in example (1). The problem is that for a pied-piping construction like (1c) it is not possible to decide which analysis is more adequate: an analysis as shown in Figure 1 where the infinitive remains within the relative sentence and only the relative pronoun is involved in the unbounded dependency, or the pied-piping analysis described in this section.

### 7.3.3.1 Complex Pied-Piping Data

So far, we have described an extraction account including a single extraction which licenses the entire infinitive including the relative pronoun at the left edge of the relative clause. The following example of a complex pied-piping construction shows that this is not sufficient:

(12) a. Dies ist der Mann, *dem    sich    zu trauen,*
    this is the man    whom himself to dare

    *die Meinung zu sagen* Hans der Mut      fehlte.
    the opinion   to say   Hans the courage lacked

    'This is the man to whom Hans did not dare to
    tell his opinion.'

  b. *Dies ist der Mann, *sich zu trauen dem die Meinung zu sagen,*
    Hans der Mut fehlte.

The fronted/pied-piped infinitive *sich zu getrauen* ('dare') subcategorizes for an infinitive complement (*die Meinung zu sagen*), and the relative pronoun *dem* is a complement of this embedded infinitive. One would expect that the pied-piping of the infinitive *zu getrauen* together with its complement results in a structure like (12b), where the relative pronoun remains within the embedded infinitive. But the only acceptable pied-piping pattern is the one shown in example (12a),[4] where the relative pronoun is at the left edge of the whole relative clause. The only explanation for this pattern is that the relative pronoun has been moved from its original position within the embedded infinitive. There are two possibilities for the position of the relative pronoun.

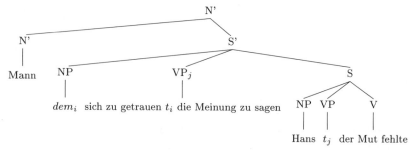

FIGURE 2  A flat structure for the pied-piping construction

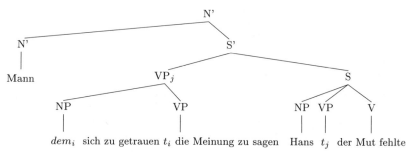

FIGURE 3  The pied-piping construction with 'internal' movement

Either the infinitive is extracted from the pied-piped infinitive and is now a sister of it as shown in Figure 2. Or it has been extracted within the pied-piped constituent so that they form one constituent at the beginning of the relative clause as shown in Figure 3.

In the following we want to show how each of these approaches can be formalized within HPSG.

---

[4]For some speakers example (12a) is only marginally acceptable, but they agree that it is much better than (12b).

## 7.4 Two HPSG Analyses

To formalize the extraction analysis of the pied-piping construction we will start by adapting an account for German relative clauses. Two analyses for relative clauses have been proposed in HPSG: the account by Pollard and Sag (1994, Ch. 5) that analyzes relative clauses as the projection of an empty head, the relativizer, and the approach by Sag (1997) where relative clauses are treated as head-filler phrases. We will show that the first approach lends itself to an analysis of the pied-piping construction as a flat structure like the one shown in Figure 2, whereas a structure like the one shown in Figure 3 can be integrated in the approach by Sag (1997).[5]

In German, contrary to English, subjects can be extracted, just like any other constituent.[6] Therefore, the accounts we propose in the following analyze all German relative clauses, including the subject ones, as unbounded dependency constructions in the sense that the relative pronoun is always extracted.

### 7.4.1 Theory 1: The Empty Pied-Piper

Building on the analysis of Pollard and Sag (1994, Ch. 5), we assume a special lexical head for relative clauses which selects the relative constituent and the relative clause containing a gap as its complements. This empty relativizer has the lexical entry shown in Figure 4.

One of the changes that was made to the original English relativizer is that the SUBCAT attribute was replaced by the valence features as proposed in Pollard and Sag 1994, Ch. 9. The selectional properties of the relativizer are now specified on the COMPS list.

Simple relative clauses, including those that contain an infinitive in its canonical position or extraposed, can be analyzed with this German relativizer.[7] To capture the special properties of the pied-piping construction, we introduce a new empty element for relative clauses with a pied-piped infinitive. In contrast to the original relativizer, which subcategorizes for two elements, the 'empty pied-piper' (EPP) selects three elements: the relative constituent, the pied-piped infinitive and the finite sentence. Its lexical entry is shown in Figure 5 on page 107.

---

[5]See De Kuthy 1996 for a discussion of further possibilities for an analysis of the pied-piping construction on the basis of these two approaches to relative clauses.

[6]It is, for example, the standard assumption that subjects in verb-second sentences, just like any other constituent preceding the verb, are fronted, i.e. take part in an unbounded dependency construction.

[7]To exclude the pied-piping construction from being analyzed as a simple relative clause with a verbal relative constituent one needs an additional constraint that requires that complements of verbs have an empty REL list.

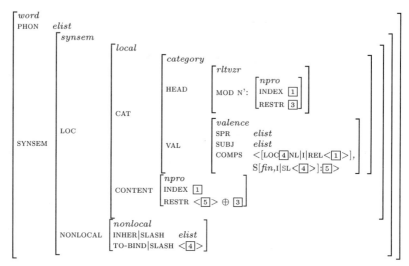

FIGURE 4 Lexical entry for the German empty relativizer

The LOCAL and INHER|SLASH values of the three elements on the COMPS list of the empty pied-piper are important. They license the two relevant filler-gap dependencies in a pied-piping construction: first, the filler-gap dependency between the fronted infinitive and the finite sentence and second, the one between the relative pronoun at the beginning of the relative clause and the fronted infinitive. The empty pied-piper ensures the first dependency via the token identity between the LOCAL value of the infinitival VP[8] on the COMPS list and the SLASH value of the finite sentence. The presence of a second filler-gap dependency is ensured via the token identity between the LOCAL value of the relative constituent, the first element on the COMPS list, and the SLASH value of the infinitival VP. Figure 6 on page 108 shows the tree licensed by this analysis for the pied piping example (1c).

---

[8] We here require the VP to have only the VFORM value *zu-inf*. This is to ensure that no other verb form, like a bare infinitive or a participle, can occur as the fronted constituent. In addition, depending on how the theory distinguishes coherent from incoherent infinitives (for an HPSG proposal distinguishing the different classes of verbs by their head-types see Meurers 1997), one needs to add a specification further restricting the VP to those headed by an incoherently constructing verb, as described in section 7.2.1.

[9] For reasons of space, we abbreviate the attribute NONLOCAL by NL, INHER-ITED by I, TO-BIND by TB, and SLASH by SL in some of the AVMs. The label H at a branch stands for head daughter, C means complement daughter, A adjunct daughter and F filler daughter. In addition, RC is an abbreviation for relative clause, which in this case is a saturated projection of the empty pied-piper.

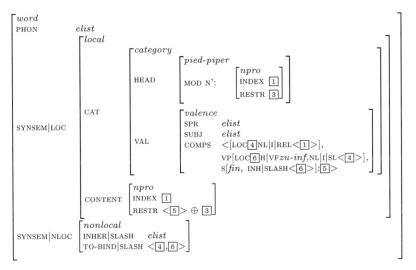

FIGURE 5  Lexical entry for the empty pied-piper

Note that although the fronted infinitive under this analysis contains a gap, we can account for the cases mentioned in examples (9) and (10) where the non pied-piping clauses should be ruled out because the infinitive may not contain a gap. We gave an example for an adjunct island constraint in section 7.3.3. In a pied-piping construction with a fronted adjunct infinitive licensed by the empty pied-piper, the pied-piped infinitive functions as the complement daughter of the whole relative clause, while only the gap inside the relative clause functions as the adjunct daughter. The empty pied-piper just requires token identity between the LOCAL value of the fronted infinitive and the inherited SLASH of the relative clause. Thus nothing prevents this fronted infinitive from having a different SLASH value than its LOCAL value. The identity of these two values is required only for the gap of the infinitive inside the relative clause.

### 7.4.2  Theory 2: The Pied-Piping Construction as Head-Filler Phrase

An analysis where the relative pronoun remains within the pied-piped infinitive can be nicely integrated into the proposal of Sag (1997). In his proposal different kinds of constituent structures are expressed via subsorts of *phrase*; relative clauses are analyzed, analogous to other UDCs, as a subsort of *head-filler-phrase*. In addition, the special properties of relative clauses are expressed via constraints on the sorts introduced for these clause types.

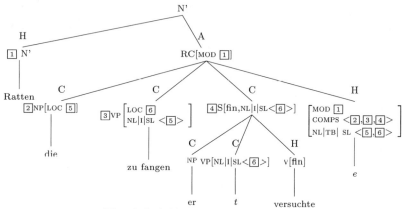

FIGURE 6  The pied-piping construction in a theory with the empty pied-piper[9]

German relative clauses can be analyzed as head-filler phrases like English non-subject relative clauses. Figure 7 shows the relevant part of the sort hierarchy.

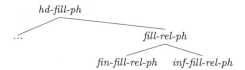

FIGURE 7  The sort hierarchy for German relative clauses

The sort *hd-fill-ph*, a subsort of *phrase*, has the subsort *fill-rel-ph* and possibly other subsorts for UDCs in German. We introduce two subsorts of *fill-rel-ph*, *fin-fill-rel-ph* and *inf-fill-rel-ph*, even though there appear to be only finite relative clauses in German. All relative clauses, including pied-piping constructions, must be instances of the sort *fin-fill-rel-ph*. The sort *inf-fill-rel-ph* is only relevant for the fronted infinitive of pied-piping constructions. If the non-head daughter[10] of a relative clause is of the sort *inf-fill-rel-ph* we get the structure for the pied-piping construction described in Figure 3.

The constraints in Figure 8 ensure that only phrases of the sort *fin-fill-rel-ph* can occur as relative clauses, whereas the non-finite coun-

---

[10]In this approach we adopt a binary branching structure, where the type of the non-head daughter can be deduced from the sort of the phrase it belongs to, e.g. the non-head daughter of a phrase of sort *fill-rel-ph* is always a filler daughter.

terparts can only serve as the filler daughter of a relative clause in a pied-piping construction.

$$\textit{fill-rel-ph} \rightarrow \left[ \text{NONHEAD-DTR} \begin{bmatrix} \text{REL} & \textit{nelist} \\ \text{QUE} & \textit{elist} \end{bmatrix} \right]$$

$$\textit{fin-fill-rel-ph} \rightarrow \begin{bmatrix} \text{SS|L|C|HEAD|MOD} & \begin{bmatrix} \text{L} & \begin{bmatrix} \text{C|HEAD} & \textit{noun} \\ \text{CONT|INDEX} & \boxed{1} \end{bmatrix} \end{bmatrix} \\ \text{HEAD-DTR} & \begin{bmatrix} \text{SS|L|C} & \begin{bmatrix} \text{HEAD|VFORM} & \textit{fin} \\ \text{V|COMPS} & \textit{elist} \end{bmatrix} \end{bmatrix} \\ \text{NONHEAD-DTR} & \begin{bmatrix} \text{REL} & <\boxed{1}> \end{bmatrix} \end{bmatrix}$$

$$\textit{inf-fill-rel-ph} \rightarrow \begin{bmatrix} \text{HEAD-DTR} & \begin{bmatrix} \text{SS|L|C} & \begin{bmatrix} \text{HEAD} & \begin{bmatrix} \text{VFORM} & \textit{zu-inf} \\ \text{MOD} & \textit{none} \end{bmatrix} \end{bmatrix} \end{bmatrix} \end{bmatrix}$$

FIGURE 8 Constraints on relative clauses

The first constraint in Figure 8 ensures that the filler daughter of any relative phrase must contain a relative pronoun, i.e. some element that has a nonempty REL list. The constraint on finite relative phrases requires the MOD value on the mother of a relative clause to be *noun-synsem*. This way a relative clause can occur as the modifier of a noun in a head-adjunct structure. In contrast, the MOD feature on non-finite relative phrases has the value *none* to ensure that phrases of this sort can never serve as a relative clause modifying a noun by themselves. For sentence (1c) this theory licenses the construction shown in Figure 9.

So far nothing ensures that the filler daughter *die zu fangen* is really of sort *inf-fill-rel-ph*. It could also be a simple head-complement phrase where the relative pronoun *die* is realized as the complement daughter of *zu fangen*. However, as we have repeatedly mentioned, in German the relative constituent always occurs at the left edge of the relative clause and is therefore always analyzed as being extracted. Thus we can impose a constraint on phrases with a verbal head[11] which requires that if the non-head daughter has a non-empty REL value then it must be the filler daughter, i.e. the phrase must be of sort *fill-rel-ph*. Figure 10 shows a formalization of this constraint. Such a constraint has several effects in our case: it rules out the possibility of having a phrase of sort

---

[11]We restrict our constraint to phrases with a verbal head as in other cases, for example in prepositional phrases serving as a relative constituent, the complement daughter may have a non-empty REL value.

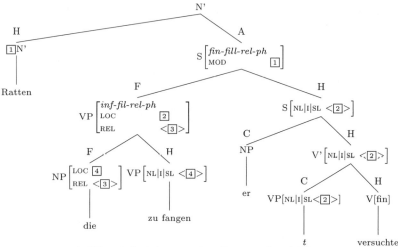

FIGURE 9  The pied-piping construction as a head-filler structure

$$\begin{bmatrix} phrase \\ \text{HEAD} \qquad verb \\ \text{NONHEAD-DTR} \begin{bmatrix} \text{REL } nelist \end{bmatrix} \end{bmatrix} \rightarrow \textit{fill-rel-ph}$$

FIGURE 10  Constraint on the distribution of REL values

*inf-fill-rel-ph* inside a normal sentence as the complement daughter of a control verb like *versuchen*. Second, it prevents the occurrence of any other phrase containing a relative pronoun inside a sentence. And it rules out the possibility of having a non-finite head complement phrase with a relativized complement daughter as the filler of a relative clause. This means that the fronted infinitive in a pied-piping construction must always be of sort *inf-fin-rel-ph*.

## 7.5   Conclusion

We started out with the question whether the pied-piping of infinitives in German relative clauses should be analyzed in a linearization-based account or by movement. Under a linearization approach only the relative pronoun is extracted from the relative clause while the fronted infinitive remains within the sentence. Problematic for such a theory are those examples where the fronted infinitive belongs to a more deeply embedded clause, and relative clauses containing a subject or adjunct infinitive where only the pied-piping construction is grammatical.

In contrast, a movement theory where both the relative pronoun and the fronted infinitive are extracted from the relative clause can account for the two problematic cases. Firstly, the fronted infinitive may be extracted from an arbitrarily deeply embedded clause. Secondly, the pied-piping construction gets a different structure than the relative clauses containing an infinitive in its canonical position or extraposed. The ungrammatical non pied-piping examples occurring with subject and adjunct infinitives are then excluded by the island constraints needed to account for the ordinary extraction data. To formalize this idea, we provided two different HPSG theories for the pied-piping construction which both capture the special properties of the fronted infinitives. Summing up, we have shown one case of a word order phenomenon where a movement analysis is preferable to a linearization-based account.

# References

Bech, Gunnar. 1955. *Studien über das deutsche Verbum infinitum.* Linguistische Arbeiten, No. 139. Tübingen: Max Niemeyer Verlag. 2nd edition, 1983.

De Kuthy, Kordula. 1996. Der Rattenfängereffekt bei Relativ- und Interrogativsätzen im Deutschen. Master's thesis, University of Tübingen.

Grewendorf, Günther. 1986. Relativsätze im Deutschen: Die Rattenfänger-konstruktion. *Linguistische Berichte* 105:409–434.

Haider, Hubert. 1985. Der Rattenfängerei muß ein Ende gemacht werden. *Wiener Linguistische Gazette* 35–36:27–50.

Kathol, Andreas. 1995. *Linearization-Based German Syntax.* Doctoral dissertation, Ohio State University.

Kiss, Tibor. 1995. *Infinite Komplementation.* Linguistische Arbeiten, Vol. 333. Tübingen: Max Niemeyer Verlag.

Lutz, Uli. 1993. Extraktion — Ein einführender Überblick. In *Extraktion im Deutschen I*, ed. F.-J. d'Avis, S. Beck, U. Lutz, J. Pafel, and S. Trissler, 1–62. Arbeitspapiere des SFB 340, No. 34. University of Tübingen.

Meurers, Walt Detmar. 1997. Statusrektion und Wortstellung in kohärenten Infinitkonstruktionen des Deutschen. In *Ein HPSG-Fragment des Deutschen. Teil 1: Theorie*, ed. E. W. Hinrichs, W. D. Meurers, F. Richter, M. Sailer, and H. Winhart. 189–248. Arbeitspapiere des SFB 340, No. 95. University of Tübingen.

Müller, Stefan. 1998. *Head-Driven Phrase Structure Grammar für das Deutsche.* Lecture Notes Computational Linguistics. Humboldt University Berlin and University of the Saarland, Saarbrücken.

Pollard, Carl, and Ivan A. Sag. 1994. *Head-Driven Phrase Structure Grammar.* University of Chicago Press.

Reape, Mike. 1994. Domain Union and Word Order Variation in German. In *German in Head-Driven Phrase Structure Grammar*, ed. J. Nerbonne, K. Netter, and C. Pollard. 151–197. CSLI lecture notes, No. 46. CSLI.

Riemsdijk, Henk van. 1985. Der Rattenfängereffekt bei Infinitiven in deutschen Relativsätzen. In *Erklärende Syntax des Deutschen*, ed. W. Abraham. Tübingen: Gunter Narr Verlag.

Ross, John R. 1967. *Constraints on Variables in Syntax*. Doctoral dissertation, MIT.

Sag, Ivan A. 1997. English Relative Clause Constructions. *Journal of Linguistics* 33(2):431–484.

Trissler, Susanne. 1991. Infinitivische w-Phrasen? In *Fragesätze und Fragen*, ed. M. Reis and I. Rosengren. Linguistische Arbeiten, Vol. 257. Tübingen: Max Niemeyer Verlag.

# 8

## Inversion and Constructional Inheritance

Charles J. Fillmore

Within a unification based grammar having grammatical constructions as its basic building blocks,[1] the formal device of CONSTRUCTIONAL IN-HERITANCE makes it possible to represent the grammar of a language as a "mere" repertory of constructions while at the same time acknowledging and representing significant grammatical generalizations. In this paper I will take the English SAI (Subject-Auxiliary Inversion) construction as the focus of an exploration of constructional inheritance, both in reference to the higher-level constructions which are the source of SAI, and a sample of the lower-level constructions which inherit it.

### 8.1 Construction Grammar

In the version of Construction Grammar that Paul Kay and I and our associates have been shaping over the last ten years, a grammar is viewed as a repertory of constructions. A construction is a set of formal conditions on morphosyntax, semantic interpretation, pragmatic function, and phonology, that jointly characterize or license certain classes of linguistic objects. A complete grammar of constructions that did everything it needed to do for a given language would provide for any well-formed linguistic object in that language at least one ensemble of grammatical constructions whose interactions account for the pairing of

This paper was written for the Grammatical Constructions panel at the 1997 HPSG conference at Cornell University. Since I am not fluent in HPSG, I have not attempted to recast my comments in its terms. I am indebted to Paul Kay, Andreas Kathol, and two anonymous reviewers for advice on a preliminary version of this paper.

[1]See Fillmore and Kay 1993, Goldberg 1995, Kay 1995, Kay and Fillmore 1994, Michaelis and Lambrecht 1996a,b.

*Lexical and Constructional Aspects of Linguistic Explanation.*
Gert Webelhuth, Jean-Pierre Koenig, and Andreas Kathol.
Copyright © 1998, Stanford University.

form and meaning which that linguistic object represents; and for any
linguistic object that was $n$-ways ambiguous it would allow $n$ ensem-
bles of constructions, each of which could assign it a different pairing of
meaning and structure.

Any phrasal and many lexical constructions will have an internal
part and an external part. The external part describes the kind of
object instances of the construction are; getting the description right
means showing what role the whole phrase can play in the rest of the
grammar. The internal part describes the kinds of objects instances of
the construction contain; getting the facts right means identifying the
kinds of constituents that can participate in the construction.

The set of constructions in a grammar includes PHRASAL CONSTRUC-
TIONS, those whose internal descriptions identify the separate parts and
the nature of their mutual dependencies of government (valence) and/or
agreement. An example of a phrasal construction is the SAI construction: for SAI we need to state that the first constituent is a finite auxiliary, the second constituent is something capable of being the subject
of that auxiliary, and the remainder, if there is anything else, will be its
non-subject complement(s).[2]

Utterances that are instances of the SAI construction can thus have
two constituents, as in (1a), three constituents, as in (1b), or four constituents, as in (1c).

(1)   a.   [Did] [you]?
      b.   [Has] [anybody] [seen them]?
      c.   [Was] [she] [here] [this morning]?

In addition to phrasal constructions there are various kinds of LEXI-
CAL CONSTRUCTIONS,. Among them we have "simple" lexical constructions, consisting of a lexical form with specification of its syntactic and
semantic properties and (where relevant) its valence. For these there
is no contrast between internal and external properties. There can be
other lexical constructions which specify as their internal structure a
particular set of lexical features, and as their outer structure a different set of lexical features, where both the "mother" constituent and the
"daughter" constituent are single lexical items. This is a construction-
grammatic way of representing "lexical rules" (and is in general the only
occasion in construction grammar for anything corresponding to "unary
branching"). Familiar examples are items which are mass nouns inter-

---

[2]Auxiliaries are treated as complement-taking verbs. In the usual case an auxiliary
verb will "take" a subject and a VP complement (*we* **have** *written the letter, she* **can**
*reach the top shelf*); but in the case of the verb BE we sometimes need to assume more
than one complement, as in example (1c). (We follow the practice of incorporating
circumstantial adjuncts among the complements in a VP.)

nally and count nouns externally (*a beer*), or vice versa (*some chicken*), or those which are proper names internally and common nouns externally (*another Jane*).

There are also LINKING CONSTRUCTIONS which license particular mappings between semantic functions (thematic roles) and grammatical functions. Some predicates, when taken "off the shelf", might have only the semantic part of their combinatorial options lexically specified (e.g., *agent, theme, recipient*); linking constructions, then, serve to assign grammatical functions, in a context-sensitive way, to constituents that can instantiate these thematically specified elements.

Lastly we can have constructions which specify dependencies between phrasal entities, independently of how they enter into phrasal constructions. This is characteristic of (lexical and syntactic) idioms.

A grammar is a repertory of constructions; but instead of being just an unstructured collection, the grammatical constructions in a language form a network connected by links of INHERITANCE. We recognize grammatical generalizations by showing the ways in which some constructions contain or are elaborations of other constructions (see Sag 1997 on relative clauses, Zwicky 1994 on constructions "invoking" other constructions). If construction C inherits construction D, then C shares all of the conditions of D while adding some of its own. We will say, for example, that a construction for Yes-No Questions inherits the SAI construction but imposes certain limitations and adds features of interpretation.[3]

## 8.2 Ancestors of SAI

I will first describe the inheritance path of constructions that leads to SAI; and then I will turn to a sampling of the constructions which inherit SAI.

All of the constructions we will be examining here are phrasal constructions. The external properties of the phrase will be represented as feature structures written in an outer box, the internal properties will be written in the constituent boxes. Constituent order in the diagrams is represented by juxtaposition of boxes.[4]

**8.2.1**　A central typological fact about English is that in phrasal constructions for which one constituent is obligatorily lexical (i.e., is a single

---

[3]We see no need for the inheritance process to incorporate defaults and overrides in the manner of Lakoff 1987 and Goldberg 1995. The equivalent of "default" values is provided by constructions that assign values to attributes whose values are otherwise unspecified.

[4]Some constructions, not described here, have constituents with unspecified order, requiring a slight modification of the representations.

word), that constituent precedes the others in the phrase.[5] The construction which captures this fact is the LEXICALLY TAGGED PHRASE construction, LTP.

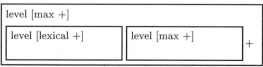

Figure 1: LTP (Lexically Tagged Phrase)

This diagram tells us that the LTP construction has a lexical (not phrasal) member on the left and one or more constituents following it. Since it is a primary construction, it does not inherit any other construction. The plus sign after the second box is a "Kleene plus", indicating one or more repetitions of the type of entity preceding the plus.[6] The feature structure "level [lexical +]" indicates that this element is obligatorily a single lexical item. The feature structure "level [max +]" means that the constituent so-marked is a "maximal" phrase, in the traditional sense.

**8.2.2**     There are two slightly less general constructions that directly inherit LTP: one of these is what can be called the LEXICALLY MARKED PHRASE, in which the first element is a "marker" and what follows is the head; and the other is the LEXICALLY HEADED PHRASE, in which the first element is a head and what follows consists of (some of) the complements of that head.

Lexically marked phrases include

(2)     a.     that   she liked it
        b.     if     you have any
        c.     to     leave home

The "markers" are the clausal subordinators *that* and *if,* and the verbal subordinator *to.* The construction:

---

[5]There are phrases containing lexical items that are not themselves expandable as phrases, but which do not constitute instances of the description of LTP. A constituent filled with the word *ago,* for example, does not require lexical membership: *ago* occupies the position that can also be filled with a prepositional phrase such as *before today,* etc.

[6]A "Kleene star"—an asterisk in the same position—would allow any number, that is, zero or more repetitions. However, we are dealing here with phrasal constructions, and for that we need at least two constituents.

| inherit LTP & HFC<br>markerlex #1[ ] | |
|---|---|
| role marker<br>markerlex #1[ ] | role head |

Figure 2: LMP (Lexically Marked Phrase)

In the description of the LMP we notice that the second element lacks the Kleene plus, since the "head" constituent is either a single clause or a single verb-phrase. Another thing to notice is that the construction specifies the projection of the lexical identity of the marker onto the parent node. This is because we need to be able to identify the phrase as a whole as a "*that*-clause", an "*if*-clause", a "*to*-marked infinitive", etc. The two instances of "#1[ ]" are unification indices, guaranteeing that whatever marker shows up in the marker position is registered with the entire constituent. The third property to notice is the inheritance of an as-yet undescribed construction called HFC, which stands for HEAD FEATURE CONSTRUCTION. That, and the attribute "role", will be described shortly.

**8.2.3**    The LEXICALLY HEADED PHRASES have valence-bearing lexical heads in phrase-initial position, the remainder constituting some (or all) of its complements. This construction requires an appeal to two other constructions, in addition to the LTP, namely the Head Feature Construction already mentioned, and the VALENCE RAISING CONSTRUCTION (VR).

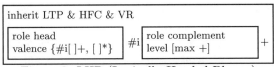

Figure 3: LHP (Lexically Headed Phrase)

One of the attributes introduced in the last two constructions is "role". The role attribute figures only in the structure of phrases, where individual constituents are marked according to their role in the phrase. The possible values of this attribute include *marker, head, complement, modifier, specifier* and *conjunct*.

The valence of a valence-bearing word is a specification of the set of elements which the presence of the valence-bearer calls for in order for the semantic and syntactic structure that is built up around it to be completed. The elements of this set are described in terms of two kinds of RELATIONAL features, their GRAMMATICAL FUNCTION (gf) and their SEMANTIC ("THEMATIC") FUNCTION (sf), together with their phrase type (NP, PP, etc.).

The valence value in the first constituent refers to the set (enclosed in wavy braces) of valence members. Some of these (one or more, as shown by the Kleene plus) are prefixed by a unification index "#i". What follows the unification index is an empty pair of square brackets standing for the feature structure which identifies a valence member. The variable "i" is understood as running through an unspecified number of elements in the valence description, and its occurrence twice in the formula means that each of the so-identified elements in the valence formula is matched by one of the constituents on the right. The remaining valence members (those represented by "[ ]*"), if there are any, are either not syntactically realized ("licensed omissions"), or are realized in a position external to the LHP. A syntactically unrealized constituent is the understood complement of *I tried*; examples of non-locally realized valence members are subjects of indicative sentences, or WH-fronted constituents.

**8.2.4** It was said that the LMP and the LTP constructions both inherit HFC, the Head Feature Construction. This is the construction which specifies that certain features of a phrasal head[7] are projected onto the mother. In positing this construction we are required to distinguish HEAD FEATURES from other kinds of features, and that requires us to say something about the architecture of the feature system we are using. Let it suffice for present purposes to say that the features we need to identify as head features are those which specify categorial and inflectional features. In particular, the set of head features does not include ROLE FEATURES (the head of a phrase is notated with the feature "role head") because the role of the mother in its own phrase is not necessarily that of "head". The set of head features does not include LEVEL FEATURES. LEXICALITY is a level feature; a phrase containing a lexical element, however, is necessarily not lexical. MAXIMALITY is a level feature; a mother and head daughter may of course differ in maximality. We also posit a level feature srs, standing for "subject requirement satisfied". A predicate phrase in an indicative sentence is [srs −] but the clause which contains it and provides it with a subject is, of course, [srs +].

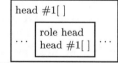

Figure 4: HFC (Head Feature Construction)

---

[7] The reader should be alerted that the word "head" occurs as a value of the attribute "role" but also as an attribute of a feature structure containing the "head" features.

This construction does not inherit LMP: the constituent providing the features projected onto the mother is identified by the role label "head" and not by position. The head in a "marker + head" construction is to the right; the head in a "head + complement" construction is to the left. Other constructions (e.g., modification), not discussed here, can have phrasal heads, and these can be leftmost or rightmost, depending on the construction.

**8.2.5** In construction grammar, the valence of a valence-bearing head is projected onto the mother node, and that is shown in the VA-LENCE RAISING construction.[8] This makes our use of the word "valence" a bit awkward, since that word was originally introduced for naming the combinatorial privileges of individual words. Instead of abandoning the word "valence", we will extend its use to include the kind of syntactic/semantic structure that can be built around a word. The valence that comes with a verb, then, is interpretable as identifying (part of) the structural potential of any clause that it heads. Similarly, the valences of non-verbs determine the syntactic/semantic structure of their phrasal projections.

The Valence Raising Construction looks like this:

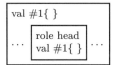

Figure 5: VR (Valence Raising)

Again, the projecting constituent is identified by its role, not its position. The valence of a verb (the leftmost constituent in its phrase) is projected to a verb phrase; the valence of a verb phrase (the rightmost constituent in its phrase) is projected to the sentence as a whole.[9]

**8.2.6** There are four major kinds of Lexically Headed Phrases, separated according to the category of the lexical head. These we will refer to as VHP (Verb-Headed Phrase), AHP, NHP, and PHP. These (perhaps awkward) names are intended to keep them distinct from the familiar and informally used VP, AP, NP and PP, since the latter are conventionally used for constituents which might be smaller than the corresponding LHP (they might not be phrasal) or they might be larger than the corresponding LHP (they might contain "specifiers" and/or "modifiers"). In

---

[8]Actually, for reasons connected with our treatment of adjuncts, a more accurate version of this rule shows a subset relation between the valence of a head daughter and the valence of the mother constituent.

[9]We ignore here the problem of valence projection in cases where the head constituent contains a conjunction of valence-bearing elements.

our representation, a word which itself serves as a maximal constituent simultaneously bears the level features [lexicalcal +] and [maximal +].

Here we exhibit only the VHP construction; the others will be identical in form but will have differ in the value of the cat ("category") attribute.

Figure 6: VHP Verb-Headed Phrase

**8.2.7**    The VHP construction can be elaborated in two ways: it underlies both the predicational VHP (as in *ate his lunch*) and the inverted clause as in *did they see us?*). The constructions specifying these elaborations are named VPC (VERBAL PREDICATE CONSTRUCTION) and, following general practice, SAI (SUBJECT-AUXILIARY INVERSION).[10]

The VPC specifies that all of the complements of the lexical head are non-subjects; the mother has the level feature [srs −]—"subject requirement not (internally) satisfied".

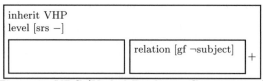

Figure 7: VPC (Verbal Predicate Construction)

**8.2.8**    The SAI construction identifies three positions. The occupant of the first has to be a finite auxiliary. The second has grammatical function subject. It is important that the constituent is not just "a subject" but is in fact the subject of the auxiliary in the first constituent, but that doesn't have to be separately specified, since the phrase as a whole is [srs +] and all other complements are specified as [gf ¬subject]. It should be noticed that the third constituent bears the Kleene star, meaning that this part of the construction might be missing, or might be multiple. Recall the examples in (1) above.

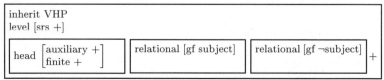

Figure 8: SAI (Subject-Auxiliary Inversion)

---

[10]In Kay & Fillmore 1994, this was called Inversion, abbreviated INV.

The full inheritance structure of SAI is displayed below:

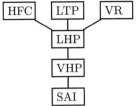

Figure 9: Inheritance structure of SAI

A complete description of SAI will have all of the properties of each of the ancestor constructions.[11]

## 8.3 Non-Interrogative Constructions Inheriting SAI

The English SAI construction is host to a large number of constructions, most famously a family of question constructions that use the SAI order. In this paper I will survey those which are not, or are not mainly, questions.[12]

**8.3.1** One heir of SAI can be called the BLESSINGS, WISHES, AND CURSES Construction, BWC. In these sentences the auxiliary is limited to the modal *may* and the sentence expresses the speaker's (real or pretended) act of calling on divine or magical forces to bring about something the speaker desires.

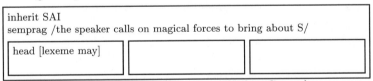

Figure 10: BWC (Blessings-Wishes-Curses)

Examples in (3):

(3)   a.   May she live forever!
      b.   May I live long enough to see the end of this job!
      c.   May your teeth fall out on your wedding night!

---

[11] The reader will have noticed that neither SAI nor any of its ancestors is provided with semantic or pragmatic information. This appears to be a major feature by which Construction Grammar and HPSG formalisms are not mutually intertranslatable: the basic "typologically relevant" constructions are not *signs* in the sense of Pollard and Sag. Whether SAI itself has a pragmatic or functional component shared by all of its inheritors is something on which I do not take a stand. (But see Michaelis & Lambrecht, 1996b.)

[12] The original version of this paper concentrated on questions, but their treatment will not be dealt with in later work.

It is important to recognize that there is no independent semantic force of SAI syntax, or any independently discoverable meaning of the modal *may,* that could explain the semantic/pragmatic force we recognize with these sentences, either compositionally or by providing the basis for a context-based interpretation. This has to be described as a separate construction.

**8.3.2**     A construction that we might call SAI-Exclamation under-lies a class of utterances which express the speaker's judgments or eval-uations of events in the speaker's personal experience. Such utterances (explored in N. A. McCawley 1973) are clearly not questions, because (i) they can be used to express experiences that addressees did not share (and therefore could not answer questions about), (ii) they do not get rendered with rising intonation, and (iii) they do not invite a response from the addressee.

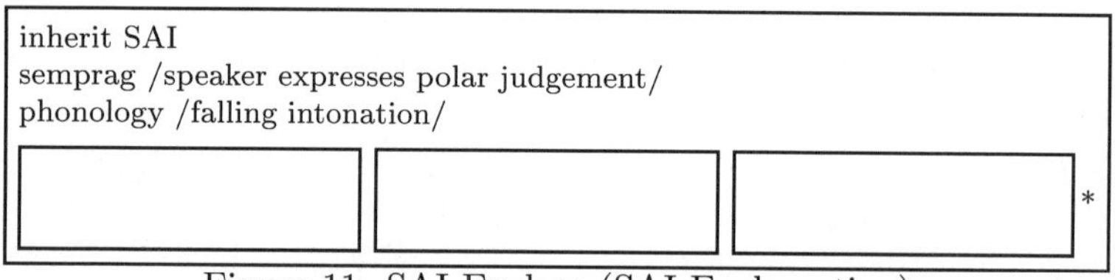

```
inherit SAI
semprag /speaker expresses polar judgement/
phonology /falling intonation/

┌──────────────┐ ┌──────────────┐ ┌──────────────┐
│              │ │              │ │              │ *
└──────────────┘ └──────────────┘ └──────────────┘
```

Figure 11: SAI Exclam (SAI Exclamation)

These utterances can be preceded by any of a number of conventional ejaculations, such as *Man!, Boy!, Wow!,* etc. Examples in (4):

(4)     a.     Boy, was I stupid!
        b.     Wow, can she sing!
        c.     Man, am I hot!

Since instances of this construction are exclamations, they typically ex-press judgments about situations that are beyond the norm on some scale. Example (4b) (even without the "Wow") suggests that it is the construction itself, not the semantics of the contained predicates, which determine the "beyond norm" interpretation. This sentence has to be interpreted as suggesting that she can sing unusually well.

**8.3.3**     There is a purely morphological construction that "uses" SAI, in the sense that it specifies SAI as the context in which it applies. This is the construction which creates the phrase *aren't I?.* The form *aren't* as the contracted form of *am not* occurs only in SAI structures. The usage specifications associated with *aren't I?* have to do with register, and are compatible with any of the various varieties of constructions in which its conditions (negative copula, present tense, occurring with first person singular subject) are met. Thus we find *aren't I?* occurring in what can be described as different sub-constructions of interrogative SAI.

(5)  a.  I'm getting closer, aren't I?
     b.  Aren't I the clever one!
     c.  Aren't I a little too old for you, honey?
     d.  Aren't I gonna get anything out of this for myself?

I offer no suggestion on how the registral information should be presented. To some speakers the form is absolutely natural, with no registral value whatever; to others it sounds cautious or pretentious; to still others it is simply bad English.

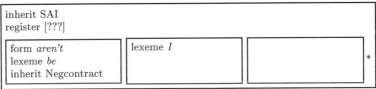

Figure 12: "Aren't I?"

The first constituent is an instance of the morphological construction NEGATIVE CONTRACTION (negcontract), the construction which produces *won't, can't, didn't,* etc., and which I will not describe.

**8.3.4**     There is a class of EMPHATIC NEGATIVE IMPERATIVES, accepting only the subject pronoun *you* and the negative form *don't,* illustrated in (6a) and (6b).

(6)  a.   Don't you even touch that!
     a'.  Don't even touch that!
     b.   Don't you dare talk to me like that!
     b'.  *Don't dare talk to me like that!

Obviously these are not questions. It appears that these are not merely Negative Imperatives (*Don't do that!*) which happen to include an overt second-person subject: sentence (6b') strikes me as ungrammatical.

```
┌─────────────────────────────────────────────────────────────┐
│ inherit SAI                                                   │
│ mood imperative                                               │
│ ┌───────────────────────┬──────────────────┬───────────────┐ │
│ │ form don't            │ lexeme you       │               │ │
│ │ lexeme do             │                  │               │ │
│ │ inherit Negcontract   │                  │               │ │
│ └───────────────────────┴──────────────────┴───────────────┘ │
└─────────────────────────────────────────────────────────────┘
```

Figure 13: ENI (Emphatic Negative Imperative)

**8.3.5**     As an alternative to versions of conditional clauses prefixed by such markers as *if* and *unless,* there is an SAI version, limited to the auxiliary forms *were, had* and *should* (and, obsolete or obsolescent, *did*).

| inherit SAI<br>semprag /conditional/ | | |
| --- | --- | --- |
| form $\left\{\begin{array}{l}\text{were}\\\text{had}\\\text{should}\end{array}\right\}$ | | |

Figure 14: Aux Cond (Auxiliary Conditional)

Examples of present counterfactual, past counterfactual, and non-past contingent Aux-Cond sentences are given in (7).

(7)  a.  Were they here now, we wouldn't have this problem.
     b.  Had we known what was in it, we wouldn't have opened it.
     c.  Should there be a need, we can always call for help.

In characterizing the construction in Figures 12 and 13, we needed to specify not just that the sentence was negative, but that the auxiliary had the neg-contracted form. By specifying the actual forms of the auxiliary in the Aux-Cond construction in Figure 14, we rule out the possibility of neg-contraction. The clause itself can be negative, however, as can be seen by comparing the affirmative sentences in (7) with the negative sentences in (8).

(8)  a.  Were it not/*Weren't it for your help, we'd be in trouble now.
     b.  Had you not/*Hadn't you invited me, I wouldn't have known about this.
     c.  Should you not/*Shouldn't you comply with this request, your permit will be taken away.

When the words inserted into the first position of Aux-Cond are *were* or *had*, an additional feature accompanies them: [mood counterfactual]; with *should*, however, it is [mood contingent]. An instance of the Aux-Cond construction can occur as a subordinate clause to a full two-part conditional sentence, as in any of the grammatical sentences in (6) or (7), or, in the case where the subjunctive is counterfactual, it also lends itself to use in a WISHING construction (not described), which, among others of its features, welcomes the word *only*.

(9)  Had I only known!

**8.3.6**     An example of a construction in which SAI can characterize one constituent of a multiple-constituent construction is the CORRELA-TIVE CONDITIONAL construction (not described here, but see Fillmore 1987), in which the second element is optionally of the SAI type. Sentence (10a) shows the presence of SAI; sentence (10b) shows the more usual form in this construction.

(10)　a.　The faster you finish eating those hot dogs, the sooner [will]
[we] [be able to claim the prize].

　　　b.　The faster you finish eating those hot dogs, the sooner we'll
be able to claim the prize.

## 8.4　Pointing to the Treatment of SAI Questions

It seems to me there are four sorts of phenomena that join with SAI to
create the kinds of questions we find: two flavors of polarity, intonation,
and (for some questions) participation in a new family of constructions
with its own inheritance hierarchy.[13] Polarity occurs on two levels: the
polarity of a sentence as a whole has to do with whether the sentence
is affirmative or negative; polarity can also color a context in respect
to the welcoming of polarity items. I will distinguish "polarity" as an
attribute having the values "affirmative" and "negative", from "polarity
context" as having the values "pospol" (positive polarity) and "negpol"
(negative polarity) or "neutral". The reason for requiring this range of
distinctions is because positive and negative polarity *contexts* can occur
distinctively in either affirmative or negative *questions*. For example:

(11)　a.　Do you want a little?　　[pol aff, polcon pos]

　　　b.　Do you want any?　　　[pol aff, polcon neg]

　　　c.　Don't you want a little?　[pol neg, polcon pos]

　　　d.　Don't you want any?　　[pol neg, polcon neg]

**8.4.1**　Underlying both real questions and a new variety of exclamatory construction, there is a general APPELLATIVE SAI construction
which specifies only appellation, a "pragmatic" feature indicating that
the speaker appeals to an addressee for a reaction. The uninformative
"semprag appellation" in the diagram below will have to be cashed out
as a scenario involving speaker intentions and certain features of illocutionary force.

---

[13]Briefly, that new family of constructions begins with what we call the "Left Isolate"
construction, by which a maximal phrase is found to the left of its valence-bearing
phrasal head. From this beginning are formed the Subject/Predicate construction,
and a large group of constructions involving the potential of "long-distance dependency" between the left-isolated constituent and the predicator whose valence requirements it satisfies. WH-MainClauseNon-SubjectQuestions, for example, inherit
LI at the top and SAI in the right sister, for questions like "What did you see?",
or WH-MainClauseSubjectQuestions inherit LI at the top and Subject/Predicate in
the right sister, as in "Who said that?".

```
┌─────────────────────────────────────────────────────────────┐
│ inherit SAI                                                   │
│ semprag appellation                                           │
│ ┌─────────────────┐ ┌─────────────────┐ ┌─────────────────┐  │
│ │                 │ │                 │ │                 │  │
│ │                 │ │                 │ │                 │  │
│ └─────────────────┘ └─────────────────┘ └─────────────────┘  │
└─────────────────────────────────────────────────────────────┘
```

Figure 15: Appellative (Appellative SAI Construction)

I will make (but leave undefended) the claim that there is a constructional contrast between NEGATIVE SAI QUESTIONS and AFFIRMATIVE SAI QUESTIONS, and, furthermore, that each of these is host to still more elaborated question types. The first of these divisions should not be surprising: grammar does not need two ways of formulating Yes/No questions, so if affirmative SAI sentences can serve that purpose, SAI questions with negative syntax are free to serve other purposes. Being precise about the difference between the plain question in (12a) and the biased question in (12b) is difficult, but there is no doubt that an important difference exists.

(12) a. Did you understand what I said?
     b. Didn't you understand what I said?

I believe that there are only partly predictable interpretations of positive and polarity contexts as they occur independently in positive and affirmative SAI questions, and that the whole range of issues includes at least the impressive collection of insights in Ann Borkin's paper of twenty-some years ago (Borkin 1977). I believe that Borkin's observations, explained in terms of the kinds of speaker intentions or attitudes expressed with the selection of positive or negative polarity items, can instead be described as conditions on constructions which create positive or negative polarity contexts within which positive or negative polarity items are welcome. A full account requires subtle and careful specification of features of intonation, mood, register, and discourse functions, as well as precise accounts of the semantics of polarity. But all of that is for another occasion.

**8.4.2**     There is at least one non-interrogative construction which inherits the feature "appellative" from the preceding construction. This is the NEGATIVE SAI EXCLAMATION CONSTRUCTION. Sentences based on this construction are negative in form but express *affirmative* judgments about some experience which speaker and addressee have shared or are sharing.

| inherit SAI-Appell<br>pragmatics exclamation | | |
|---|---|---|
| inherit Negcontract | head [definite +] | (*see discussion*) |

Figure 16: NegSAI Exclam ("Negative" SAI Exclamation)

Instances of this construction are compatible with falling or rising intonation, but in either case they assume addressee assent, or seek addressee validation, on the *affirmative* version of the proposition underlying the sentence. Unlike the positive SAI Exclam construction of Figure 11, this one isn't used with completely private judgments: if I exclaim *Wasn't I hot!*—as opposed to *Was I hot!*—the chances are I'm asking for confirmation of my fine performance on the basketball court rather than seeking confirmation of my degree of discomfort from the heat.

Sentences of the type in question include those in (13).

(13)  a.  Isn't she amazing!
      b.  Wasn't that awful!
      c.  Aren't they beautiful.

The description of this construction will clearly have to include semantic constraints on the predicate phrases. A corpus search[14] for sentences which began with neg-contracted auxiliaries and did not end in question marks yielded predicates that tended to have a clear end-of-scale character. A sampling of the adjectivals: *amazing, brilliant, disgusting, extraordinary, fabulous, fantastic, glorious, hopeless, horrible, huge, incredible, ludicrous, magnificent, marvellous, splendid, stupendous, terrific,* and *wonderful.* With predicate nominals one finds *a grand girl, a hideous thought, a scream,* etc., and the exclamatory *something* (as in *Isn't that something!*).

## 8.5   Closing

A major intellectual challenge in writing a construction grammar of a language is found in the problem of figuring out whether newly encountered phenomena can be accounted for by the constructions already posited for the grammar, in standard unificational and compositional ways, or by exploiting the possibilities of contextual interpretations, or whether the newly considered phenomena require the positing of a new construction. At times researchers will discover ways in which certain postulated constructions can be dissolved by showing that all of

---

[14]Using the British National Corpus, made available to me at the International Computer Science Institute through the courtesy of Oxford University Press.

their properties "fall out from" constructions or principles that can be independently called on to analyze the phenomena. But at the same time researchers will continue discovering layers of conventionalization in linguistic forms that superficially appear to be plainly derivable by familiar means, and therefore will find themselves positing new constructions. It seems to me that a theory of grammar which uses grammatical constructions and posits a rich network of inheritance relations among them gives a point to such reformulations, in that the before and after stages of such recastings will show a clear difference between two important kinds of linguistic discoveries—finding generalizations where previous scholars wrongly posited idiosyncracy, and finding new levels of conventionalization where previous scholars wrongly posited generality.

## References

Borkin, Ann. 1976. Polarity in Questions. *Chicago Linguistic Society* 7:53–62.

Fillmore, Charles J. 1987. Varieties of Conditional Sentences. *Proceedings of the Third Eastern States Conference on Linguistics*, Columbus: Ohio State University. 163–182.

Fillmore, Charles J., and Paul Kay. 1993. Construction Grammar (ms). UC Berkeley.

Goldberg, Adele. 1995. *Constructions: A Construction Grammar Approach to Argument Structure*. Chicago: University of Chicago Press.

Kay, Paul. 1995. Construction Grammar. *Handbook of Pragmatics*, eds. Jef Verschueren, Jan-Ola Östman, and Jan Blommaert. John Benjamins.

Kay, Paul, and Charles J. Fillmore. 1993. Grammatical Constructions and Linguistic Generalizations: The *What's X doing Y?* Construction (ms), UC Berkeley.

Lakoff, George. 1987. *Women, Fire and Dangerous Things*. University of Chicago Press.

McCawley, Noriko A. 1973. Boy, is Syntax Easy! *Chicago Linguistics Society* 9:369–377.

Michaelis, Laura, and Knud Lambrecht. 1996a. Toward a Construction-Based Theory of Language Function: The Case of Nominal Extraposition. *Language* 72:215–247.

Michaelis, Laura, and Knud Lambrecht. 1996b. The Exclamative Sentence Type in English. *Conceptual Structure, Discourse and Language*, ed. Adele Goldberg. CSLI: Stanford.

Sag, Ivan A. 1996. English Relative Clause Constructions, *Journal of Linguistics* 33(2):431–484.

Zwicky, Arnold. 1994. Dealing out Meaning: Fundamentals of Syntactic Constructions. *Proceedings of the Twentieth Annual Meeting of the Berkeley Linguistics Society*. 611–625.

# 9

# German Partial-VP Topicalization Revisited

Walt Detmar Meurers

## 9.1 Introduction

The topicalization of partial verbal projections in German (henceforth: PVP topicalization) has received much attention because the variable constituency it displays is a challenge to the traditionally central role of constituent structure. In the HPSG framework, Pollard (1996, orig. ms. 1990), and more recently Hinrichs and Nakazawa (1994) and Nerbonne (1994) met this challenge with a variety of mechanisms and drew conclusions for the general architecture: Pollard showed how the extended notion of valence introduced by argument raising (Hinrichs and Nakazawa 1989) can be used to license the required multiple structures. Nerbonne introduced a non-monotonic device to relax certain requirements for fronted constituents and claimed that only a traceless analysis can provide a satisfactory account. Hinrichs and Nakazawa based their analysis on a special lexical rule constructing new constituents for topicalization only and strengthened the unbounded dependency mechanism to be able to license topicalized constituents containing a gap.

The purpose of this short paper is to reexamine whether the phenomenon of PVP topicalization supports these conclusions and which consequences should be drawn for the general architecture of HPSG.

I want to thank Tilman Höhle, Stefan Müller, Kordula De Kuthy, Frank Richter, Manfred Sailer, Erhard Hinrichs, Gerald Penn, and the anonymous reviewers for their comments.

## 9.2    PVP Topicalization and HPSG Theory

It has become standard to analyze German verb-second sentences as verb-first structures from which an element has been topicalized. Leaving aside few classes of exceptions, the topicalized element is (a) a single constituent which (b) could also occur in non-topicalized position.

Under these two assumption (henceforth: topicalization assumptions), the phenomenon of PVP topicalization is problematic. To see why this is the case, consider the sentences in (1).[1] Example (1a) is an ordinary verb-first question. In (1b) the main verb and one object has been fronted, with the other object remaining in its "base position". In (1c) the main verb and the auxiliary is topicalized, leaving both objects behind. The problem is that under the two topicalization assumptions, no single structure can be found for (1a) that allows both topicalizations.

(1)    a.    Wird    er     ihr     einen    Ring     schenken    können?
               will     he     her     a        ring     give        be-able-to
               'Will he be able to give her a ring?'

       b.    *Einen Ring schenken* wird er ihr können.

       c.    *Schenken können* wird er ihr einen Ring.

Pollard (1996) proposes an HPSG theory using optional argument raising for auxiliaries in the style of Hinrichs and Nakazawa (1989) and a standard UDC mechanism employing traces. He shows that such an analysis can account for the data he discusses, but also points out that this is done at the cost of licensing multiple structures for sentences like (1a)—such as structures in which the accusative object *einen Ring* forms a constituent with the verb *schenken,* corresponding to the constituent topicalized in (1b), and others in which *schenken* and *können* form a constituent, as motivated by examples like (1c). Since these multiple structures are not independently motivated, they are spurious ambiguities which under most concepts of linguistic theory should be eliminated.

This is where Nerbonne 1994 and Hinrichs and Nakazawa 1994 pick up. Common to both proposals is that they keep the first topicalization assumption, i.e., that only a single constituent can be topicalized, but relax the second, the assumption that a topicalized constituent can also occur in non-fronted position. The basic idea thus is to license partial constituents only in fronted position. Reducing the two proposals to the essentials, we believe there are two key ingredients needed to exclude the spurious structures of the Pollard's analysis:

---

[1]The example basically follows those discussed by Nerbonne (1994, ex. (1)) and Hinrichs and Nakazawa (1994, ex. (17)).

1. Instead of *optional* argument raising, which introduces the many subcategorization possibilities at the basis of the spurious structures, some version of *obligatory* argument raising must be employed.
2. The topicalized verb phrase must be exempt from this requirement.

We first turn to the different possibilities for enforcing obligatory argument raising.

### 9.2.1 Enforcing Obligatory Argument Raising

Two versions of obligatory argument raising are proposed. Nerbonne (1994) proposes to raise *all complements* of the embedded verb and assumes flat structures with no verbal complex.[2] Hinrichs and Nakazawa (1994) raise only *all non-verbal complements* and assume a contoured, left-branching verbal complex.

The way to achieve obligatory argument raising is basically the same in both approaches. A new attribute LEX[3] is introduced with the idea of marking a verbal constituent as [LEX −] if it has realized either one or more complements (in the flat Nerbonne approach) or one or more non-verbal complements (in the contoured Hinrichs/Nakazawa approach). To enforce obligatory argument raising, it then suffices to specify the lexical entries of auxiliaries so that they require their verbal complement to be [LEX +].

In the Nerbonne approach, the idea of marking all verbal constituents in which complements are realized as [LEX −] is easily formalized by requiring every *phrase* to be [LEX −]. To obtain a theory enforcing a contoured verbal complex, Hinrichs and Nakazawa (1994) propose a slightly more complicated encoding. The head-complement schema is split up into a binary branching "Verbal Complex Schema" (their Figure (6), p. 4) licensing [LEX +] constituents as the combination of a *word* head with a single verbal complement and a "Head-NP-Complement ID Schema" (their Figure (21), p. 11) licensing [LEX −] constituents consisting of a head combining with any number of non-verbal constituents plus an optional verbal complement. Furthermore, the verbal complements are excluded from argument raising by specifying the elements raised to be non-verbal signs.

---

[2]Nerbonne (1994, 141) suggests that one might consider extending his proposal to accommodate a contoured verbal complex.

[3]Hinrichs and Nakazawa (1994) name the attribute NPCOMP and interpret its value as the polar opposite of the value of LEX. To have a uniform setup, we will call the attribute LEX throughout the paper; but note that different connotations were associated with the attribute name of the original proposal.

## 9.2.2   Relaxing the Requirement for Topicalization

With two methods for enforcing obligatory argument raising on our hands, the remaining issue is to find a way to relax the obligatory argument raising between an auxiliary and its topicalized verbal complement. Regarding this issue, Nerbonne says of his theory:

> "Phrasal PVPs are licensed in the Vorfeld first because they are licensed by a SLASH specification generated via the complement extraction rule (Pollard and Sag 1994, 446), with an important modification—the feature LEX is nonmonotonically relaxed on SLASII specifications. It is this nonmonotonic relaxing of LEX which ultimately explains the lack of perfect correspondence between Vorfeld "fillers" and Mittelfeld "sources"."   (Nerbonne 1994, 127)

Hinrichs and Nakazawa (1994) introduce a new lexical rule, the "PVP-Topicalization Lexical Rule" (their Figure (19), p. 10, henceforth: PVPTLR). This rule does not extract a constituent to be topicalized, but rather it creates a new verbal element for topicalization only. This "hand assembled" constituent is specified to share some selected properties with a verbal element subcategorized for by the input of the lexical rule. Furthermore, the PVPTLR uses a modified UDC mechanism to require complements missing from the topicalized verb phrase to be realized in the Mittelfeld. For this purpose, the SLASH feature is changed to take a set of *signs* as value instead of the more restrictive *local* objects usually assumed.

Looking back at the task to be achieved—to relax the obligatory argument raising requirement—a rather simple alternative solution comes to mind. Even though the LEX attribute has traditionally been assumed to be appropriate for *category* objects, to our knowledge no real arguments why this needs to be the case have been given. Thus, it is unproblematic to make LEX appropriate for *synsem* objects instead. The standard UDC mechanism only identifies the *local* properties of a filler and a trace so that having LEX as attribute of *synsem* objects will have the effect that the LEX property is no longer shared between a filler and its trace.[4] As a result, the topicalized constituent does not have to obey the obligatory argument raising enforced by [LEX +] on its trace. Note that this makes argument raising optional only for the topicalized constituent itself; argument raising remains obligatory for the subconstituents of the topicalized element.

---

[4]Independently, Müller (1996) also came up with the idea to relocate the LEX attribute to *synsem* in order to relax the LEX restriction on topicalized PVPs.

Before we can show how this idea is spelled out by describing how the original Pollard 1996 proposal can be modified to exclude the spurious structures, there are two relevant issues left to discuss: the use of traces and the directionality of branching in contoured verbal complexes.

### 9.2.3 Related Issues

#### 9.2.3.1 Traces

The theory proposed by Nerbonne (1994) employs a complement extraction lexical rule to obtain a traceless theory of unbounded dependencies. In connection with this choice, he makes the following claim:

> "The key to eliminating the spurious ambiguity problem [...] is the elimination of traces in favor of an analysis in which long distance dependence is grounded not in a missing constituent, but rather in an unrealized functor-argument relation." (Nerbonne 1994, 117)

On closer inspection, this claim turns out to be false. A PVP topicalization account works equally well with traces. The trace can stand for a topicalized constituent which happens to be a partial-VP. Due to argument raising, the verbal head selecting the trace then attracts the complements not yet realized in the topicalized constituent. To illustrate this, the theories discussed in Section 9.3.2 all make use of a standard UDC mechanism employing traces.

On pp. 147f. Nerbonne (1994) notes independent motivation for abandoning traces. He claims that in an analysis employing traces, another kind of spurious ambiguity can arise, e.g., in complex VPs, because "there is no nonarbitrary single location at which a "trace" might be posited." However, if only the phonologies are ordered, as assumed in standard HPSG (cf., Pollard and Sag 1987, 169ff.), this is not the case since the phonology of a trace is the empty list and therefore *a trace is not linearized* at all.[5] The phonology of each sign is a list of phonological symbols. It is these symbols that are linearized, not the lists themselves. Traces have an empty list as phonology.

#### 9.2.3.2 Left- and Right-Branching Verbal Complexes

Two different styles of verbal complexes have been proposed for German. Hinrichs and Nakazawa employ a traditional left-branching structure for the verbal complex. Kiss (1992) proposes a right-branching one, in which the auxiliaries combine one by one and the main verb is

---

[5]A discussion on the point that empty constituents have no word order properties is also provided by Pollard and Moshier (1990, 291f.). Kathol (1995, 152f) comes to the same conclusion for a linearization-based variant of HPSG explicitly encoding domain objects.

added at the end.[6] Kiss (1992, 281ff.) himself states that the analysis he proposes cannot account for VP-topicalization if the two topicalization assumptions are made, because the constituent structure needed for topicalization is not contained in the structure he assigns to a verb-first sentence. However, if we take a closer look at the problem his analysis has with VP-topicalization, it turns out to be the same problem which we discussed for the PVP-topicalization analyses avoiding spurious ambiguities above—namely that one has to allow elements which do not form a constituent in the structure assumed for verb-first sentences to be topicalized as a constituent. Thus, as shown in Section 9.3.2.3, our analysis idea for PVP topicalization carries over to an analysis of (P)VP topicalization using the right-branching structures of Kiss.

## 9.3  Modifying the Theory of Pollard (1996)

This section provides a more formal proposal of how Pollard's original theory can be modified to exclude the spurious structures. First, we review the basic ingredients of Pollard's theory. Then, we discuss the modifications which are necessary to obtain a theory licensing only flat structures in the style of Nerbonne. Finally, we introduce the modifications of Pollard's theory needed to obtain theories licensing contoured structures à la Hinrichs/Nakazawa and à la Kiss.

### 9.3.1  Pollard's Original Theory

We briefly review the lexical entries of auxiliaries and the ID schemata proposed by Pollard (1996). The principles (Head-Feature Principle, Subcat Principle, ... ) Pollard uses are rather standard and carried over without discussion.

Figure 1 shows the lexical entry of the non-finite form of the perfect auxiliary *haben*.[7] While the verbal complement is encoded on SUB-CAT, the subject valence of non-finite verbs is encoded on a separate SUBJECT attribute. The structure sharing of ⊡ between the SUB-JECT attribute and that of the selected verbal complement indicates that *haben* is analyzed as a subject-raising verb. Finally, the valence requirements encoded on the SUBCAT attribute of the selected verbal complement are raised by unioning them to subcategorization requirements of *haben*.[8]

---

[6]Some additional motivation for a right-branching verbal complex structure is discussed in Meurers 1997a.

[7]Here and throughout the paper, the following attributes for space reasons sometimes are abbreviated by their initial letter: SYNSEM, LOCAL, NONLOCAL, IN-HERITED, TO-BIND, CAT, and HEAD. Additionally, SBC abbreviates SUBCAT.

[8]Traditionally argument raising is explicitly specified in the lexical entries of an intuitively understood lexical class, like in the lexical entry shown in Figure 1. Meur-

$$
\begin{bmatrix}
\text{PHON} & \langle haben \rangle \\
\text{S}\,|\,\text{L}\,|\,\text{C} & 
\begin{bmatrix}
\text{HEAD} & \begin{bmatrix} verb \\ \text{VFORM} \;\; bse \end{bmatrix} \\
\text{SUBJECT} & \{\boxed{1}\} \\
\text{SUBCAT} & \left\{ (P)VP_{psp} \left[ \text{L}\,|\,\text{C} \begin{bmatrix} \text{SUBJECT} & \{\boxed{1}\} \\ \text{SUBCAT} & \boxed{2} \end{bmatrix} \right] \right\} \cup \boxed{2}
\end{bmatrix}
\end{bmatrix}
$$

FIGURE 1   Pollard 1996, 300: Lexical entry for a base-form auxiliary

Figure 2 shows the lexical entry of the finite future auxiliary *wird*. The SUBCAT set of finite auxiliaries consists of two elements, the sub-

$$
\begin{bmatrix}
\text{PHON} & \langle wird \rangle \\
\text{S}\,|\,\text{L}\,|\,\text{C} & 
\begin{bmatrix}
\text{HEAD} & \begin{bmatrix} verb \\ \text{VFORM} \;\; fin \end{bmatrix} \\
\text{SUBCAT} & \left\{ \boxed{1}NP_{nom}, (P)VP_{bse} \left[ \text{L}\,|\,\text{C} \begin{bmatrix} \text{SUBJECT} & \{\boxed{1}\} \\ \text{SUBCAT} & \boxed{2} \end{bmatrix} \right] \right\} \cup \boxed{2}
\end{bmatrix}
\end{bmatrix}
$$

FIGURE 2   Pollard 1996, 299: Lexical entry for a finite auxiliary

ject NP and the non-finite verbal complement from which, just like in the non-finite case, the complements are raised.

The two relevant ID Schemata are shown in Figure 3.[9]   Schema B' licenses non-finite verbal projections where the head is a *word* and combines with any number of its complements. Schema C licenses finite verbal projections in which all of the complements are realized.

$$
\begin{bmatrix} phrase \\ \text{DTRS} \;\; headed\text{-}struc \end{bmatrix} \rightarrow
\begin{bmatrix}
\text{S}\,|\,\text{L}\,|\,\text{C}\,|\,\text{SUBJ} & \{\boxed{1}\} \\
\text{DTRS}\,|\,\text{HEAD-DTR} & \begin{bmatrix} word \\ \text{S}\,|\,\text{L}\,|\,\text{C}\,|\,\text{SUBJ} \; \{\boxed{1}\} \end{bmatrix}
\end{bmatrix}
$$   (Schema B')

$$
\vee \begin{bmatrix} \text{S}\,|\,\text{L}\,|\,\text{C} & \begin{bmatrix} \text{SUBJ} & \{\} \\ \text{SUBCAT} & \{\} \end{bmatrix} \end{bmatrix}
$$   (Schema C)

$$\vee \qquad \ldots$$   (Schemata D, E, F)

FIGURE 3   Pollard 1996: ID Schemata B' and C

---

ers (1997b) shows how argument raising can be introduced by lexical principles as a theoretical generalization over a class of words.

[9]The schemata A and B (without prime) "missing" here are introduced in Pollard 1996 for English only.

To illustrate this, the two structures for example sentence (1a) discussed in Section 9.2 are shown in Figures 4 and 5.

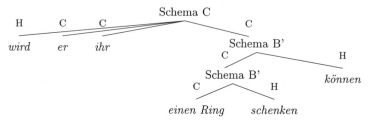

FIGURE 4   A structure for (1a) with [*einen Ring schenken*] as constituent

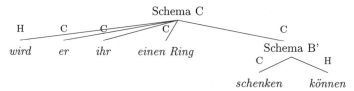

FIGURE 5   One of the structures for (1a) with [*schenken können*] as constituent

In Figure 4, *schenken* combines with its accusative complement, while its dative complement is raised to become a complement of *können* and further raised to become a complement of *wird*, as which it is finally realized. In Figure 5, on the other hand, *schenken* combines directly with *können*, which raises both of the NP arguments. Those are then raised further to *wird*, in order to be realized as complements of that auxiliary.

### 9.3.2   Three Theories for PVP Topicalization

We base the three theories introduced below on the proposal of Pollard 1996 and change only those aspects of direct relevance to the issues under discussion. In the feature geometry, the *boolean*-valued attribute LEX is introduced for *synsem* objects as discussed in Section 9.2.2. For ease of notation, we make one further modification: Following a suggestion in Kiss 1992, Pollard's attribute SUBJ is introduced for *head* instead of for *category*. As a result, the Head-Feature Principle takes care of the correct percolation of SUBJ in non-finite verb projections and no separate mention of SUBJ in the schemata is needed.

### 9.3.2.1 Theory 1: Flat Structures

In a theory licensing completely flat structures, as proposed by Nerbonne, we need to ensure that all phrases are [LEX −]. Rather than adding this specification to the mother in Pollard's head-complement schemata B' and C (and the other schemata), we can express this in the simple principle shown in Figure 6.

$$phrase \rightarrow \left[ \text{SYNSEM} \mid \text{LEX} \ - \right]$$

FIGURE 6  Theory 1: A simple principle constraining phrases

The lexical entries of the auxiliaries are modified to require their verbal complement to be [LEX +].[10] We thus obtain the lexical entry for the finite future auxiliary *wird* shown in Figure 7.

$$\left[ \begin{array}{l} \text{PHON} \ \langle wird \rangle \\ \text{S} \mid \text{L} \mid \text{C} \left[ \begin{array}{l} \text{HEAD} \left[ \begin{array}{l} verb \\ \text{VFORM} \ fin \end{array} \right] \\ \text{SUBCAT} \left\{ \boxed{1} NP_{nom}, \ VP_{bse} \left[ \begin{array}{l} \text{LEX} \ + \\ \text{LOC} \mid \text{CAT} \left[ \begin{array}{l} \text{HEAD} \mid \text{SUBJECT} \ \{\boxed{1}\} \\ \text{SUBCAT} \ \boxed{2} \end{array} \right] \end{array} \right] \right\} \cup \boxed{2} \end{array} \right] \end{array} \right]$$

FIGURE 7  Theory 1: Lexical entry for the finite auxiliary *wird*

This minimally modified Pollard theory succeeds in eliminating the spurious ambiguity problem. But a completely flat analysis can also be achieved with only one head-complement schema replacing Pollard's schemas B' and C, which is shown in Figure 8.[11] This schema licenses all head-complement constructions whose head daughter is a *word*.

$$\left[ \begin{array}{l} phrase \\ \text{DTRS} \ headed\text{-}struc \end{array} \right] \rightarrow \quad \left[ \text{DTRS} \mid \text{HEAD-DTR} \ word \right] \qquad \text{(HC Schema)}$$

$$\vee \quad \ldots \qquad \text{(Schemata D, E, F)}$$

FIGURE 8  Theory 1: One head-complement ID schema

To illustrate this first theory using the single head-complement schema, the structure licensed for the PVP topicalization example (1b)

---

[10]Note that here it is not possible to eliminate the LEX attribute by requiring the verbal complements to be of type *word* since the SUBCAT set only contains *synsem* objects.

[11]The original theory of Nerbonne 1994 also contains two head-complement schemata since he uses a special schema to license topicalized constituents.

is shown in Figure 12 (appendix). Note that just as in Pollard's original theory, the analysis uses a standard UDC mechanism employing traces.

### 9.3.2.2 Theory 2: Left-Branching Verbal Complexes

To obtain a theory licensing "Hinrichs/Nakazawa-style" left-branching verbal complexes, in addition to the schema for [LEX −] constituents we need a second head-complement schema to license binary branching verbal complexes. So we define a variant of Hinrichs/Nakazawa's Verbal Complex ID Schema. Both schemata are shown in Figure 9.

$$
\begin{bmatrix} phrase \\ \text{DTRS} \quad headed\text{-}struc \end{bmatrix} \rightarrow \quad \begin{bmatrix} \text{S} \mid \text{LEX} & - \\ \text{DTRS} \mid \text{HEAD-DTR} & word \end{bmatrix} \quad \text{(HC)}
$$

$$
\vee \quad \begin{bmatrix} \text{S} \mid \text{LEX} \ + \\ \text{DTRS} \begin{bmatrix} \text{HEAD-DTR} & word \\ \text{COMP-DTRS} \ \big\langle [\text{S} \mid \text{L} \mid \text{C} \mid \text{HEAD} \ \ verb] \big\rangle \end{bmatrix} \end{bmatrix} \quad \text{(VC)}
$$

$$
\vee \qquad \ldots \qquad \text{(Schemata D, E, F)}
$$

FIGURE 9  Theory 2: Two head-complement ID schemata

Since we cannot force all phrases to be [LEX −] as done in the first theory, we need to explicitly require this in the HC Schema. Our second schema licenses binary branching head-complement constructions marked [LEX +] whose head daughter is a *word* and whose complement daughter's head value is *verb*.

As discussed in Section 9.2.1, we also need to change the specification of the lexical entries of auxiliaries to exclude verbal complements from argument raising. We require this indirectly by adding a specification to the lexical entries of auxiliaries which requires each argument raised to be [LEX −].

To illustrate the resulting proposal, the structure of the PVP topicalization example (1b) as assigned by this second theory is shown in Figure 13 (appendix). In this figure, the tree in which the auxiliary *können* combines with the trace is licensed by the binary head-complement schema.

### 9.3.2.3 Theory 3: Right-Branching Verbal Complexes

Finally, to get a theory licensing a structure with a "Kiss-style" right-branching verbal complex, we need to specify two different head-complement schemata. The first head-complement schema licenses constructions marked [LEX −] with a head daughter of type *word* and complement daughters marked [LEX −]. The verbal-complex schema licenses binary branching head-complement constructions marked [LEX −] whose complement daughter is marked [LEX +] and has the HEAD value *verb*. The two schemata are shown in Figure 10.

$$
\begin{bmatrix} phrase \\ \text{DTRS} \ headed\text{-}struc \end{bmatrix} \rightarrow
\begin{bmatrix} \text{S} \mid \text{LEX} \ - \\ \text{DTRS} \ \begin{bmatrix} \text{HEAD-DTR} & word \\ \text{COMP-DTRS} & list\!\left(\begin{bmatrix}\text{S}\mid\text{LEX} \ -\end{bmatrix}\right) \end{bmatrix} \end{bmatrix} \quad \text{(HC)}
$$

$$
\vee \ \begin{bmatrix} \text{S} \mid \text{LEX} \ - \\ \text{DTRS} \ \begin{bmatrix} \text{COMP-DTRS} & \left\langle \begin{bmatrix} \text{S} & \begin{bmatrix} \text{L}\mid\text{C}\mid\text{HEAD} & verb \\ \text{LEX} & + \end{bmatrix} \end{bmatrix} \right\rangle \end{bmatrix} \end{bmatrix} \quad \text{(VC)}
$$

$$
\vee \qquad \ldots \qquad \text{(Schemata D, E, F)}
$$

FIGURE 10  Theory 3: Two head-complement ID schemata

As lexical entries for the auxiliaries, this third theory uses those of Pollard's original theory shown in Figures 1 and 2, which do not make reference to the LEX attribute. Obligatory argument raising in this theory follows from the interaction of the LEX specification in the two head-complement schemata alone.

Again, we illustrate this third theory by showing the structure of the PVP topicalization example (1b) in Figure 14 (appendix). However, while Figure 14 shows the relevant distribution of specifications, the example is not complex enough to actually show the difference in structure between a left- and the right-branching theory. Figure 11 therefore illustrates the structures assigned to the verbal complex of the same sentence with one more modal auxiliary: *Einen Ring schenken wird er ihr können müssen* ('It must be the case that he will be able to give her a ring').

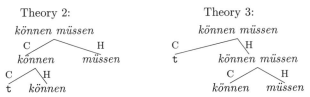

FIGURE 11  Left-branching and right-branching verbal complex structures

## 9.4  Summary

On the basis of two recent proposals for PVP topicalization, Hinrichs and Nakazawa 1994 and Nerbonne 1994, we identified two essential ingredients that are required to exclude the spurious structures licensed by Pollard's (1996) original proposal: obligatory instead of optional argument raising, and a method to exclude the relation which holds between the topicalized constituent and the verb of which it is a complement from this requirement. While both proposals successfully introduce a version of obligatory argument raising, the conclusions drawn in connection with the second issue were shown to be less convincing. In particular, we showed that there is no need for a nonmonotonic device to relax specifications or "hand-assembled" constituents since it is sufficient to make LEX appropriate for *synsem* instead of for *category* in order to make argument raising non-obligatory for topicalized constituents.

We backed up our claim that the identified ingredients are the essential ones by illustrating that it is sufficient to introduce them into the original theory of Pollard (1996) to eliminate the spurious ambiguities. Since this proposal makes use of traces, we thereby falsified Nerbonne's claim that traces are the source of the problem; both a traceless analysis and an analysis employing traces are equally possible.

Finally, in formalizing three different theories, we showed that a flat structure without a verbal complex, a structure with a left-branching verbal complex, and a structure with a right-branching verbal complex are equally suitable for PVP topicalization. This shows that in an approach employing argument raising, the selectional properties encoded in the valence attributes and the constituent structure are related much more indirectly than traditionally assumed.

## References

Hinrichs, Erhard, and Tsuneko Nakazawa. 1989. Flipped Out: Aux in German. In *Papers from the 25th Regional Meeting of the CLS*, 193–202. Chicago, Illinois.

Hinrichs, Erhard, and Tsuneko Nakazawa. 1994. Partial-VP and Split-NP Topicalization in German - An HPSG Analysis. In: E. Hinrichs, D. Meurers, and T. Nakazawa: *Partial-VP and Split-NP Topicalization in German— An HPSG Analysis and its Implementation*. SFB 340 Arbeitspapier Nr. 58, Univ. Tübingen.

Kathol, Andreas. 1995. *Linearization-Based German Syntax*. Doctoral dissertation, Ohio State University.

Kiss, Tibor. 1992. *Infinite Komplementation: Neue Studien zum deutschen Verbum infinitum*. Doctoral dissertation, University of Wuppertal.

Meurers, Walt Detmar. 1997a. Statusrektion und Wortstellung in kohärenten Infinitkonstruktionen des Deutschen. In *Ein HPSG-Fragment des Deutschen. Teil 1: Theorie*, ed. E. Hinrichs et.al. 189–248. SFB 340 Arbeitspapier Nr. 95, Univ. Tübingen.

Meurers, Walt Detmar. 1997b. Using Lexical Principles in HPSG to Generalize over Valence Properties. In *Proceedings of the Third Conference on Formal Grammar*. Aix-en-Provence, France.

Müller, Stefan. 1996. Yet another Paper about Partial Verb Phrase Fronting in German. In *Proceedings of COLING 96*, 800–805. Copenhagen.

Nerbonne, John. 1994. Partial Verb Phrases and Spurious Ambiguities. In *German in Head-Driven Phrase Structure Grammar*, ed. John Nerbonne, Klaus Netter, and Carl Pollard. 109–150. Stanford: CSLI Publications.

Pollard, Carl. 1996. On Head Non-Movement. In *Discontinuous Constituency*, ed. Harry Bunt and Arthur van Horck. Berlin, New York: Mouton de Gruyter. (published version of a ms. dated January 1990).

Pollard, Carl, and Drew Moshier. 1990. Unifying Partial Descriptions of Sets. In *Information, Language and Cognition*, ed. P. Hanson. 285–322. Vancouver: University of British Columbia Press.

Pollard, Carl, and Ivan A. Sag. 1987. *Information-Based Syntax and Semantics, Vol. 1*. Stanford: CSLI Publications.

Pollard, Carl, and Ivan A. Sag. 1994. *Head-Driven Phrase Structure Grammar*. Chicago: University of Chicago Press.

# Appendix

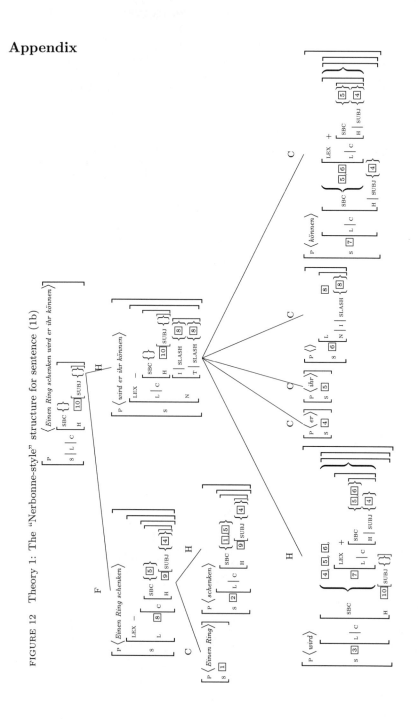

FIGURE 12   Theory 1: The "Nerbonne-style" structure for sentence (1b)

FIGURE 13    Theory 2: The "Hinrichs/Nakazawa-style" structure for sentence (1b)

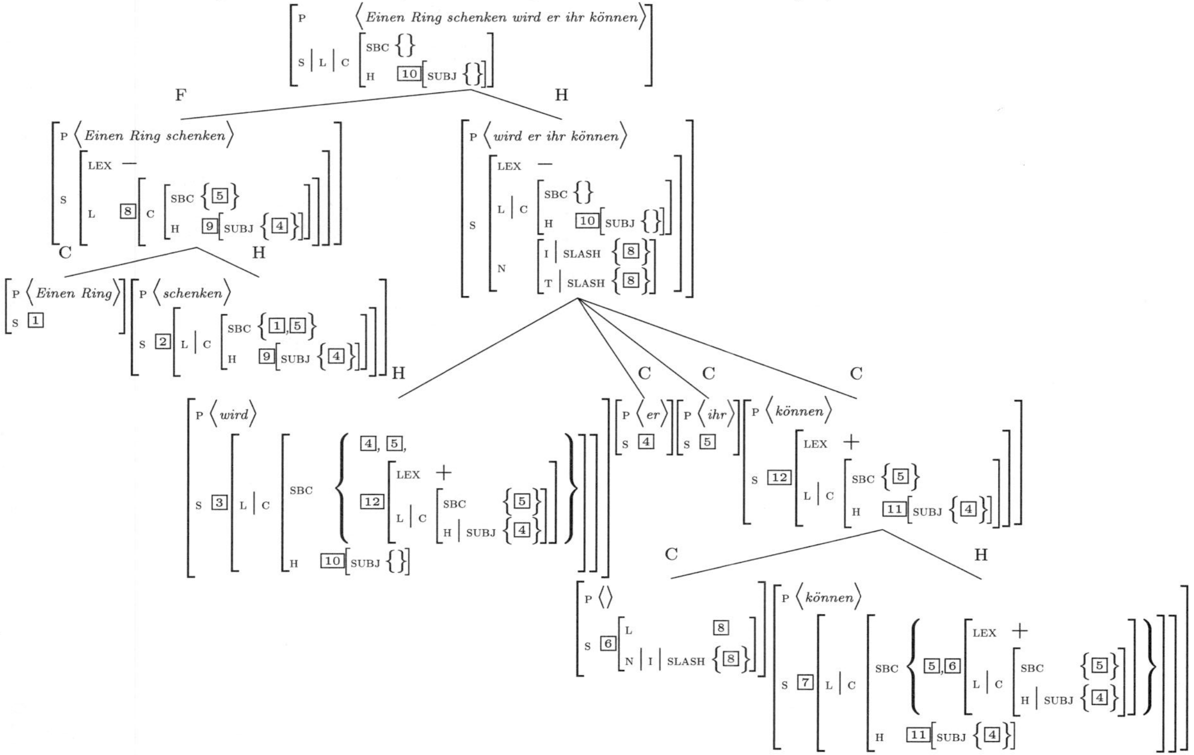

FIGURE 14   Theory 3: The "Kiss-style" structure for sentence (1b)

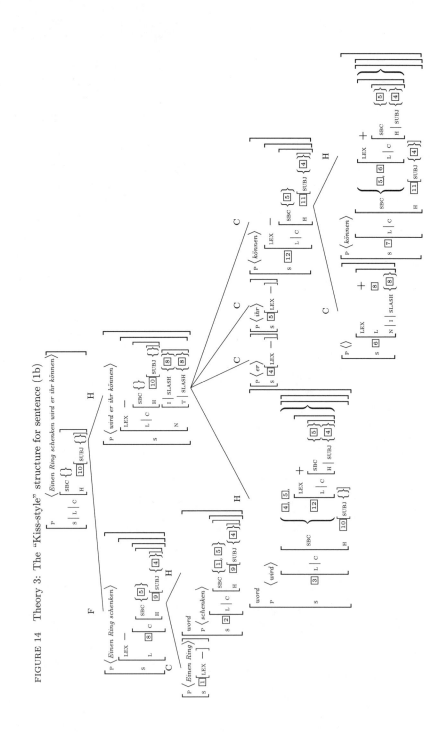

# 10

# English Number Names in HPSG

Jeffrey D. Smith

## 10.1 Introduction and Initial Assumptions

The purpose of this paper is to verify that complex English number names such as *two hundred twelve thousand twenty two* can be represented quite naturally in HPSG as phrases rather than as lexical items. The properties of these phrases are predictable from their lexical heads just as are properties of other phrases in HPSG. No machinery unmotivated elsewhere in English is needed except for new subsorts and features defined on these subsorts.

This representation allows a major reduction in the size of the lexicon compared to the case where all represented integers require at least one lexical entry.

Many of the observations in this paper are independent of HPSG and generalize easily to other syntactic theories. Many generalize beyond number names to related expressions. Expressions involving number names and related expressions present interesting data for any theory of syntax, although little or no relevant literature on the syntax of English number names has appeared since the 1970s and the days of unconstrained transformations.

Within HPSG, the deviations given as Assumptions 1–3 from the version given in Pollard and Sag 1994 are assumed. Each of these is built into the implementation of HPSG maintained by the Linguistic Grammars Online (LinGO) project at the Center for the Study of Language and Information (CSLI), Stanford University, for the Verbmobil

This paper has benefited from discussions with Dan Flickinger, Emily Bender, Ivan Sag, and other members of the LinGO project. Thanks are also due to several anonymous reviewers for the HPSG-97 conference, and for this volume.

*Lexical and Constructional Aspects of Linguistic Explanation.*
Gert Webelhuth, Jean-Pierre Koenig, and Andreas Kathol.
Copyright © 1998, Stanford University.

machine translation project (Kay et al. 1994). The work described in this paper was conceived as a contribution to that project.

**Assumption 1** *The* SUBCAT *list is split into a* SUBJ *list and a* COMPS *list. An additional* SPR *feature is available. There is a schema corresponding to a head-specifier structure. In other words, the modifications to* HPSG *discussed in Chapter 9 of Pollard and Sag 1994 are adopted.*

**Assumption 2** *Specifiers precede heads in English, while complements follow. Specifiers need not be semantic heads in head-specifier constructions that are not determiner-noun constructions.*[1] *There is no* SPEC *feature, but heads may select their specifier by means of the* SPR *feature. Each head has only one specifier in English.*

**Assumption 3** *Multiple inheritance is allowed in sort hierarchies.*

In this paper the terms *attribute* and *feature* are used interchangeably. The U.S. system of numeration is assumed.

## 10.2 Syntax

This paper is concerned primarily with the internal syntax of number names themselves, rather than that of larger phrases that might contain them, or with their categorial status. A natural starting point is to ask whether these number names are headed constructions.

Determining which constituent might be the head of an English number name is difficult to accomplish by means of the usual tests. For example, most of the tests of Zwicky 1993 are inconclusive due to the impoverished morphology of English and the specialized nature of the data. The one test that does give some evidence is the *external representative test*, if this is interpreted to mean, as in Zwicky 1985, that the distribution of the entire phrase is predictable from that of the head rather than that of the nonhead constituent.[2]

The distribution of *two hundred* and the minimally different phrases *three hundred* and *two thousand* may be seen in (1–3). The distributions of *two hundred* and *three hundred* may be seen to be identical. The distribution of *two hundred* differs from that of *two thousand*. In other words, the distribution of *two hundred* is predictable from the distribu-

---

[1] This weakening of the Semantics Principle from Pollard and Sag 1994 has independent motivation, at least inside the LinGO project, from such examples as *very tall* or *foot long*, treated as specifier-head constructions in which the left constituent is a specifier but the semantics comes fundamentally from the right constituent. In what follows we assume that specifiers are not semantic heads inside integer expressions.

[2] In Zwicky 1993 this is actually a test for his *B* element, which is shared by heads in head-argument constructions and by the specified in specifier-specified constructions.

tion of *hundred*, but not from the distribution of *two*. Thus *hundred* may be taken to be the head of *two hundred*.

(1)   a.   four thousand two hundred
      b.   four thousand three hundred
      c.   *four thousand two thousand

(2)   a.   two hundred thousand
      b.   three hundred thousand
      c.   ??two thousand thousand

(3)   a.   *two hundred four hundred
      b.   *three hundred four hundred
      c.   two thousand four hundred

In the absence of any notion of predication or of clauses in this construction, an analysis as a subject-head construction is not feasible. Similarly, the obligatory nature and the impossibility of iteration of the non-head constituent, together with the head-final nature of the construction, suggest a specifier-head analysis rather than a modifier-head analysis. In particular, the data of (1–3) are perfectly consistent with an interpretation of *two* and *three* as alternate specifiers of *hundred*.

Data on the distribution of *two hundred five* as well as the minimally different expressions *three hundred five*, *two thousand five*, and *two hundred six* are given in (4–5). Here the phrases containing *hundred* have the same distribution, which is different than that of the phrase containing *thousand*. The distribution is not predictable from the assumption that *two* or *five* is the head of *two hundred five*. The data is consistent, and consistent only, with *hundred* being the head of *two hundred five*, which is in turn consistent with the analysis of (1–3).

(4)   a.   two hundred five thousand
      b.   three hundred five thousand
      c.   *two thousand five thousand
      d.   two hundred six thousand

(5)   a.   four thousand two hundred five
      b.   four thousand three hundred five
      c.   *four thousand two thousand five
      d.   four thousand two hundred six

An account that considered either *two* to be the head of (6) would have trouble explaining why the other *two* couldn't be replaced by a phrase that it heads, giving the unacceptable (7).

(6)   two hundred two

(7)   *two hundred two hundred two

Thus the evidence, together with Assumption 2, leads to a treatment of *hundred* as a head that takes an obligatory specifier and an optional complement. A similar argument applies to *thousand* and its powers.

Analogous tests involving the distribution of *twenty five* are less conclusive—*twenty five* has the same distribution as both *twenty six* and *thirty five*. However in (8), the constituents that coordinate easily are precisely those that have been identified above as complements rather than specifiers or heads. This generalization can be extended to the data of (9) if the larger number corresponds to the head.

(8)　a.　two hundred three or four
　　　b.　*[two hundred or three hundred] three
　　　c.　*[two or three] hundred three
　　　d.　*[two hundred or three thousand] four

(9)　a.　twenty five or six
　　　b.　*[twenty or thirty] five

Also, that *twenty five* has a distribution more like *twenty* than like *five* (cf. (10)) would be awkward to explain under an analysis in which *five* is treated as the head of *twenty five*. But if instead *twenty* is the head, then this observation can be explained as a consequence of optional complementation of the head.

(10)　a.　two thousand five hundred
　　　b.　*two thousand twenty five hundred
　　　c.　*two thousand twenty hundred

Thus in what follows we treat *twenty five* as a left-headed construction. Once again, the absence of notions of predication or clauses, the noniterability, and the generalizations about ordering in English headed constructions suggest a more particular interpretation, in this case as a head-complement construction. This interpretation preserves a powerful generalization, stated below as Property 1.

**Property 1** *In English integer expressions, constructions with multiplicative semantics are specifier-head constructions. Constructions with additive semantics are head-complement constructions.*

Property 1 by itself does not determine the shape of parse trees for long integer expressions. It does imply that all specifiers correspond to integers less than 1000 (since all left factors do), and thus are of bounded complexity. We consider first the structure of expressions that contain these specifiers, and then that of these specifiers themselves.

Consider for example the integer 123,456,789. Property 1 requires the factors *one hundred twenty three* and *four hundred fifty six* to be constituents, giving the partial bracketing suggested by (11). Treating *seven hundred eighty nine* as a constituent for the time being, there are still two possible high-level bracketings, given in (12), for the expression representing the entire integer. Note that in (a), *million* has two complements, while in (b) *million* has one and *thousand* has one.

(11)  [ [123] million [456] thousand 789 ]

(12)  a.  [ [123] million [ [456] thousand ] [789] ]
      b.  [ [123] million [ [456] thousand [789] ] ]

The natural generalization of the strategy of (a) would allow each successively larger complement-taker to have one more complement, so that there would be no principled upper bound on the number of complements a head could have. If *seven hundred eighty nine* were not treated as a constituent in (12), the situation would only be worse.

In (b), not only would there be a bounded number of complements (in fact, at most one complement), but the constraint on complements would be simpler—the integer corresponding to the complement would have to have value strictly less than that of the head. Thus in what follows we assume the strategy of (b).

As for the specifiers themselves, since each represents an integer less than 1000, there are at most five possible binary bracketings. Those for *three hundred forty five* are given in (13). Of these, only in (c) and (d) does the specifier combine with the head after all the complements do.

(13)  a.  [[[three hundred] forty] five]
      b.  [[three [hundred forty]] five]
      c.  [three [[hundred forty] five]]
      d.  [three [hundred [forty five]]]
      e.  [[three hundred] [forty five]]

There are several objections to (c), the case in which both *forty* and *five* are complements of *hundred*. For example, *forty* must not itself take a complement. This arbitrary stipulation is awkward in any syntactic theory, but is particularly problematic within HPSG, where access to the constituency of complements is highly constrained.

In addition, the appropriate lexical entry or entries for *hundred* would have to allow zero, one, or two complements. In the case of two complements, extra stipulation would be required to get the first of them to correspond to a multiple of 10 less than 100, and the second to an integer less than 10, in order to handle the data of (14).

(14)  a.  *one hundred nine five
      b.  *one hundred thirty forty
      c.  *one hundred eight fifty

By contrast, in the case of (13d) there is just a single (optional) complement, whose head also has a single optional complement. This single complement of *hundred* once again has the property that the integer corresponding to the complement is bounded above by the integer corresponding to the head. In summary, there are several desirable properties of the current approach, given as Properties 2–6.

**Property 2** *All integer words have at most one complement and at most one specifier. All specifiers are obligatory[3]. All complements are optional.*

**Property 3** *In English integer expressions, the lexical head is that lexical item representing the largest integer.*

**Property 4** *All saturated constituents may appear independently as numbers. All numbers may appear as complements.*

**Property 5** *Semantics is compositional in the sense that a head may treat the semantics of its complement or specifier as an unanalyzed whole.*

**Property 6** *All constraints on specifiers and complements can be expressed in terms of upper bounds on the corresponding integers.*

That Property 5 holds will actually not be established until the relevant lexical entries are presented. The danger is that when heads combine with specifiers, the integer corresponding to the specifier needs to multiply with that corresponding to the *uncomplemented* head, since the multiplication required by the specifier must precede the addition required by the complement. Thus it appears that access to the constituency of the semantic representation of the complemented head is needed.

The desirability of Property 6 comes from the fact that the conjunction of two or more constraints defined in terms of upper bounds on integers is itself a constraint of the same type. Thus no other types of constraints are ever needed. By contrast, imagine an approach in which, say, *five* is the head of both *fifty five* and *two hundred five*, but not *five hundred*. In this approach, constraints on specifiers for *hundred* would be stated in terms of upper bounds as in the approach actually adopted. However since possible specifiers of *five* are numbers greater than 10, a second type of constraint, one stated in terms of lower bounds, would be needed for these specifiers. A third type of constraint would arise from conjunction of constraints of these two different types.

---

[3]Although it is true that in isolated number names specifiers are never optional in English, it is plausible that in *the hundred books*, *the* is the specifier of *books* rather than of *hundred*.

| representative | sort | complement | specifier |
|---|---|---|---|
| two | *1-digit* | - | - |
| twelve | *2-digit* | - | - |
| twenty | *2-digit* | (*up-to-1-digit*) | - |
| hundred | *3-digit* | (*up-to-2-digits*) | *up-to-1-digit* |
| thousand | *6-digit* | (*up-to-3-digits*) | *up-to-3-digits* |
| million | *9-digit* | (*up-to-6-digits*) | *up-to-3-digits* |
| ... | ... | ... | ... |
| $10^{3k}$ | *[3k + 3]-digit* | (*up-to-[3k]-digits*) | *up-to-3-digits* |
| hundred | *4-digit* | (*up-to-2-digits*) | *2-digit* |
| thousand | *7-digit* | (*up-to-3-digits*) | *4-digit* |

FIGURE 1  Patterns of specification and complementation

## 10.3   The Lexicon

In this section, we sketch, with the aid of the properties above, a treatment of the appropriate portion of the lexicon. The approach of the previous section suggests the following lexical classes for cardinals:

- { one, two, ..., nine }
- { twenty, thirty, ..., ninety }
- { eleven, twelve, ..., nineteen }
- { hundred }
- { thousand }
- { million }
- ...

The pattern of specification and complementation for each class is given in Figure 1. In this figure the first column gives a representative for each class. The second column gives a constraint corresponding to the number of digits of a maximal projection for each class. In HPSG terms, each constraint gives the sort of the HEAD value of the associated lexical entry. The entries in the third and fourth columns describe the sort of the HEAD value of the complements and specifiers respectively. The rows of the figure correspond to the classes above, except for the final two rows, inserted to allow expressions such as *twelve hundred* and *twelve hundred thousand*. By Assumption 2, there is no need for a SPEC feature in the table. All complements are optional.

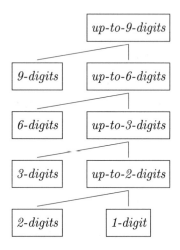

FIGURE 2 Partial sort hierarchy for English number words

The entries in the third and fourth columns are constraints (again stated in terms of the sorts of HEAD values) on the lengths of specifiers and complements—in particular on their lengths in digits. As upper bounds, these constraints are consistent with Properties 2 and 6 and with (12b) and (13d).

The subsort hierarchy for the sorts above is implicit in their names. For $j < k$, the sorts *k-digits* and *up-to-j-digits* are subsorts of *up-to-k-digits*. The sort *1-digit* may be identified with the sort *up-to-1-digit*. A diagram of a portion of the sort hierarchy is given in Figure 2. All sorts in Figure 1 are subsorts of a subsort *integer* of sort *head*.

For example, *twelve* may be a complement of *hundred*, since the sorts *2-digit* and *up-to-2-digits* are consistent. However *two thousand* may not be a complement of *hundred*, since *6-digit* and *up-to-2-digits* are incompatible.

## 10.4 Semantics

The exact form of the semantic representation for English number names and for the lexical entries that compose them inevitably depends on the precise semantic theory adopted. For purposes of exposition we first assume an informal tree-based representation like that of Figure 3.

By Property 5, a representation like that of Figure 3 should be constructible by unifying local trees available in lexical entries, using the

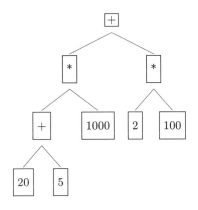

FIGURE 3  A tree representation of 25,200

Semantics Principle. That is, the local trees of such a representation need to be partitioned among the individual lexical entries.

Property 1 suggests that local trees whose root corresponds to a multiplication be contributed by those lexical entries requiring a specifier. Local trees whose root corresponds to an addition should be contributed by those lexical entries taking a complement. The local tree corresponding to a lexical entry that takes neither a complement nor a specifier consists solely of a root. In particular, there is a significant difference between complement-taking and complement-free lexical entries for the same word, although the difference is small and predictable enough to allow the entries to be related by lexical rule.

Lexical entries taking both a specifier and a complement will need a representation slightly more general than a local tree, since they are responsible both for the requirement of a multiplication and for the requirement of an addition. It will be convenient, however, to retain the term 'local tree' in this case. For example, the local tree for the lexical entry for *thousand* of Figure 3 would look like that of Figure 4(d). Here the value $c4$ is intended to unify with the root of the complement's local tree and the value $s4$ with the root of the specifier's local tree. These trees appear respectively in (a) and (e) of the figure.

The importance of Assumption 2 can now be explained. Note that the root of the tree of Figure 3 corresponds to the root of the tree of Figure 4(d). This means that the semantics of the expression *twenty five thousand two hundred* comes from the syntactic head *thousand*. Sim-

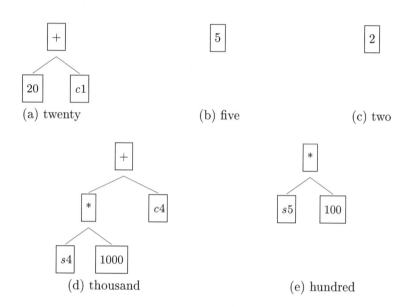

FIGURE 4  Lexical semantics for number words

ilarly, syntactic heads must always be semantic heads in the current approach, even in head-specifier constructions. If instead the specifier had to be the semantic head, then for example in the expression *two hundred thousand,* both *two* and *two hundred* would have to have the same semantic head as the expression itself. This would be inconsistent with the current representation.

The apparent conflict noted in connection with Property 5 in Section 10.2 between complementation preceding specification, and multiplication preceding addition, can also now be resolved. The observation is simply that lexical entries for numbers taking both complements and specifiers have positions for both (cf. $c4$ and $s4$ in Figure 4), and that both positions appear in the correct place in the overall representation. Thus by the monotonicity of unification, they don't care which they combine with first.

The local trees for the other lexical entries required for Figure 3 are also given in Figure 4. The natural generalization of the notational convention described above for (d) of the figure suggests that the value

$c1$ would unify with the root of the tree of (b) and that the value $s5$ would unify with the root of (c). When these unifications are combined with those described above for $c4$ and $s4$, the tree of Figure 3 results.

The local trees for the lexical entries of Figure 1 not represented in Figure 4 would look as follows: the local trees for *twelve* and uncomplemented *twenty* would look like that of *two*. That of uncomplemented *thousand* would be as in Figure 4(e). Those of uncomplemented *million*, *billion*, etc., would be similar. Those of complemented *hundred*, *million*, etc., would look like that of Figure 4(d).

Translation of the notion of node unification into HPSG depends on which semantic representation is used. One appropriate representation, used in the LinGO implementation, is Minimal Recursion Semantics (Copestake et al. 1995) , or MRS. In HPSG terms, the effect of assuming an MRS representation is to require CONTENT values to be defined in terms of attributes HANDEL and LISZT. The value of the LISZT attribute is an unordered list of elements of sort *relation*. Typically these elements will be of different subsorts. This allows the equivalent of a flat representation.

The HANDEL attribute in general captures scope information that cannot be represented in a flat structure. However for purposes of this paper, the value of the HANDEL attribute may be thought of as a pointer to a relation; here we identify relations with the tree nodes of Figure 3 and HANDELs with pointers to these nodes.

To embed the original approach into MRS, we define new relation sorts *plus-rel*, *times-rel*, and *const-rel*, all subsorts of *quant-rel* (the sort for quantifier relations) and all inheriting a HANDEL feature (from the sort *relation*). The new attribute VALUE is defined for *const-rels*, new features TERM1 and TERM2 are defined for *plus-rels*, and new features FACTOR1 and FACTOR2 are defined for *times-rels*. Features TERM1, TERM2, FACTOR1, and FACTOR2 have values of the same sort as HANDEL (that is, take as their values handels of other relations).

In MRS, the AVM representing 25,200, corresponding to the tree of Figure 3, would have a LISZT attribute containing the nine relations of Figure 5. The handel $h0$, corresponding to the root of the tree, is shared with the HANDEL value of the AVM's CONTENT.

The LISZT values for the complement-free and complemented lexical entries for *twenty* are given in Figure 6. In both cases, the handel $h1$ of the first relation would be shared with the HANDEL of the entire lexical entry. In the complemented case (b) of the figure, the handel $h3$ would be shared with the HANDEL of the complement.

Figure 7 is similar to Figure 6, except that it gives the two lexical entries suggested in Figure 1 for *hundred*. The structure sharing is en-

$$
\left\langle
\begin{bmatrix}
\textit{plus-rel} \\
\text{HANDEL} \quad h0 \\
\text{TERM1} \quad h1 \\
\text{TERM2} \quad h2
\end{bmatrix}
\begin{bmatrix}
\textit{times-rel} \\
\text{HANDEL} \quad h1 \\
\text{FACTOR1} \quad h3 \\
\text{FACTOR2} \quad h4
\end{bmatrix}
\begin{bmatrix}
\textit{plus-rel} \\
\text{HANDEL} \quad h3 \\
\text{TERM1} \quad h5 \\
\text{TERM2} \quad h6
\end{bmatrix}
\right.
$$

$$
\begin{bmatrix}
\textit{times-rel} \\
\text{HANDEL} \quad h2 \\
\text{FACTOR1} \quad h7 \\
\text{FACTOR2} \quad h8
\end{bmatrix}
\begin{bmatrix}
\textit{const-rel} \\
\text{HANDEL} \quad h4 \\
\text{VALUE} \quad 1000
\end{bmatrix}
\begin{bmatrix}
\textit{const-rel} \\
\text{HANDEL} \quad h5 \\
\text{VALUE} \quad 20
\end{bmatrix}
$$

$$
\begin{bmatrix}
\textit{const-rel} \\
\text{HANDEL} \quad h6 \\
\text{VALUE} \quad 5
\end{bmatrix}
\begin{bmatrix}
\textit{const-rel} \\
\text{HANDEL} \quad h7 \\
\text{VALUE} \quad 2
\end{bmatrix}
\left.
\begin{bmatrix}
\textit{const-rel} \\
\text{HANDEL} \quad h8 \\
\text{VALUE} \quad 100
\end{bmatrix}
\right\rangle
$$

FIGURE 5  Part of an MRS representation for 25200

$$
\left\langle
\begin{bmatrix}
\textit{const-rel} \\
\text{HANDEL} \quad h1 \\
\text{VALUE} \quad 20
\end{bmatrix}
\right\rangle
$$

(a) for complement-free *twenty*

$$
\left\langle
\begin{bmatrix}
\textit{plus-rel} \\
\text{HANDEL} \quad h1 \\
\text{TERM1} \quad h2 \\
\text{TERM2} \quad h3
\end{bmatrix}
\begin{bmatrix}
\textit{const-rel} \\
\text{HANDEL} \quad h2 \\
\text{VALUE} \quad 20
\end{bmatrix}
\right\rangle
$$

(b) for complemented *twenty*

FIGURE 6  LISZT values of lexical entries for *twenty*

$$\left\langle \begin{bmatrix} times\text{-}rel \\ \text{HANDEL} & h1 \\ \text{FACTOR1} & h3 \\ \text{FACTOR2} & h2 \end{bmatrix} \begin{bmatrix} const\text{-}rel \\ \text{HANDEL} & h2 \\ \text{VALUE} & 100 \end{bmatrix} \right\rangle$$

(a) for complement-free *hundred*

$$\left\langle \begin{bmatrix} plus\text{-}rel \\ \text{HANDEL} & h1 \\ \text{TERM1} & h4 \\ \text{TERM2} & h3 \end{bmatrix} \begin{bmatrix} times\text{-}rel \\ \text{HANDEL} & h4 \\ \text{FACTOR1} & h5 \\ \text{FACTOR2} & h2 \end{bmatrix} \begin{bmatrix} const\text{-}rel \\ \text{HANDEL} & h2 \\ \text{VALUE} & 100 \end{bmatrix} \right\rangle$$

(b) for complemented *hundred*

FIGURE 7  LISZT values of lexical entries for *hundred*

forced in the same way as for Figure 6, except that $h3$ (in (a)) and $h5$ (in (b)) would be shared with the HANDEL value of the specifier.

The LISZTs for the lexical entries for *two* and *twelve* would be similar to those of Figure 6(a). The LISZTs for the lexical entries for *thousand*, *million*, etc., would be similar to those of Figure 7.

## 10.5  Related Phenomena

Several phenomena related to English number names have undergone only preliminary investigation and are not yet included in the LinGO implementation. These preliminary analyses are as sketched below.

English ordinals have the property that ordinal morphology constrains the interpretation of an entire phrase, even though it appears only on the rightmost word. An analysis in terms of a phrasal affix *-th* would be in danger of predicting the acceptability of the expressions of (15), as well as being awkward to implement. So it's worth giving an alternative analysis, which would still allow sharing of lexical entries between *twenty* and *twenty first*.

(15)  a. *twenty oneth
      b. *twenty three or fourth

This may be done in terms of a head feature [±ORDINAL] (and perhaps a semantic counterpart). Words with ordinal morphology would be [+ORDINAL]. Other lexical items without complements would be [−ORDINAL]. Lexical items taking complements would share their ORDINAL value with their complement (and with their mother, by the Head Feature Principle). For example, the complement-taking lexical entry for *twenty* would be unspecified for ORDINAL, and could be used in both *twenty one* and *twenty first*. In the first case, it would receive the value [−ORDINAL] from *one*; in the second case it would receive the value [+ORDINAL] from *first*.

The feature ORDINAL, and therefore the sharing of its value, would be restricted to lexical items with HEAD values of sort *integer*. Lexical entries for ordinals would not take complements, and their specifiers would have to be [−ORDINAL].

A similar account can be given for the NUMBER feature. This feature would then have an unspecified value for ordinals and for complement takers. A perhaps unexpected property is that since complement-taking cardinals are all plural and take their NUMBER value from their complements, all complements would have to be plural. In particular, the legal complement *one* would have to have a life as a plural.[4]

The pseudo-coordinate structures of (16) suggest that lexical entries for numbers less than or equal to 90 may be optionally marked with *and*. Lexical entries for numbers greater than or equal to 100 may take either marked or unmarked complements. Other numbers must take unmarked complements.

(16)  a.  two hundred and five
      b.  two hundred and twenty five
      c.  two thousand and twenty five
      d.  *two thousand and two hundred
      e.  *twenty and five

(17)  a.  zwei und zwanzig
          two  and twenty
      b.  *zwei zwanzig

In German, lexical entries for numbers less than 10 may be marked with *und*; lexical entries for words from 20 through 90 must take com-

---

[4]In treatments like that of the LinGO implementation in which numbers may be either determiners or adjectives, there is a danger of spurious ambiguity if the plural *one* mentioned above is added to the singular adjective *one* and to the singular determiner *one*. In *the one book*, the first and third of these entries may be ruled out by giving them MOD values *none*. In *one book*, the first may be ruled out by making it an adjective. And in *twenty one*, the third may be ruled out by requiring complements to be adjectives, and the second by giving it a HEAD value of a sort incapable of satisfying a subcategorization frame (this is the equivalent of treating it as if it had infinitely many digits).

plements so marked (cf. (17)). That complements precede their heads in this construction is consistent with other head-final behavior in German. Words of the *zwanzig* class would have one lexical entry with ordinal morphology specified as [+ORDINAL] and one lexical entry without ordinal morphology and specified as [−ORDINAL]. Both entries would have cardinals as complements and specifiers.

True coordination in the current context is best exemplified by constructions with *or*, as in (18). Under the current account, coordination always is of constituents. This is not true in other possible approaches. For example, (g) and (h) would be awkward in an consistent head-final approach, where *three hundred twenty nine* in isolation would have head *nine* and specifier *three hundred twenty*, while *three hundred thirty* in isolation would have head *thirty* and specifier *three hundred*.

(18)   a.   [two or three] hundred
       b.   twenty [one or two]
       c.   [twenty or thirty] thousand
       d.   one hundred [ten or eleven]
       e.   *[twenty or thirty] five
       f.   *two [hundred or thousand]
       g.   three hundred [twenty nine or thirty]
       h.   three hundred [twenty or twenty one]

The failure to observe coordination where it might be expected can be explained by a pragmatic/semantic constraint involving definiteness. The approximate generalization is that indefinite heads cannot take a specifier or complement, and that expressions agree with their specifiers or complements on definiteness, where coordinate structures and some lexical items are automatically indefinite. In the case of heads taking both specifiers and complements, it appears that the specifier must be definite while the complement need not be, as in (19). One possible exception is given in (e).

(19)   a.   two hundred [three or four]
       b.   [two or three] hundred
       c.   two thousand odd
       d.   *several thousand twenty
       e.   [two or three] hundred odd

As in the case of ORDINAL and NUMBER, this behavior may be obtained in HPSG by using one or more head features for definiteness, where heads agree on definiteness with their complements if there are any, and otherwise with their specifiers if there are any.

# References

Copestake, Ann, Dan Flickinger, Robert Malouf, Susanne Riehemann, and Ivan A. Sag. 1995. Translation using Minimal Recursion Semantics. In *Proceedings of The Sixth International Conference on Theoretical and Methodological Issues in Machine Translation*. Leuven.

Kay, Martin, Jean Mark Gawron, and Peter Norvig. 1994. *Verbmobil: A Translation System for Face-to-Face Dialog*. Stanford: CSLI Publications.

Pollard, Carl, and Ivan A. Sag. 1994. *Head-Driven Phrase Structure Grammar*. Stanford: CSLI Publications.

Zwicky, Arnold. 1985. Heads. *Journal of Linguistics* 21:1–29.

Zwicky, Arnold. 1993. Heads, Bases, and Functors. In *Heads in Grammatical Theory*, ed. Greville G. Corbett, Norman M. Fraser, and Scott McGlashan. 292–315. Cambridge: Cambridge University Press.

# Part III

## Binding Theory

# Long-Distance Reflexives and the Binding Square of Opposition

ANTÓNIO BRANCO AND PALMIRA MARRAFA

## 11.1 Introduction

We present data showing that, unlike other long-distance anaphors widely documented in the literature, *ele próprio* in Portuguese is not subject-oriented. This supports a reformulation of Principle Z, a fourth binding principle, to cover both subject-oriented and non-subject-oriented long-distance anaphors. The remarkable internal congruence among the resulting four principles of binding theory argues that binding symmetries are far richer than the distributional symmetry between anaphors and pronouns that has commonly been assumed to be the only one in past research in this area. In particular, adequate formalisation of those symmetries uncovers a classical square of oppositions between the four principles, which enhances our understanding of binding phenomena by opening new promising paths of inquiry into the logical and quantificational structure of binding theory.

We also discuss how the data involving the Portuguese long-distance anaphor add to the growing evidence that the generalisations forming

For helpful discussion, we are grateful to the participants of the *11th Pacific Asia Conference on Language, Information and Computation,* Kyung Hee Univ., Seoul, December 1996, the *Long-Distance Reflexives Workshop,* and the *4th International Conference on Head-Driven Phrase Structure Grammar,* both held in Cornell University, Ithaca, July 1997, in particular to Peter Cole, Gabriella Hermon, Jeffrey Lidz, Arild Hestvik, and Haihua Pan. Special thanks are due to Hans Uszkoreit for his comments and support. This work was supported in part by Fundação Luso-Americana and the PRAXIS XXI Programme of the Portuguese Ministry of Science and Technology.

*Lexical and Constructional Aspects of Linguistic Explanation.*
Gert Webelhuth, Jean-Pierre Koenig, and Andreas Kathol.
Copyright © 1998, Stanford University.

the basis for mainstream approaches to long-distance anaphora are not supported by the empirical facts.

## 11.2 The Irreducibility of Long–Distance Anaphora

Long-distance anaphors have recently been a major focus of inquiry for theories of binding. These are expressions that have to get their interpretation from suitable antecedents occurring either inside or outside the relevant local domain. Their behavior, however, is not accounted for by any of the three "classic" binding principles, established primarily on the basis of empirical evidence from English. Following Pollard and Sag (1994), Principle A requires o-binding of an anaphor by a suitable antecedent occurring *in the relevant local domain*; Principles B and C concern themselves with requirements of *o-freeness* for pronouns and nonpronominals.

The continued insistence in taking the distributional symmetry between (short-distance) anaphors and pronouns as the empirical touchstone to be accounted for by binding theory has had its impact, both theoretically and methodologically, on the way in which long-distance anaphora have been dealt with. In accordance with the unique central role assigned to this distributional symmetry, the phenomenon of long-distance anaphora has been given marginal status and has been considered in the Government-Binding (GB) framework as simply a successive-cyclic association of short-distance "links".[1]

This has had the side effect of funneling attention to a specific set of empirical correlations which, in turn, have became the "standard" empirical basis for GB research on long-distance anaphora. However different the several alternative proposals may be in their details, they all share the conviction that the central facts to be accounted for in the study of long-distance anaphora center around the correlation between so-called "morphologically simple" anaphors, long-distance binding, subject-orientation, and blocking of binding possibilities by intervening subjects.

The different accounts share the following basic assumptions. Simplex anaphors have a kind of "inflectional deficit" which must be supplemented by some kind of local "link" (e.g., movement, coindexing, etc.) to the Inflection of the local subject. This explains subject-orientedness. Links of the same sort across different successively subordinated clauses may be connected, which explains the long-distance behavior. Finally,

---

[1]Some examples: in Cole and Sung 1994 (as well as many references cited therein) the anaphor undergoes head movement to Infl at LF; in Huang and Tang 1991 there is no head movement but adjunction to IP; in Progovac 1993 the movement is replaced by coindexation with the Agr node.

in some languages such as Chinese, the concatenation of these links is interrupted when there is a subject in a higher clause which does not support the relevant kind of link. This provides the explanation for the blocking of long-distance binding by intervening subjects.

Leaving aside the blocking effect, which has been thoroughly discussed only for Chinese, the relevant correlations, assumed to be universal, can be summarized in the following table:

| | Subject-oriented | Not Subject-oriented | Morphological simplicity | Morphological complexity |
|---|---|---|---|---|
| Short-distance reflexives | | X | | X |
| Long-distance reflexives | X | | X | |

### 11.2.1 The Portuguese LD Reflexive

As we argue in this section, Portuguese has a long-distance reflexive which does not appear to behave according to the pattern outlined above.

In Portuguese, *si próprio* ('*si* own') is the third person short-distance anaphor while *ele* ('he') is the third person pronoun. It is well known that their behaviour as referentially dependent expressions closely parallels that of English *himself* and *he,* respectively. As we show in (1–7), in addition to these two expressions, Portuguese has also the long-distance anaphor *ele próprio* ('he own').

The contrast in (1) illustrates that, like short-distance anaphors, *ele próprio* is a referentially dependent expression which requires an antecedent (with identical feature values for person, number, and gender).

(1)    O   Carlos$_i$ gosta d**ele próprio**$_{*j/i}$.
       the Carlos  likes  of_he own
       'Carlos likes himself.'

(1) and (2b), in turn, show that *ele próprio* must be o-bound. The examples in (2a,b) illustrate the parallelism between *ele próprio* and the short-distance anaphor, while (2b,c) demonstrate the difference between *ele próprio* and the pronoun with respect to the requirement of o-binding by the antecedent.

(2)    a. *[As pessoas que falaram com a Ana$_i$] gostam de
          the people  who talked   with the Ana like     of
          **si própria**$_i$.
          SI own
          '[People who talked with Ana$_i$] like herself$_i$.'

b. *[As pessoas que falaram com a Ana$_i$] gostam
   the people  who talked  with the Ana like
   **dela própria$_i$**.
   of_she own
   '[People who talked with Ana$_i$] like herself$_i$.'

c. [As pessoas que falaram com a   Ana$_i$] gostam **dela$_i$**.
   the people  who talked  with the Ana  like    of_she
   '[People who talked with Ana$_i$] like her$_i$.'

The examples in (3) illustrate the ability of *ele próprio* to function as a long-distance anaphor;

(3)   a.  O  Pedro$_i$ convenceu a   Ana de [que o   Carlos$_j$ gosta
           the Pedro  convinced the Ana of  that the Carlos  likes
           **dele próprio$_{i/j}$**].
           of_he own
           'Pedro$_i$ convinced Ana [that Carlos$_j$ likes him$_i$/himself$_j$].'

     b.  O  João$_i$ disse-me [que tu  achas [que o   Carlos$_j$ gosta
           the João  told me  that you think that the Carlos  likes
           **dele próprio$_{i/j}$**]].
           of_he own
           'João$_i$ told me [that you think [Carlos$_j$ likes him$_i$/himself$_j$]].'

The contrast in (4) provides further evidence for the status of *ele próprio* as a long-distance anaphor. The example shows that even when coindexed with an antecedent outside the local domain, *ele próprio* has to be o-bound, contrary to the behaviour of pronouns.

(4)   a. *[O  apartamento que o   Carlos ofereceu à     Ana$_i$]
         the apartment    that the Carlos offered  to_the Ana
         mostra que ele pensa **nela   própria$_i$**.
         shows  that he  thinks in_she own
         '[The apartment that Carlos offered to Ana$_i$] shows that he cares about herself$_i$.'

     b. [O  apartamento que o   Carlos ofereceu à     Ana$_i$]
         the apartment    that the Carlos offered  to_the Ana
         mostra que ele pensa **nela$_i$**.
         shows  that he  thinks in_she
         '[The apartment that Carlos offered to Ana$_i$] shows that he cares about her$_i$.'

The data shown in (1–4) support standard diagnostics for the anaphoric status of long-distance referentially dependent expressions. In the case of Portuguese, object clitic doubling provides an additional test, cf. (5,6):

(5)  a.  O  Pedro$_i$ viu-se          a **si próprio**$_i$ no      espelho.
         the Pedro  saw-CLIT.ANAPH to si own       in_the mirror
         'Pedro$_i$ saw himself$_i$ in the mirror.'
     b.  O  Pedro$_i$ viu-se          a **ele próprio**$_i$ no      espelho.
         the Pedro  saw-CLIT.ANAPH to he own          in_the mirror
         'Pedro$_i$ saw himself$_i$ in the mirror.'
     c.  *[A  mãe     do      Pedro$_i$] viu-se          a **ele próprio**$_i$
         the mother of_the Pedro    saw-CLIT.ANAPH to he own
         no      espelho.
         in_the mirror
         '[Pedro's$_i$ mother] saw himself$_i$ in the mirror.'
(6)  a.  [O  pai     da      Ana$_i$] viu-a          a **ela**$_i$ no
         the father of_the Ana    saw-CLIT.PRON to she  in_the
         espelho.
         mirror
         '[Ana's$_i$ father] saw her$_i$ in the mirror.'
     b.  [O  pai     da      Ana$_i$] viu-a          a **ela própria**$_i$
         the father of_the Ana    saw-CLIT.PRON to she own
         no      espelho.
         in_the mirror
         '[Ana's$_i$ father] saw her$_i$ in the mirror.'

The data show that *ele próprio* can double both anaphoric and pronominal clitics. Interestingly, it is apparent that *ele próprio* assumes anaphoric status if it doubles anaphoric clitics (cf. the contrast in (5)) while it assumes pronominal status if it doubles pronominal clitics (cf. (6)). This shows that the status of the clitics carries over to *ele próprio*. Although this does not directly render any support to claims about the anaphoric or pronominal nature of *ele próprio*, it is worth noting that even when it doubles pronominal clitics, locally o-commanded *ele próprio* retains its inability to support deictic reference:

(7)  a.  O  Pedro viu-a          a **ela** no      espelho.
         the Pedro saw-CLIT.PRON to she in_the mirror
         'Pedro saw her in the mirror.'
     b.  *O  Pedro viu-a          a **ela própria** no      espelho.
         the Pedro saw-CLIT.PRON to she own        in_the mirror
         'Pedro saw herself in the mirror.'

After having shown that *ele próprio* is a long-distance anaphor, we turn now to its distinctive feature of lack of subject orientation. The examples in (8) illustrate that this expression may have antecedents that are not subjects:

(8)  a.  O  Pedro descreveu a Maria$_i$  a **ela própria$_i$**.
the Pedro described the Maria to she own
'Pedro described Maria to herself.'

   b.  O  Pedro convenceu a Ana$_i$  de que o Carlos  gosta
the Pedro convinced the Ana of that the Carlos likes
**dela própria$_i$**.
of_she own
'Pedro convinced Ana$_i$ that Carlos likes her$_i$.'

   c.  O  Pedro disse à    Ana$_i$ que o Carlos   gosta
the Pedro said to_the Ana  that the Carlos likes
**dela própria$_i$**.
of_she own
'Pedro said to Ana$_i$ that Carlos likes her$_i$.'

The data exhibited in this section thus show that there is a long-distance anaphor in Portuguese, which, contrary to the universal correlation standardly assumed by GB accounts of long-distance reflexives, is morphologically complex (i.e., with a full overt inflectional paradigm) and is not subject-oriented.

## 11.2.2   World Reflexivity

The question which follows naturally and deserves subsequent scrutiny is whether *ele próprio* is an isolated exception to the "standard" correlation assumed in GB accounts of long-distance anaphora.

### 11.2.2.1   Long-Distance Reflexives

The long-distance reflexive *sig* of Icelandic provides a good example of the "standard" correlation: it is morphologically simple and it is subject-oriented (Cole and Sung 1994, ex. (11)):

(9)   Jón$_i$ sagði Maríu$_j$ að   þu  elskaðir  **sig$_{i/*j}$**.
Jon told Maria that you loved-SUB self
'Jon$_i$ told Maria$_j$ that you loved him$_{i/*j}$.'

In the literature on long-distance reflexives it is, however, not hard to find several counterexamples to that correlation.

In Finnish the long-distance reflexive *hän itse* is subject-oriented but it is morphologically complex (van Steenbergen 1991, ex. (11)):[2]

---

[2]Unlike Portuguese, the long-distance status in Finnish seems to be available only across tenseless clauses that are successively subordinated. For details see van Steenbergen 1991.

(10)  Pekka$_i$ sanoi Jusille$_j$ Matin       katsovan
      Pekka  said  Jussi   Matin-GEN watch-PTC-GEN
      **häntä itseään**$_{i/*j}$
      he self-POSS
      'Pekka$_i$ said to Jussi$_j$ that Matti watched him$_{i/*j}$.'

Chinese *ziji* is morphologically simple but it also turns out not to be subject-oriented (Cole and Wang 1996, ex. (4)):

(11)  Zhangsan$_i$ yiwei Lisi$_j$ hui ba ni$_k$ ling hui  **ziji**$_{i/j/k}$ de jia.
      Zhangsan think Lisi  will BA you lead back self      DE home
      'Zhangsan$_i$ thought Lisi$_j$ would take you$_k$ back to his/your home$_{i/j/k}$.'

Together with *ele próprio,* the above long-distance reflexives actually exhibit all the possible correlations between morphological complexity/simplicity and subject/non-subject-orientedness:

| Subject-oriented | Not Subject-oriented | Morphological simplicity | Morphological complexity | |
|---|---|---|---|---|
| X | | X | | Icelandic |
| X | | | X | Finnish |
| | X | X | | Chinese |
| | X | | X | Portuguese |

### 11.2.2.2   Short-Distance Reflexives

Turning now to short-distance reflexives, English *himself* is the classic illustration of the "standard" correlation: it is morphologically complex and it is not subject-oriented. But for this type of reflexive as well, a survey of the literature reveals that the possibilities are not confined to that constellation.

| Subject-oriented | Not Subject-oriented | Morphological simplicity | Morphological complexity | |
|---|---|---|---|---|
| | X | | X | English |
| X | | | X | Norwegian, Icelandic |
| | X | X | | Hungarian |
| X | | X | | Czech |

Norwegian *seg selv* and Icelandic *sjálfur sig* are complex but subject-oriented (Koster and Reuland 1991b, exs. (12,13)). Hungarian *maga* is not subject-oriented but is not complex (Marácz 1989, referred to in Koster and Reuland 1991b, ex. (19)). Finally, Czech *se* is subject-oriented and morphologically simple (Toman 1991).

A few important conclusions follow from these observations. First, it is clear that standard GB accounts of long-distance anaphora are flawed in their basic assumptions. On the one hand, they explicitly exclude three quarters of the possible correlations between morphological complexity and subject-orientedness, both for long- and short-distance reflexives. On the other hand, the explanatory machinery employed does not appear to lend itself well to subsequent improvement. The idea of reducing long-distance anaphora to a recursive effect of some sort of short-distance relation appears to be based entirely on theory-internal considerations, without strong empirical motivation.

Second and more importantly, the crosslinguistic survey suggests strongly that subject-orientedness is not correlated with long- nor short-distance anaphoric binding. Therefore we conclude that there is no reason to bring the eventual solution for subject-orientedness into the formulation of binding principles proper.

## 11.3　The Fourth Principle

Building on Pollard and Sag's (1992) proposal, Xue, Pollard and Sag (1994) sketch a treatment of long-distance anaphora whose major innovative feature is its departure from the desideratum of reducing long-distance binding to a recursive effect of short-distance relations. They consider data involving Chinese *ziji,* which is classified as a so-called "z-pronoun", and observe that "z-pronouns must be o-bound" (Principle Z), adding the "provisional" stipulation that "antecedents of z-pronouns should be subjects".

We argue in this section that this is a suitable basis for a generalized account of long-distance anaphora provided that, on the one hand, a more empirically adequate formulation is given for Principle Z, and, on the other hand, a separation between binding and subject-orientation requirements is established.

### 11.3.1　Long-Distance Exemption

One of the most interesting features of Pollard and Sag's research on binding theory is the discovery of contexts where anaphors turn out to be exempt from the usual locality requirement for their antecedents. This has led them to render Principle A in the form of a conditional statement (*an anaphor must be locally o-bound* **if it is locally o-commanded**), which defines the exemption contexts as those where the anaphor is not locally o-commanded.

A natural extension of this approach is to test whether exemption contexts can also be found for long-distance anaphors and whether they are the same as those for short-distance anaphors.

As the following data from Portuguese show, *ele próprio* is exempt from the binding requirement if it is not o-commanded, closely paralleling short-distance reflexives. In such cases it may have a logophoric interpretation.

(12) a. **Ele próprio** pagou a    conta.
        he own        paid   the bill
        'He paid the bill.'

    b. [Se o Carlos$_i$  gostasse da      Ana], **ele próprio**$_i$
        if  the Carlos liked       of_the Ana,  he own
        lho            diria.
        CLIT.to_her_it tell
        '[If Carlos$_i$ liked Ana], he$_i$ would tell it to her.'

    c. O  amigo da      Ana$_i$ disse que o   jornalista [que
        the friend of_the Ana  said that the journalist that
        **ela própria**$_i$ convidou] pagou a    conta.
        she own          invited   paid   the bill
        'Ana's$_i$ friend said that the journalist [she$_i$ invited] paid
        the bill.'

    d. *O  jornalista [que viu  a    Ana$_i$] disse ao      Carlos que
        the journalist who saw the Ana    told  to_the Carlos that
        **ela própria**$_i$ dançou na       festa.
        she own          danced in_the party
        The journalist who saw Ana$_i$ told Carlos that herself$_i$ danced
        in the party'

The grammatical examples in (12a–c) show that when the reflexive is not o-commanded, it is not required to be o-bound: in (12a) *ele próprio* has no possible antecedent, in which case it is able to support a deictic use; in (12b) and (12c) the reflexive has an antecedent which does not o-command it. These data should be contrasted with (2b), (4a), or (12d), where o-commanded but not o-bound occurrences of *ele próprio* are ungrammatical.

These data suggest that Principle Z should be given the following definition:

(13)  PRINCIPLE Z
      An o-commanded anaphoric pronoun[3] must be o-bound.

This formulation of Principle Z, which applies to Portuguese, is very likely to have general character. In light of this formulation, let us reconsider the data from Chinese, a language completely unrelated to

---

[3]We have been using the terms *long-distance reflexive* and *long-distance anaphor* interchangeably. In view of the usual classification of NPs in terms of [±ANAPHORIC] and [±PRONOMINAL] features, we use the term *anaphoric pronoun* in the definition of Principle Z.

Portuguese.[4] Consider the contrast (14), taken from Xue *et al.* 1994, exs. (11,21).

(14) a. [Zhangsan$_i$ de xin]   biaoming Lisi$_j$ hai-le   **ziji** $*i/j$.
Zhangsan DE letter indicate Lisi harm-ASP self

'[Zhangsan's$_i$ letter] indicates that Lisi$_j$ harmed him$_i$/himself$_j$.'

b. [Zhangsan$_i$ de hua]   anshi [Lisi$_j$ de xin]   zai yingshe **ziji**$_{?i/j}$.
Zhangsan DE speech imply Lisi DE letter ASP allude-to self

'[Zhangsan's$_i$ words] implied that [Lisi's$_j$ letter] was alluding to him$_{?i}$/himself$_j$.'

Xue *et al.* explain this contrast on the basis of an analogy with the unlike-person blocking effect assumed to hold in Chinese for discourse anaphora. The impossibility of *ziji* being bound by *Zhangsan* in (14a), but not in (14b), is claimed to be due to "...the unlike-person blocking, ...a pragmatic or discourse processing effect of animate blocking."

In contrast, we tentatively propose a different explanation based on the new formulation of Principle Z. We take the contrast in (14) as evidence that in Chinese the requirement of o-binding for long-distance reflexives also holds only in case the reflexive is o-commanded. Since *ziji* is [+animate] and hence requires a [+animate] antecedent, its o-commanders must also be [+animate] in order to qualify as o-commanders for the application of Principle Z. Since *ziji* is o-commanded by *Lisi,* the coindexation of *ziji* with *Zhangsan* in (14a) is ruled out because the long-distance anaphor is required to be o-bound and this constraint is not satisfied under this coindexing. In (14b), in turn, coindexation with *Zhangsan* or *Lisi* would be acceptable due to the fact that *ziji* is not o-commanded (by a [+animate] o-commander) and it is therefore exempt from binding requirements, which allows it to logophorically pick antecedents that do not o-command it.

An important consequence of this solution is that we can dispense with Xue *et al.*'s assumption that, on a par with "syntactic *ziji*", ruled by Principle Z, there is a "discourse *ziji*", whose apparent distinctive feature would be its ability to allow subcommanding antecedents. It will be interesting to check the adequacy of our hypothesis against further empirical evidence from Chinese and other languages which have long-distance anaphors.

---

[4]For languages like Finnish (see footnote 2), however, some restriction should be imposed on the domain in which Principle Z holds. See Branco 1998 for discussion on how this can be done in a principled way.

Xue *et al.* (1994, ex. (26)) provide yet a further piece of evidence which supports our analysis. They present an example from Wang 1990 in which *ziji* does not need to have a (commanding or subcommanding) antecedent:

(15)  Mama de shu   ye    bei **ziji** de pengyou touzoule.
      mother DE book also BEI self DE friend    steal-ASP
      'Mother's$_i$ book was also stolen by his$_k$ friend.'

In (15) *ziji* is not o-commanded (by a [+animate] o-commander) and, just like *ele próprio* in (12a), it is claimed to be able to support a deictic use in the absence of overtly available antecedents in the sentence.

### 11.3.2  Dissociating LD Anaphora and Subject-Orientation

Turning now to the issue of subject-orientation, we argue that this property can be explained on the basis of an independently motivated principle without resorting to any specific stipulation, provisional or not. We suggest that the new formulation of Principle Z be complemented with the proposal that the obliqueness hierarchy relevant to binding theory may have a non-linear ordering, as argued for in Branco 1996. This solution builds on Manning and Sag's (1995) proposal for dissociating argument structure (coded in the new ARG-ST feature) and grammatical relations (coded in valence features such as SUBJ and COMPS), and for checking binding principles in the former and subcategorisation principles in the latter.

Following Branco 1996, obliqueness hierarchies may be given a non-linear ordering where subjects are the only o-commanders of any other argument, both in single-clause constructions (exemplified in (16a) with a representation in AVM format) and multiclausal ones (sketched in (16b) in a slightly modified Hasse diagram):

(16)  a.  $\left[ \text{ARG-ST} \quad \langle arg1, \{arg2, \ldots, argn\} \rangle \right]$

     b.

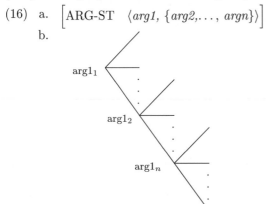

Accordingly, in languages with subject-orientation, i.e., with a non-linear obliqueness hierarchy in the ARG-ST value of predicators, plausibly by virtue of parametric choice, Principle Z as stated in (13) makes the correct predictions because only subjects can be the o-binders of any other argument.

Notice furthermore that the distinction between predicators having a linear obliqueness order vs. those having a non-linear obliqueness order can be active within a particular language, as it seems to be the case for Dutch (Bredenkamp 1996, ex. (3.26)):

(17)  a.  $\text{Jan}_i$ vertelde $\text{Piet}_j$ een verhaal over  $\textbf{zichzelf}_{i/*j}$.
          Jan told      Piet  a    story  about self

      b.  $\text{Jan}_i$ vroeg $\text{Piet}_j$ een verhaal over  $\textbf{zichzelf}_{i/j}$.
          Jan asked Piet  a    story  about self

## 11.4   The Binding Square of Oppositions

We now reach a point where it is possible and important to assess the merits of the new formulation of Principle Z not only in terms of its empirical adequacy, but also as regards its impact on binding theory as a whole. Under our proposal, Principle Z is not merely an extra binding constraint, but is given the status of a fourth principle of the theory, on an equal footing with the three "classic" principles A, B, and C. This gives rise to a striking natural symmetry between the four principles:

(18)  A:  A *locally o-commanded* anaphor must be *locally o-bound*.
      Z:  An *o-commanded* anaphoric pronoun must be *o-bound*.
      B:  A personal pronoun must be *locally o-free*.
      C:  A nonpronoun must be *o-free*.

Both anaphoric and non-anaphoric expressions now have two binding principles governing them. The opposition of *local* vs. *nonlocal* can be given a more fine-grained interpretation. Principle Z is the nonlocal (extended) variant of Principle A, in the same sense that Principle C can be understood as the nonlocal (extended) variant of Principle B; however, Principle B may also be taken as the non-"local" (complement) variant of Principle A in the same sense that Principle C can be understood as the non-"local" (complement) variant of Principle Z.

The elegance and heuristic value of the suggested relations can be brought into even sharper focus if the exact correlations between the four principles are made evident in a more formally precise way. Specifically, once reference to the relevant subtype of (potentially) referentially dependent element is removed from the binding principles proper, the basic properties of binding theory can be given a characterization in the form of a classical square of oppositions:

(19)  X is locally bound    X is free

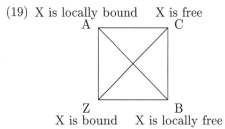

X is bound    X is locally free

There are two pairs of *contradictory* constraints (one is true iff the other is false), which are formed by the two diagonals, (A, B) and (C, Z). One pair of *contrary* constraints (they can be both false but they cannot both be true) are given by the upper horizontal edge, (A, C). One pair of *compatible* constraints (they can be both true but cannot be both false) are given by the lower horizontal edge, (Z, B). Finally, two pairs of *subcontrary* constraints (the first coordinate implies the second, but the second does not imply the first) are obtained by the vertical edges, (A, Z) and (C, B).

Consequently, by enlarging our data sample to encompass both subject-oriented and non-subject-oriented long-distance anaphors, we obtain a more general and empirically adequate account of long-distance anaphora. But it is worth pointing out that as an unexpected side-effect, we arrive at a more integrated binding theory as well.

We suspect that the formal oppositions between the four principles made evident are only the beginning of a further inquiry into unsuspected properties of binding phenomena. Questions such as the following call for undertaking promising new paths of research into the nature of the meaning of nominal referentially dependent expressions.[5]

> Does (19) indicate a subjacent quantificational structure for binding theory? Is there a corresponding square of duality? Does the universal nature of binding theory stem in any interesting way from its possible quantificational structure? Will this justify a new standpoint on referential dependence that is convergent with the lexicalisation of binding requirements (in line with Dalrymple 1993)?

## 11.5   Conclusions

A generalised approach to long-distance anaphora has been developed by means of a new formulation of Principle Z together with the adoption of non-linear obliqueness ordering for valence lists. This led to a significant reorganization of our understanding of the internal structure

---

[5]For subsequent research on these issues and positive answers to some of these questions, see Branco 1998.

of binding theory in general, and to a more fine-tuned and formally precise characterisation of the distinction between locality and nonlocality in binding requirements in particular. Since the binding principles have been shown to constitute a logical square of oppositions, new directions for the research on binding may have been suggested as well.

## References

Branco, António. 1996. Branching Split Obliqueness at the Syntax-Semantics Interface. *COLING-96 Proceedings of The 16th International Conference on Computational Linguistics,* Copenhagen: Center for Sprogteknologi. 149–156.

Branco, António. 1998. *The Logical Structure of Binding.* Unpublished Manuscript, Saarbrücken: DFKI.

Bredenkamp, Andrew. 1996. *Towards a Binding Theory for Head-Driven Phrase Structure Grammar.* Doctoral Thesis. University of Essex.

Cole, Peter, and Li-May Sung. 1994. Head Movement and Long-Distance Reflexives. *Linguistic Inquiry* 25:355–406.

Cole, Peter, and Chengchi Wang. 1996. Antecedents and Blockers of Long-Distance Reflexives: The Case of Chinese *Ziji. Linguistic Inquiry* 27:357–390.

Dalrymple, Mary. 1993. *The Syntax of Anaphoric Binding.* Stanford: CSLI Publications.

Hellan, Lars. 1991. Containment and Connectedness Anaphors. In Jan Koster and E. Reuland (1991a), 27–48.

Huang, C.-T. James, and C.-C. Jane Tang. 1991. The Local Nature of the Long-Distance Reflexive in Chinese. In Jan Koster and E. Reuland (1991a), 263–282.

Koster, Jan, and E. Reuland, eds. 1991a. *Long-Distance Anaphora.* Cambridge: Cambridge University Press.

Koster, Jan, and E. Reuland. 1991b. Long-Distance Anaphora: An Overview. In Jan Koster and E. Reuland (1991a), 1–25.

Manning, Christopher, and Ivan A. Sag. 1995. Dissociations between Argument Structure and Grammatical Relations. ms., paper presented at the Tübingen Workshop on HPSG, University of Tübingen.

Marácz, Laszlo. 1989. *Asymmetries in Hungarian.* Doctoral Dissertation, University of Groningen.

Pollard, Carl, and Ivan Sag. 1992. Anaphors in English and the Scope of Binding Theory. *Linguistic Inquiry* 20:365–424.

Pollard, Carl, and Ivan A. Sag. 1994. *Head-Driven Phrase Structure Grammar.* Stanford: CSLI Publications.

Progovac, Ljiljana. 1993. Long-Distance Reflexives: Movement to Infl versus Relativized SUBJECT. *Linguistic Inquiry* 24:755–772.

van Steenbergen, Marlies. 1991. Long-Distance Binding in Finnish. In Jan Koster and E. Reuland (1991a), 231–244.

Toman, Jindřich. 1991. Anaphors in Binary Trees: An Analysis of Czech Reflexives. In Jan Koster and E. Reuland (1991a), 151–171.

Wang, J.-H. 1990. *Ziji*—A Chinese Long-Distance Anaphor. Unpublished Manuscript. Carnegie Mellon University.

Xue, Ping, Carl Pollard, and Ivan A. Sag. 1994. A New Perspective on Chinese *Ziji*. In *Proceedings of the West Coast Conference on Formal Linguistics*, vol. 13. Stanford: CSLI Publications.

# 12

# HPSG, GB, and the Balinese Bind

STEPHEN WECHSLER

## 12.1   The Myth of the Notational Variant

In comparing two analyses of the same phenomenon within HPSG and
GB (Government/Binding theory or its descendants such as Principles
and Parameters and Minimalism), one sometimes finds a rough parallelism between the descriptive mechanisms of each theory. (Such parallel
analyses are occasionally incorrectly referred to as 'notational variants'.)
While parallelism is not surprising when the object of inquiry is identical,
such cross-framework comparisons are nevertheless valuable.

However, as will be shown below, the apparent parallelism in simple
cases can mask crucial underlying differences which lead to radically
divergent empirical consequences when the data set is extended. This
paper is a case study in the illusion of parallelism between HPSG and
GB. The empirical basis for this study is the interaction of voice-marking
and anaphoric binding in Balinese (Austronesian), as described in joint
work conducted with I Wayan Arka (Arka 1988; Arka and Wechsler 1996;
Wechsler and Arka 1996, 1997a, 1997b, 1998). First I will present our
HPSG analysis as well as the 'standard' GB analysis of Austronesian
voice-marking, the latter based on Guilfoyle, Hung, and Travis 1992
(see also Bittner and Hale 1996). I will point out the close parallels
between the two approaches and show that they handle basic anaphoric
binding facts equally well. Then I will expand the data set to include
raising constructions. There we will see as radical a divergence as one

All of the descriptive work and much of the analysis for this paper was carried out
in collaboration with Wayan Arka. For their comments and discussion I wish to
thank Lisa Travis, Knud Lambrecht, Jean-Pierre Koenig, and Ralph Blight. I am
also grateful to an anonymous NLLT reviewer (of Wechsler and Arka 1998), who,
as a mythologist of the notational variant, provided the initial inspiration for this
paper.

*Lexical and Constructional Aspects of Linguistic Explanation.*
Gert Webelhuth, Jean-Pierre Koenig, and Andreas Kathol.
Copyright © 1998, Stanford University.

can imagine. The HPSG analysis extends automatically to cover such constructions, while the GB analysis runs into serious problems: not only does it fail to extend properly, it cannot be modified to allow for the extension without an overhaul of basic tenets of GB binding theory.

## 12.2   Balinese Voice-Marking and Binding

Like many of its Austronesian relatives, Balinese has a voice system (sometimes called 'focus-marking') whereby morphology on the verb determines which argument is selected to be the subject. Balinese verbs can appear in either of two voices: (i) Objective Voice (OV) which is morphologically unmarked as in (2a); and (ii) Agentive Voice (AV) which is formed by substituting a homorganic nasal for the stem-initial consonant or prefixing *ng-* [ŋ] to a vowel-initial stem, as in (2b). Intransitive verbs are unmarked, as in (1).

(1)    Ia    pules.
       3rd sleep

       '(S)he is sleeping.'

(2)    a.    Bawi adol    ida.
             pig    OV.sell 3sg

             '(S)he sold a pig.'
       b.    Ida ng-adol bawi.
             3sg AV-sell pig

             '(S)he sold a pig.'

(3rd = third person pronoun, unmarked for number or gender). Notice that the voice marking determines the order of arguments: the OV sentence has the order Theme-Verb-Agent, while the AV sentence has it Agent-Verb-Theme. We have argued elsewhere that the preverbal NPs in (2a) and (2b) are the surface subjects and the postverbal ones are complements, so that Balinese canonically has SVO order, regardless of whether the verb is OV or AV (Artawa 1994; Wechsler and Arka 1998). In other words, (2a) and (2b) are not just word order variants; rather, the voice markers regulate the mapping between arguments (agent, theme, etc.) and grammatical relations (subject, object, etc.). Our evidence for this view is quite extensive, drawing on relativization, Subject-to-subject raising, Subject-to-object raising, Control, Extraposition, quantifier float, and other phenomena in the syntax of Balinese. We will not review those arguments here, however, but refer the reader to Wechsler and Arka 1998.

## 12.3  HPSG Analysis

The Balinese voice alternation can be described in HPSG by assigning an
ARG-ST value to each verb stem, then allowing the voice morphology to
determine which ARG-ST item maps to the SUBJ value. The term 'A-
subject' refers to the first (leftmost) item in the ARG-ST list (following
Manning 1994). The rules for Balinese subject selection are as follows.
When the verb is in AV form, the A-subject maps to the SUBJect.
For example, suppose the ditransitive (applicativized) verb stem *beliang*
'buy for' has the following ARG-ST:

(3)     verb stem *beliang* 'buy for':

$$
\begin{bmatrix}
\text{ARG-ST} & \langle NP_i, NP_j, NP_k \rangle \\
\text{CONTENT} & \begin{bmatrix} buy\text{-}rel \\ \text{AGENT} & i \\ \text{GOAL} & j \\ \text{THEME} & k \end{bmatrix}
\end{bmatrix}
$$

As seen in (3), the agent argument is the A-subject. The AV form of
this verb takes the agent argument as its subject (in the AV form the
homorganic nasal /m/ substitutes for the stem-initial /b/):

(4)     Ia   meli-ang      I    Wayan potlot-e     ento.
        3rd AV.buy-APPL ART Wayan pencil-DEF that

        '(S)he bought Wayan the pencil.'

Also, for any intransitive verb, whatever its voice marking, the sole NP
argument is the subject. On the other hand, the subject of a mono- or
ditransitive OV verb is any term (NP) argument *except* the A-subject.
Thus a ditransitive OV verb has two linking possibilities (in (5a,b) the
agent is realized as the 3rd person pronominal clitic =*a*):

(5)     a.  Potlote      ento beli-ang=a      I    Wayan.
            pencil-DEF that OV.buy-APPL=3 Art Wayan

            '(S)he bought Wayan the pencil.'

        b.  I    Wayan beli-ang=a        potlote      ento.
            Art Wayan OV.buy-APPL=3 pencil-DEF that

            '(S)he bought Wayan the pencil.'

        c.  *Ia   beli-ang       I    Wayan potlot-e      ento.
            3rd OV.buy-APPL Art Wayan pencil-DEF that

            '(S)he bought Wayan the pencil.'

These rules are formalized as follows. Verb signs are sorted as in (6).

(6)    Sort hierarchy for verbs

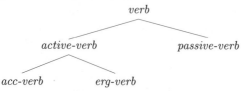

For any verb (modulo pro-drop, pronoun incorporation, etc.) the SUBJ
list contains one NP and the ARG-ST value is the *sequence union* ($\cup_{<>}$)
of the SUBJ and COMPS values (i.e. the non-SUBJ arguments are
mapped to COMPS, preserving order):[1]

(7)    *verb:*
$$\begin{bmatrix} \text{VALENCE} & \begin{bmatrix} \text{SUBJ} & \boxed{1}\langle\text{NP}\rangle \\ \text{COMPS} & \boxed{2} \end{bmatrix} \\ \text{ARG-ST} & \boxed{1}\ \cup_{<>}\ \boxed{2} \end{bmatrix}$$

Active verbs are sorted into accusative and ergative (passives will not
be treated here, but are analyzed in Wechsler and Arka 1998). For an
accusative verb, the A-subject is the SUBJect (8a). The sort declaration
for ergative verb, shown in (8b), can be satisfied in either of two ways:
(i) the verb is intransitive (only one NP in its ARG-ST list); or (ii) any
NP *except* the A-subject maps to SUBJ. (A negated description ¬A is
satisfied by any feature structure which fails to satisfy description A.)

(8)    a.    *acc-verb:*
$$\begin{bmatrix} \text{SUBJ} & \langle\boxed{1}\rangle \\ \text{ARG-ST} & \langle\boxed{1},\dots\rangle \end{bmatrix}$$

       b.    *erg-verb:*
$$\neg\begin{bmatrix} \text{SUBJ} & \langle\boxed{1}\rangle \\ \text{ARG-ST} & \langle\boxed{1},\dots,\text{NP},\dots\rangle \end{bmatrix}$$

See also Manning and Sag (this volume) for a similar proposal. A crucial
feature of this analysis of the AV/OV alternation is that the ARG-
ST list ordering is constant for a particular verb stem, irrespective of
voice. In that respect the AV/OV alternation differs from the more
familiar active/passive alternation, which is typically analyzed in terms
of a shuffling of the ARG-ST list. For example, in (5a,b) above, the agent
(the third person clitic =a) is still the first (leftmost) item in ARG-ST,
even though it does not appear as subject. In other words, while the
agent is 'demoted' in the passive, the agent is not 'demoted' in OV.

    Important evidence for this view comes from anaphoric binding,
since binding is defined at ARG-ST. As in many west Austronesian lan-

---

[1]Given two lists $L_1$ and $L_2$, the list $L_1 \cup_{<>} L_2$ contains all and only the elements
of $L_1$ and $L_2$, preserving ordering on $L_1$ and on $L_2$ but freely intermingling their
elements. For example: $\langle a, b\rangle \cup_{<>} \langle 1, 2\rangle = \langle a, b, 1, 2\rangle \vee \langle a, 1, b, 2\rangle \vee \langle a, 1, 2, b\rangle \vee$
$\langle 1, a, b, 2\rangle \vee \langle 1, a, 2, b\rangle \vee \langle 1, 2, a, b\rangle$. See Reape 1994.

guages, anaphoric binding conditions in Balinese depend on argument role, and not on grammatical relations (see Andrews 1985; Kroeger 1993; Schachter, 1984, inter alia). In (9a) the subject binds the object while in (9b) the object binds the subject. But in each case, the agent can bind a theme (and not vice versa), irrespective of grammatical function.[2]

(9)   a.   Ida nyingakin ragan idane.
             3sg AV-see     self
             '(S)he saw himself/herself.'
      b.   Ragan idane cingakin ida.
             self           OV.see 3SG
             '(S)he saw himself/herself.'

As noted by Manning (1994), this follows straightforwardly on the HPSG theory of anaphoric binding (adapted from Pollard and Sag 1992):

(10)   HPSG(3) Binding Theory
      Principle A. An a-commanded anaphor must be locally a-bound.
      Principle B. A personal pronoun must be locally a-free.
      Principle C. A non-pronoun must be a-free.

      Definitions:
      In [ARG-ST $\langle \ldots, x, \ldots, y, \ldots \rangle$], $x$ is said to *a-command* $y$.
      $x$ *locally a-binds* $y$ = $x$ a-commands $y$, $x$ and $y$ coindexed
      $x$ *a-binds* $y$ = $x$ a-commands some $z$ dominating $y$, $x$ and $y$ coindexed
      $x$ is (locally) *a-free* = $x$ is not (locally) a-bound

In both (9a) and (9b), the SEER argument a-commands the SEEN, so the reflexive is locally a-bound in each sentence. (11) gives simplified HPSG lexical signs for *nyingakin* 'see (AV)' and *cingakin* 'see (OV)' as in (9a) and (9b) respectively (cp. Manning and Sag, this volume). Note that the ARG-ST and CONTENT features are identical across the two voices, while the VALENCE features differ:

---

[2]Example (9) is in Balinese 'high register', while most of the other examples are in the low register. In the low register sentence corresponding to (9b), the OV agent pronoun would be cliticized to the verb, so high register is used in order to simplify the descriptions in (11). ARG-ST is identical irrespective of whether a pronoun is incorporated or free, so binding is unaffected by this distinction. Pronoun incorporation is analyzed in Wechsler and Arka 1996.

(11)  a.*nyingakin* ('AV.see'):        b.*cingakin* ('OV.see'):

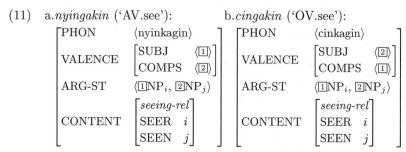

In addition to the AV/OV forms, Balinese has a passive construction, with an optional agent by-phrase. Assuming the standard analysis of passive as a shuffling of the ARG-ST list, the passive agent is more oblique than its coarguments. This predicts that binding facts will differ for OV (where the Agent is leftmost in ARG-ST) and passive clauses, respectively. This prediction is confirmed for Balinese, but this will not be presented here for lack of space (see Wechsler and Arka 1998).

To sum up this section, we have analyzed the Balinese voice morphology as regulating the mapping between the ARG-ST list and the VALENCE lists. On this view ARG-ST is invariant across OV and AV voices. This explains why binding appears not to depend on grammatical function (subject, etc.). Next we look at a GB analysis of the same facts.

## 12.4  GB Analysis

To our knowledge GB theory has not been applied to Balinese (except Travis 1997; see Section 12.7 below). The following analysis essentially follows the account of Austronesian voice-marking in (Guilfoyle, Hung, and Travis 1992) (hereafter 'GHT'), which is based on data from Tagalog, Indonesian, and Malagasy. Numerous more recent studies of Austronesian have the same general structure (see, e.g. Bittner and Hale 1996), and my comments apply equally to all of them that I am familiar with.

As in much recent GB work, GHT assume that all theta-roles are discharged within the VP. Their [Spec,IP] position, to which an argument sometimes moves for Case, corresponds to our 'subject', the single element of the SUBJ list. Applying this theory to Balinese, syntactically ergative (OV) or accusative (AV) clauses would be generated by moving the theme or agent, respectively, into [Spec,IP]. In either case, the verb moves to Infl:

(12)   a. OV clause:               b. AV clause:

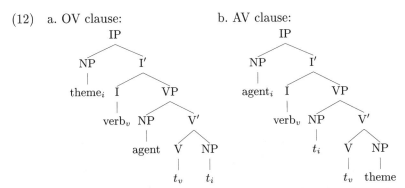

Now consider binding. GB binding theory is based on configurational relations defined on phrase structure representations. Specifically, given two constituents $x$ and $y$, $x$ A-binds $y$ iff $x$ is in an A-position (argument position), $x$ and $y$ are coindexed, and $x$ c-commands $y$. The set of items in A-positions (in GB) roughly corresponds to the set of items in our ARG-ST list (in HPSG), and the relative c-command relations holding between those items (in GB) corresponds to the ordering on the elements in ARG-ST, namely a-command (in HPSG). Thus a crucial issue for any GB account of binding is just which phrase structure positions are assumed to be A-positions.

GHT do not investigate binding in detail, but they note that binding in the Austronesian languages they consider appears to be 'theta sensitive' in that, e.g., 'Agents are always possible antecedents of reflexives.' (p. 392). They suggest that their analysis makes available a structural account of binding (p. 392). Given the binding facts, GHT must assume that the set of A-positions are the VP-internal positions, while [Spec,IP] is an A′ position (non-A-position). On that assumption, in both (12a) and (12b), the highest A-position in the agent chain (namely [Spec,VP]) c-commands the highest A-position in the theme chain (namely the complement of V). This gives the desired result: the agent asymmetrically binds the theme regardless of which one is subject. In other words, since binding depends on A-positions, we effectively abstract away from the effects of A′ movement, returning each argument to the highest A-position in its chain.

Now let us compare the two representations of the voice-marking alternation, in HPSG (11) and GB (12). There are clear parallels. In both frameworks the arguments are hierarchically organized for the purpose of various processes such as anaphoric binding, whether represented by an ARG-ST list or by the set of A-positions arranged in a hierarchical phrase structure. Subjecthood of an argument is represented by structure-sharing with the SUBJ item or by movement into the subject position ([Spec,IP]). The correspondences are summarized here:

(13)     <u>HPSG</u>                     <u>GB</u>
         ARG-ST list items           items in A-positions ('arguments')
         a-command                   c-command (between A-positions)
         structure-sharing w/ SUBJ    movement to [Spec,IP]

There are also important differences between the respective representations. Empirical differences between binding theories based on a-command and c-command have been discussed extensively elsewhere (Bresnan 1995; Pollard and Sag 1992). Also, the tree structure representation of hierarchy is considerably richer than the list representation, begging the question of whether that added richness is ever linguistically relevant. Does the grammar ever appeal to any properties of the VP in (12), other than the fact that the agent c-commands the theme? For example, does it matter that the V$'$ is a constituent; V and its object are sisters; V$'$ and its specifier are sisters; and so on? If not, then by Occam's Razor it should be abandoned in favor of the list representation.

Apart from suffering from this 'embarrass de richesse', the GB analysis appears to be substantially similar to that of HPSG. However, this apparent similarity turns out to be illusory, as we will see when we expand our coverage to include raising constructions.

## 12.5   Raising

Balinese has many subject-to-subject raising (SSR) and subject-to-object raising (SOR) predicates. These allow raising only of the downstairs subject (as noted by Artawa (1994)). Consider embedded transitive verbs, first an OV verb (14):

(14)   a.   Ngenah sajan [kapelihan-ne      engkebang ci].
           seem     much mistake-3POSS OV.hide    2nd

            'It is very apparent that you are hiding his/her wrongdoing.'

      b.   Kapelihan-ne     ngenah sajan engkebang ci.
          mistake-3POSS seem     much OV.hide    2nd

      c.?*Ci   ngenah sajan kapelihan-ne      engkebang.
          2nd seem     much mistake-3POSS OV.hide

In the non-raised example (14a) the bracketed clause is the complement of the predicate *ngenah* 'seem'/'apparent'. Since the embedded verb *engkebang* 'hide' is in OV form, its theme *kapelihan-ne* 'his/her mistake' is the subject and its agent *ci* 'you' is the object. Being the embedded subject, the theme *kapelihan-ne* can be raised, as shown in (14b), while the embedded agent *ci,* being a non-subject, cannot raise, as shown in (14c).

When the embedded verb *ngengkebang* 'hide' appears in its AV form, the arguments are reversed from (14a). Now the agent *ci* is the embedded subject and the theme *kapelihan-ne* is the object:

(15)  a.  Ngenah sajan [ci   ngengkebang kapelihan-ne].
        seem      much 2nd AV.hide      mistake-3POSS

        'It is very apparent that you are hiding his/her wrongdoing.'
    b.  Ci   ngenah sajan ngengkebang kapelihan-ne.
        2nd seem    much AV.hide      mistake-3POSS
    c.?*Kapelihan-ne    ngenah sajan ci   ngengkebang.
        mistake-3POSS seem    much 2nd AV.hide

As expected, the embedded agent *ci,* being the subject, can raise (as in (15b)), while the theme *kapelihan-ne,* being a non-subject, cannot raise (as in (15c)).

Now consider the Balinese SOR construction (example from Artawa 1994, 148):

(16)  a.  Nyoman Santosa tawang    tiang mulih.
        Nyoman Santosa OV.know 1st    go.home

        'I knew that Nyoman Santosa went home.'
    b.  Tiang nawang    Nyoman Santosa mulih.
        1st    AV-know Nyoman Santosa go.home

        'I knew that Nyoman Santosa went home.'

The SOR verb *tawang* 'know' is transitive, hence participates in the OV/AV voice alternation. Specifically, the 'raised' NP appears in the subject position of an OV SOR verb (as in (16a)) or the object position of an AV SOR verb (as in (16b)). (In that sense 'subject-to-object raising' is a misnomer; rather it involves, so to speak, 'raising to A-object', i.e. to the second position in ARG-ST.) This alternation follows from our account of voice-marking, assuming that the 'raised' NP and the following open complement (here, the predicate *mulih* 'go home') are both complements of the matrix verb (Pollard and Sag 1994, Ch. 3). The verb *tawang* 'know' has the following ARG-ST list and semantic content:

(17)  *tawang*:

$$\begin{bmatrix} \text{ARG-ST} & \langle \text{ NP}_i, \boxed{2}\text{NP, VP[SUBJ } \langle\boxed{2}\rangle]{:}j\rangle \\ \\ \text{CONTENT} & \begin{bmatrix} \textit{know-relation} \\ \text{KNOWER} & i \\ \text{PROPOSITION} & j \end{bmatrix} \end{bmatrix}$$

From the linking rules in (8) we see that when the SOR verb appears in OV voice a non-A-subject term must be the subject; the only element qualifying for subject is the second item in ARG-ST, $\boxed{2}$NP. The result is (16a). In AV voice the A-subject is the subject, yielding (16b).

As with SSR, only the lower subject can raise into the higher clause in the SOR construction. This generalization obtains for all four combinations of AV and OV on the matrix and embedded predicates, but space does not allow for presentation of the relevant data (see Wechsler and Arka 1998).

## 12.6  Binding in Raising Constructions

Now consider binding in raising constructions. As in English, the Balinese SSR verb meaning 'seem' optionally takes a PP complement to express the agent. In Balinese (19), as in English (18), the raised NP can bind a reflexive in the PP, and cannot bind a pronominal in that position.

(18)  I wonder whether he$_i$ seems to {himself$_i$/him$_{*i}$} to be ugly.

(19)  Takonang tiang apa ia$_i$ ngenah sig {awakne$_i$/ia$_{*i}$} jelek sajan.
      OV.ask   1st   Q   3rd seem   to self         bad  very
      'I asked (him) whether he seemed to himself/him to be very ugly.'

In HPSG these facts follow from the ARG-ST for *ngenah* 'seem', in which the raised NP a-commands the PP:

(20)  *ngenah*:
$$\begin{bmatrix} \text{ARG-ST} & \langle \boxed{1}\text{NP}_i, \text{PP[sig]}:ana_i/ppro_{*i}, \text{VP[SUBJ } \langle\boxed{1}\rangle]:j \rangle \\ \text{CONTENT} & seem(i,j) \end{bmatrix}$$

The raised NP can alternatively bind an embedded NP complement reflexive which it a-commands on the downstairs ARG-ST list:

(21)  a.  Ia$_i$ ngenah pesan sig cange ngajum-ngajum awakne$_i$/ia$_{*i}$
         3rd seem   very  to me    AV.boast-boast  self
         'He$_i$ seems to me to boast of himself$_i$/him$_{*i}$.'

      b.  ARG-ST lists for (21a)
$$\begin{bmatrix} \text{'seem'} & \langle \boxed{1}\text{NP}, \text{PP}, \text{VP[SUBJ } \langle\boxed{1}\rangle]\rangle \\ \text{'AV.boast'} & \langle \boxed{1}\text{NP}_i, \text{NP}:ana_i/ppro_{*i} \end{bmatrix}$$

The ARG-ST lists for *ngenah* 'seem' and *ngajum-ngajum* 'AV.boast', as they occur in example (21a), are shown in (21b). Here and in subsequent diagrams, the tags indicate structure-sharing between elements in the respective ARG-ST lists when these words occur in the relevant sentence.

If the embedded predicate is in OV form, then the embedded agent can bind a raised reflexive:

(22) a. Awakne$_i$ ngenah pesan sig cange ajum-ajum=a$_i$
    self      seem  very  to me    OV.boast-boast=3

    'He$_i$ seems to me to boast of himself$_i$.'

b. ARG-ST lists for (22a)

$$\begin{bmatrix} \text{'seem'} & \langle \boxed{1}\text{NP, PP}[sig], \text{VP[SUBJ } \langle\boxed{1}\rangle]\rangle \\ \text{'OV.boast'} & \langle \text{NP}_i, \boxed{1}\text{NP}:ana_i\rangle \end{bmatrix}$$

Note that binding in this case takes place on the ARG-ST list for the embedded predicate *ajum-ajum* 'OV.boast', although the bound anaphor is raised into the matrix subject position.

Unlike SSR verbs, SOR verbs are transitive so they exhibit the OV/AV alternation, leading to further complication. But these facts also follow directly from our theory. As shown in (17) above, the agent ('knower') argument of 'know' a-commands the raised NP. We predict that the agent can bind a raised reflexive but not a raised pronoun. This is confirmed for 'think' in its AV form ((23a)) and OV form ((23b)):

(23) a. Cang ngaden   {awak cange/*cang} suba    mati.
    1sg    AV.think myself/*me         already dead

    'I believed myself/*me to be dead already.'

b. {Awak cange/*cang} kaden    cang suba    mati.
    myself/*me         OV.think 1sg  already dead

    'I believed myself/*me to be dead already.'

c. ARG-ST lists for examples (23a,b)

$$\begin{bmatrix} \text{'AV/OV.think'} & \langle \text{NP}_i, \boxed{1}\text{NP}:ana_i/ppro_{*i}, \text{XP[SUBJ } \langle\boxed{1}\rangle]\rangle \\ \text{'dead'} & \langle \boxed{1}\text{NP}\rangle \end{bmatrix}$$

Since voice marking on the matrix verb does not affect the ARG-ST list, we can collapse (23a) and (23b) into one diagram, shown in (23c).

In (24) the embedded transitive verb is OV, so the theme is the subject which is raised. As in the previous example, a raised reflexive argument can be bound by the upstairs agent while a raised pronoun cannot be (irrespective of whether the SOR verb is AV as in (24a) or OV as in (24b)):

(24) a. Ia$_i$ nawang  {awakne$_i$/ia$_{*i}$} lakar tangkep   polisi.
    3rd AV.know self/3rd       FUT OV.arrest police

b. {Awakne$_i$/*Ia$_i$} tawang=a$_i$   lakar tangkep   polisi.
    self/3rd         OV.know=3 FUT OV.arrest police

    'He$_i$ knew that the police would arrest self$_i$./him$_{*i}$.'

c. ARG-ST lists for examples (24a,b)

$$\begin{bmatrix} \text{'AV/OV.know'} & \langle \text{NP}_i, \boxed{1}\text{NP}:ana_i/ppro_{*i}, \text{VP[SUBJ } \langle\boxed{1}\rangle]\rangle \\ \text{'OV.arrest'} & \langle \text{NP}, \boxed{1}\text{NP}\rangle \end{bmatrix}$$

The preceding examples illustrate binding on the matrix ARG-ST list. The raised argument can alternatively participate in binding relations with its semantic coarguments on the embedded ARG-ST list. In (25) the raised argument (*ia*) binds the downstairs reflexive (*awakne*) but not a pronoun, regardless of whether the matrix verb is AV (placing the raised argument in object position, as in (25a)) or OV (placing the raised argument in subject position, as in (25b)).

(25) a. Cang ngaden ia$_i$ suba ningalin awakne$_i$/ia$_{*i}$
     1sg  AV.think 3rd already AV.see self/3rd
     'I believe him$_i$ to have seen himself$_i$/him$_{*i}$.'

    b. Ia$_i$ kaden cang suba ningalin awakne$_i$/ia$_{*i}$
      3rd OV.think 1sg already AV.see self
      'I believe him to have seen himself.'

    c. ARG-ST lists for examples (25a,b)

$$\begin{bmatrix} \text{'AV/OV.think'} & \langle \text{NP}, \boxed{1}\text{NP}_i, \text{VP[SUBJ } \langle\boxed{1}\rangle]\rangle \\ \text{'AV.see'} & \langle\boxed{1}\text{NP}, \text{NP}:ana_i/ppro_{*i}\rangle \end{bmatrix}$$

Or the raised argument can be bound on the downstairs ARG-ST, as in (26):

(26) a. Cang ngaden awakne$_i$ suba tingalin=a$_i$.
     1sg  AV.think self$_i$ already OV.see=3
     'I believe him to have seen himself.'

    b. Awakne$_i$ kaden cang suba tingalin=a$_i$.
      self$_i$ OV.think 1sg already OV.see=3
      'I believe him to have seen himself.'

    c. ARG-ST lists for examples (26a,b)

$$\begin{bmatrix} \text{'AV/OV.think'} & \langle \text{NP}, \boxed{1}\text{NP}, \text{VP[SUBJ } \langle\boxed{1}\rangle]\rangle \\ \text{'AV.see'} & \langle \text{NP}_i, \boxed{1}\text{NP}:ana_i\rangle \end{bmatrix}$$

The raised reflexive *awakne* is bound by the downstairs agent, the clitic =*a*.

Examples (24), (25), and (26) point up a slight vagueness in the interpretation of HPSG binding theory, which must be resolved. If, due to raising, an anaphor is simultaneously a-commanded on two ARG-ST lists, must it be bound on both lists, or is one sufficient? Must a pronoun in this situation be free on both lists? Since an anaphor needs only one antecedent, it would be illogical to expect it to be bound on more than one ARG-ST list, so we adopt an 'existential' interpretation of Principle A: An a-commanded anaphor must be locally a-bound on *some* ARG-ST list (we call this 'Principle A$_\exists$'; the universal version will be designated 'Principle A$_\forall$'). On the other hand, Principle B dictates the obviation domain for pronouns, so we take the strongest ('universal quantification') interpretation of Principle B: a pronominal must be locally a-free in all ARG-ST lists in which the pronominal appears. To put it differently: an anaphor satisfies Principle A if it is locally a-bound (on any list); a pronoun violates Principle B if it is locally a-bound (on any list).

This interpretation gives the correct results for Balinese. For example, the anaphor in (26) is a-bound only on the ARG-ST list for 'see', and not on the list for 'think'.

An anonymous reviewer has suggested that certain facts involving clitic climbing in French causative constructions cast doubt on the universality of Principle A∃. The reviewer notes that the ungrammaticality of the following example could be explained by assuming the universal interpretation instead.

(27) *Jean se      fera      pincer à Marie.
     Jean REFL make-fut pinch  to Marie

The sentence is ill-formed on either construal of the reflexive clitic: 'Jean will make Marie pinch Jean' or 'Jean will make Marie pinch herself.' French clitic climbing (the appearance of certain clitics on a higher verb than the one subcategorizing them) has been analyzed in HPSG in terms of argument composition (cp. 'clause union', 'argument attraction'): through its lexical specification the causative verb *faire,* in effect, 'attracts' the arguments of its complement infinitive verb onto its own ARG-ST list (Abeillé, Godard, and Sag, to appear). In (27) the clitic *se* would be a-commanded on two lists, those of *faire* and *pincer*:

(28)   ARG-ST lists for ex. (27)
$$\begin{bmatrix} \text{faire:} & \langle \text{'Jean'}, \boxed{1}\text{se, 'pincer', 'a Marie'}_i \rangle \\ \text{pincer:} & \langle \text{NP}_i, \boxed{1} \rangle \end{bmatrix}$$

Assuming Principle A∀ (instead of A∃, as assumed here) such examples are ruled out since the reflexive cannot possibly be bound on both lists (this would entail that Jean and Marie are coreferential).

While the explanation for (27) is clearly outside the scope of the present paper, it should be noted that there are problems with the reviewer's proposal (there is currently no definitive analysis of this specific point by the HPSG 'French group', according to Ivan Sag (personal communication, Feb. 27, 1998)). First of all, non-third person clitics resist climbing regardless of whether they are reflexive or not (Hyman and Zimmer 1976; Koenig 1994):

(29) *Marc m'a      fait    raccompagner à Jacques.
     Marc 1p'aux make bring.back      to Jacques

     'Marc made Jacques bring me back.'

This suggests that the explanation for (27) may be unrelated to anaphoric binding (as indeed Koenig (1994) argues). Also some dialects allow se-climbing as in (27); see (Koenig 1994, 314) for attested examples from texts.

In any case it is important to understand that the universal/existential issue, while interesting, is completely orthogonal to the point being made in this paper. My argument does not rest on a claim to universality for the binding rules given here; indeed, it is well-known that binding systems vary across languages (Dalrymple 1993, inter alia). Rather, the purpose of this paper is to compare HPSG and GB approaches to binding in Balinese. The problems which Balinese raising constructions pose for GB binding theory are deeper, and would not be ameliorated by either an existential or universal interpretation of (GB) Principle A. This is shown in the following section.

## 12.7 Implications of Raising for the GB Analysis

Crucial to any GB account of binding is the designation of which positions are A-positions and which are A$'$ positions. In GB terms we have demonstrated in the previous section that the raised NP acts, for purposes of binding within the matrix clause, as if it is in an A-position. For example, the raised subject in (19) can bind the matrix PP.

Hence the matrix [Spec,VP] and/or [Spec,IP$^1$] position in (30) below is necessarily an A-position.[3] This follows because the anaphor *awakne* must be a-bound, that is, coindexed with a c-commander in an A-position. Now consider the status of the lower subject position, that is, the [Spec,IP$^2$] position in (30). Normally one would assume that the raised item has passed through the [Spec,IP$^2$], as indicated by the trace $t'_i$ in (30). This assumption is needed in order to capture the generalization that only subjects can be raised. Movement from A$'$ position to A-position is prohibited as improper movement (it is technically ruled out because of improper A-binding of the variable in the [Spec,IP$^2$] position). From this we deduce that [Spec,IP$^2$] is necessarily an A-position.

---

[3] Various modifications of the structure in (30) are imaginable: having the moved element skip [Spec,VP]; positing different functional projections; eliminating ternary branching, and so on. As far as I can tell they would have no effect on our argument.

(30)

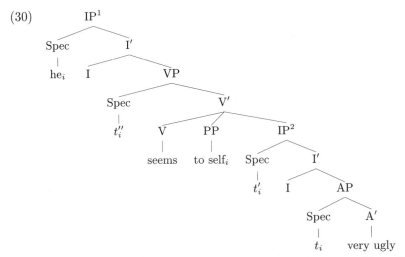

However, as explained in Section 4 above, that subject position ([Spec,IP])
must be an A′ position if we are to account for binding in simplex clauses
(see example (9,12) above). This leads to a contradiction: for the purpose of binding by a raised argument in the higher clause, the lower
subject position must be an A-position, while for binding in a simplex
clause that same position must be an A′ position. This contradiction
arises regardless of what precise position we assume as the landing site
for movement in SSR and SOR constructions (e.g. [Spec,AgrO] in the
latter case).

This paradox, which I call 'the Balinese bind', goes to the heart of
the GB binding theory and cannot, to my knowledge, be solved with a
simple technical fix. In particular, let us try universal and existential
versions of Principle A, as discussed in the previous section. In (30)
the anaphor does not move, so the existential/universal distinction has
no effect; on either version [Spec,IP] must be an A-position to allow
this sentence. So let us designate [Spec,IP] as an A-position, thus solving (19,30), and consider simplex clauses. GB Principle $A_\forall$ (*every* link
in an anaphor chain must be A-bound in a local domain) cannot be
right, as it would incorrectly rule out simple transitive OV sentences
like (9b,12a), since the head of the anaphor chain is not A-bound. Now
try GB Principle $A_\exists$: *some* link in an anaphor chain must be bound
in a local domain. This seems to solve the problem now for (9b,12a):
the *trace* of the reflexive is bound, in accord with Principle A. But now
other problems arise. First, the reflexive in (9b), now assumed to be in
an A-position, improperly binds the pronoun, a Principle B violation.
Moreover, exchanging the pronoun and reflexive in (9b) (but maintain-

ing the OV verb form) is predicted to produce a good sentence, since the reflexive, now in [Spec,VP], would be bound by the pronoun in [Spec,IP]. But in fact such a sentence is impossible.

In the spring of 1997 Lisa Travis became aware of our Balinese data, and discovered that a similar problem arises for Malagasy raising. Travis(1997) outlines possible foundational changes to GB binding theory which would address this problem. Travis' proposal involves (at least) the following innovations: (i) binding is based on theta-positions instead of A-positions; (ii) certain functional heads assign an abstract theta role to their Spec positions 'in the syntax'; and (iii) an argument may move into such a theta-marked Spec position (despite the theta-criterion). In this way the raised position (cp. [Spec, IP$^1$] in (30)) becomes a theta-position so the raised argument can bind the reflexive. It is beyond the scope of this paper to assess this proposal. The present point is rather that the new proposal, in contrast to Guilfoyle, Hung, and Travis 1992, no longer has any apparent parallels to the present HPSG analysis. Indeed, as far as I can tell, the HPSG analysis presented above cannot be 'translated' into GB in any straightforward fashion.

## 12.8   Conclusion

It is commonplace in some circles to trivialize apparently minor (or so-called 'notational') differences between comparable analyses in different frameworks. The case of the 'Balinese bind' illustrates the fallacy of this practice.

## References

Abeillé, Anne, Danièle Godard, and Ivan A. Sag. to appear. Two Kinds of Composition in French Complex Predicates. In *Complex Predicates in Nonderivational Syntax,* edited by E. Hinrichs, A. Kathol, and T. Nakazawa. New York: Academic Press.

Andrews, Avery. 1985. The Major Functions of the Noun Phrase. In *Language Typology and Syntactic Description, vol. I: Clause Structure,* edited by T. Shopen, 62-154. Cambridge, England: Cambridge University Press.

Arka, I Wayan. 1988. *From Morpho-Syntax to Pragmatics in Balinese.* PhD, Department of Linguistics, The University of Sydney, Sydney, Australia.

Arka, I Wayan, and Stephen Wechsler. 1996. Argument Structure and Linear Order in Balinese Binding. Paper read at Workshop on Lexical-Functional Grammar, at Grenoble, France.

Artawa, Ketut. 1994. *Ergativity and Balinese Syntax.* PhD dissertation, La Trobe University, Bundoora, Australia.

Bittner, Maria, and Ken Hale. 1996. Structural Determination of Case and Agreement. *Linguistic Inquiry* 27.1:1–68.

Bresnan, Joan. 1995. Linear Order, Syntactic Rank, and Empty Categories: On Weak Crossover. In *Formal Issues in Lexical-Functional Grammar,* edited by M. Dalrymple, R. M. Kaplan, J. T. Maxwell III, and A. Zaenen. Stanford, CA: CSLI Publications.

Dalrymple, Mary. 1993. *The Syntax of Anaphoric Binding.* Stanford, CA: CSLI Publications.

Guilfoyle, Eithne, Henrietta Hung, and Lisa Travis. 1992. SPEC of IP and SPEC of VP: Two Subjects in Austronesian Languages. *Natural Language and Linguistic Theory* 10.3:375–414.

Hyman, Larry, and Karl Zimmer. 1976. Embedded Topic in French. In *Subject and Topic,* edited by C. Li, 191–211. New York: Academic Press.

Koenig, Jean-Pierre. 1994. *Lexical Underspecification and the Syntax/Semantics Interface.* UC Berkeley PhD Dissertation.

Kroeger, Paul. 1993. *Phrase Structure and Grammatical Relations in Tagalog.* Stanford: CSLI Publications.

Manning, Chris. 1994. *Ergativity: Argument Structure and Grammatical Relations.* PhD, Linguistics Dept., Stanford University, Stanford. (also published by CSLI Publications, 1996).

Pollard, Carl, and Ivan Sag. 1992. Anaphors in English and the Scope of Binding Theory. *Linguistic Inquiry* 23 (2):261–303.

Pollard, Carl, and Ivan Sag. 1994. *Head-Driven Phrase Structure Grammar.* Stanford and Chicago: CSLI Publications and University of Chicago Press.

Reape, Michael. 1994. Domain Union and Word Order Variation in German. In *German in Head-Driven Phrase Structure Grammar,* edited by J. Nerbonne, K. Netter and C. Pollard, 151–197. Stanford: CSLI Publications.

Schachter, Paul. 1984. Semantic-Role-Based Syntax in Toba Batak. In *Studies in the Structure of Toba Batak,* edited by P. Schachter. UCLA Occasional Papers in Linguistics No. 5. Los Angeles: UCLA.

Travis, Lisa. 1997. Theta-Positions and Binding in Balinese and Malagasy. Paper read at the Fourth Annual Meeting of the Austronesian Formal Linguistics Association, UCLA, April 27, 1997.

Wechsler, Stephen, and I Wayan Arka. 1996. Balinese Argument Structure and Valence. Paper read at Third International Conference on Head-Driven Phrase Structure Grammar, at Marseille, France.

Wechsler, Stephen, and I Wayan Arka. 1997a. Balinese Binding. Manuscript.

Wechsler, Stephen, and I Wayan Arka. 1997b. Balinese Binding and Raising. Paper read at 4th Annual Meeting of the Austronesian Formal Linguistics Association, at UCLA.

Wechsler, Stephen, and I Wayan Arka. 1998. Syntactic Ergativity in Balinese: an Argument Structure Based Theory. To appear in *Natural Language and Linguistic Theory.*

# Part IV

## Case and Agreement

# 13

# Peripheral Constructions and Core Phenomena: Agreement in Tag Questions

Emily Bender and Dan Flickinger

Many "peripheral" constructions in English have received little study in recent generative linguistics, despite their high degree of irregularity and attendant potential for illuminating the full range of distinctions needed in the grammar. This neglect is most striking in lexicalist frameworks which should be well suited to capture both the regularities and the idiosyncrasies of such constructions. Tag questions in English, for example, were the subject of vigorous study in earlier transformational grammar, but largely ignored for the past twenty years. This paper presents an HPSG account of this construction using a lexical rule for the auxiliary verbs, and demonstrates how syntactic and semantic distinctions observed in core phenomena interact with this rule to predict many of the properties of tag questions. Based on this analysis, we argue that the grammar of English must draw a systematic distinction between

Bender's contribution to this paper is based upon work supported under a National Science Foundation Graduate Research Fellowship. Any opinions, findings, conclusions, or recommendations expressed herein are those of the authors and do not necessarily reflect the views of the National Science Foundation. Flickinger gratefully acknowledges for this work the support of both the National Science Foundation under grant number IRI-9612682, and the German Federal Ministry of Education, Science, Research, and Technology (BMBF) in the framework of the VerbMobil project under grant FKZ:01IV7024. We are grateful for the insights and critique provided by the members of the Linguistic Grammar Online project at CSLI as we developed the analysis presented here, and two anonymous reviewers for their helpful comments, though we hold them all blameless for any flaws that might be found.

two kinds of agreement. This conclusion is independently supported by examples with intrasentential anaphoric binding.

## 13.1 Introduction

It is characteristic of current work in generative grammar that little attention is given to so-called "peripheral constructions," with efforts concentrated instead on describing "core" linguistic phenomena. There are, however, notable exceptions to this generalization, particularly within the framework of Construction Grammar. Indeed, Charles Fillmore and Paul Kay (see e.g., Kay 1995) argue that the distinction is likely to be artificial, both in terms of its location and of its supposed discreteness. Their research employs a strategy of working in from the extreme edge of the periphery. Only once we have a more complete description of the full range of linguistic phenomena, they argue, will it become clear whether there is any concrete distinction to be made between core and periphery, what the nature of that distinction is, and where it lies.

Earlier work in generative grammar, in contrast, reflected a strong interest in the periphery, including analyses of the unusual phenomenon of tag questions in English. Klima (1964) proposed an early transformational analysis of tag questions which engendered a lively debate about the negative polarity properties of tags. This debate largely ended in the mid-seventies with Hudson's (1975) study of interrogatives, in which he asserts that "the syntax of tags is unpredictable," and that they may be unique to English.

Culicover 1992 provides a rare exception to the ensuing neglect of tags. Working within the Principles and Parameters framework, he endeavors to predict both the presence and form of English tag questions on the basis of Universal Grammar and independently-motivated English-specific properties. While we find this to be an interesting approach to the study of peripheral constructions, it is the converse that we are advocating here: namely, using in-depth analysis of peripheral phenomena to illuminate aspects of the core grammar. For this purpose, we need a more explicit formalization of the phenomena and of the relevant grammatical principles than that provided in Culicover 1992, which is why we present our analysis within the HPSG framework.

## 13.2 Properties of Tag Questions

This section outlines the familiar and straightforward, though intricate, properties of tag questions.

In their basic structure, tag questions consist of an auxiliary verb followed by a pronoun, where the pronoun agrees in person, number, and gender with the subject of the main clause.

(1)     Sara slept, didn't she/*Sara/*he/*they/*I/*$\phi$?

The auxiliary verb in the tag is drawn from the set of inverted auxiliaries (see Gazdar et al. 1982), as evidenced by the fact that both sets share irregular forms (2) and accidental gaps (3).

(2)     a.    I'm still invited, aren't/*amn't I?
        b.    Aren't/*Amn't I invited to that party?

(3)     a.    You better not be late.
        b.    *Better you not be late?
        c.    *You better not be late, better you?

The pronoun in the tag must be of nominative case, non-reflexive, and not possessive:

(4)     My sister slept, didn't she/*her/*herself/*mine?

In addition, the pronoun must be referential if the subject of the main clause is referential, and must be a matching expletive if not:

(5)     a.    Sara is sleeping, isn't she/*there/*it?
        b.    There is a meeting, isn't there/*it/*he?

If the main clause is headed by an auxiliary verb, then the auxiliary in the tag question must match (modulo negation). If the main clause's head verb is not an auxiliary, then the tag's auxiliary must be the verb *do*. In addition, the tag's auxiliary must match the tense of the head verb in the main clause:

(6)     a.    Sara will sleep, won't/*can't/*doesn't she?
        b.    Sara sleeps, doesn't/*didn't/*won't/*slept she?

Tags attach only to matrix clauses that are not interrogative:

(7)     a.    Bob knows that Sara will win, doesn't he?
        b.    *Bob knows that Sara will win, won't she?
        c.    Sara will sleep, won't she?
        d.    Sleep, won't you?
        e.    *Will Sara sleep, won't she?

## 13.3   Further Properties of Tag Questions

In addition to the relatively straightforward properties discussed in the preceding section, tag questions also have some more surprising properties.

As discussed in most of the work on tag questions, from Klima 1964 through to Culicover 1992, tag questions usually show the opposite polarity for negation relative to the main clause. When both are positive as in (8c), the sentence has a reading distinct from a sentence with an opposite polarity tag.

(8)     a.   Sara slept, didn't she?
         b.   Sara didn't sleep, did she?
         c.   Sara slept, did she?
         d.   *Sara didn't sleep, didn't she?

The analysis presented here will not cover the distinctions in (8), but should be able to be extended appropriately once there is an analysis of the general problem of polarity phenomena in place.[1]

One class of unexpected data are the examples where the tag agrees in all of the relevant ways with the embedded clause, not with the matrix clause, as in (9).

(9)     a.   I suppose Sara will win, won't she?
         b.   *I suppose Sara will win, don't I?

These embedded tags occur only with a small class of 'hedge' verbs such as *suppose, guess, imagine, reckon*, which we assume to have separate lexical entries which are unusual in being restricted to heading main clauses, and in their ability to license tag questions on their complement clause. A more detailed analysis of these unusual verbs would take us too far afield here, but see Emonds 1976 for relevant data and discussion.

In the literature on English tag questions, much less attention has been devoted to apparent violations to the agreement generalization:

(10)    a.   Everyone wins, don't they?
        b.   No one left yet, did they?
        c.   A person's supposed to make a living, aren't they?
        d.   Well, someone's sure to say something, aren't they?

We return to this problem after describing our analysis of the basic data.

## 13.4  Analysis

### 13.4.1  Basic Structure

We analyze tags as modifiers on matrix clauses, where the auxiliary verb heading the tag is related by lexical rule to the regular inverted auxiliary form.[2] The tag phrase must modify the full sentence, attaching at S rather than at VP, for three reasons. First, tags appear outside of

---

[1] William Ladusaw (p.c.) points out the following example, which will constrain the analysis of polarity in tags:

(i)     She saw nobody, *didn't she/did she?
       [Aggressive reading only.]

[2] Here we are only concerned with the inverted auxiliaries that appear in matrix questions, and we leave open the question of whether the same lexical entries for

elements extraposed from subject NPs (examples due to Tom Wasow, p.c.):

(11)  a.  A review appeared of Chomsky's latest book, didn't it?
      b.  That movie bombed that you really liked, didn't it?

The phrases *of Chomsky's latest book* and *that you really liked* are extraposed from the subject NP, presumably attaching at S, not VP, and since the tags appear outside of the extraposed phrases, the tags must also attach at S.[3] Second, tags are possible on some coordinated sentences. In this example, that the tag is attaching to the highest, coordinated S is shown by the fact that *they* takes *Kim* and *Sandy* together as its antecedent.

(12)  Kim left and Sandy stayed, didn't they?

Finally, we observed above that tags must attach only to matrix clauses. We assume that the matrix/embedded distinction is only relevant for S, not VP, reinforcing the argument that tags attach to S, where this constraint can be imposed.

This gives us the basic phrase structure in (13),[4] where $V_{tag}$ indicates that *didn't* is the output of the lexical rule for tag auxiliaries (described in the following pages).

(13)

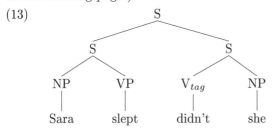

The details of our analysis are captured in the lexical rule *tag_lr* (Figure 1) which relates the auxiliary verbs that head tag questions to

---

inverted auxiliaries might also be used for other non-question inversion constructions such as the locative inversion in *In the corner stood an old grandfather clock*.

[3]Rochemont and Culicover 1990, 35 argue that extraposition from subject can attach either at S or at VP, citing examples like (i) involving stress with VP ellipsis:

(i)    A MAN came in who had lived in Boston, and a WOMAN did too.

We do not find the data convincing. However, if their analysis is correct, it only means that extraposition provides no evidence for tag attachment. On the other hand, our other arguments still stand.

[4]Tags must appear to the right of the sentence they modify; this linear precedence property is not captured in the analysis we give here, but should follow from more general semantic/pragmatic constraints on ordering adjuncts relative to heads.

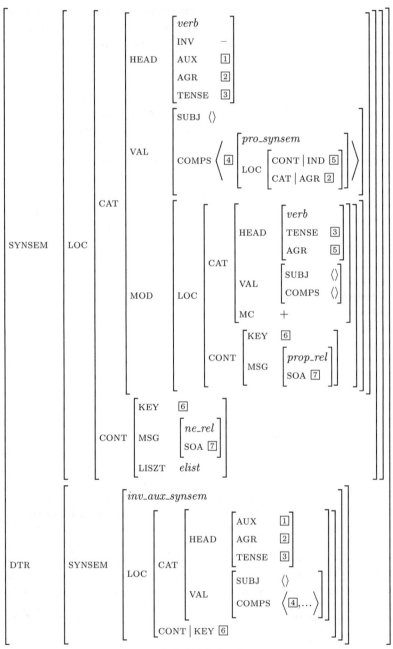

FIGURE 1  *tag_lr*

ordinary inverted auxiliaries.[5] Apart from these constraints and the ones for agreement in the discussion to follow, our analysis employs just the standard properties of the English Resource Grammar[6] as it has been developed on the basis of independent motivations. Note especially that there is no need for a special schema to build the tag phrase; an already existing subtype of the Head-Complement schema will do. The lexical rule given here is the rule for tags on declaratives. Tags on imperatives are produced by a related but slightly different lexical rule which we do not elaborate here.

We account for the similarities between tag auxiliaries and regular inverted auxiliaries by deriving the tag entry from the inverted entry. One difference between the two is that while a regular inverted auxiliary may have complements after the subject, the tag auxiliary may not. Accordingly, the derived COMPS list consists solely of the first member of the "input" COMPS list (the subject of the inverted auxiliary).[7]

Another difference is that, while ordinary inverted auxiliaries are [ INV + ], the *tag_lr* creates tag auxiliaries which are [ INV − ]. The reason for this has to do with the type of construction that tag auxiliaries head. In the larger HPSG grammar within which this analysis is embedded, the analysis of clauses provides distinct subtypes of each of the standard phrasal schemata corresponding to different clause types.[8] The partial hierarchy in Figure 2 illustrates the basic idea.[9]

The candidates for tag phrases in this grammar are two subtypes of the Head-Complement schema, namely the one for main clause yes-no questions (*hcomp_yn_mc*) and the one for non-clausal head-complement phrases (*hcomp_nc*). In addition to their clausal status, these two

---

[5]This rule could be streamlined by creating a type *tag_aux_synsem* in the *verb_synsem* hierarchy. Some of the specifications on the output would then be inherited from higher types, and the rule could be stated as a relationship between words with *inv_aux_synsems* and words with *tag_aux_synsems*. In this case, only a few instances of structure sharing would need to be stipulated. For purposes of exposition, we present the full set of relevant constraints in the single feature structure given in Figure 1.

[6]That is, the HPSG grammar for English implemented by the Linguistic Grammars Online (LinGO) project. Demonstration available at:
http://hpsg.stanford.edu/hpsg.

[7]We ignore here the additional variant of negated tags as in *Sara left, did she not?*, which will have both the subject and the negation particle on the COMPS list. These forms are the result of the interaction of three lexical rules that apply to the auxiliary (neg-addition, inversion, and tag). Space considerations preclude describing that interaction here. For background on the neg-addition and inversion rules, see Warner 1993 and Kim and Sag 1995.

[8]For more on this theory of clauses, see Sag 1997 and Ginzburg and Sag 1998.

[9]The boxes around HEADED_PHRASE and CLAUSALITY indicate a cross-classification. All construction types inherit from some subtype of each of these.

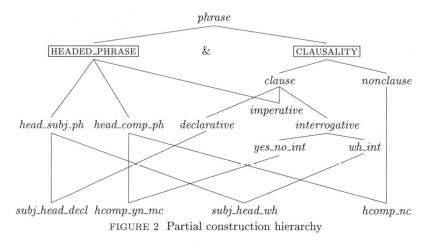

FIGURE 2 Partial construction hierarchy

schemata differ on the value of INV required of the head daughter. Using *hcomp_yn_mc* would result in generating extra parses for elliptical sentences such as *Didn't he?*. More importantly, tags do not have the distribution of other clauses. For example, no verb takes a tag phrase as a complement. Thus, we analyze tag phrases as instances of *hcomp_nc*, and accordingly assign [ INV − ] to the "output" of *tag_lr*.

### 13.4.2 Semantics

Following Ginzburg and Sag 1998, we include a feature MESSAGE in our analysis of the semantics of clauses. The value of MESSAGE is what distinguishes the semantics of questions from propositions and from commands based on the same *soa*. We take advantage of this feature twice in this analysis. On the one hand, we use it to make sure that tags attach to only declaratives (in this case) or imperatives (in the case of the other closely related type of tag), and not to interrogatives, by restricting the value of MESSAGE in the tag's MOD value. On the other hand, we also use MESSAGE in integrating the contribution of the tag with the meaning of the sentence.[10]

For this discussion, we employ the flat declarative semantic representations of Minimal Recursion Semantics (MRS) presented in Copestake et al. 1997. In MRS, lexical entries (and some phrases or constructions) contribute one or more *relations* which are gathered composition-

---

[10]Although tag auxiliaries, and thus tag phrases, will have contentful MESSAGE values, the SOA feature of those messages will come from the sentences the tags modify. This is another reason to see tag phrases as non-clausal.

ally. The collection of relations for a phrase, its LISZT value,[11] is the append of the LISZTs of its daughters, plus any relations contributed by the phrasal schema. These relations are organized in a hierarchy of types to reflect semantically motivated grammatical distinctions, including constraints on complements like the directional locative PP selected by verbs like *put*, and restrictions on the applicability of lexical rules such as the one for causatives. Each sign (word or phrase) identifies one distinguished relation in its LISZT as its KEY relation. The KEY of a phrase is identified with that of its head daughter; this relation is used for semantic subcategorization constraints such as verb-preposition dependencies. The feature MESSAGE takes as its value a relation from the *message* subhierarchy of the relation hierarchy, or else the type *no_rel*, indicating that the sign does not carry a message.

The only semantic contribution a tag makes to its sentence is through its message. In particular, it does not include the auxiliary verb relation of its KEY attribute in its LISZT, as would be the case for other auxiliaries.[12] The additional relation that does appear in the semantics of sentences containing tags is of type *ne_rel*,[13] which is specified as the value of the tag auxiliary's MESSAGE. The type *ne_rel* is a subtype of *int_rel*, which is, in turn, the subtype of *message* that builds questions. This *ne_rel* is differentiated from *int_rel* to reflect its slightly different semantic contribution. While *int_rel* is used for both polar questions and *wh*-questions, the semantic similarity between tag questions and polar questions is captured via the PARAMS feature. In polar and tag questions, the value of PARAMS is the empty set, indicating that they are not parameterized questions (see Ginzburg and Sag 1998).

The semantic contribution of a tag gets into the LISZT of the semantics (CONT) for the full sentence via the same mechanisms used for all MESSAGE values. In particular, the message of a sign gets added to a LISZT if the sign is for the main clause of a sentence or if the sign is selected by a clause-selecting head. Tags on matrix sentences contribute

---

[11]LISZTs are formally interpreted as bags. In the implementation, they are represented as lists, but where nothing makes reference to the order.

[12]In keeping with this conception of the desired meaning for tag questions, the *pron_rel* contributed by the "subject" pronoun in the tag phrase should also not make it onto the LISZT of the sentence as a whole. This could be achieved in a grammar where the semantics of a lexical entry "amalgamated" the contributions of its complements, analogous to the amalgamation for SLASH proposed in Sag 1996. This would mean the semantics of a phrase would only need to draw from the semantics of its head daughter, enabling lexically idiosyncratic suppression of the contribution of a complement daughter, as needed for the subjects of tag auxiliaries.

[13]So named because both German and Japanese have particles similar in function to English tag questions spelled *ne*. As it happens, Potawatomi also has a question particle of the same spelling.

their *ne_rel* via the former mechanism, while tags on sentences embedded under hedge verbs like *suppose* make use of the latter. In both cases the *ne_rel* gets passed from the tag auxiliary to the sign including the sentence and the tag by virtue of the phrasal schemata involved: The nonclausal Head-Complement schema identifies the MESSAGE value of the mother with that of the head daughter, and the Head-Adjunct schema takes the MESSAGE value of the adjunct (semantic head) daughter as that of the mother.[14]

In order for the semantic analysis to be complete, some account should also be given for the intuition that a reversed-polarity tag, at least, conveys some degree of confidence on the part of the speaker of the truth of the clause modified by the tag. The feature CONTEXT could probably be used for this kind of information. However, such an analysis would require both a fuller treatment of contextual information as well as a more detailed understanding of this aspect of the meaning of tags than we have time or space for here. Hence we leave this issue for further development, and focus instead on another important characteristic of tag questions that has not been discussed in previous work.

### 13.4.3 Agreement

The various forms of agreement between the tag and its sentence are captured by letting the tag select for the sentence via its MOD value. Tense agreement is effected by identifying the TENSE values of the auxiliary and the modified sentence (③ in Figure 1). Similarly, the matching between the head of the sentence and the tag auxiliary, illustrated in (6) above, is ensured by unifying the values of the KEY attributes (⑥). We assume that the relation hierarchy is such that all relations contributed by main verbs inherit from a common supertype which is distinct from that for those of auxiliary verbs. Most auxiliaries have a specific value for KEY, so the structure-sharing of the KEYs entails an identical auxiliary in the modified sentence. The auxiliary *do* is special in that its KEY value is the supertype to all main verb relations, and hence will unify with any main verb's relation, but not with that of any other auxiliary verb. As such, it can function in the tag for any sentence headed by a main verb or by *do* itself, but not by any other auxiliary. We see no main verbs in tags because the *tag_lr* only applies to auxiliaries.

The final and most interesting aspect of tag agreement we discuss here is the matching of subjects. Given the structure we have proposed

---

[14]Most modifiers identify their MESSAGE with the MESSAGE of what they modify, but tag auxiliaries and perhaps speaker attitude adverbs like *frankly* or *hopefully* do not.

in (13), the tag phrase modifies a sentence, so the SUBJ attribute of the modified phrase is empty. Under standard assumptions, this means that the information needed by the tag to ensure agreement between its pronoun and the subject of the main clause is not accessible through the tag auxiliary's MOD value. One's first guess in such a situation might be that the agreement is of the usual sort between coreferential pronouns across clauses. However, there is evidence that the relationship is, in Pollard and Sag's (1994) terms, one of coindexing and not of coreference.

First, as discussed above, we take the semantic contribution of the tag to be only its *ne_rel*. It follows that the pronoun should not be contentful.

Second, as noted in Section 13.2, the agreement also applies to expletives:

(14)   There is a meeting, isn't there/*it?

As expletives do not refer in the first place, they presumably cannot corefer either.

Finally, there is evidence from the sort of sentences that Pollard and Sag use to argue for the notion of *index* in the theory of agreement in the first place. In particular, they find examples such as those reproduced in (15) (1994, 73) where one and the same referent can be referred to by expressions with distinct indices, as long as those expressions do not stand in a grammatical anaphoric relation to each other.

(15)   a.   That dog is so ferocious, it even tried to bite itself.
       b.   That dog is so ferocious, he even tried to bite himself.
       c.   *That dog is so ferocious, it even tried to bite himself.
       d.   *That dog is so ferocious, he even tried to bite itself.

Similar examples with tag questions show the same pattern:

(16)   a.   What a little dog.   It certainly is cute, isn't it?
       b.   What a little dog.   He certainly is cute, isn't he?
       c.   What a little dog.   *It certainly is cute, isn't he?
       d.   What a little dog.   *He certainly is cute, isn't it?

We conclude that the relationship between the subject of the sentence and the pronoun in the tag is one of coindexing rather than coreference. This means that information about the subject must be made available at the S node. We would prefer to do this without losing other locality predictions of the current feature geometry.

In fact, such a mechanism has already been proposed by Kathol (in press). Kathol examines a wide range of morphosyntactic data from German and the Romance languages and concludes that both agreeing elements (e.g., subject NP and verb) should bear an AGR feature, and further that this is a HEAD feature. This account of agreement differs from that developed in Chapter 2 of Pollard and Sag 1994 in two ways. First, on Pollard and Sag's account, verbs do not bear an AGR feature of their own. Rather, they record their agreement specifications by constraining certain features of the nouns they select for. Second, Pollard and Sag argue that, in the case of English, all agreement phenomena can be accounted for with the *index* as the single locus of agreement.[15] While Kathol finds evidence to distinguish two kinds of agreement in other languages, he maintains Pollard and Sag's analysis of English by stipulating that all nouns in English identify (the relevant sub-features of) their INDEX and AGR values.

In investigating a precise account of tag questions, we find evidence from English for an account similar to Kathol's[16] on both dimensions in which it differs from that of Pollard and Sag 1994.

First, the coindexing found in tag questions supports the position that AGR is a head feature of verbs as well as of nouns. Once we place the constraint shown in (17) on the type *verb_synsem*, we have the necessary information about the subject available at the S level.

(17)
$$
\begin{bmatrix}
verb\_synsem \\
\text{LOCAL} \begin{bmatrix} \text{CAT | HEAD} \begin{bmatrix} verb \\ \text{AGR} \quad \boxed{1} \end{bmatrix} \\ \text{ARG-ST | FIRST | LOCAL | CAT | HEAD | AGR} \quad \boxed{1} \end{bmatrix}
\end{bmatrix}
$$

The next question to ask is, how much information about the subject must be passed up by the AGR feature? Here, the behavior of expletives in tags is illuminating:

(18)  a.  There is a meeting, isn't there?
　　　b.  *There is a meeting, isn't it/he?
　　　c.  *He's here, isn't it/there?

Given Pollard and Sag's (1994) view of nominal indices, propagating the (typed) index of the subject allows us to block sentences like (18a,b) while still allowing ones like (18a) because expletives are distinguished from each other and from referential NPs by their index types:

(19)

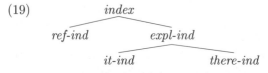

---

There is also evidence for distinguishing AGR and INDEX even in English. So far we have seen that tag questions must attach to a matrix S, and that a succinct and precise analysis can be given by treating tags as modifiers that select for this matrix S via their MOD value. Information about the subject of the modified sentence must be available in order for the tag to ensure matching between the subjects, and this is effected by the *index*-valued AGR feature. Against this background, we present evidence for distinguishing two kinds of agreement in English. Consider (10a), repeated here:

(20)   Everyone wins, don't they?

In its agreement with *everyone*, *they* is apparently singular, but in its agreement with *don't*, *they* is apparently plural. That is, one token is showing two different agreement patterns simultaneously. We can only conclude that English does have two different kinds of agreement, and argue that the distinction must be represented in the grammar.

In light of the relevance of indices to tag agreement, we propose that subject-verb agreement in English be constrained via the syntactic feature AGR, though for most nouns the value of AGR will be identified with that of the INDEX, resulting in the agreement properties given by Pollard and Sag (1994).

In order to capture the example in (20), we propose that there are two lexemes *they*. One is the ordinary *they*, which like most English nouns, identifies its AGR and INDEX values.

$$(21) \quad \begin{bmatrix} they\_1 \\ \dots \mid \text{AGR} \quad \boxed{1} \\ \dots \mid \text{INDEX} \quad \boxed{1} \begin{bmatrix} \text{NUM} & pl \\ \text{PERS} & 3 \end{bmatrix} \end{bmatrix}$$

The other *they* is the one found in sentences like (20). It is unusual in having distinct AGR and INDEX values.[17]

---

[17]This *they* has been in the language since at least the time of Shakespeare (Bodine 1975), as shown by the following example from *Much Ado About Nothing*, Act 3, Scene 4:

(i)       MARGARET:     Nothing I; but God send every one their
                      heart's desire!

(22)
$$\begin{bmatrix} they\_2 \\ \\ \ldots \mid \text{AGR} \quad \begin{bmatrix} \text{NUM} & pl \\ \text{PERS} & 3 \end{bmatrix} \\ \\ \ldots \mid \text{INDEX} \quad \begin{bmatrix} \text{NUM} & sg \\ \text{GEND} & andro \\ \text{PERS} & 3 \end{bmatrix} \end{bmatrix}$$

*They_2* is specified as [ GENDER *andro* ] (for 'androgynous', distinct from *neuter*). This makes it compatible with words like the pro-form *everyone*,[18] but not others, such as *he*, so the grammar accepts example (20) while still correctly blocking (23):

(23)  *He wins, don't they?

As illustrated in Figure 3, the final piece of the analysis of (20) is that the tag auxiliary identifies its subject's INDEX value with the AGR value of the clause the tag modifies (④), which in turn is identified with the AGR value of the subject of that clause. This, in turn, is usually identified with the INDEX of that subject. At the same time, the tag behaves like any other verb in identifying its own AGR value with its subject's (③), ensuring plural agreement morphology with the gender-neutral *they* subject.

This analysis extends easily to cover examples involving binding of anaphora such as (24). As binding is taken to be identification of indices, we expect to find the gender-neutral *they* able to be bound by *everyone*, since the INDEX value for both is [ NUMBER *sg* ].

(24)  Everyone thinks they're happy.

The alignment of binding with tag agreement supports the choice of the more semantic INDEX feature for these as opposed to the more syntactic AGR feature for subject-verb agreement.

## 13.5  Summary

We have found that the pursuit of a precise account of tag questions and gender-neutral *they* has led us to insights on the basic phenomenon of agreement in English which would not be apparent from core con-

---

[18]The value for the feature GENDER on *everyone* should be *human*, supertype to *masculine*, *feminine*, and *andro*. This is because (i) and (ii) are both grammatical and natural, especially when the group relevant to the interpretation of *everyone* is all male or all female, respectively:

(i)    Everyone$_i$ thinks he$_i$ will win.
(ii)   Everyone$_i$ thinks she$_i$ will win.

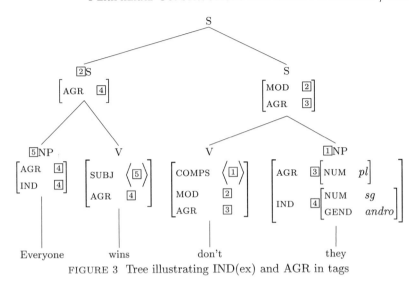

FIGURE 3  Tree illustrating IND(ex) and AGR in tags

structions alone. We believe that this is not an isolated case, but rather illustrative of a more general point: the idiosyncrasies of peripheral constructions will illuminate basic aspects of grammar which are underdetermined by the well-studied, core phenomena.

## References

Bodine, Ann. 1975. Androcentrism in Prescriptive Grammar: Singular 'they', Sex-Indefinite 'he', and 'he or she'. *Language in Society* 4:129–146.

Copestake, Ann, Daniel Flickinger, and Ivan A. Sag. 1997. Minimal Recursion Semantics: An Introduction. ms., Stanford University.

Culicover, Peter. 1992. English Tag Questions in Universal Grammar. *Lingua* 88:193–226.

Emonds, Joseph. 1976. *A Transformational Approach to English Syntax*. New York: Academic Press.

Gazdar, Gerald, Geoffrey Pullum, and Ivan A. Sag. 1982. Auxiliaries and Related Phenomena in a Restricted Theory of Grammar. *Language* 58:591–638.

Ginzburg, Jonathan, and Ivan A. Sag. 1998. English Interrogative Constructions. ms., Hebrew University of Jerusalem and Stanford University.

Hudson, Richard A. 1975. The Meaning of Questions. *Language* 51:1–32.

Kathol, Andreas. in press. Agreement and the Syntax-Morphology Interface in HPSG. In *Readings in HPSG*, ed. R. Levine and G. Green. Cambridge: Cambridge University Press.

Kay, Paul. 1995. Construction Grammar. In *Handbook of Pragmatics: Manual*, ed. J. Verschueren, J.-O. Ostman, and J. Blommaert. Amsterdam: John

Benjamins.

Kim, Jong-Bok, and Ivan A. Sag. 1995. The Parametric Variation in English and French Negation. In *Proceedings of the West Coast Conference on Formal Linguistics*, ed. Jose Camacho et al., 303–318. Stanford. CSLI.

Klima, Edward S. 1964. Negation in English. In *The Structure of Language*, ed. J. Fodor and J. Katz. Englewood Cliffs, NJ: Prentice Hall.

Pollard, Carl, and Ivan A. Sag. 1994. *Head-Driven Phrase Structure Grammar*. Chicago: Chicago University Press.

Rochemont, Michael, and Peter Culicover. 1990. *English Focus Constructions and the Theory of Grammar*. Cambridge: Cambridge University Press.

Sag, Ivan A. 1996. Constraint-Based Extraction (without a Trace). *Korean Journal of Linguistics* 21:57–91.

Sag, Ivan A. 1997. English Relative Clause Constructions. *Journal of Linguistics* 33(2):431–484.

Warner, Anthony. 1993. *English Auxiliaries: Structure and History*. Cambridge: Cambridge University Press.

# 14

# Locus Agreement in American Sign Language

KEARSY CORMIER, STEPHEN WECHSLER, AND
RICHARD P. MEIER

## 14.1 Introduction

For the past several years, syntacticians have used HPSG to analyze
many of the world's spoken languages. Recent analyses of signed languages have been based largely on Government and Binding theory
(Aarons, Bahan, Kegl & Neidle 1992, Bahan 1996, Lillo-Martin 1986,
Lillo-Martin 1991); no work has been done on a signed language within
a constraint-based grammar. Like many spoken languages, signed languages typically have rich morphological agreement systems. In this
paper we use HPSG to shed new light on the agreement properties of
one particular signed language, American Sign Language (ASL). One
consequence of this study is that it may lend support to the theory of
index agreement due to Pollard and Sag (1994).

ASL is a natural language used by most deaf people in the United
States and Canada. For deaf children of deaf parents, ASL is generally
acquired just as naturally as any spoken language (Newport & Meier
1985, Meier 1991). For deaf children of hearing parents, ASL is acquired
through contact with other children at residential schools for the deaf.
ASL shares characteristics with many spoken languages. It is a topic-
oriented language much like Chinese (cf. Lillo-Martin 1991) and has a

This research is supported in part by a grant (R01 DC01691-05) from the National
Institute on Deafness and Other Communication Disorders, National Institutes of
Health, to RPM. All original illustrations by Tony McGregor (copyright RPM).
Thanks to Gene Mirus for his native signer intuitions and to Perry Connolly, the
model for the illustrations. We thank Karen Emmorey, Carol Neidle, and Ben Ba-
han for their comments on an earlier draft of this paper.

*Lexical and Constructional Aspects of Linguistic Explanation.*
Gert Webelhuth, Jean-Pierre Koenig, and Andreas Kathol.
Copyright © 1998, Stanford University.

classifier system comparable to Navajo's (Klima & Bellugi 1979). ASL is typically SVO, but due to its agreement inflection, many other word orders are possible (Fischer 1975).

## 14.2 Description of ASL

### 14.2.1 Lexical Items

Loosely speaking, a manual sign (i.e., a lexical item) in ASL consists of a particular handshape, a location, a movement, and a palm orientation. Some signs maintain the same general handshape and location throughout the articulation of the sign. Other signs involve changes in handshape and/or movement and/or location. For example, the verb LIKE starts with a 5 handshape (all 5 fingers extended and spread) at or contacting the center of the chest, and closes to an 8 handshape (contact between middle finger and thumb, with other fingers extended) in the neutral space in front of the chest. (Neutral space consists of the area in front of the signer's torso, within approximately a forearm's length from the body.) This distinct change of location from the signer's chest to neutral space in front of the signer is an example of path movement, a feature of many ASL signs including LIKE. Path movement will be relevant to our description of agreement morphology below.

### 14.2.2 Nouns

Before looking at the verbal system of ASL, it is important to understand how nominals are signed in space. An NP can consist of a noun by itself (e.g., BOY),[1] or a pronominal pointing sign as shown in Figure 1.[2] When a pointing sign occurs in a construction with a noun, it functions as a determiner instead of a pronoun (Bahan 1996). The determiner can occur immediately before the noun, immediately after it (see Figure 2), or perhaps even concurrently with the noun if that noun is one-handed.[3]

The pointing sign ($_x$PT), whether functioning as a pronoun or determiner, acts as a discourse marker. By using a pointing sign, a signer can associate a noun or a pronoun with a distinct location in space. Any subsequent signs that point to a location established in this manner are interpreted as being coreferential. If the referent is physically

---

[1] As is conventional in ASL literature, English glosses appear in small caps.

[2] $_x$PT is a pointing sign, with x being the location toward which the point is directed. In the illustrations containing more than one lexical sign, the dotted lines indicate the sign that is articulated first, followed by the sign shown in solid lines.

[3] Other researchers have claimed that pointing signs occurring before the noun function as determiners, while pointing signs occurring after the noun function adverbially (Bahan et al. 1995, Bahan 1996, MacLaughlin 1997). However, we will assume for the purposes of this paper that both prenominal and postnominal pointing signs can function as determiners.

Figure 1

₁PT
'he/she/it'

Figure 2

BOY  ₁PT
boy  the
'the boy'

present, the signer points to its location. If the referent is not present, the signer may arbitrarily choose a location in neutral space for it.[4] These locations remain throughout the discourse until actively changed (Lillo-Martin 1986).

### 14.2.3   Verb Agreement

Some verbs in ASL, called agreement verbs, make use of the association between NPs and distinct locations (Padden 1983). Since ASL lacks case marking and word order is fairly free, the agreement morphology on the verb is often what identifies the subject and object. These verbs generally distinguish subject and object locations in one of two ways: i) through palm orientation or ii) through path movement between locations. STARE-AT is a verb that shows agreement through changes in palm orientation. In this sign, the palm is oriented toward the location associated with the object NP and the back of the hand is oriented toward the location associated with the subject NP. Subject and object can also be distinguished by differences in the location of the verb. Verbs such as HELP have path movement that begins with the location associated with the subject NP and ends with the location associated with the object NP, as in Figure 4 where the subject and object NPs refer to signer and addressee, respectively. The $S$ and $A$ subscripts on HELP indicate that the verb is marked for subject agreement with the signer and object agreement with the addressee (Figure 3).

Agreement verbs fall into two subclasses, referred to as single-agreement and double-agreement verbs (Meier 1982, Padden 1983). Single-agreement verbs agree only with the object, while double-agreement verbs can agree with both the subject and object.[5] For example, HELP is a double-agreement verb and agrees with its subject and object, as in Figure 4. SEE (Figure 5) is a single-agreement verb; it agrees only with its object. (The lack of an initial subscript on SEE in Figure 5 indicates that this verb is not marked for subject agreement.) Single-agreement verbs tend to be body-anchored. That is, their articulation begins on the signer's body. It is not possible for the initial location of such a verb to match the location of the subject (i.e., $*_i$SEE$_j$). However, some single agreement verbs are not body-anchored (e.g., TEACH, for some signers).

---

[4]Other researchers have claimed that there are other factors that determine where a locus is established in signing space (e.g., discourse factors, semantic affinity with another referent, conventional location, etc.). Thus, the establishment of loci is rarely arbitrary (Engberg-Pedersen 1993).

[5]Double-agreement verbs agree with the notional indirect object if there is one (e.g., GIVE). If there is no indirect object, the verb agrees with the direct object (e.g., HELP).

Figure 3

<sub>S</sub>PT    <sub>S</sub>HELP<sub>A</sub>
I        I-help-you
'I help you.'


Figure 4

<sub>i</sub>PT    <sub>i</sub>HELP<sub>j</sub>
she    she-help-him
'She helps him.'

Figure 5

iPT    SEEj
she    see-him
'She sees him.'

This suggests that the verb classes (see 10 below) are not completely predictable on the basis of phonological form.

Figure 6a                    Figure 6b

iHELPj                       iPT    iHELPj
she-help-him                 she    she-help-him
'She helps him.'                 'She helps him.'

These two subclasses both allow subject pro-drop. In both Figures

6a and 6b, for example, the verb HELP begins at the location of the subject and ends with the location of the object. The overt subject pronoun in Figure 6b is optional.

Subject pro-drop for single-agreement verbs patterns closely with pro-drop in Chinese. That is, because both ASL and Chinese are topic-prominent languages (versus subject-prominent languages like English), overt subjects are not required if the topic (usually the subject) is clear from context (Lillo-Martin 1991).

Both single-agreement verbs and double-agreement verbs allow object pro-drop. Thus, examples (7a–d) are grammatical.

(7)  a.  $_i$PT $_i$HELP$_j$
     b.  $_i$PT $_i$HELP$_j$ $_j$PT
     c.  $_i$PT SEE$_j$
     d.  $_i$PT SEE$_j$ $_j$PT

The contexts in which overt object pronouns may be favored over non-overt object pronouns (and vice-versa) is not clear; we leave this issue for further research.

So far only third-person translations for the $i$ and $j$ indices have been used. Signer/addressee agreement works exactly the same way as third person agreement shown above.[6] The only difference is that for every signer, there is a particular location associated with the signer him/herself, and likewise for every addressee there is a particular location that is associated with the addressee, as illustrated in Figure 8 and in (9).[7]

(9)    $_A$PT $_A$HELP$_S$.
       You you-help-me
       'You help me.'

Agreement verbs make up one of three major classes of verbs in ASL: plain verbs, spatial verbs, and agreement verbs (Padden 1983).

(10)  Types of ASL Verbs
         I. plain
         II. spatial
         III. agreement
              a. single (e.g., SEE)
              b. double (e.g., HELP)

---

[6]Since the status of person in ASL is a matter of some controversy (Meier 1990, Lillo-Martin & Klima 1990), "first person" and "second person" will not be used when referring to the speaker and addressee loci. "Third person" here simply means a location not associated with the speaker or addressee.

[7]Some verbs (e.g., FINGERSPELL-TO, & TEACH for some signers) lack a first-person object form. For such verbs speaker agreement would need to be precluded.

Figure 8

sPT    sHELPₐ
I      I-help-you
'I help you.'

Plain verbs show no agreement with the subject or the object; these verbs require overt subject and object arguments. An example of a plain verb is LIKE, as described above in 14.2.1. Spatial verbs are verbs of motion and show agreement with locations associated with the initial and final positions of motion, *not* with the subject or object. Spatial verbs are a complex issue and beyond the scope of this paper.

In summary, agreement verbs in ASL involve either i) a distinct palm orientation in which the palm faces away from one location and toward another location, or ii) path movement from one location to another. For double-agreement verbs, these locations must be the subject location and the object location, respectively.[8] For single-agreement verbs, the final location must be associated with the object.

## 14.3 HPSG Analysis of ASL Agreement

Agreement in HPSG depends on structure-sharing of the index value of one expression with the index value of another expression. For most spoken languages, these index values must include some combination of the categories person, number and gender. But as we have seen in the

---

[8]The reverse is true of a subclass of double agreement verbs called *backwards verbs* (Meir, in press). For these verbs, the initial location must be associated with the object and the final location with the subject. Examples include TAKE and BORROW.

above description, ASL agreement depends heavily on location, or *locus*. Therefore I propose the following sort declaration for *index*:[9]

(11)  *index*: [LOCUS *locus*]
      Partition of *locus*: *S, A, other*
      Partition of *other*: *i, j, k, ...*

Following Meier 1990, *S* and *A* will be used to refer to locations associated with the signer and addressee, respectively. *S* (signer) is the location directly in front of the signer's chest. *A* (addressee) is the location within the signer's own sign space but toward and associated with the addressee. The index values *i, j, k, ...* represent distinct locations in neutral space.

### 14.3.1  Verbal Lexical Entries

The lexical entry for an agreement verb stem specifies only the ARG-ST list (not the SUBJ and COMPS list) and coindexes the NPs with their appropriate semantic roles in CONTENT. Thus the lexical entry represents the verb stem, unmarked for any agreement morphology. Each lexical entry simply gives the valence features of the verb and cross-references those valence features with the semantic roles that the verb takes. The lexical entries also assign verbs to their appropriate agreement types, so that SEE is of the sort *single-agr-vstem*, and HELP is of the sort *double-agr-vstem*.

(12)  Lexical entry for SEE:

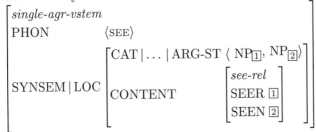

---

[9]ASL also has number agreement, which may also be explained to a certain extent in terms of locus agreement. However, this issue needs to be further analyzed.

(13)   Lexical entry for HELP:

$$
\begin{bmatrix}
double\text{-}agr\text{-}vstem \\
\text{PHON} \qquad \langle \text{HELP} \rangle \\
\text{SYNSEM} \,|\, \text{LOC}
\begin{bmatrix}
\text{CAT} \,|\, \dots \,|\, \text{ARG-ST} \; \langle \text{NP}_{\boxed{1}},\ \text{NP}_{\boxed{2}} \rangle \\
\text{CONTENT}
\begin{bmatrix}
help\text{-}rel \\
\text{HELPER} \; \boxed{1} \\
\text{HELPEE} \; \boxed{2}
\end{bmatrix}
\end{bmatrix}
\end{bmatrix}
$$

## 14.3.2   Verbal Sort Declarations

To account for the pro-drop patterns mentioned above in 14.2.3, each type of verb has a sort declaration that specifies valence features of all possible surface forms. Below are the sort declarations for single-agreement and double-agreement verbs.

(14)   Sort declaration for *single-agr-verb* (e.g., SEE$_j$):

$$
\begin{bmatrix}
\text{PHON} \quad F_{single}(\boxed{3}, y) \\
\text{SYNSEM} \; \boxed{4} \,|\, \dots \,|\, \text{CAT}
\begin{bmatrix}
\text{VAL}
\begin{bmatrix}
\text{SUBJ} \quad \langle (\boxed{1}\text{NP}) \rangle \\
\text{COMPS} \; \langle (\boxed{2}\text{NP}) \rangle
\end{bmatrix} \\
\text{ARG-ST} \; \langle \boxed{1}\text{NP},\ \boxed{2}\text{NP}_{[\text{LOCUS } y]} \rangle
\end{bmatrix} \\
\text{STEM}
\begin{bmatrix}
single\text{-}agr\text{-}vstem \\
\text{PHON} \quad \boxed{3} \\
\text{SYNSEM} \; \boxed{4}
\end{bmatrix}
\end{bmatrix}
$$

where $F_{single}(\alpha, \beta) = \alpha_\beta$

(15)   Sort declaration for *double-agr-verb* (e.g., $_i$HELP$_j$):

$$
\begin{bmatrix}
\text{PHON} \; F_{double}(x, \boxed{3}, y) \\
\text{SS'M} \quad \boxed{4} \,|\, \dots \,|\, \text{CAT}
\begin{bmatrix}
\text{VAL}
\begin{bmatrix}
\text{SUBJ} \quad \langle (\boxed{1}\text{NP}) \rangle \\
\text{COMPS} \; \langle (\boxed{2}\text{NP}) \rangle
\end{bmatrix} \\
\text{ARG-ST} \; \langle \boxed{1}\text{NP}_{[\text{LOCUS } x]},\ \boxed{2}\text{NP}_{[\text{LOCUS } y]} \rangle
\end{bmatrix} \\
\text{STEM}
\begin{bmatrix}
double\text{-}agr\text{-}vstem \\
\text{PHON} \quad \boxed{3} \\
\text{SYNSEM} \; \boxed{4}
\end{bmatrix}
\end{bmatrix}
$$

where $F_{double}(\alpha, \beta, \gamma) =_\alpha \beta_\gamma$

These sort declarations expand the lexical entries for the verbs.[10] For both single and double-agreement verbs, the SUBJ list member as well as the first member of the COMPS list are optional. Unexpressed ARG-ST list items (those which are not structure-shared with valence list items) are interpreted as pronouns.

The functions $F_{single}$ and $F_{double}$ specify the morphological operations whereby loci associated with ARG-ST list items are affixed to the verb. The $x$ and $y$ tags represent items of sort *locus*, hence range over the full set of loci, $\{S, A, i, j, k, \ldots\}$. Thus, these sort declarations account for agreement with any locus. No separate specifications are needed for speaker and addressee agreement.

### 14.3.3 Origins of Locus Values

As mentioned above, NPs can be set up in space whether or not the referent is present. If the referent is present, the locus of the pronoun or determiner *must* correspond to the actual location of the referent. We can set up a separate restriction on the anchoring of indices to handle this; however, we will not examine this issue here.

If the referent is not present, then loci are set up arbitrarily.[11] In this case, the index values originate within the CONTENT of the pointing sign $_i$PT (whether it functions as a pronoun or a determiner), not within the CONTENT of the noun; cf. (16) and (17).

(16)  Lexical entry for pronoun/determiner $_i$PT:

$$
\begin{bmatrix}
\text{PHON} & \langle _i\text{PT} \rangle \\
\text{SYNSEM} \,|\, \text{LOC} &
\begin{bmatrix}
\text{CAT} &
\begin{bmatrix}
\text{HEAD } noun \\
\text{VAL} &
\begin{bmatrix}
\text{SUBJ} & \langle \, \rangle \\
\text{COMPS} & \langle (\text{NP}[\boxed{3}]npro) \rangle \\
\text{SPR} & \langle \, \rangle
\end{bmatrix}
\end{bmatrix} \\
\text{CONTENT} &
\begin{bmatrix}
\text{INDEX} & \boxed{2}[\text{LOCUS } i] \\
\text{RESTR} & \{\boxed{3}[\text{INST } \boxed{2}]\}
\end{bmatrix}
\end{bmatrix}
\end{bmatrix}
$$

---

[10] Other factors such as eye gaze, shift in body position, and other non-manual signals also play a part in ASL verb agreement (cf. Aarons et al. 1992). However, given the high degree of subtlety and variation associated with these non-manual signals, only manual information is included in the verbal sort declarations in this paper.

[11] See Footnote 4.

(17)   Lexical entry for the noun BOY:

$$\begin{bmatrix} \text{PHON } \langle \text{BOY} \rangle \\ \text{SYNSEM} \,|\ldots|\, \text{CONTENT} \begin{bmatrix} \textit{nom-obj} \\ \text{RELN } \textit{boy} \end{bmatrix} \end{bmatrix}$$

(18)   Sort declaration for *npro*:

$$\textit{npro:} \begin{bmatrix} \text{RELN } \textit{rel} \\ \text{INST } \textit{index} \end{bmatrix}$$

(19)   Sort declaration for *ppro*:

$$\textit{ppro:} \begin{bmatrix} \text{INDEX } \textit{index} \\ \text{RESTR } \textit{set(psoa)} \end{bmatrix}$$

The index, and hence the locus feature, lexically originates in the pronoun, while the common noun supplies only the relation (here, the *boy* relation). This means that an NP consisting of a noun without a determiner either lacks a locus value altogether or receives its locus in some manner other than through the determiner.[12] In example (20b), we have assumed that no mechanism (pointing or otherwise) has assigned a locus value to the noun BOY.

To summarize, if ₁PT subcategorizes for a nonpronoun complement, then it is a determiner. If, on the other hand, ₁PT does not subcategorize for a complement, then it functions as a pronoun. Therefore the lexical entries in (16) and (17) allow for three main types of NPs, shown in (20).

(20)   Possible NPs in ASL

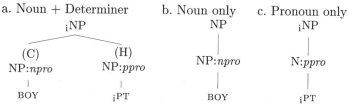

a. Noun + Determiner     b. Noun only     c. Pronoun only

## 14.4   Conclusions

The analysis presented here accounts for the basic agreement properties of ASL verbs. The verbal sort declarations account for the pro-drop properties described above by allowing for different combinations of overt and non-overt pronominal arguments. The agreement functions specify

[12]Other methods of assigning a noun a locus value, apart from the use of a determiner, include body shift (i.e., shifting the body toward a locus), eye gaze (i.e., gazing at a certain location in space), and articulating the noun at a certain location in neutral space (this is particularly true of fingerspelled names and is not possible with body-anchored nouns).

the index value of certain members of the ARG-ST list, regardless of the overt/non-overt nature of the arguments. These functions ensure that the locus values of the verb are token identical to the locus values of the verb's arguments.

This analysis lends support to Pollard & Sag's (1994) account of index agreement, according to which agreement features attach to the index or discourse marker. The ASL locus functions exactly as a discourse marker (see Lillo-Martin & Klima 1990), even though locus is not normally considered a phi-feature like the other agreement features of person, number and gender. The fact that locus participates in verb agreement provides interesting evidence for index agreement.

Also, the fact that locus functions as a phi-feature in ASL but not in any spoken language suggests that phi-features as we know them are not universal. In order to encompass both signed and spoken languages, the inventory of phi-features would therefore need to be expanded to include these spatial loci.

Although ASL does share many characteristics with spoken languages, there are many differences as well. One difference is the number of possible values for agreement features in spoken languages versus locus in ASL. Person, number, and gender each consist of a finite set of values. ASL can have an infinite number of possible locus values (Lillo-Martin 1991, Meier 1990). The number of loci that a signer might actually use is limited by perceptual and memory-related constraints, but theoretically an infinite number of loci is possible.

Turning to another point of comparison with spoken languages, ASL agreement appears to violate Greenberg's (1966) markedness universal, according to which subject agreement is less marked than object agreement (see also Everett 1996). While ASL has both subject and object agreement (and thus accords with Greenberg's claim that languages with object agreement also have subject agreement), ASL object agreement is less marked in the sense that some verbs have only object agreement but none have only subject agreement. This unexpected and quite interesting difference between ASL and spoken languages still awaits an explanation.

The question of whether this and other peculiarities of ASL can be attributed to modality (signed versus spoken) will be answered by comparing agreement systems in other signed languages. We leave this matter for future research (see Engberg-Pedersen 1993 and Supalla (In prep) on agreement verbs in non-ASL signed languages such as Danish Sign Language).

## 14.5 Appendix: Notation

The subscripts *S, A, i, j, k,* etc. represent distinct locations in space—see (11). Verbs are translated in present tense for clarity. ASL does mark aspect and can mark tense, but often tense is not marked if it is understood in context. Also, different genders are used here to distinguish between different locations, although ASL does not grammatically distinguish gender.

VERB    A verb unmarked for agreement; verb stem
$_x$VERB$_y$    A verb marked for subject and object agreement.
VERB$_y$    A verb marked for only object agreement.

## References

Aarons, Debra, Ben Bahan, Judy Kegl, and Carol Neidle. 1992. Clausal Structure and a Tier for Grammatical Marking in American Sign Language. *Nordic Journal of Linguistics* 15.103–142.

Bahan, Ben. 1996. *Non-Manual Realization of Agreement in American Sign Language*. Doctoral dissertation, Boston University.

Bahan, Ben, Judy Kegl, Dawn MacLaughlin, and Carol Neidle. 1995. Convergent Evidence for the Structure of Determiner Phrases in American Sign Language, in L. Gabriele, D. Hardison and R. Westmoreland, eds., *Proceedings of the Sixth Annual Meeting of the Formal Linguistics Society of Mid-America*, Volume Two. Bloomington, IN: Indiana University Linguistics Club Publications, 1–12.

Engberg-Pedersen, Elisabeth. 1993. *Space in Danish Sign Language: The Semantics and Morphosyntax of the Use of Space in a Visual Language.* (International Studies on Sign Language and Communication for the Deaf 19). Hamburg: Signum.

Everett, Daniel. 1996. *Why There Are No Clitics.* Dallas: Summer Institute of Linguistics.

Fischer, Susan. 1975. Influences on Word Order Change in American Sign Language, in C. Li, ed., *Word Order and Word Order Change.* Austin: University of Texas Press, 1–25.

Greenberg, Joseph. 1966. *Language Universals, with Special Reference to Feature Hierarchies.* The Hague: Mouton.

Klima, Edward and Ursula Bellugi. 1979. *The Signs of Language.* Cambridge, MA: Harvard University Press.

Lillo-Martin, Diane and Edward Klima. 1990. Pointing Out Differences: ASL Pronouns in Syntactic Theory, in S. Fischer and P. Siple, eds., *Theoretical Issues in Sign Language Research: Vol. 1: Linguistics.* Chicago: University of Chicago Press, 191–210.

Lillo-Martin, Diane. 1986. Two Kinds of Null Arguments in American Sign Language. *Natural Language and Linguistic Theory* 4.415–444.

Lillo-Martin, Diane. 1991. *Universal Grammar and American Sign Language.* Boston: Kluwer.

MacLaughlin, Dawn. 1997. *The Structure of Determiner Phrases: Evidence from American Sign Language.* Doctoral dissertation, Boston University, Boston, MA.

Meier, Richard P. 1982. *Icons, Analogues and Morphemes: The Aquisition of Verb Agreement in ASL.* Doctoral dissertation, University of California, San Diego.

Meier, Richard P. 1990. Person Deixis in ASL, in S. Fischer and P. Siple, eds., *Theoretical Issues in Sign Language Research: Vol.1: Linguistics.* Chicago: University of Chicago Press, 175–190.

Meier, Richard P. 1991. Language Acquisition by Deaf Children. *American Scientist* 79:60–70.

Meir, Irit. In press. Syntactic-Semantic Interaction in Israeli Sign Language Verbs: The Case of Backwards Verbs. *International Journal of Sign Linguistics.*

Newport, Elissa L. and Richard P. Meier. 1985. The Acquisition of American Sign Language, in D. Slobin, ed., *The Crosslinguistic Study of Language Acquisition. Volume 1: The Data.* Hillsdale, NJ: Lawrence Erlbaum, 881-938.

Padden, Carol. 1983. *Interaction of Morphology and Syntax in American Sign Language.* Doctoral dissertation, University of California, San Diego.

Pollard, Carl and Ivan Sag. 1994. *Head-Driven Phrase Structure Grammar.* Chicago: University of Chicago Press.

Supalla, Ted. In prep. An Implicational Hierarchy in Verb Agreement in American Sign Language. Unpublished manuscript. University of Rochester, Rochester, NY.

Wilbur, Ronnie. 1994. Foregrounding Structures in American Sign Language. *Journal of Pragmatics* 22.647–672.

# 15

---

# On Case Assignment and "Adjuncts as Complements"

Adam Przepiórkowski

## 15.1 Introduction

Pollard and Sag (1994) say that in HPSG, "[t]here is no separate theory of case (or Case). Nominative case assignment takes place directly within the lexical entry of the finite verb." However, they add in a footnote that "for languages with more complex case systems, some sort of distinction analogous to the one characterized in GB work as 'inherent' vs. 'structural' is required." In fact, many HPSG accounts of various phenomena from various languages assume just such a distinction.[1]

The aim of this paper is twofold: to present a general technique of case assignment in HPSG avoiding various problems of previous accounts, and to show that case assignment facts provide strong evidence for the "Adjuncts as Complements" (AasC) approach to modification.

We present some motivation for a separate case module and mention several problems with previous accounts in Section 15.2. Then, in Section 15.3 we put forward our proposal, which is free from these flaws. In Section 15.4, we show that, assuming AasC, this approach deals easily with case assignment to adverbials. Finally, in Section 15.5 we argue that no other combination of case assignment / modification approaches in the current HPSG literature can deal with the adverbial data in a straightforward way.

I am grateful to the audiences of Marseilles'96 and Ithaca'97 for useful comments. The work presented in this paper was partly supported by the Polish Committee for Scientific Research (KBN) grant 8 T11C 011 10.

[1]For lack of space, we cannot extensively discuss previous HPSG analyses of case assignment here, but see Przepiórkowski In preparation for such a discussion.

*Lexical and Constructional Aspects of Linguistic Explanation.*
Gert Webelhuth, Jean-Pierre Koenig, and Andreas Kathol.
Copyright © 1998, Stanford University.

## 15.2  Case Assignment in HPSG

### 15.2.1  Why?

Why do we need a separate case module in HPSG at all? The bulk of
the motivation in the HPSG work on case assignment has roughly the
same form: there are certain case alternations which would be difficult
(if not impossible) to account for without the notion of syntactic (structural) case assigned in the syntax rather than in the lexicon. By way of
example, consider German (1) from Pollard 1994:

(1)   a.   [Den  Wagen zu reparieren] wurde    versucht.
           the$_{acc}$ car    to repair       pass-pst tried
           'One tried to repair the car.'
      b.   [Zu reparieren versucht] wurde    der     Wagen lange Zeit.
           to repair       tried       pass-pst the$_{nom}$ car     long  time
           'One has been trying to repair the car for a long time.'

Subject-controlled equi verbs such as *versuchen* are assumed to optionally attract the arguments of their verbal complements, i.e., they subcategorize either for a phrase VP[*inf*], or for a word V[*inf*] and all the
arguments of this word. (1a) illustrates the former case: it is the VP[*inf*]
complement of *versucht* that becomes the subject of the passive construction. On the other hand, in (1b), *versucht* subcategorizes for the
infinitive verb *zu reparieren* and for its NP complement, which becomes
the subject *der Wagen* of the passive.

Now, assuming case assignment in the lexicon only, as in Pollard and
Sag 1994 (henceforth, PS'94), what should the case specification of the
NP complement in the lexical entry for *reparieren* be? It cannot be the
nominative (it is accusative in (1a)), but it also cannot be the accusative
(it is nominative in (1b)). Leaving the case of NPs on infinitive verbs
unspecified in the hope that these NPs will be raised and their case will
be resolved by a finite verb (Pollard 1994) does not work either: the
complement of the infinitive *reparieren* in (1a) is never raised, and yet
it unambiguously receives the accusative.

What seems needed to account for cases like these is a syntactic case
principle assigning case to arguments on the basis of their syntactic realization: *den Wagen* in (1a) receives the accusative because it is realized
as a direct object, while *der Wagen* in (1b) gets the nominative because
it is the surface subject.

### 15.2.2  How?

The clearest and most influential HPSG case theory is that of Heinz and
Matiasek 1994 (henceforth, HM'94). Their account (based on German)
consists of three parts. First, a sort hierarchy for *case* specifies that, syn-

tactically speaking, there are *structural* cases and *lexical* cases, with a particular morphological case being either always structural (e.g., nominative in German), always lexical (e.g., dative), or ambiguous between the two (e.g., genitive). For example, HM'94 posit a case hierarchy as in (2).

(2)

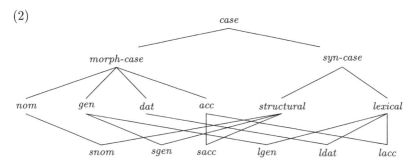

Second, lexical entries subcategorize either for specific lexical NPs (e.g., lexical genitive), or for underspecified structural NPs. For example, the SUBCAT specification of the lexical entry for *helfen* 'help' is $\langle NP[structural], NP[ldat]\rangle$.

Third, a configurational constraint (Case Principle) resolves structural cases to specific morphological cases on the basis of their syntactic realization. For example, one clause of the Case Principle of HM'94 says that for any Head-Subject Schema, if the subject daughter is a structural NP, it must be nominative. See HM'94 for details.

### 15.2.3 Problems

There are two theory-internal problems with the case theory summarized above. The first is noted by Pollard (1994), who tentatively considers a case principle similar to that of HM'94: such a principle would be against the "traditional aversion within HPSG theory to tree-configurationally-based notions." This might look like a non-problem but there is a conceptual side to it. Case assignment is generally viewed as a local phenomenon. If this is so, it would be desirable to model it via strictly local means, with as little recourse to constituent structure as possible.

Secondly, the theory of HM'94 is ill-suited to traceless dialects of HPSG. If there are no traces in the tree structure (e.g., because extraction is handled by lexical rules as in ch. 9 of PS'94) and case is assigned configurationally, the case of the filler must be resolved at the level of the Head-Filler Schema, i.e., when the information about the grammatical function of the filler (as well as about its governor) is no longer available. Thus, there is no way to predict the ungrammaticality of (3):

(3)  *Whom$_{acc}$ do you think _ likes him?

One way to recover from this problem (cf. Grover 1995) is to have, apart from the configurational case assignment rules, separate rules operating at the same level as the CELR and the SELR (or to hard-wire structural case assignment into these extraction lexical rules). This is, however, a clear case of a missed generalization as most case assignment rules have to be stated twice: for arguments realized via the Valence Principle, and for extracted arguments. This problem is further aggravated by the existence of the third mode of argument realization, i.e., as pronominal affixes (see, e.g., Miller and Sag 1997, Calcagno and Pollard 1997).

Another way of solving this problem would be to assign case at the Head-Filler Schema. However, in order to do so, the case assignment rules would have to traverse the tree to find the place from which the filler is extracted (and thus learn about the grammatical function of the extracted element, about the category of its governor, etc.). Apart from sharing with the previous tentative solution the problem of redundancy (missed generalization), this account would have to rely on global complex relations, thus giving up any pretence of locality. A variant of this solution (suggested by Carl Pollard, p.c., Tübingen, July 1997) would be to package all the information necessary to assign case to the filler into the SLASH value and carry it all the way up to the Head-Filler Schema. Again, in order for this idea to work, we would have to (unnecessarily, as we show below) multiply the number of case assigning rules.

### 15.2.4  Conclusion

In Section 15.2.1, we exemplified the claim that some configurational information has to be taken into account in case assignment (see the contrast in (1)). However, the solution (dominant in HPSG) presented in Section 15.2.2 seems to be 'too configurational': as discussed in Section 15.2.3, not only does it have to be formalized as a constraint on trees, but it is also not clear how it can be extended to account for arguments realized as fillers (a problem for the traceless analyses of extraction) or pronominal affixes.

### 15.3  Non-Configurational Case Assignment

In this section, we present a case assignment technique free from the problems mentioned above.

First of all, we adopt the division of morphological cases into (at least) syntactic (structural) and lexical (inherent, quirky). Formally, this is rendered by rich language-specific type hierarchies for *case*, such as (2) above.[2] As in, e.g., HM'94, we assume that lexical items subcategorize either for specific lexical cases (e.g., *lgen*), or for the underspecified *structural* case. And again, a separate constraint will resolve this structural case to a given morphological case (e.g., *snom* or *sgen*).

### 15.3.1 Locus of Case Assignment

Where our analysis crucially differs from the previous approaches is in the locus of case assignment: in our approach structural case gets resolved on argument structure (ARG-ST), rather than tree-configurationally. Moreover, we claim that under the current HPSG assumptions this is the **necessary** locus of any homogeneous case theory for the simple reason that only ARG-ST contains all the arguments of a lexical head.

As discussed in Section 15.2.3, the configurational case assignment technique of HM'94 and others cannot be maintained because some arguments never surface configurationally (pronominal affixes), while others appear so 'far' from their base positions that additional (and relatively complex) logistics are necessary. Even if these problems were solved, any such case theory would be redundant in the sense that the case of, say, extracted objects, those *in situ*, and those realized as pronominal affixes would have to be resolved by three separate principles, even though case assignment does not depend on the mode of realization.

For similar reasons, structural case cannot be resolved on VALENCE attributes: some case-bearing arguments never appear there (cf., e.g., the use of a *noncan* subtype of *synsem* in Miller and Sag 1997 and Abeillé et al. 1997). The only place in the current HPSG feature geometry where all the arguments (or even dependents, see Sections 15.4–15.5) do appear is ARG-ST.

Moreover, assigning case on ARG-ST seems not to be just a technical HPSG-internal necessity. It can be viewed as one way of instantiating and formalizing the intuitions behind the influential "case in tiers" theory of surface case of Yip et al. 1987.[3]

---

[2]We envisage the possibility of enriching such case hierarchies in various ways, e.g., to account for morphological case syncretisms or by adding further subsorts of *syn-case* such as thematic/semantic case. We leave this, however, for future research.

[3]"It seems likely that [case-argument] association must be defined on grammatical (or thematic) relations... perhaps universally" (Yip et al. 1987, p.220). See also the discussion of Maling 1993 below.

### 15.3.2 Global Information on ARG-ST

The conclusion of the previous section, i.e., that structural case should be resolved on ARG-ST, seems to contradict the conclusion of Section 15.2.1, namely that case cannot be assigned without taking into consideration syntactic realization of the assignee. Consider again example (1) on page 232. Recall that in (1a), the complement of *reparieren* is realized as its direct object and hence gets the accusative, while in (1b) this complement is raised first to the (ARG-ST of) *versucht*, and then to the subject position (of the ARG-ST) of *wurde*, from which it is realized and hence gets the nominative.[4] Thus, what matters for case assignment to an NP is the grammatical function of this NP at the point of syntactic realization. In other words, when assigning case to an NP, only the ARG-ST from which this NP is syntactically realized should be considered. Or, equivalently, when assigning case to structural NPs on a given ARG-ST, only those NPs should be considered which are syntactically realized from this ARG-ST.

It seems then that the only 'non-local' information we need is binary: whether the argument is realized locally, or whether it is raised to be realized higher up. We formalize this conclusion by minimally enriching the information present on ARG-ST as well as on VALENCE lists: we assume that values of these attributes are lists of objects of sort *arg*(ument), for which two attributes are appropriate, the *synsem*-valued ARGument and the binary REALIZED.

(4)
$$\begin{bmatrix} argument \\ \text{ARGUMENT } synsem \\ \text{REALIZED } bool \end{bmatrix}$$

(5)
$$\begin{bmatrix} category \\ \text{VALENCE} \begin{bmatrix} \text{SUBJECT list}(argument) \\ \text{SPECIFIER list}(argument) \\ \text{COMPLEMENTS list}(argument) \end{bmatrix} \\ \text{ARGUMENT-STRUCTURE list}(argument) \end{bmatrix}$$

What remains to be said is how to ensure proper instantiation of the REALIZED feature. In order to do so, we have to explicate our assumptions about the relation between ARG-ST and VALENCE. Following much of the HPSG literature, we assume here that ARG-ST is present on *word*s only, and it is the concatenation of the VALENCE features, plus perhaps gaps (arguments extracted at a given word) and arguments realized as pronominal affixes (Miller and Sag 1997, Abeillé et al. 1997). Thus, in essence, there are three ways of realizing an ar-

---

[4]We do not claim that this is the proper analysis of partial VP topicalization and/or passivization in German. We use Pollard's analysis simply to illustrate our point.

gument on ARG-ST: via the Valence Principle, via extraction lexical rules (assuming no traces), and via whatever mechanism is responsible for pronominal affixation. Each of these three mechanisms has to mark the corresponding arguments as [REALIZED +]. Specifically:

(6)     The Valence Principle of PS'94 (p.392) has to be reformulated in the following way: In a headed phrase, for each valence feature F, the F value of the head daughter is the concatenation of the phrase's F value with the list of [REALIZED +] SYNSEM values of the F-DTRS value.

(7)     Extraction lexical rules, which remove arguments from the VALENCE features, mark these arguments as [REALIZED +].

(8)     Assuming the approach to pronominal affixation of Miller and Sag 1997, arguments whose ARG values are of type *affix* must be [REALIZED +].

Note that, although some of these processes (the valence principle and the extraction lexical rules) resolve the value of REALIZED on VALENCE, at the same time they resolve it on ARG-ST: this is guaranteed by the structure sharing of (some of) the word's arguments between ARG-ST and VALENCE.

On the other hand, care must be taken to ensure that the arguments which are not locally realized (e.g., because they are raised) are marked as [REALIZED −] and, hence, exempt from the Case Principle. The common characteristics of such unrealized arguments is that they are present on a VALENCE attribute of a subcategorized element.[5] In other (Pollard's, p.c., July 1997) words, they are valents' valents. Thus, we need a principle stating that valents' valents are [REALIZED −].[6]

(9)

$$
valence \rightarrow \left[ F_1 \; list\left( \left[ \begin{array}{l} arg \\ ARG \; \left[ \begin{array}{l} synsem \\ L|C|VAL|F_2 \; list\left( \left[ \begin{array}{l} arg \\ REALIZED \; - \end{array} \right] \right) \end{array} \right] \end{array} \right] \right) \right]
$$

We will illustrate the mechanisms just introduced with examples (1) and (3). Consider (3) first. Both arguments of *likes* become [REALIZED +], although by different means: *him* is marked as + by the Valence Principle, while the argument corresponding to *whom* is marked by the SELR. Also the object of *reparieren* in (1a) is marked as + via the Valence Principle. On the other hand, the object of *reparieren* in

---

[5]Consider, for example, the raising verb *seem*: it subcategorizes for a VP complement, i.e., for a synsem with non-empty VALENCE|SUBJ.

[6]In (9), $F_1$ and $F_2$ range over {SUBJ, SPR, COMPS}.

(1b) is marked via the constraint (9) as [REALIZED −] because it is present on a VALENCE attribute ($F_2$ = COMPS) of a synsem corresponding to *reparieren*, which is itself present on a VALENCE attribute ($F_1$ = COMPS) of *versucht*. The argument corresponding to *der Wagen* is [REALIZED −] also on the ARG-ST of *versucht*, and for the same reason: it is a valent of the word *versucht*, which itself is the valent of the word *wurde*. (Recall that we assume an analysis in which the object of *reparieren* is raised to *versucht* and further to *wurde*.) Finally, *der Wagen* is realized as a subject of *wurde*, i.e., it is marked as [REALIZED +] on the ARG-ST of this word by the Valence Principle. The careful reader will notice that the important assumption we make here is that what is raised in the raising constructions is not an element of ARG-ST (or VALENCE), but only the synsem which is the value of ARGUMENT of this element. Thus, the REALIZED values of the controllee and the controller may differ.

### 15.3.3 Case Principle

Now, the Case Principle (CP) for a given language consists of a series of constraints resolving structural cases of locally realized NPs depending on the grammatical function of the NP, the category of the governor, etc. For example, two clauses of the CP for German may (assuming a case hierarchy as in (2)) be as in (10)–(11).

$$(10) \quad \begin{bmatrix} cat \\ \text{HEAD } verb \\ \text{ARG-ST } \langle \begin{bmatrix} \text{ARG NP}[str] \\ \text{REALIZED } + \end{bmatrix} \rangle \oplus \boxed{2} \end{bmatrix} \rightarrow$$
$$\begin{bmatrix} \text{ARG-ST } \langle \begin{bmatrix} \text{ARG NP}[snom] \end{bmatrix} \rangle \oplus \boxed{2} \end{bmatrix}$$

$$(11) \quad \begin{bmatrix} cat \\ \text{HEAD } verb \\ \text{ARG-ST } \boxed{1}_{ne\_list} \oplus \langle \begin{bmatrix} \text{ARG NP}[str] \\ \text{REALIZED } + \end{bmatrix} \rangle \oplus \boxed{2} \end{bmatrix} \rightarrow$$
$$\begin{bmatrix} \text{ARG-ST } \boxed{1} \oplus \langle \begin{bmatrix} \text{ARG NP}[sacc] \end{bmatrix} \rangle \oplus \boxed{2} \end{bmatrix}$$

Note that the interaction of (10)–(11) with the principles (6)–(9) responsible for instantiation of REALIZED correctly models the data in (1). *Den Wagen* is accusative in (1a) because its synsem is a non-initial [REALIZED +] structural argument on the ARG-ST of *reparieren*, while *der Wagen* is nominative in (1b) because it is the initial [REALIZED +] argument of *wurde*. Moreover, although the synsem of *der Wagen* is also present on the ARG-ST of *reparieren* and *versucht*, it is marked as [REALIZED −] there, so the CP does not apply (and there are no clashing constraints).

## 15.4 Case Assignment to Adverbials

It has been recently argued by many that certain adverbials (characterized by Wechsler and Lee (1996) as 'extensive measure adverbials') get their case assigned syntactically by the same processes which are responsible for case assignment to arguments. Such claims were made with respect to, e.g., Korean (cf. Maling 1989, Kim and Maling 1993, Kim and Maling 1996, Wechsler and Lee 1996), Chinese (Li 1990), Russian (Babby 1980, Fowler 1987) and Polish (Przepiórkowski 1998).[7] In this paper, however, we will be concerned with the Finnish data presented by Maling (1993).

Finnish is famous for its rich case system involving 15 different morphological cases. As in many other languages, these are divided into syntactic cases (e.g., nominative, accusative, partitive) and lexical cases (e.g., genitive and illative). A given predicate may subcategorize either for a structural case (resolved syntactically), or for a given lexical case.

A verb's dependents which are not marked by the verb as bearing a lexical case receive either nominative or accusative.[8] Maling (1993) notes the following generalization about syntactic case assignment: only one NP dependent of the verb receives the nominative, namely the one which has the highest grammatical function; other dependents receive the accusative. Thus, if none of the arguments bears inherent case, the subject is in the nominative and other dependents are in the accusative (12), but if the subject bears an idiosyncratic case, it is the object that gets nominative (13). Furthermore, if all arguments (if any) bear inherent case, the next 'available' grammatical function is that of an adjunct, thus one of the adjuncts receives the nominative (14)–(15).

(12) Liisa    muisti    matkan vuoden.
Liisa$_{nom}$ remembered trip$_{acc}$ year$_{acc}$
'Liisa remembered the trip for a year.'

(13) Lapsen  täytyy lukea kirja    kolmannen kerran.
child$_{gen}$ must  read book$_{nom}$ [third    time]$_{acc}$
'The child must read the book for a 3rd time.'

(14) Kekkoseen  luotettiin yksi kerta.
Kekkonen$_{ill}$ trust$_{pass}$ [one time]$_{nom}$
'Kekkonen was trusted once.'

(15) Kekkoseen  luotettiin yhden kerran  yksi vuosi.
Kekkonen$_{ill}$ trust$_{pass}$ [one  time]$_{acc}$ [one year]$_{nom}$
'Kekkonen was trusted for one year once.'

---

[7]Maling (1993) also mentions Warumungu and Classical Arabic.

[8]We abstract away here from issues to do with another syntactic case, partitive, and with case assignment to subordinate clauses.

On the basis of facts such as (12)–(15), Maling (1993) concludes that syntactic case is assigned on the basis of a grammatical hierarchy and that (at least some) adjuncts belong to this hierarchy. Moreover, as evidenced by (14)–(15), adjuncts do not form a single class in this hierarchy: although the multiplicative adverbial[9] *yksi kerta* is nominative in (14), the duration adverbial in (15) wins in the competition for the nominative case. Taking into consideration also the partitive of negation facts (measure adverbials, but not duration or frequency adverbials, behave like direct objects in the sense that they take partitive case under sentential negation), Maling (1993) extends the grammatical function hierarchy for Finnish in the following way:

(16) SUBJ > OBJ > MEASURE > DURATION > FREQUENCY

It should be clear by now that the Finnish case assignment facts (or, in general, case assignment to adverbials) can be easily modelled in our approach provided that the relevant adverbials are present on ARG-ST: the nominative is simply assigned to the first structural NP on ARG-ST, the accusative to any following structural NP. Thus, the facts discussed above provide some evidence for the Adjuncts-as-Complements approach to modification in which (at least some) adjuncts are put on ARG-ST and COMPS via a lexical process.[10] In the following section we make a stronger claim, namely that other approaches to modification currently available on the HPSG market can deal with these facts only at a very prohibitive cost.

## 15.5 Evidence for Adjuncts as Complements?

Consider first the standard (PS'94) approach to adjuncts and recall that adjuncts are supposed to modify phrases, i.e., they select (via MOD) synsems with empty COMPS.[11] Now, assuming the minimalist approach to case of PS'94, bare NP adverbials would have to originate in the lexicon with their case specified, thus there would be two lexical entries for each adverbial taking part in the alternations exemplified in (12)–

---

[9]We call adverbials such as *once*, *third time*, etc. 'multiplicative' to distinguish them from other frequency adverbials such as 'every day', which might have different case-taking properties as discussed Wechsler and Lee 1996.

[10]This idea has been formalized in, e.g., Miller 1992, van Noord and Bouma 1994, Kim and Sag 1996, Abeillé and Godard 1997, Przepiórkowski 1997. It should be noted that also Pollard and Sag 1987 propose that adjuncts be selected by the head. Moreover, Bouma et al. 1997 have recently proposed a separate feature encoding a head's DEPENDENTS; as far as we can see, our approach is compatible with theirs on the assumption that the locus of case assignment is DEPENDENTS rather than ARG-ST.

[11]Our argument is orthogonal to the improvements by Kasper (1997).

(15): one in the nominative, and another in the accusative. Consider what the MOD value of, say, a nominative multiplicative adverbial such as *yksi kerta* 'one time' should be. It can modify only those verbs, which do not have a structural subject or structural object, and which are not modified by a duration adverbial. But there is no way this information can be encoded in the MOD value. Since adjuncts modify phrases, the COMPS value of the MOD synsem is an empty list, so the adjunct has no information about whether there is a structural complement on this verb or not. Even worse, the adjunct has no information about other adjuncts, which might have stronger claims to the nominative.

One way of solving this problem would be to let adjuncts 'blindly' modify any phrase, and posit global well-formedness constraints ruling out, say, structures with a nominative multiplicative adverbial whenever there is a structural subject, object or duration adverbial. Such constraints can, in principle, be stated although they would have to be formulated as constraints on maximal projections (to ensure that no more adjuncts are attached), and would be fairly complex. Moreover, the simple empirical generalization that the nominative is assigned to the highest available grammatical function, and the accusative to any other available grammatical function, would be lost without a trace.

Note that adopting the configurational case assignment technique of HM'94 and others does not help. Their approach, although configurational, is local in the sense that their Case Principle operates on local trees: it never traverses the tree. However, in order to model the Finnish data, exactly such a traversal would be necessary. To see why, consider again a multiplicative adverbial attaching to a VP. Let us assume that such adverbials are specified as *structural* in the lexicon. What would a constraint resolving the case of such a structural adverbial have to look like? There is no information about the head's complements at the level of the Head-Adjunct Schema, so this constraint would have to go down along the projection path to the *word* level. This, however, is still not enough as there might be a duration adverbial attached higher than our multiplicative adverbial. Thus, this constraint would also have to 'look up'. This is technically impossible so, again, the Case Principle would have to be formulated not as a constraint on *phrase*, but rather as a global constraint on maximal projections. This shares all the problems with the standard (PS'94) approach to case.

Let us now consider another approach to modification, namely that of Kasper 1994. The main idea of his proposal (based on German *Mittelfeld* facts) is to replace the Head-Complement Schema and the Head-Adjunct Schema with a single schema realizing complements (on COMP-DTRS) as well as adjuncts (on ADJ-DTRS), so that adjuncts modify *words*, rather than *phrases*. Adjuncts are ordered on ADJ-DTRS according to scope: the first one has the widest scope, the last one scopes immediately over the predicate. Moreover, all adjuncts syntactically select the head, while semantically, they select the next adjunct on ADJ-DTRS (or the head, in case of the last adjunct). Let us again consider in turn the approaches to case assignment of PS'94, and of HM'94 and others.

Assume first PS'94, i.e., no specialized case module, and consider again the question of what kind of verbs can be modified by a nominative multiplicative adverbial. It is now easy to state part of the necessary condition, namely that there cannot be any structural NPs among the arguments of the word: the MOD value of such an adverbial would have to be a synsem, whose VALENCE features (or ARG-ST) do not contain such NPs. However, it is still impossible for multiplicative adverbials to select heads not modified by durational adverbials. Thus, again, we would have to resort to well-formedness checking principles. However, this time this checking could be stated as a constraint on the Head-Complement Schema (assuming that **all** relevant adjuncts are sisters to complements), thus avoiding the problem of global constraints.

Also assuming the approach of HM'94, the problem of global constraints would be evaded: the Case Principle could operate on Head-Complement phrases. However, this CP would have to be (again) fairly complex: it would have to look into VAL|SUBJ to check if the verbal phrase expects a structural subject, and then into COMP-DTRS and ADJ-DTRS, and calculate cases of all structural dependents with regards to other dependents. For example, in order to assign nominative to a multiplicative adverbial, such a principle would have to make sure that (i) the element of VAL|SUBJ is not an NP[*str*], (ii) there are no NP[*str*] among elements of COMP-DTRS, (iii) there are no duration adverbials on ADJ-DTRS.

Although it is an improvement over the standard theory of modification, the approach of Kasper 1994 is not without its problems. First, again, case assignment has to be tree-configurational (although pretty local). Second, and more importantly, the generalization captured by Maling 1993 would be lost again: instead of assigning the nominative to the first structural NP on a certain list and the accusative to all the other structural elements, the Case Principle would have to do quite a lot of calculation. It seems that in order not to miss the generalizations, an additional attribute would have to be introduced whose value would be the concatenation of the subject, the complements and the adjuncts, in this order: then the nominative could be assigned to the first structural NP on this list, etc.[12] What is striking about this solution, however, is that the only purpose of this attribute would be to encode the obliqueness hierarchy among (some of) the dependents of the word, a clear case of unwelcome theoretical redundancy (ARG-ST already fulfills this function with respect to arguments!). Even if these problems were solved, one remaining problem would be more difficult to deal with: the order of adjuncts on ADJ-DTRS assumed by Kasper 1994 (adjuncts of wider scope earlier on the list) is not reconcilable with the grammatical function order postulated by Maling 1993. For example, if both frequency and duration adverbials are present, two different orders on ADJ-DTRS correspond to two different scoping relations between them, wrongly predicting that the case of these adverbials depends on their scope.

What we hope to have shown is that no combination of the existing HPSG accounts of modification (i.e., adjuncts via Head-Adjunct Schema of PS'94 and adjuncts as sisters to complements by Kasper 1994) with the existing approaches to case assignment (i.e., strictly lexical by PS'94 and configurational by HM'94 and others) can elegantly account for the case assignment to adverbials in Finnish (and, by extension, in other languages). Although, technically, there are ways of saving these accounts, the price to be paid is prohibitive: loss of the linguistic insights and non-negligible complexity of such accounts.[13]

## 15.6 Conclusion

In this paper, we provided a general case assignment technique (Section 15.3) which was designed to meet various demands on case assignment present in the HPSG and non-HPSG literature: it is non-tree-configurational (Pollard 1994), it is compatible with both traced and traceless approaches to extraction, and it is based on the notion of obliqueness / grammatical function hierarchy (Yip et al. 1987, Maling 1993). Moreover, on our approach, unlike on previous approaches suggested in the HPSG literature (cf. fn. 1), case assignment does not

---

[12]The function of this attribute would be similar to the function of SUBCAT, retained in ch. 9 of PS'94 to handle BT facts; thus it is not technically necessary but it is very useful for a straightforward and intuitively appealing account.

[13]The other four combinations of modification / case assignment accounts which we reject without discussion are: (i), (ii) case assignment on ARG-ST with either of the two non-AasC approaches to modification (for the obvious reason that structural case is resolved on ARG-ST, and adverbials never make it to any ARG-ST); and (iii), (iv) AasC approach to modification with either of the two previous approaches to case assignment (minimally, because they share the case assignment problems mentioned in Section 15.2.3).

depend on the mode of realization: the same principle assigns case to locally realized NPs, to extracted elements and to pronominal affixes.

In the second part of the paper (Sections 15.4–15.5), we argued that facts from case assignment to adverbials call for a single level of representation for a head's dependents. We showed that assuming such a representation, e.g., a variant of the Adjuncts-as-Complements approach, our case theory elegantly accounts for these facts. On the other hand, none of the other two approaches to modification in the HPSG literature can model these facts in a satisfying way.

## References

Abeillé, Anne, and Danièle Godard. 1997. The Syntax of French Negative Adverbs. In *Negation*, ed. Paul Hirschbühler and France Martineau. Benjamins. Forthcoming.

Abeillé, Anne, Danièle Godard, and Ivan A. Sag. 1997. Two Kinds of Composition in French Complex Predicates. Version of June 29, 1997. To appear in Erhard Hinrichs, Andreas Kathol, and Tsuneko Nakazawa, eds., *Complex Predicates in Nonderivational Syntax*. New York: Academic Press.

Babby, Leonard. 1980. The Syntax of Surface Case Marking. In *Cornell Working Papers in Linguistics*, ed. W. Harbert and J. Herschensohn. 1–32. Department of Modern Languages and Linguistics, Cornell University.

Bouma, Gosse, Rob Malouf, and Ivan Sag. 1997. Satisfying Constraints on Extraction and Adjunction. Draft of July 1, 1997.

Calcagno, Mike, and Carl Pollard. 1997. The Structure of French Causatives. Abstract for HPSG97.

Fowler, George Hayden. 1987. *The Syntax of the Genitive Case in Russian*. PhD dissertation, University of Chicago, Chicago, Illinois.

Grover, Claire. 1995. *Rethinking Some Empty Categories: Missing Objects and Parasitic Gaps in HPSG*. PhD dissertation, University of Essex.

Heinz, Wolfgang, and Johannes Matiasek. 1994. Argument Structure and Case Assignment in German. In Nerbonne et al. 1994, 199–236.

Kasper, Robert. 1994. Adjuncts in the Mittelfeld. In Nerbonne et al. 1994, 39–69.

Kasper, Robert. 1997. Semantics of Recursive Modification. To appear in the *Journal of Linguistics*.

Kim, Jong-Bok, and Ivan A. Sag. 1996. French and English Negation: A Lexicalist Alternative to Head Movement. Unpublished manuscript. Version of July 22, 1996.

Kim, Soowon, and Joan Maling. 1993. Syntactic Case and Frequency Adverbials in Korean. In *Harvard Studies in Korean Linguistics V*, 368–378.

Kim, Soowon, and Joan Maling. 1996. Case Assignment in the *siphta* Construction and Its Implications for Case on Adverbials. In *Description and*

*Explanation in Korean Linguistics*, ed. Ross King. 141–179. Cornell University Press.

Li, Audrey Yen-hui. 1990. *Order and Constituency*. Studies in Natural Language and Linguistic Theory, Vol. 19. Dordrecht: Kluwer Academic Publishers.

Maling, Joan. 1989. Adverbials and Structural Case in Korean. In *Harvard Studies in Korean Linguistics III*, ed. Susumu Kuno, Ik-Hwan Lee, John Whitman, Syng-Yun Bak, Young-Se Kang, and Young-joo Kim, 297–308. Cambridge, Massachusetts.

Maling, Joan. 1993. Of Nominative and Accusative: The Hierarchical Assignment of Grammatical Case in Finnish. In *Case and Other Functional Categories in Finnish Syntax*, ed. Anders Holmberg and Urpo Nikanne. 51–76. Dordrecht: Mouton de Gruyter.

Miller, Philip. 1992. *Clitics and Constituents in Phrase Structure Grammar*. New York: Garland.

Miller, Philip H., and Ivan A. Sag. 1997. French Clitic Movement Without Clitics or Movement. *Natural Language and Linguistic Theory* 15(3):573–639.

Nerbonne, John, Klaus Netter, and Carl Pollard (ed.). 1994. *German in Head-Driven Phrase Structure Grammar*. Stanford: CSLI Publications.

Pollard, Carl. 1994. Toward a Unified Account of Passive in German. In Nerbonne et al. 1994, 273–296.

Pollard, Carl, and Ivan A. Sag. 1987. *Information-Based Syntax and Semantics, Volume 1: Fundamentals*. Stanford: CSLI Publications.

Pollard, Carl, and Ivan A. Sag. 1994. *Head-Driven Phrase Structure Grammar*. Chicago: Chicago University Press.

Przepiórkowski, Adam. 1997. Quantifiers, Adjuncts as Complements, and Scope Ambiguities. Unpublished manuscript. Version of December 2, 1997.

Przepiórkowski, Adam. 1998. On Complements and Adjuncts in Polish. To appear in: R. D. Borsley and A. Przepiórkowski (eds.), *Slavic in HPSG*, CSLI Publications.

Przepiórkowski, Adam. In preparation. *Case Assignment and the Complement-Adjunct Dichotomy: A Constraint-Based Approach*. PhD dissertation, Universität Tübingen. Working title.

van Noord, Gertjan, and Gosse Bouma. 1994. Adjuncts and the Processing of Lexical Rules. In *Fifteenth International Conference on Computational Linguistics (COLING '94)*, 250–256. Kyoto, Japan, August.

Wechsler, Stephen, and Yae-Sheik Lee. 1996. The Domain of Direct Case Assignment. *Natural Language and Linguistic Theory* 14:629–664.

Yip, Moira, Joan Maling, and Ray Jackendoff. 1987. Case in Tiers. *Language* 63(2):217–250.

# Part V

## Formal and Computational Issues

# 16

# "The Importance of Being Lazy"— Using Lazy Evaluation to Process Queries to HPSG Grammars

Thilo Götz and Walt Detmar Meurers

## 16.1 Introduction

Linguistic theories formulated in the architecture of HPSG can be very precise and explicit since HPSG provides a formally well-defined setup. However, when querying a faithful implementation of such an explicit theory, the large data structures specified can make it hard to see the relevant aspects of the reply given by the system. Furthermore, the system spends much time applying constraints which can never fail just to be able to enumerate specific answers. In this paper we want to describe lazy evaluation as the result of an off-line compilation technique. This method of evaluation can be used to answer queries to an HPSG system so that only the relevant aspects are checked and output.

The paper is organized as follows. The next section describes three different ways to check grammaticality. In Section 16.3, we introduce our lazy compilation method and compare it to a more standard compilation. We examine the theoretical properties of our approach in Section 16.4 and conclude in Section 16.5.

## 16.2 Three Ways to Check Grammaticality

Formally speaking, a HPSG *grammar* consists of a *signature* defining the linguistic ontology and a *theory* describing the grammatical objects.

The authors are listed alphabetically. We would like to thank Dale Gerdemann and the anonymous reviewers for helpful comments.

A grammar G *admits* some term $\phi$ just in case G has a model that satisfies $\phi$.

**Checking Grammaticality I: Enumerating models** The simplest possibility to answer a query to a HPSG grammar is to construct the models of the grammar which satisfy the query and enumerate all possibilities. The algorithm proposed in Ch. 15 of Carpenter 1992 is an example for this method. It is implemented in the type constraint part of the ALE 2.0 system (Carpenter and Penn 1994). Another computational system which can proceed in this way is TFS (Emele and Zajac 1990).[1] Since such systems give full models as answers to queries, no additional knowledge of the signature or theory is needed to interpret the answers.

While enumerating models is a correct way to check grammaticality, it has a severe disadvantage: The answers are not compact in the sense that much information which could be left underspecified is made fully explicit. This concerns in particular information that could be deduced from the signature. For example, when querying an English HPSG grammar for the lexical entry of a finite past tense verb like *walked*, a system under the simple approach enumerates solutions for every person and number assignment instead of leaving those agreement properties underspecified in the answer.[2]

**Checking Grammaticality II: Satisfying all constraints of the theory** We can avoid explicit model construction by using constraint solving techniques. This can be thought of as 'enriching' the query until all theory constraints are satisfied. For the example of *walked* above this means that no agreement information is provided in the answer if there are no grammar constraints on the agreement features of that lexical entry. Computational approaches implementing this approach are, for example, the compiler described in Götz and Meurers 1995 or the WildLIFE system (Aït-Kaci et al. 1994) . Since these systems answer queries with descriptions satisfying both theory and query, and not with full models,[3] to interpret the replies the user needs to fill in some ontological information from the signature.

---

[1]The TFS system in version 6.1 (1994) has several evaluation options, including an undocumented "lazy narrowing" mode, which seems to implement a lazy evaluation strategy similar to that described in this paper.

[2]Since ALE uses an open world interpretation of the type hierarchy only all appropriate attributes, but not the different subtypes will be filled in. However, standard HPSG (Pollard and Sag 1994) uses a closed world interpretation of the type hierarchy. Cf. Gerdemann and King 1993 and Meurers 1994 for some discussion.

[3]Some approaches even remove information deducible from the signature to keep datastructures small (Götz 1994).

While this mode of processing queries does improve on the first approach, there still are many cases in which the system does more than necessary. Consider the lexical entry of an auxiliary verb employing an argument raising technique in the style of Hinrichs and Nakazawa (1989). Such entries are being used in most current HPSG theories for German, Dutch, French, or Italian. The idea is to specify the auxiliary to subcategorize for a verbal complement plus those arguments of that verbal complement which have not yet been saturated. As a result, the lexical entry of the auxiliary subcategorizes for an underspecified number of arguments. If the raised arguments have to obey grammar constraints, e.g., in the theory of Hinrichs and Nakazawa (1994) they are required to be non-verbal signs, this results in an infinite number of solutions to the query for such a lexical entry. The reason is that the constraints enforced by the theory need to be checked on each member of the subcategorization list, and the list is of underspecified length.

The example points out a problematic aspect of the second approach to answer queries: the system checks constraints which can never clash with the information specified in the query. To avoid making these checks, we propose to use a lazy evaluation technique.

**Checking Grammaticality III: Lazy evaluation**  The basic idea of lazy evaluation is that nodes with *more information content* should be preferred in evaluation over nodes with less information content. This suggests an on-line strategy for goal selection based on the idea of laziness. However, we would like to take a compilation approach to laziness. Instead of reordering goals on-line, we compute off-line which nodes need to checked *at all* to guarantee there is a solution. This means that our on-line proof strategy is exactly identical to the non-lazy case, but it needs to do less work.

Lazy compilation can quite easily be integrated, e.g., into the compilation method translating HPSG theories into definite clause programs described in Götz and Meurers 1995. In the next section we discuss a small HPSG example to illustrate this.

Theoretically, on the other hand, lazy evaluation changes our perspective on program semantics. Whereas the programs previously had the property of *persistence* (any term subsumed by a solution was also a solution), the compilation technique for lazy evaluation abandons this property to be able to compute more efficiently. It simply demands that if $\phi$ is a solution and there are terms more specific than $\phi$, then *some* of these more specific terms must also be solutions. Such an interpretation is only correct if we impose a well-formedness condition on our grammars. This idea is due to Aït-Kaci et al. (1993), who impose a strong syntactic restriction on their theories, which will be discussed in Section 16.4.1. We replace this restriction by a weaker semantic one, which demands that the grammar has some model where every type has a non-empty denotation. From the viewpoint of the user of such a system this means that not every instantiation of an answer given by the system actually is grammatical. We will illustrate this in Section 16.3.2.

## 16.3  An HPSG Example

To illustrate the second and third method to check grammaticality introduced in the last section, we want to discuss a small HPSG example: a grammar dealing with part of the agreement paradigm of German adjectives discussed by Pollard and Sag (1994, 64–67).[4] The grammar deals with the adjectival agreement pattern shown in Figure 1.

|  | fem | masc |
|---|---|---|
| strong | *kleine Sorge* | *kleiner Erfolg* |
| weak | *(die) kleine Sorge* | *(der) kleine Erfolg* |

FIGURE 1  Part of the paradigm of nominative adjectives

The signature of our example grammar is shown in Figure 2.

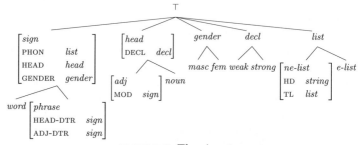

FIGURE 2  The signature

In Figure 3 the lexicon is defined. It contains lexical entries for the adjective *klein* ('small') and for the nouns *Erfolg* ('success') and *Sorge* ('worry'). Note that the entry for the female form of the adjective, *kleine*, is underspecified for the declension pattern.

Figure 4 shows a head-adjunct ID schema including the effect of

---

[4]The small example grammar presented here only serves to illustrate the different methods of checking grammaticality. It differs in many respect from the linguistic theory developed by Pollard and Sag (1994, 88-91).

$$
word \rightarrow
\begin{bmatrix}
\text{PHON} & \langle kleine \rangle \\
\text{HEAD} & adj \\
\text{GENDER} & fem
\end{bmatrix}
\lor
\begin{bmatrix}
\text{PHON} & \langle kleine \rangle \\
\text{HEAD} & \begin{bmatrix} adj \\ \text{DECL} & weak \end{bmatrix} \\
\text{GENDER} & masc
\end{bmatrix}
\lor
$$

$$
\begin{bmatrix}
\text{PHON} & \langle kleiner \rangle \\
\text{HEAD} & \begin{bmatrix} adj \\ \text{DECL} & strong \end{bmatrix} \\
\text{GENDER} & masc
\end{bmatrix}
\lor
\begin{bmatrix}
\text{PHON} & \langle Erfolg \rangle \\
\text{HEAD} & noun \\
\text{GENDER} & masc
\end{bmatrix}
\lor
\begin{bmatrix}
\text{PHON} & \langle Sorge \rangle \\
\text{HEAD} & noun \\
\text{GENDER} & fem
\end{bmatrix}
$$

FIGURE 3 The word principle

the HFP and the Semantics Principle to percolate the gender (which normally is part of the content's index).

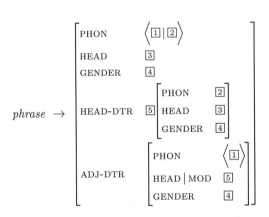

FIGURE 4 A simple head-adjunct ID schema

Finally, a principle is included to ensure that the declension class of the modified head is identical to that of the modifier.

$$
adj \rightarrow
\begin{bmatrix}
\text{MOD} \mid \text{HEAD} \mid \text{DECL} & \boxed{1} \\
\text{DECL} & \boxed{1}
\end{bmatrix}
$$

FIGURE 5 A principle for adjective declension

The tree in Figure 6 is an example for an agreement mismatch in a structure with two adjectives.[5] The above grammar correctly rules out this ungrammatical example, since the principle in Figure 5 enforces tags 3 and 3′ in the description of *kleine* to be identical, which results in an inconsistent structure.

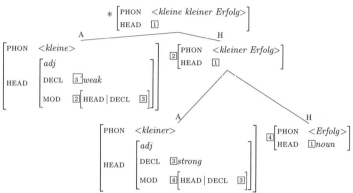

FIGURE 6  An example for an agreement mismatch

### 16.3.1  Non-Lazy Compilation

In the following, we first show how the grammar defined above is compiled in a setup checking grammaticality by method II. In Section 16.3.2 we then discuss how the grammar code produced by a compiler for laziness differs and how this changes processing.

A compiler, such as the one described in Götz and Meurers 1995, takes the HPSG grammar defined in the last section, determines which nodes in a structure of a certain type need to be checked, and produces code for checking these nodes. More specifically, this compiler translates constraints into clauses whose bodies are just tags that occur in the head of the clause. In the following we're interested in the question *which* nodes should be checked.

Figure 7 shows our example grammar 'in compiled form'.[6] The nodes which need to be checked are indicated with double boxes. For example, to make sure that a *word* with phonology *kleiner* is grammatical, we need to check that the *adjective* head value meets the principle for adjective declension. In Figure 7 this is marked by tag C.

Now that we have a compiled grammar, let us take a look at how a

---

[5]The GENDER values are left out for space reasons. They are all *masc.*

[6]We here ignore the optimizations discussed in Götz and Meurers 1995 since they are independent of the lazy evaluation issue discussed in this paper. Briefly said, the compiled example grammar produced by the optimized version of the compiler

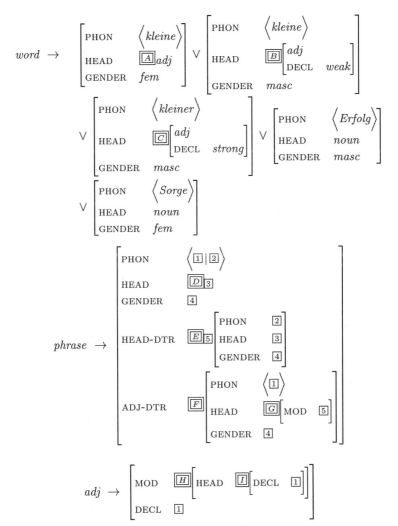

FIGURE 7 The compiled example grammar

query is processed. Figure 8 shows the trace of the query for a *word*, i.e., a lexical entry. In the first step, the constraint on *word* is applied. There are several disjuncts; we take the first one, the lexical entry for *kleine* (leaving a choice point behind). The disjunct chosen contains the tag Ⓐ, a call to the definition of *adj*. Upon execution of that call in

would not include the tags Ⓓ, Ⓔ, and Ⓖ, since those nodes will be checked when the *word* constraint is checked on node Ⓕ. The same holds for Ⓘ.

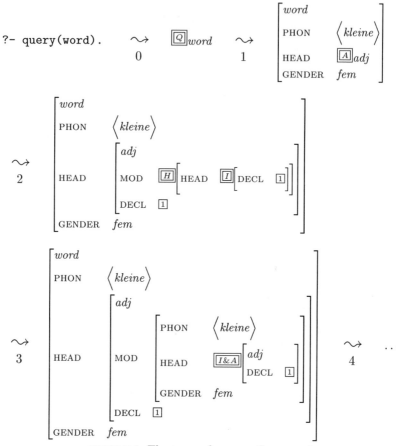

FIGURE 8 The trace of a query for a *word*

step 2, we unify in the definition of *adj*, which adds ▣H▣, a call to *sign*, to the goal list to ensure that the sign below the MOD attribute is also a grammatical sign. Executing the call to *sign*, we again have a choice, this time between the two constrained subtypes *word* and *phrase*. So in step 3 we again choose the first disjunct of *word*, which brings us into a state where we again have to check that the *adj* at ▣I&A▣ satisfies the grammar - and we see that we're in an infinite loop.

To obtain some answer, e.g., in step 1 we can chose another disjunct in the definition of *word* such as the lexical entry of either noun instead of the lexical entry of an adjective. There are no calls in the lexical entry of these nouns and there are none left on our goal list, so in the next state we're done. However, such a 'correct' order in which to try disjuncts needs to be specified by hand and in any case the system will still find infinitely many solutions for the above example.

### 16.3.2 Lazy Compilation

The lazy compilation method is almost the same, except that *no nodes without features are marked*. As mentioned in the beginning, the on-line proof strategy is identical to the non-lazy case, but since less nodes are marked, it needs to do less work. Essentially, the lazy compilation algorithm can be described as follows:

> For each $t \rightarrow \Phi$ in the theory
>> For each node $q$ in $\Phi$ (except the root node)
>>> If the type of $q$ subsumes a constrained type and
>>> at least one feature is defined on $q$
>>> Then mark $q$

For the example grammar in Figure 7, this means that the indices $\boxed{A}$ and $\boxed{D}$ go away. The intuition derives from the property we require grammars to obey for lazy compilation: *type consistency*. A grammar is type consistent iff it has a model where every type has a non-empty denotation. If there are no features defined on a node, then by type consistency, models satisfying that node exist and we don't need to search any further. We will take a closer look at this condition in Section 16.4.

Returning to the example, consider the lexical entry for the feminine form of the adjective *klein* repeated in Figure 9a.

a. $\begin{bmatrix} \text{PHON} & \langle \textit{kleine} \rangle \\ \text{HEAD} & \boxed{A}\textit{adj} \\ \text{GENDER} & \textit{fem} \end{bmatrix}$  b. $\begin{bmatrix} \text{PHON} & \langle \textit{kleine} \rangle \\ \text{HEAD} & \textit{adj} \\ \text{GENDER} & \textit{fem} \end{bmatrix}$

FIGURE 9 Normal and lazily compiled lexical entry of feminine *klein*

The HEAD value is specified to be *adj*, a constrained type. However, there is no feature specified for the HEAD value, and so the entry in the grammar after lazy compilation is simply as shown in Figure 9b.

In the lazy approach, a query is also processed by the lazy compiler. This leads to interesting behavior: If we pose the same query as in the last section (Figure 8), namely just *word*, the system immediately comes back with the answer *word*, without further instantiating the query. This is because, by type consistency, objects of type *word* are known to exist, and no further inferences are necessary. We have to be more specific if we want to see a specific *word*. Figure 10 shows what happens if ask for a *word* with the PHON value <*kleine*>. With the lazily compiled

$$?\text{- query}(\begin{bmatrix} word \\ \text{PHON} \quad \langle kleine \rangle \end{bmatrix}). \quad \underset{0}{\rightsquigarrow} \quad \boxed{Q}\begin{bmatrix} word \\ \text{PHON} \quad \langle kleine \rangle \end{bmatrix}$$

$$\underset{1}{\rightsquigarrow} \quad \begin{bmatrix} word \\ \text{PHON} \quad \langle kleine \rangle \\ \text{HEAD} \quad adj \\ \text{GENDER} \quad fem \end{bmatrix}$$

FIGURE 10  The evaluation of a more specific query

grammar, we don't go into an infinite loop anymore on the unspecified HEAD value. Thus, our method of lazy evaluation not only results in an efficiency increase, but actually leads to better termination properties. Of course, lazy compilation can not solve all termination problems. The problem remains for the masculine form of *klein*, whose compiled form is still as shown in Figure 11, since the HEAD value has the feature DECL specified.

$$\begin{bmatrix} \text{PHON} \quad \langle kleine \rangle \\ \text{HEAD} \quad \boxed{A}\begin{bmatrix} adj \\ \text{DECL} \quad strong \end{bmatrix} \\ \text{GENDER} \quad masc \end{bmatrix}$$

FIGURE 11  The lazily compiled lexical entry of the masculine form of *klein*

Reconsider the answer the system gave to the query in Figure 10. We know that our grammar contains a constraint on the type *adj* which has not been applied to the answer. In fact, precisely this constraint was at the basis of the infinite loop in non-lazy evaluation. The user therefore has to be aware of the fact that only certain *adj* objects are grammatical and that this information is not provided in the answer. The system only checks on nodes with features since those nodes are the only ones that can lead to an inconsistency.

## 16.4  Theoretical Aspects

In this section, we will briefly look at the theoretical aspects of the proof method proposed in this paper. Specifically, we will compare our approach to the one of Aït-Kaci et al. (1993), from which we differ in two respects:

- Our basic formalism is different. We use a closed world interpretation of the type hierarchy, and we allow disjunction and negation. The basic formalism we employ therefore is the same as that used in standard HPSG. This difference has consequences for the well-formedness condition on grammars we propose as an alternative to the one given by Aït-Kaci et al. (1993).
- We compile the information about lazy evaluation off-line. The actual proof method is then very similar to SLD resolution. Aït-Kaci et al. (1993) use a more sophisticated, on-line method. Our method is essentially a simplification of theirs.

From a theoretical point of view, the most interesting aspect of a lazy evaluation method is its soundness. Since we do less work in our proofs, we need to ensure that we don't stop resolving too early. We must make sure that when our proof terminates, there are no contradictions hidden in the search space that we just didn't get to because of our laziness. The example theory in Figure 12 will illustrate that lazy evaluation is not sound in general.

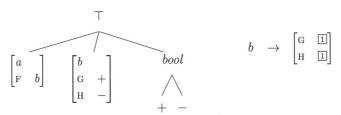

FIGURE 12 Unsoundness of lazy evaluation for non-type consistent grammars

$$\begin{bmatrix} a & \\ \text{F} & b \end{bmatrix}$$

FIGURE 13 A query for the unsoundness example

Consider the query in Figure 13. Our method will say that there's nothing to prove here: There are no constraints on $a$, and the $b$ node is a terminal node and thus it does not need to be checked. However, the constraint on $b$ is clearly inconsistent. There can never be any models of this grammar with objects of type $b$ in them. By the appropriateness conditions it follows that there can not be any objects of type $a$, either. So our proof system should really come back with the answer **no**.

Aït-Kaci et al. (1993) solve this problem by giving a sufficient syntactic condition for grammars that ensures soundness, i.e., by restricting the class of grammars that they can handle. Indeed, it is very hard to imagine a lazy proof system that is sound for all grammars. We will thus also restrict our attention to a proper subset of possible grammars. However, instead of using the syntactic restriction of Aït-Kaci et al. (1993), called *well-formedness*, which we suggest below to be too strong for HPSG grammars, we will use a weaker semantic one. We say that a grammar is *type consistent* iff for every type $t$, there is a model of the grammar that contains at least one object of type $t$. That is a very reasonable restriction, since one might expect the grammar writer not to introduce any types that never denote anything. One can show that our lazy resolution method is sound with respect to type consistent grammars.

### 16.4.1   Well-Formedness vs. Type Consistency

The condition of type consistency is properly weaker than that of well-formedness, the syntactic condition of Aït-Kaci et al. (1993). Every grammar that is well-formed is also type consistent, but not vice versa. We conjecture that the soundness result of Aït-Kaci et al. (1993) also holds for theories that are only type consistent. However, the stronger syntactic condition has the advantage of being checkable—it is decidable if a given theory is well-formed or not. It is in general undecidable if a theory is type consistent. But note that it is also undecidable whether a given theory can be transformed into an equivalent one that meets the syntactic condition of Aït-Kaci et al. (1993). For theoretical considerations, it is still useful to use our semantic restriction, since it is the weakest possible condition for soundness of the kind of lazy evaluation that we use, i.e., it is a necessary condition. We can thus try to find weaker, checkable sufficient conditions that are more suitable for the kind of linguistic applications that we have in mind. As long as they entail type consistency, they will always guarantee soundness of lazy constraint solving.

We will now illustrate the difference between well-formedness and type consistency with two examples. The first one is trivial and shows the general idea, the second one is more practical and involves disjunction. Simplifying somewhat, the condition of well-formedness requires that for each consequent in the grammar, unfolding the type constraints for each node exactly once would not add any new information, i.e., the new consequent is logically equivalent to the old one.

Suppose we have a type hierarchy of types $a$, $b$ and $c$, which are minimally ordered such that $a$ subsumes $b$ and $c$. Consider the constraint shown in Figure 14. This theory is not well-formed (unfolding the node labeled $b$ will bump the node labeled $a$ to $b$), but it is type consistent. Moreover, the theory can not be brought into well-formed format through partial evaluation: the process will not terminate. However, one could substitute the equivalent $b \rightarrow \begin{bmatrix} \text{F} & b \end{bmatrix}$ to obtain a well-formed theory.

$$b \rightarrow \begin{bmatrix} \text{F} & \begin{bmatrix} b \\ \text{F} & a \end{bmatrix} \end{bmatrix}$$

FIGURE 14  A theory that is not well-formed

A more realistic example is the junk slot encoding of the append relation (Aït-Kaci 1984). We here assume an appropriate extension of the well-formedness condition to disjunctive theories.

$$append \rightarrow \begin{bmatrix} \text{ARG1} & \langle\rangle \\ \text{ARG2} & L \\ \text{ARG3} & L \end{bmatrix} \vee \begin{bmatrix} \text{ARG1} & <H \mid T1> \\ \text{ARG2} & L \\ \text{ARG3} & <H \mid T2> \\ \text{JUNK} & \begin{bmatrix} append \\ \text{ARG1} & T1 \\ \text{ARG2} & L \\ \text{ARG3} & T2 \end{bmatrix} \end{bmatrix}$$

FIGURE 15  The junk-slot encoding of append

The theory in Figure 15 is not well-formed, although type consistent. Consider what happens if we try to unfold this type definition with respect to itself as shown in Figure 16. Unfortunately, the result is still not well-formed, and indeed we can not get a well-formed type constraint for *append* by unfolding or any other transformation.

We conclude that in a setup without disjunction and with open-world reasoning, like the one originally proposed by Aït-Kaci et al. (1993), well-formedness is a useful strengthening of type consistency. In a HPSG setup, using closed world reasoning and disjunction[7], well-formedness appears to be too strong. Therefore, a more liberal syntactic restriction

---

[7]Note that disjunction does not increase the expressive power of a system under closed world reasoning, since disjunction can be expressed via the type hierarchy. This is different in an open world setup, where disjunction is needed to enforce a choice of subtypes.

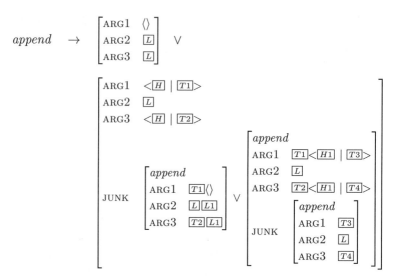

FIGURE 16 The junk-slot encoding of append after one unfolding step

needs to be found. In the meantime, the grammar writer needs to ensure that our semantic condition, type consistency, is met.

## 16.5 Conclusion

In this paper, we have discussed three possibilities to answer queries to a HPSG grammar. We described a compiler that takes a HPSG grammar and compiles it such that standard evaluation yields a lazy strategy. Lazy evaluation in our approach therefore is not an on-line goal reordering strategy, but the result of an optimizing compiler. This removes the overhead of on-line goal reordering from processing. We showed that lazy compilation has advantages both for efficiency of processing and the termination properties of HPSG grammars.

Theoretically, we justified our approach by giving the weakest possible condition that guarantees soundness of lazy evaluation: type consistency. We argued that this simplifies the search for stronger, checkable conditions. One only needs to show that a candidate condition is stronger than type consistency; no separate soundness proof is required.

The lazy compiler described has has been fully implemented as part of the ConTroll system (Götz et al. 1997). So far it has been tested with two complex HPSG grammars for German: one implementing the theory proposed in Pollard 1996 and the other focusing on the phenomena of aux-flip and PVP-topicalization Hinrichs and Nakazawa 1989, 1994.

Lazy evaluation for these grammars led to efficiency gains of up to 30% compared to the non-lazy approach described in Götz and Meurers 1995.

## References

Aït-Kaci, Hassan. 1984. *A Lattice Theoretic Approach to Computation Based on a Calculus of Partially Ordered Type Structures.* Doctoral dissertation, University of Pennsylvania.

Aït-Kaci, Hassan, Bruno Dumant, Richard Meyer, Andreas Podelski, and Peter van Roy. 1994. The Wild LIFE Handbook (prepublication edition). Technical report. Digital Equipment Corporation.

Aït-Kaci, Hassan, Andreas Podelski, and Seth Copen Goldstein. 1993. Order-Sorted Theory Unification. Technical Report 32. Digital Equipment Corporation.

Carpenter, Bob. 1992. *The Logic of Typed Feature Structures - With Applications to Unification Grammars, Logic Programs and Constraint Resolution.* New York: Cambridge University Press.

Carpenter, Bob, and Gerald Penn. 1994. ALE—The Attribute Logic Engine, User's Guide, Version 2.0.1, December 1994. Technical report. Carnegie Mellon University: Computational Linguistics Program, Philosophy Department.

Emele, Martin, and Rémi Zajac. 1990. Typed Unification Grammars. In *Proceedings of the 13th Conference on Computational Linguistics (COLING)*, ed. Hans Karlgreen. Helsinki.

Gerdemann, Dale, and Paul John King. 1993. Typed Feature Structures for Expressing and Computationally Implementing Feature Cooccurrence Restrictions. In *Proceedings of 4. Fachtagung der Sektion Computerlinguistik der Deutschen Gesellschaft für Sprachwissenschaft*, 33–39.

Götz, Thilo. 1994. A Normal Form for Typed Feature Structures. Arbeitspapiere des SFB 340 Nr. 40. Universität Tübingen.

Götz, Thilo, Detmar Meurers, and Dale Gerdemann. 1997. *The ConTroll Manual (ConTroll v.1.0β, Xtroll v.5.0β)*. Seminar für Sprachwissenschaft, Universität Tübingen.

Götz, Thilo, and Walt Detmar Meurers. 1995. Compiling HPSG Type Constraints into Definite Clause Programs. In *Proceedings of the Thirty-Third Annual Meeting of the ACL*. Boston. Association for Computational Linguistics.

Hinrichs, Erhard, and Tsuneko Nakazawa. 1989. Review of Word Order and Constituent Structure by Hans Uszkoreit. *Language* 65:141–149.

Hinrichs, Erhard W., and Tsuneko Nakazawa. 1994. Partial-VP and Split-NP Topicalization in German - An HPSG Analysis. In: Erhard W. Hinrichs, W. Detmar Meurers, and Tsuneko Nakazawa: *Partial-VP and Split-NP Topicalization in German—An HPSG Analysis and its Implementation.* Arbeitspapiere des SFB 340 Nr. 58, Universität Tübingen.

Meurers, W. Detmar. 1994. On Implementing an HPSG Theory—Aspects of the Logical Architecture, the Formalization, and the Implementation of Head-Driven Phrase Structure Grammars. In: Erhard W. Hinrichs, W. Detmar Meurers, and Tsuneko Nakazawa: *Partial-VP and Split-NP Topicalization in German—An HPSG Analysis and its Implementation*. Arbeitspapiere des SFB 340 Nr. 58, Universität Tübingen.

Pollard, Carl. 1996. On Head Non-Movement. In *Discontinuous Constituency*, ed. Harry Bunt and Arthur van Horck. Berlin, New York: Mouton de Gruyter. (published version of a ms. dated January 1990).

Pollard, Carl, and Ivan Sag. 1994. *Head-Driven Phrase Structure Grammar*. University of Chicago Press.

# 17

# Inside-Out Constraints and Description Languages for HPSG

JEAN-PIERRE KOENIG

An important contrast between most current syntactic frameworks and Head-Driven Phrase Structure Grammar or Lexical Functional Grammar (hereafter HPSG and LFG respectively) is the common insistence of the latter two on the need to distinguish between the mathematical structures which model utterance types and the logical formulas which describe these structures (see Kaplan and Bresnan 1982, Pollard and Sag 1994, Kaplan 1995 *inter alia*). Grammars are viewed as sets of constraints expressed in a description language whose denotata serve as models of linguistic utterances. In such frameworks, it is possible to change the description language—and the possible grammars which can be written within it—without altering the modeling domain (the linguistic ontology). In this paper, I present a particular class of examples for which this distinction between the modeling domain and the formulas which describe it proves crucial. My goals are two-fold. Empirically, I wish to argue for the need to include a kind of constraints in our models of natural language only sparsely mentioned in previous literature. Methodologically, I want to illustrate the usefulness to linguistic theorizing of the afore mentioned distinction by showing how modeling this new kind of constraints does not require an enrichment of our linguistic ontology, but a change in our descriptive metalanguage.

## 17.1 A Few Examples of Inside-Out Constraints

The class of phenomena with which I am concerned is best introduced by looking back at the notion of subcategorization, first discussed within generative linguistics in Chomsky 1965. The basic idea was that it is

*Lexical and Constructional Aspects of Linguistic Explanation.*
Gert Webelhuth, Jean-Pierre Koenig, and Andreas Kathol.
Copyright © 1998, Stanford University.

useful to keep a record of its complements on a predicator's lexical entry. What this paper illustrates is that from time to time we need the converse, namely keep a record on an argument of the type of predicators it can complement. I am thus interested in cases where certain non-heads are constrained with respect to the environments in which they must be phrase-structurally embedded. I call this class of constraints inside-out after Dalrymple 1993 for reasons that will become clear shortly. References to such an idea appear here and there in the literature (cf. Lakoff's (1987) notion of bound constructions, Kay's (1994) concept of conscription, and particularly Dalrymple's (1993) notion of inside-out functional uncertainty), but for the most part scholars have not systematically gathered such cases. This paper attempts to remedy the situation. My evidence for the linguistic need for inside-out constraints comes from three grammatical areas: predicate-argument relations, binding theory, and morphology. Although it is possible that better analyses of some of these data exist which do not require their introduction, I take their apparent relevance to several different areas as further evidence of their usefulness.

### 17.1.1  Predicate-Argument Inside-Out Constraints

My first class of examples of inside-out constraints concerns predicate-argument relations and is closest to the subcategorization parallel with which I informally introduced them.

*The Dative Predication construction:* (1) and (2) illustrate the first class of sentences whose account seems to require inside-out constraints. These sentences exemplify a French construction which I call the Dative Predication construction (DP hereafter), which was discussed by Ruwet (1982) and Koenig (1994).

(1)  Je crois    des    circonstances  atténuantes
     I  believe  some   circumstances  mitigating
     à    certains  criminels.
     to   certain   criminals.
     'I believe some criminals have mitigating circumstances.'

(2)  Il a    une Toyota? Je lui      croyais  une R18.
     he has  a   Toyota. I  to.(s)he believed a    R18
     'He has a Toyota. I thought he/she had a R18.'

The DP applies to sixty so-called object to subject raising verbs and can always be paraphrased in English by a sentential complement whose main predicate is *have*. Koenig (1994) argues that the best account of (1–2) assigns to the preposition *à* or the corresponding dative clitics *lui* or *leur* a meaning parallel to English *belong*. That is, *à* in (1) denotes a possession relation (but see below for more details), the NP *des circonstances atténuantes* satisfies its possessed role and the NP *certains criminels* its possessor role. This analysis assigns a meaning to *à*, following the analysis of non-spatial prepositions as semantically potent in Wechsler 1994 and Davis 1996. The closest English parallel would be the preposition *to* which complements the verb *belong*. The DP is not the only case where a PP headed by *à* in French is semantically potent and denotes a possession relation. Some other examples of such semantically potent uses of *à* are given in (3) and (4).

(3)  a.  La  table  est  à   lui.
         the table  is   to  him/her
         'The table belongs to him/her.'

     b.  La  table  lui          appartient.
         the table  to.him/her   belongs
         'The table belongs to him/her.'

(4)  La   police  lui          a     retiré son permis de conduire.
     The  police  to.him/her   have  take  his permit of drive
     'The police took away his driving permit.'

Crucially, though, which kind of possession relation is denoted by *à* or the corresponding clitics depends on which verb the PP headed by *à* complements, thus providing our first example of an inside-out constraint—here, an instance where a complement PP selects for the head it complements. The need to restrict the *à* PP to the appropriate class of verbs is apparent when we look closely at the particular range of possession relations denoted by the use of *à* or *lui* in (1) or (2): the range is less restricted for DP sentences than for other uses of *à* or *lui* which encode a relation of possession. I present two cases here and refer the reader to Koenig 1993 and Koenig 1994 for more details.

(5)  a.  Je  lui      aimerais  davantage  d'  enthousiasme.
         I   to.him   like.cond  more        of  enthusiasm
         'I would like him to have more enthusiasm.'

     b.  *Du      charme  est  à   lui.
         of.the  charm   is   to  her
         'She has some charm.'

(6)  a.  Nous  lui      savons  plusieurs  contacts  au        pentagone.
         We    to.her   know    several    contacts  at.the    Pentagon
         'We know that she has several contacts at the Pentagon.'

     b.  *Plusieurs  contacts  au       pentagone  lui       appartiennent.
         several     contacts  at.the   Pentagon   to.him    are
         'He has several contacts at the Pentagon.'

Whereas *à* when used in the DP construction can express possession of an abstract property, it cannot when complementing the copula, as the contrast between (5a) and (5b) shows. Similarly, *lui* in (6a) expresses the idea that someone *has* contacts, but the same notion cannot be expressed by *lui* in the non-DP context in (6b). To cover these contrasts and other similar ones, we must restrict the use of *à* or *lui* to mark *non-literal* notions of possession to examples such as (1–2), that is to sentences where it complements verbs such *croire* 'to believe' or more generally, verbs of propositional attitude and verbs of saying. We thus need to include in the grammar of French the statement in (7), our first example of an inside-out constraint.

(7)   'If a phrase is headed by a *dative-predication* sign, it must complement a verb whose semantic content is a relation of type *say* or *represent*.'

*Romance faire-infinitive construction:* The Romance *faire*-infinitive construction illustrated in (8) provides the second example of inside-out statements.

(8)   Marc  a    fait   arrêter Paul par la   police.
      Marc  has  made   arrest  Paul by  the  police
      'Marc had the police arrest John.'

As is well-known, this use of *faire* involves clause-union, which HPSG models through the composition of the argument structures of *faire* and its verbal complement (see Abeillé et al. 1997 and Koenig 1994, among many others). The relevant fact for us here is that the demotion of the external-argument of the verbal complement to *faire* (*arrêter* in (8)) takes place within the complement verb's argument structure (or maximal projection in GB approaches), "before" it is composed with that of *faire*. The sensitivity of the adjunct expressing the demoted external-argument to the Aktionsart of the complement verb shows this unequivocally. The contrast between (9) and (10) shows that a PP headed by *de* can only express the external argument of stative verbs, whereas a PP headed by *par* must express the external argument of dynamic verbs. The same contrast holds for the *faire*-infinitive construction: the PP headed by *de* can only express the external argument of stative verbal complement to *faire* and the PP headed by *par* that of dynamic verbal complements (see the contrast between (11) and (12)). Since *faire* is consistently dynamic, the PP selection must take place within the argument-structure of the complement verb, and, consequently, so must the demotion of the external argument.

(9)  Jean  a    été  volontairement  suivi    *de/par  Paul.
     Jean  has  been  voluntarily     followed  of/by   Paul
     'Jean was voluntarily followed/preceded by Paul.'

(10) Le    poisson  a    été  suivi     de/*par  rôtis.
     The   fish     has  been  followed  of/by    roasts
     'The fish was followed/preceded by roasts.'

(11) Marc  a    fait  volontairement  suivre  Jean  *de/par  Paul.
     Marc  has  made  voluntarily     follow  Jean  of/by    Paul
     'Marc had Jean followed/preceded by Paul voluntarily.'

(12) Marc  a    fait  suivre  le    poisson  de/*par  rôtis.
     Marc  has  made  follow  the   fish     of       roasts
     'Marc had the fish be followed/preceded by a roast.'

I conclude that, as argued by Moore (1991) and several scholars within HPSG (see op.cit.), in *faire*-infinitive structures the complement verb's external argument is demoted. But such 'spontaneous demotion' is strictly restricted to the context of verbal complements of clause-union verbs. Conditions must therefore be attached to verbs whose external arguments undergo 'spontaneous demotion' to indicate they must complement clause-union verbs so as to rule out the ungrammatical (13).

(13) *Marc  a     arrêté     par  la   police.
      Marc  have  arrested   by   the  police
      'Marc was arrested by the police.'     (intended meaning)

To effect this restriction, one possibility is to assume that the valence-wise passive, but morphologically active class of verbs that complement *faire* in the *faire*-infinitive construction must have an empty SUBJ list (this is the solution proposed by Koenig (1994) within Construction Grammar). Even though it is descriptively adequate, this solution relies on theory-internal and parochial assumptions. Another possibility is that we bite the bullet and directly model the descriptive fact by attaching an inside-out constraint to the entry of the complement verb of a *faire*-infinitive clause-union pattern. One formulation of such a constraint is given in (14).

(14) 'If a verb is valence-wise passive, but morphologically active, it must be the complement of a verb that belongs to the *clause-union* class.'

### 17.1.2 Binding Domain 'Inside-Out' Constraints: Body-Part Binding in French

Let me know turn to the second class of phenomena for which 'inside-out' constraints are needed. As much recent work has shown, different anaphors can select different binding domains within a single language (see Manzini and Wexler 1987, Dalrymple 1993 among others). Binding domains within which anaphors must be bound must therefore be lexically specified. We must attach to the lexical entries of particular anaphors a record of the phrase-structural domain within which their antecedent must be located. The need for such constraints was at the root of the introduction of inside-out functional uncertainty within LFG (see Dalrymple 1993). In this section, I illustrate this need with a less well-known example of anaphors which pertains to an entire class of nouns. My example comes from French again, and the basic pattern is illustrated in (15) (from Zola, *Son excellence Eugène Rougon*, p.140.)

(15) '*Il* haussait **le menton**, comme si
he raised the chin, as if

**le cou** *lui* avait fait du mal.
the neck to.him had caused some pain

'He was raising his chin as if his neck hurt him.'

The NPs denoting body parts in bold face in (15) contain an unexpressed inalienable possessor argument which is co-indexed with the NPs in italics. I call *body-part*-NP*s* NPs which denote body-parts and which do not contain a complement satisfying the inalienable possessor argument of their head noun, such as *le menton* 'the chin' in (15) (to be contrasted with *son menton* 'his chin'). The co-indexing of the unexpressed arguments of body-part-NPs with their antecedents is subject to two inside-out constraints. The first is a binding domain constraint and simply says that the unexpressed possessor argument of the body-part noun must be bound within the minimal predicative phrase (the minimal complete nucleus in Dalrymple's terms). Its effects are illustrated in the contrast between (16a) and (16b) and between (17a) and (17b) (subscripts indicate co-indexing between the antecedent and the unexpressed possessor argument of the 'body-part-NP'). The possessor of the NP *la main* in (16) can be bound to the (local) subject of *lever*, but not to the subject of *persuadé*, indicating it must be bound within the first phrase containing a subject. The contrast between (17a) and (17b) shows that the constraint cannot be reduced to a pragmatic 'first available antecedent' condition, but is indeed a syntactic locality condition: *il* is the first available antecedent in (17b), but is too far syntactically to serve as antecedent of the unexpressed possessor argument.

(16)  a.  Je  l'$_i$   ai    persuadé  de  lever  la   main$_i$.
          I   her$_i$  have  persuaded  of  raise  the  hand
          'I persuaded her to raise her hand.'
      b. *Je$_i$  l'   ai    persuadé  de  lever  la   main$_i$.
          I$_i$    her  have  persuaded  of  raise  the  hand
          'I persuaded her to raise my hand.'

(17)  a.  Il  croit   que  le  vin  lui$_i$    barbouille  l'   estomac$_i$.
          he  believes  that  the  wine  to.her$_i$  upsets      the  stomach$_i$
          'He believes that the wine upset her stomach'
      b. *Il$_i$  croit   que  le  vin  barbouille  l'   estomac$_i$.
          he$_i$  believes  that  the  wine  upsets      the  stomach$_i$
          'He believes that the wine upset his stomach'

The second constraint on the construction is semantic in nature. To simplify, the body-part must be instrumental in the possessor argument's antecedent satisfying its semantic role (it must be what Langacker (1984) calls its *active-zone*). The constraint is illustrated in (18). Marc's feet are instrumental to his movement in (18a), but not to his bathing (18b). *Marc* can therefore bind the possessor argument of *les pieds* 'les pieds' in the former but not the latter. Note that adding a dative reflexive clitic playing an affected entity role as in (18c) reverses the grammaticality of (18b). In this case, the possessor of *pieds* is indeed instrumental in the reflexive satisfying an affected entity role and can therefore be bound by it.

(18)  a.  Marc$_i$  a    avancé        le   pied$_i$.
          Marc$_i$  has  moved.forward  the  foot$_i$
          'Marc$_i$ moved his$_i$ foot forward$_i$'
      b. *Marc$_i$  a    lavé   les  pieds$_i$.
          Marc$_i$  has  washed  the  feet$_i$
          'Marc$_i$ washed his$_i$ feet'
      c.  Marc$_i$  s'$_i$  est  lavé    les  pieds$_i$.
          Marc$_i$  self$_i$  is   washed  the  feet$_i$
          'Marc$_i$ washed his$_i$ feet'

To express these two constraints on French body-part NPs, we need to define a new lexical type corresponding to what I called body-part NPs, say the type *body-part-noun*—and have it be subject to the two inside-out constraints expressed in (19). One is identical to Dalrymple's minimal nucleus domain constraint. The other is particular to the construction under discussion.

(19)  a.  'If an anaphor is a *minimal complete nucleus anaphor*, it must
      be bound within its minimal complete nucleus (Dalrymple,
      op.cit).'

      b.  'If a phrase is headed by a *body-part-noun*, the body-part must
      be instrumental in the antecedent's referent satisfying its se-
      mantic role.'

### 17.1.3  Inside-Out Constraints in Morphology: Bound-Roots

My third class of examples comes from morphology and is illustrated by
the well-known data from English in (20). Even though *aggression* and
*aggressive* are derived stems formed through the affixation of *-ion* and
*-ive* respectively, the base to which these suffixes attach does not exist
in modern English. Inkelas (1989) proposes that a bound root selects for
a particular morphological context, alongside the affix's subcategorizing
for the root. She suggests that *aggressive* is formed by suffixing *-ive*
to *aggress* (*-ive*, as most affixes, subcategorizes for a class of stems in
Inkelas' approach). To insure that we cannot use the root *\*aggress* by
itself, she proposes to attach the prosodic domain condition in (20b) to
the entry for *aggress*. (20b) says that *aggress* must attach to a prosodic
domain of type $\alpha$ to form another prosodic domain of type $\alpha$. The particulars of her analysis are not the concerns of this paper. It is sufficient
to note that her account of bound roots requires one form of inside-out
constraints: the non-head of a morphological tree (its base) selects for
the morphological (prosodic) constituent structure within which it must
be embedded. (21) expresses the relevant constraint in more theory-
neutral terms.

(20)  a.  *\*aggress, aggression, aggressive*

      b.  $[_\alpha$ aggress  $[_\alpha$  ] ]

(21)  'The stem *aggress* must be the morphological daughter of a mul-
      timorphemic word'

As suggested by an anonymous reviewer, we could forego the constraint in (21) by dividing stems into two classes, *real-stem* and *fake-
stem* and requiring stems of the class of *simple-lexeme* words to be of
type *real-stem*. The *simple-lexeme* *\*aggress* would then be ill-formed
because the stem on which it is based is of type *fake-stem*. Note, that
this solution crucially relies on the existence of a distinct class of *simple-
lexeme* words to properly differentiate the ill-formed *\*aggress* from the
well-formed *aggression* or *aggressive*. Only the former belongs to the
category *simple-lexeme* and is subject to the constraint that its stem be
a *real-stem*. I know of no independent evidence that would justify this
division among words. In general, the "derivational history" of word for-

mation is morphologically irrelevant; the crucial division between simple and complex-lexemes required by this proposal would be morphologically unmotivated.

Before closing this section, let me briefly mention a fourth area where 'inside-out' constraints might be useful. I owe the example to Carl Pollard and Adam Przepiórkowski. Pollard and Yoo ((to appear)) observe that *wh*-phrases which do not appear *in situ* cannot have wider scope than that indicated by their surface position. The formulation of the relevant constraint is given in (22). Now, if we assume lexical retrieval of quantifiers as proposed in Manning et al. (to appear) and Przepiórkowski 1997, we cannot attach the constraint to a phrasal constituent as in (22). Przepiórkowski rephrases the constraint lexically as in (23).

(22)   'At any filler-head node, if the filler has a nonempty QUE value, then its member must belong to the node's RETRIEVED value.'

(23)   'If QUANTS of a *psoa* contains a *wh*-quantifier, there must be a projection with the same *psoa* involving a left-periphery *wh*-phrase.'

Clearly, the constraint in (23) is yet another example of 'inside-out' condition—it requires lexical items at which interrogative quantifiers are retrieved to be inserted in certain phrase-structural contexts. By contrast with previous examples, the motivation for an inside-out constraint is more theory-internal here, since it depends on the theory of quantifiers retrieval we adopt. But the usefulness of inside-out conditions in yet another grammatical area is still significant to my general point in this section, namely that such constraints must be recognized as part and parcel of the grammars of natural languages.

In this section, I have presented five phenomena from four different grammatical areas (predicate-argument relations, binding constraints, morphology, quantifier scoping) where something like inside-out constraints are needed. Now, leaving aside the admittedly more theory-internal case of quantifier scoping, there are still various ways in which we could handle the cited phenomena without appealing to inside-out statements. One only needs a little ingenuity and a willingness to introduce otherwise unmotivated features. But I think this is the wrong approach. By contrast to, say, subcategorization features, such putative new features one would need to introduce to handle the data are not linguistically motivated. They are not grounded in the unescapable predicate/argument organization of semantic information; furthermore, they are not a general property of words, like subcategorization. The addition of new properties to our inventory of lexical features to mimic the effects of inside-out constraint is therefore not optimal from a linguist's perspective: their functional load would simply be too small. In the next section, I propose that instead of resorting to new features in our modeling domain, we allow inside-out statements in our metalanguage describing linguistic structures. Our linguistic ontology is thus left unchanged, although not our linguistic metalanguage.

## 17.2  A Description Language for Inside-Out Constraints

If, as just suggested, inside-out constraints ought to receive a 'metalinguistic' rather than ontological treatment, how shall we model them? What makes inside-out constraints interesting methodologically is that their inclusion in our description language is not equally easy for all languages used to formalize HPSG. In fact, as I show in this section, some description languages typically assumed for HPSG grammars cannot directly express inside-out constraints.

### 17.2.1  The Sorted Rounds-Kasper Description Language

The description languages typically assumed to underlie typed feature structures and HPSG are either a (sorted) Rounds-Kasper style logic (hence RKL) or King's Speciate Reentrant Logic (hereafter SRL).[1] Since the numerous points of difference between these two types of description languages are irrelevant to my point, I focus on only one in this paper, RKL, for simplicity. RKL recognizes four types of formulas:

(24)  a.  $\sigma$ is a description, $\sigma$ a type
      b.  $\pi : \sigma$ is a description, $\pi$ a path of attributes, $\sigma$ a type
      c.  $\pi = \pi'$ is a description, $\pi$, $\pi'$ two paths of attributes
      d.  $\phi \wedge \psi$, $\phi \vee \psi$ are descriptions, $\phi$, $\psi$ descriptions

The crucial property of RKL for our purposes is that although feature structures are individuals of the universe of discourse, there are no terms (variables or constants) of the description language which denote them. The graph-theoretic interpretation of HPSG constraints is built in the description language via an isomorphism between paths (sequences of labels) and sequences of edges in the denoted graphs. Consider the conjoined description in (25).

(25)  $sign \wedge$ SYNSEM : $synsem$

The first conjunct describes feature structures whose root vertex is of type $sign$; the second conjunct describes feature structures with an edge labeled SYNSEM stemming from the root vertex and pointing toward a vertex whose type is $synsem$. The zero length of the path in the first conjunct entails that the type is true of the root vertex

---

[1]See Kasper and Rounds 1990, Pollard 1991, Carpenter 1992, among others for the former, and King 1994 for the latter.

of feature structures it describes; the fact that the path in the second conjunct is of length one entails that the type *synsem* is true of the vertex at the end of the edge stemming from the root vertex. Because of this built-in isomorphism grammatical constraints on feature-structures expressed in RKL must always take an outside-in form—that is, go from the root of the overall graph to its leaves. Inside-out constraints of the kind discussed in Section 17.1 contravene this built-in isomorphism and cannot be expressed.

### 17.2.2  Predicate-Calculus Inspired Description Languages

RKL-style languages are not the only description languages for feature structures. There is at least one other class of languages which is inspired by first-order predicate logic (see Johnson 1988, Smolka 1992). As I show in this section, such description languages are well-adapted to our problem, as one could surmise from the fact that LFG uses this kind of languages to describe inside-out functional uncertainty (see Dalrymple et al. 1995).[2]

The distinguishing characteristic of first-order predicate-logic inspired languages is that they include terms that refer to feature structures. Because of the inclusion of these terms, reference to two different feature structures within a formula can be made without relying on path-position. Space considerations prevent me from adequately discussing Johnson's or Smolka's features logics. So as to ease the comparison with a RKL-style language, I define in (26) a quantifier-free first-order language (henceforth QFFOP) corresponding to the RKL language introduced in (24). (27) adds regular expressions and conditionals descriptions to the language. The relevant satisfaction relation for the language defined in (27) is given in (28).

(26)  a.  $(\sigma x)$ is a description, $\sigma$ a type, $x$ a variable  
     b.  $(\pi x_1) \approx x_2$ is a description, $\pi$ a path, $x_1$, $x_2$ variables  
     c.  $\phi \wedge \psi$, $\phi \vee \psi$ are descriptions, if $\phi$, $\psi$ are descriptions

(27)  a.  $(\sigma x)$ is a description, $\sigma$ a type, $x$ a variable  
     b.  $(\pi x_1) \approx x_2$ is a description, $\pi$ a path, $x_1$, $x_2$ variables  
     c.  $(r x_1)$, $r$ a regular expression over paths  
     d.  $\phi \wedge \psi$, $\phi \vee \psi$, $\phi \rightarrow \psi$ are descriptions, $\phi$, $\psi$ descriptions

*Satisfaction of basic formulas for a model* $\mathcal{M} = <F, g>$, *F a Typed*

---

[2]Carl Pollard pointed out to me (p.c.) that the Relational Speciate Re-entrant Logic of Frank Richter and Manfred Sailer (see Richter 1997) also allows for the statement of inside-out constraints. As other description languages discussed in this section, it crucially includes terms denoting feature structures.

*Feature Structure* $F = < Q, \bar{q}, \theta, \delta >$, $g$ *an assignment function from variables into* $Q$:[3]

(28)  a.  $\mathcal{M} \models (\sigma\ x)$ if $\sigma$ is a type, $[\![x]\!]^{\mathcal{M}} = q$ and $\sigma \sqsubseteq \theta(q)$
b.  $\mathcal{M} \models (\pi\ x_1) \approx x_2$ if $\delta^*(\pi, [\![x_1]\!]^{\mathcal{M}}) = [\![x_2]\!]^{\mathcal{M}}$
c.  $\mathcal{M} \models (r\ \ x_1) \approx x_2$ if there is a path $\pi \in r$ such that
$\delta^*(\pi, [\![x_1]\!]^{\mathcal{M}}) = [\![x_2]\!]^{\mathcal{M}}$
d.  $\mathcal{M} \models \phi \wedge \psi$ if $\mathcal{M} \models \phi$ and $\mathcal{M} \models \psi$
e.  $\mathcal{M} \models \phi \vee \psi$ if $\mathcal{M} \models \phi$ or $\mathcal{M} \models \psi$
f.  $\mathcal{M} \models \phi \rightarrow \psi$ if it is not the case that $\mathcal{M} \models \phi$ or $\mathcal{M} \models \psi$

Crucially, because of the presence of variables that help keep track of the described feature structures, we can now directly encode in our description language inside-out constraints. (29), for example, represents within the just introduced language the constraint on *\*aggress* informally stated in (21). The constraint reads: if a feature structure $x_1$ is of type *aggress*, a feature structure $x_2$ of type *complex-lexeme* must have $x_1$ as the value of its STEM attribute. (30) represents the more complex Dative Predication constraint informally stated in (7) in all its HPSG details; (31) expresses the same constraint semi-formally using an AVM notation. The constraint reads: if a feature structure $x_1$ is of type *dative-predication*, then a feature structure $x_2$ of type *phrase* must have the SYNSEM of $x_1$ as one element of its subcategorization list as well as have a head-daughter whose semantic nucleus is of type *say-rel* or *represent-rel*.[4]

(29)  $(aggress\ x_1) \longrightarrow ((complex\text{-}lexeme\ x_2) \wedge (\text{STEM}\ x_2) \approx x_1)$

(30)  $(dative\text{-}predication\ x_1) \longrightarrow ((phrase\ x_2) \wedge (\text{DGHTERS}\ x_2) \approx x_3$
$\wedge\ (\text{HEAD-DGHTER}\ x_3) \approx x_4 \wedge (\text{SYNSEM}\ x_4) \approx x_5 \wedge (\text{LOCAL}\ x_5)$
$\approx x_6 \wedge (\text{CONTENT}\ x_6) \approx x_7 \wedge (\text{NUCLEUS}\ x_7) \approx x_8 \wedge ((say\text{-}rel\ x_8) \vee$
$(represent\text{-}rel\ x_8)) \wedge (\text{CATEGORY}\ x_6) \approx x_9 \wedge (\text{ARG-ST}\ x_9) \approx x_{10} \wedge$
$((\text{REST}^*).\text{FIRST}\ x_{10}) \approx x_{11} \wedge (\text{SYNSEM}\ x_1) \approx x_{11})$

---

[3]As is customary, Q is a non-empty, finite set of states, $\bar{q}$ is the start state, $\delta$ is a partial transition function, and $\theta$ is a type assignment function. $\delta^*$ is defined as follows: for empty paths $p$, $\delta^*(p, x) = x$, for non-empty paths $p = lp'$, $\delta^*(p, x) = \delta^*(p', \delta(l, x))$.

[4]Clearly, the statement in (30) is partial. It only includes information which cannot be inferred from general principles or the grammar of French.

(31)  $x_1$

$$\begin{bmatrix} dat\text{-}predication \\ \text{SYNSEM} \quad x_{11} \end{bmatrix}$$

$\longrightarrow$

$x_2$

$$\begin{bmatrix} \text{DGTRS} \mid \text{HD-DGTR} \begin{bmatrix} \text{SYNSEM} \mid \text{LOCAL} \begin{bmatrix} \text{CONTENT} & say\text{-}rel \vee represent\text{-}rel \\ \text{CAT} & \begin{bmatrix} \text{ARG-ST} \langle \dots, x_{11}, \dots \rangle \end{bmatrix} \end{bmatrix} \end{bmatrix} \end{bmatrix}$$

Now that I have briefly introduced a predicate logic based language within which inside-out constraints can be stated, the reader might wonder what the logical properties of the languages defined in (26) and (27) are. Firstly, note that adopting a quantifier-free first-order description language is not 'conservative' with respect to sorted RKL. RKL logics rely on the partiality of denoted objects and unification. Conjunction of formulas, in particular, corresponds to unification of the conjuncts' denotata. But in QFFOP conjuncts do not have to share variables and conjoined formulas in general are not insured to denote connected graphs. Conjunction of formulas cannot therefore translate model-theoretically into unification of denotata. More generally, as in Johnson's AVL or King's SRL, we cannot rely on partiality of information and unification. An immediate consequence is that we cannot directly translate Pollard (1991) or Carpenter's (1992) axiomatization of sorted RKL, since these logics depend on the correspondence between conjunction and unification. Secondly, the satisfiability of a QFFOP formula without functional uncertainty is decidable only if appropriateness conditions on types are not included as axioms in the logic (as mentioned in Johnson 1995). Finally, whether the satisfiability of a formula with functional uncertainty is decidable depends on how negative descriptions are interpreted (the same restriction applies to LFG-style equations for inside-out functional uncertainty, Ron Kaplan (p.c.)).

## 17.3 Conclusion

I have argued in this paper that grammars must include a new kind of constraints which attach to stems and words and stipulate the phrase-structural environment in which they can appear. I suggested that the existence of these constraints should not prompt us to change anything in the structures that model information associated with strings (our linguistic ontology). The needed change is in the metalanguage of linguistic descriptions. I then showed that within current path-based descriptions languages for HPSG such constraints cannot be expressed, but they can within a quantifier-free first-order predicate logic-based description language (more generally, languages that include terms denoting feature structures). Aside from their inherent grammatical interest, inside-out constraints thus provide us with a methodological lesson. By distinguishing between modeling domains and description languages, HPSG and LFG enable us to differentiate between two methods for modeling descriptive generalizations we uncover: by augmenting our repertoire of linguistic objects and their properties or by adding to our list of constraints on those objects. Which course is better depends on the particulars of the case at hand. It is important, though, that we are provided with the choice.

## References

Abeillé, Anne, Danièle Godard, Philip Miller, and Ivan Sag. 1997. French Bounded Dependencies. In *Romance in* HPSG, ed. Luca Dini and Sergio Balari. Stanford: CSLI.

Carpenter, Bob. 1992. *The Logic of Typed Feature Structures*. Cambridge: Cambridge University Press.

Chomsky, Noam. 1965. *Aspects of the Theory of Syntax*. Cambridge, MA: MIT Press.

Dalrymple, Mary. 1993. *The Syntax of Anaphoric Binding*. Chicago: CSLI.

Dalrymple, Mary, John T. Maxwell III, and Annie Zaenen. 1995. Modeling Syntactic Constraints on Anaphoric Binding. In *Formal Issues in Lexical-Functional Grammar*, ed. Mary et al. Dalrymple. 167–175. Stanford: CSLI.

Davis, Anthony. 1996. *Linking and the Hierarchical Lexicon*. Doctoral dissertation, Stanford University, Stanford.

Inkelas, Sharon. 1989. *Prosodic Constituency in the Lexicon*. Doctoral dissertation, Stanford University, Stanford.

Johnson, Mark. 1988. *Attribute-Value Logic and the Theory of Grammar*. Stanford: CSLI.

Johnson, Mark. 1995. Logic and Feature Structures. In *Formal Issues in Lexical-Functional Grammar*, ed. Mary Dalrymple, Ronald M. Kaplan, John T. Maxwell III, and Annie Zaenen. 369–380. Stanford: CSLI.

Kaplan, Ronald. 1995. The Formal Architecture of Lexical-Functional Grammar. In *Formal Issues in Lexical-Functional Grammar*, ed. Mary et al. Dalrymple. 7–27. Stanford: CSLI.

Kaplan, Ronald, and Joan Bresnan. 1982. Lexical-Functional Grammar: A Formal System for Grammatical Representation. In *The Mental Representation of Grammatical Relations*, ed. Joan Bresnan. 173–281. Cambridge, MA: MIT Press.

Kasper, Robert, and William Rounds. 1990. The Logic of Unification in Grammar. *Linguistics and Philosophy* 13:35–58.

Kay, Paul. 1994. Anaphoric Binding in Construction Grammar. In *Proceedings of BLS 20*. Berkeley. Berkeley Linguistics Society.

King, Paul. 1994. An Expanded Logical Formalism for Head-Driven Phrase Structure Grammar. Technical report. Tübingen. Seminar für Sprachwissenschaft Technical Report.

Koenig, Jean-Pierre. 1993. Semantic Constraints on Binding Conditions: The French and German Inalienable. In *Proceedings of WECOL XXIII*.

Koenig, Jean-Pierre. 1994. *Lexical Underspecification and the Syntax/Semantics Interface*. Doctoral dissertation, University of California at Berkeley, Berkeley.

Lakoff, George. 1987. *Women, Fire and Dangerous Things*. Chicago: The University of Chicago Press.

Langacker, Ron. 1984. Active Zones. In *Proceedings of the Tenth Meeting of the Berkeley Linguistic Society*, 172–188. Berkeley. Berkeley Linguistics Society.

Manning, Christopher, Ivan Sag, and Masayo Iida. (to appear). The Lexical Integrity of Japanese Causatives. In *Readings in* HPSG, ed. Georgia Green and Robert Levine. Cambridge: Cambridge University Press.

Manzini, Maria Rita, and Kenneth Wexler. 1987. Parameters, Binding, and Learnability. *Linguistic Inquiry* 18:413–444.

Moore, John. 1991. *Reduced Constructions in Spanish*. Doctoral dissertation, University of California at Santa Cruz. PhD Thesis.

Pollard, Carl. 1991. Sorts in Unification-Based Grammars and What They Mean. Ohio State University.

Pollard, Carl, and Ivan Sag. 1994. *Head-Driven Phrase-Structure Grammar*. Chicago: Chicago University Press.

Pollard, Carl, and Eun Jung Yoo. (to appear). A Unified Theory of Scope for Quantifiers and *wh*-Phrases. *Journal of Linguistics*.

Przepiórkowski. 1997. Quantifiers, Adjuncts as Complements, and Scope Ambiguities. Manuscript.

Richter, Frank. 1997. Die Satzstruktur des Deutschen und die Behandlung langer Abhängigkeiten in einer Linearisierungsgrammatik. In *Ein HPSG-Fragment des Deutschen. Teil 1: Theorie*, ed. Erhard Hinrichs et al. Chap. 2, 13–188. Tübingen, Germany: SFB 340, Universität Tübingen, April.

Ruwet, Nicolas. 1982. Le datif épistémique en français et la Condition d'opacité de Chomsky. In *Grammaire des insultes et autres études*. 172–204. Paris: Seuil.

Smolka, Gert. 1992. Feature-Constraint Logics for Unification Grammars. *Journal of Logic Programming* 12:51–87.

Wechsler, Stephen. 1994. Preposition Selection Outside the Lexicon. In *Proceedings of WCCFL XIII*, ed. et al. Aranovich, Raul. 416–431. Stanford: CSLI.

# 18

---

# Strong Generative Capacity in HPSG

Carl J. Pollard

## 18.1 Introduction

Grammars exist in the real world, more specifically the part of the world inside language knower's minds; utterance tokens are events, also in the real world but external (at least in part) to minds. Formal linguists create mathematical idealizations of both these things. A formal grammar, a certain kind of logical theory, is a mathematical idealization of the mental grammar; and utterance tokens which are judged grammatical by native language knowers are idealized as certain mathematical structures, in such a way that distinct utterances which are linguistically indistinguishable, e.g., two utterances of *Poor John ran away*, are idealized as isomorphic structures. What I think ties all these things together is that, given an appropriate scheme of semantic interpretation for formal grammars, and assuming it is a good grammar, the mathematical structures which idealize the grammatical utterance tokens will be (certain kinds of) *models* of the grammar. We can state this equivalently in terms of prediction: a formal grammar is a scientific theory which predicts that an utterance token will be judged grammatical if and only if it is (or more precisely, is idealized as) a model of the grammar (more specifically, a model which is *singly generated*, in a sense to be explained below).

---

I owe a profound debt of gratitude to Paul King, whose ideas pervade this paper. Indeed, King authored a draft of which this paper is a radical revision. The only reason King's name does not appear on the byline is that he is unsympathetic to the way that strong generative capacity is defined, for reasons explained in King in prep. Thanks are also due to Frank Richter, who pointed out a number of errors in an earlier draft.

*Lexical and Constructional Aspects of Linguistic Explanation.*
Gert Webelhuth, Jean-Pierre Koenig, and Andreas Kathol.
Copyright © 1998, Stanford University.

On the other hand, generative grammarians are accustomed to thinking of a formal grammar as *generating* a set of structures, called the *strong generative capacity* (SGC) of the grammar. This set is usually considered to have the following two properties: (1) no two of its members are structurally isomorphic; and (2) if the grammar is making good predictions, then utterance tokens whose structures are isomorphic to members of the SGC will be judged grammatical.

Now consider the following two questions. First, recall that immediately above we considered two token utterances of *Poor John ran away*. The question is: precisely what, if anything, is this mysterious entity *Poor John ran away* of which our two utterance tokens are instances, and should we (as linguists) care? The second question is: what, if anything, is the SGC of a grammar? In this paper, we propose answers to these questions. Most of the paper is formal in character, but the intuition behind the formalities can be stated simply along the following lines.

As for the first question, one may be tempted to say that *Poor John ran away* is a type, or property, of which distinct token utterances are instances. Alas, in what sense such types exist, if at all, is a question that is answered differently in different ontologies. Fortunately, though, nothing about the nature of linguistic theory requires us to take a stand on this question one way or the other. On the other hand, it would be nice to have a name for the isomorphism class of structures which includes (the structures that idealize) all these tokens; we could perfectly well call it the *Poor John ran away* isomorphism class without accepting the reality of a *Poor John ran away* type. For that matter, there is a well-known technique—to be explained below—for selecting from an isomorphism class of structures (at least, for the kinds of structures we are dealing with), a canonical representative. We are going to take the liberty of using *Poor John ran away* as the name of the canonical representative of the isomorphism class discussed immediately above. Thus, according to the practice we are adopting, *Poor John ran away* is a canonical representative of a certain isomorphism class of singly generated models of our formal grammar.

Second, what does our grammar generate? Well, *Poor John ran away*, among other things. More generally, we will *define* the **strong generative capacity (SGC)** of a grammar to be the set of canonical representatives of the isomorphism classes of singly generated models of the grammar. This notion of SGC satisfies the two criteria mentioned above, without entailing any ontological commitment to utterance types.

## 18.2 Then and Now

In early HPSG (Pollard and Sag 1987, hereafter, HPSG'87), the formalization of grammar was based on the use of 'intuitionistic' feature structures to model *partial information* about linguistic entities. On that approach, pioneered by Pereira and Shieber (1984), Kasper and Rounds (1986), and Moshier (1988), feature structures are essentially canonical forms for logical equivalence classes of linguistic descriptions. The linguistic descriptions themselves (which may be informal attribute-value matrices or expressions in a formal feature logic) can be thought of as preordered by relative informativeness (with more informative elements lower in the preorder); here the descriptions are analogous to formulas in an intuitionistic propositional logic. Identifying informationally equivalent descriptions (which is the same as forming the Lindenbaum algebra of the feature logic), we obtain a Heyting algebra $H$, and it is elements of this algebra that were employed in early HPSG as lexical entries, grammar rules, and well-formedness principles. Now suppose that, within this algebra, we limit our attention to the subset of *coprime* elements, i.e., the equivalence classes of noncontradictory nondisjunctive formulas, but now ordered with the (restriction of the) dual ordering (i.e., with relatively more informative elements higher). Then the resulting partial order turns out to be isomorphic to the set of finite feature structures under the subsumption ordering. So in a precise mathematical sense, feature structures and feature descriptions are interdefinable.[1]

By contrast, and in accordance with the general trend in feature logic from the late 1980's on (cf. Johnson 1988, Smolka 1988, King 1989), the HPSG of Pollard and Sag 1994 (hereafter, HPSG'94), distinguishes sharply between feature descriptions and feature structures. On this more recent approach, feature structures are now employed only as (total) mathematical idealizations of linguistic entities, and the information ordering holds only among descriptions. As explained below, descriptions are employed in grammars in order to pick out that subset of the feature structures that will be regarded as (idealizations of)

---

[1]To be precise, the relationship is as follows: the set of (abstract) feature structures (including ones with infinite node sets) under the subsumption ordering is a (Scott) domain whose set of Scott compact-open subsets (i.e., finite unions of principal filters generated by finite feature structures) ordered by inclusion is isomorphic to $H$. In the other direction, the feature structure domain is recoverable is the *spectrum* (i.e., the set of prime ideals) of $H$. Thus we have a Stone duality (in the sense of Johnstone 1982, 66) between the feature structure domain and the (Lindenbaum algebra of) the feature logic. In this setting, a grammar is a finite set of sort-description pairs, and its denotation is determined by a certain fixed-point construction on a Cartesian power of the feature structure domain. For details, see Pollard and Moshier 1990 and Pollard to appear.

possible well-formed linguistic entities. Crucially, in order for negative and implicative constraints to work as intended, the underlying feature logic must now be classical (in contrast with the intuitionistic logic of the earlier approach). Now very roughly speaking, the relationship between an HPSG grammar and its SGC is analogous to the relationship between a first-order theory and its models. There are, however, some subtle differences, and it is something of an embarrassment that there is as yet no place in the literature where the relationship between an HPSG'94 grammar and its SGC is given a precise characterization. In the course of this paper we intend to fill that gap.

The remainder of this paper is organized as follows. In Section 18.3, we introduce a particular formal logic, SRL, which will be used for writing linguistic descriptions and grammars, together with a certain kind of algebraic interpretation of descriptions and grammars which is analogous in certain respects to the standard set-theoretic interpretation of classical logic. However, the models yielded by this kind of interpretation do not correspond directly to the usual linguistic notion of SGC. Section 18.4 digresses briefly from our main agenda to explain the relationship between the formal grammars of Section 18.2 and informal grammars along the lines of HPSG'94. In Section 18.5, we explain in informal terms how to use the models of Section 18.3 to construct a more satisfactory mathematical embodiment of the notion of SGC. Finally, in Section 18.6, we synopsize the mathematics that legitimates the informal approach of Section 18.5.

## 18.3 Descriptions, Theories, Interpretations, and Models

In feature-based grammatical frameworks (such as HPSG), linguistic entities are idealized of as structured objects, i.e., things with identifiable parts. An obvious example is that the constituents of a phrase can be regarded as parts. A second example is that the different 'levels of representation' or aspects of linguistic structure (phonology, morphology, syntax, semantics, pragmatics, etc.) of a linguistic expression can be viewed as parts of the expression; such a view is particularly appropriate within nonderivational frameworks (such as HPSG) where the different levels are considered to 'exist in parallel' (as opposed to one or more of the levels being sequentially derived by operating on or transforming an earlier level). A third example is that the morphosyntactic features of a word (such as the case of a noun or the inflectional form of a verb) can be considered a part of the word. In HPSG all these notions of part (inter alia) play a significant role.

The two fundamental ontological assumptions that give HPSG theory much of its distinct flavor are (1) the closed world assumption, and (2) the assumption of total well-typedness. The closed world assumption is simply that there is a fixed set of disjoint ontological categories (species) which partition the universe of linguistic entities. Total well-typedness means that (a) for each species, there is a fixed inventory of identifiable immediate subparts (features) such that every entity of that species has those and only those features; and (b) for each species and for each feature appropriate to that species, there is a fixed set of species to which the corresponding immediate subpart can belong. Simply put: different kinds of things (species) have different kinds of identifiable parts (features), which in turn must be of certain kinds (other species). Thus, e.g., linguistic expressions have various levels of representation; phrases (as opposed to words) have syntactic immediate constituents, each of which must be a word or a phrase; and the parts of speech of different classes of expressions have different morphosyntactic features, etc. In order to talk about species and their features with precision, both in describing linguistic entities and in writing grammars that predict what linguistic entities are well-formed, we will employ a particular logic, SRL (King 1989), that is specially designed for this purpose.[2]

Syntactically, an SRL language is determined by specifying two disjoint sets of nonlogical symbols (species and features) and a notion of appropriateness that relates them to each other; semantically, for a given SRL language, there will be a class of interpretations each of which provides meanings for the nonlogical symbols and for descriptions (formulas of the language). Unlike the case of many familiar logics (e.g., the first-order predicate calculus), an SRL description, when interpreted, is taken to denote not a truth value but rather a subset of the points in the interpretation. Let us make this more precise.

A **signature** is a triple $\Sigma = \langle \mathsf{S}, \mathsf{F}, \mathsf{A} \rangle$, where $\mathsf{S}$ and $\mathsf{F}$ are sets, whose members are called **species** and **features** respectively, and $\mathsf{A}$ is a total function from $\mathsf{S} \times \mathsf{F}$ to $Pow(\mathsf{S})$, called the **appropriateness** function. A **interpretation** of $\Sigma$ is a triple $I = \langle U, S, F \rangle$, where $U$ is a set, $S$ is a

---

[2]SRL is very similar in character to the attribute-value logic (AVL) of Johnson 1988, and to the feature logic (FL) of Smolka 1988; for detailed comparison, see King 1989. The most significant difference between SRL and these other logics is that the fundamental ontological assumptions (closed world and total well-typedness) are directly built into the notion of interpretation (see below), i.e., there are no interpretations for SRL in which closed world and total well-typedness do not hold. In addition, SRL is essentially equivalent to the typed feature logic of Carpenter 1992 as long as the latter is equipped with axioms of inequation-resolvedness, total well-typedness, and closed world, and as long as feature structures with infinite node sets are permitted.

total function from $U$ to $S$, $F$ is a total function from $F$ to the set of partial functions from $U$ to $U$, and for each $\varphi \in F$, for each $v \in U$,

$F(\varphi)(v)$ is defined iff $A(S(v), \varphi) \neq \emptyset$, and

if $F(\varphi)(v)$ is defined then $S(F(\varphi)(v)) \in A(S(v), \varphi)$.

The three components of the interpretation are called its **universe**, **species interpretation function**, and **feature interpretation function**, respectively; and the members of the universe are called its **objects**.[3] Informally, each species denotes a set of objects, each object is in the denotation of exactly one species, and $S$ assigns to each object the unique species to whose denotation the object belongs; thus species $\sigma$ denotes the set $\{v \in U \mid S(v) = \sigma\}$. Each feature denotes a partial function from objects to objects, and $F$ assigns to each feature the partial function it denotes; thus the feature $\varphi$ denotes the partial function $F(\varphi)$.

The appropriateness function encodes—and the definition of an interpretation enforces—a strict relationship between the denotations of species and features: if $A(\sigma, \varphi) = \emptyset$ then the domain of $F(\varphi)$ does not intersect the denotation of $\sigma$; but if $A(\sigma, \varphi) \neq \emptyset$ then that domain includes the denotation of $\sigma$ and maps it into the union of the denotations of the species in $A(\sigma, \varphi)$. For example, one would put $A(monarchy, \text{MONARCH}) = \{king, queen\}$ to indicate that each monarchy has a monarch that is either a king or a queen, and put $A(republic, \text{MONARCH}) = \emptyset$ to indicate that each republic has no monarch. For convenience, we henceforth assume that none of the logical symbols :, $\sim$, $\approx$, $\neg$, $\wedge$, $\vee$, $\rightarrow$, [ and ] is a species or a feature. In the remainder of this paper, we will assume a fixed signature $\Sigma = \langle S, F, A \rangle$.

We now define by simultaneous recursion the sets of **terms**, $T_\Sigma$, and **descriptions**, $D_\Sigma$.[4] These are the smallest sets such that

$: \in T_\Sigma$,

for each $\tau \in T_\Sigma$, for each $\varphi \in F$, $\tau\varphi \in T_\Sigma$,

for each $\tau \in T_\Sigma$, for each $\sigma \in S$, $\tau \sim \sigma \in D_\Sigma$,

for each $\tau_1 \in T_\Sigma$, for each $\tau_2 \in T_\Sigma$, $\tau_1 \approx \tau_2 \in D_\Sigma$,

for each $\delta \in D_\Sigma$, $\neg\delta \in D_\Sigma$,

for each $\delta_1 \in D_\Sigma$, for each $\delta_2 \in D_\Sigma$, $[\delta_1 \wedge \delta_2] \in D_\Sigma$,

for each $\delta_1 \in D_\Sigma$, for each $\delta_2 \in D_\Sigma$, $[\delta_1 \vee \delta_2] \in D_\Sigma$, and

---

[3]Mathematically, an interpretation is a sorted unary partial algebra, with species as sorts and feature denotations as operations, with special conditions on the domains and ranges of the operations. For this reason they are also often known as **feature algebras**.

[4]Terms and descriptions are also often called **paths** and **formulas**, respectively.

for each $\delta_1 \in D_\Sigma$, for each $\delta_2 \in D_\Sigma$, $[\delta_1 \to \delta_2] \in D_\Sigma$.

For a fixed interpretation $I = \langle U, S, F \rangle$ of $\Sigma$, we now explain how the terms and descriptions are interpreted. First, the **term interpretation function**, $T_I$, maps terms to partial functions from $U$ to $U$ as follows:

for each $v \in U$,

$\quad T_I(:)(v)$ is defined and $T_I(:)(v) = v$,

for each $\tau \in T_\Sigma$, for each $\varphi \in F$, for each $v \in U$,

$\quad T_I(\tau\varphi)(v)$ is defined iff $T_I(\tau)(v)$ is defined and $F(\varphi)(T_I(\tau)(v))$ is defined, and

$\quad$ if $T_I(\tau\varphi)(v)$ is defined then $T_I(\tau\varphi)(v) = F(\varphi)(T_I(\tau)(v))$

Informally, : denotes the identity function on the universe, and other terms, which are nonnull strings of features, denote the function composition of the functions denoted by those features.

Next, the **description interpretation function**, $D_I$, maps descriptions to subsets of the universe as follows:

for each $\tau \in T_\Sigma$, for each $\sigma \in S$,

$$D_I(\tau \sim \sigma) = \left\{ v \in U \left| \begin{array}{l} T_I(\tau)(v) \text{ is defined and} \\ S(T_I(\tau)(v)) = \sigma \end{array} \right. \right\},$$

for each $\tau_1 \in T_\Sigma$, for each $\tau_2 \in T_\Sigma$,

$$D_I(\tau_1 \approx \tau_2) = \left\{ v \in U \left| \begin{array}{l} T_I(\tau_1)(v) \text{ is defined,} \\ T_I(\tau_2)(v) \text{ is defined, and} \\ T_I(\tau_1)(v) = T_I(\tau_2)(v) \end{array} \right. \right\},$$

for each $\delta \in D_\Sigma$, $D_I(\neg\delta) = (U \setminus D_I(\delta))$,

for each $\delta_1 \in D_\Sigma$, for each $\delta_2 \in D_\Sigma$, $D_I([\delta_1 \wedge \delta_2]) = D_I(\delta_1) \cap D_I(\delta_2)$,

for each $\delta_1 \in D_\Sigma$, for each $\delta_2 \in D_\Sigma$, $D_I([\delta_1 \vee \delta_2]) = D_I(\delta_1) \cup D_I(\delta_2)$,

for each $\delta_1 \in D_\Sigma$, for each $\delta_2 \in D_\Sigma$,

$\quad D_I([\delta_1 \to \delta_2]) = (U \setminus D_I(\delta_1)) \cup D_I(\delta_2)$.

Informally, $\tau \sim \sigma$ denotes those objects from which an object of species $\sigma$ is reached by following the path $\tau$; $\tau_1 \approx \tau_2$ denotes those objects from which the paths $\tau_1$ and $\tau_2$ lead to the same object; and the boolean connectives work as in classical propositional logic.

It is crucial to bear in mind that descriptions denote subsets of the interpretation, not truth values. To put it another way, unlike the situation with (say) first-order logic, we speak not of truth in an interpretation, but rather of truth at an object in an interpretation. That is, for a fixed interpretation, we say that a description is **true** at an object of the interpretation just in case the object is in the denotation of the description.

We extend the notions of denotation and truth to **theories** (sets of descriptions) in the obvious way: the denotation of a theory $\theta$, $\Theta_I(\theta)$, is the intersection of the denotations of the descriptions in $\theta$, i.e.,

$$\text{for each } \theta \subseteq D_\Sigma, \ \Theta_I(\theta) = \{ v \in U \, | \, \text{for each } \delta \in \theta, \ v \in D_I(\delta) \},$$

and a theory is **true** at an object just in case each of its descriptions is. (An important special case of this is the **theory of** an object, which is defined as the set of all descriptions true at that object.) And an interpretation is called a **model** of a theory just in case the denotation of the theory (relative to that interpretation) is the whole universe. Equivalently, a model of a theory is an interpretation such that the theory is true at every object. Finally, a **grammar** is a pair $\langle \Sigma, \theta \rangle$, where $\Sigma$ is a signature and $\theta \subseteq D_\Sigma$.[5]

It might be expected that a model of the grammar (or, more precisely, of the grammar's theory) could be employed as the SGC of the grammar. Such a notion of SGC has the virtue of mathematical simplicity, but it suffers from a number of defects. First, there can be many models of a given grammar, and these need not all be isomorphic. Second, some models of a grammar are 'too small', in the sense that the natural language whose grammar we are trying to write might have some grammatical expressions that do not correspond to any object of the model. And third, models may differ from each other in ways that make no linguistic difference, e.g., the number of objects in the model which correspond to the sentence *Poor John ran away*. There is a clear intuitive sense in which this should not matter linguistically; we want a notion of SGC which abstracts away from how many 'instances' or 'tokens' of a given expression there are, and instead is sensitive only to isomorphism classes. In Section 18.5 we will address these problems, and present an informal argument that, as far as SGC is concerned, it is not really the models of the grammar that are of interest, but rather a certain set of feature structures associated with certain 'sufficiently large' models (viz., the **exhaustive** models). But first, we digress briefly to explain the connection between the formal notion of grammar just presented and the informal notion of grammar in the sense in which it is usually employed in HPSG practice.

---

[5]Because we are concerned primarily with issues of grammar interpretation in this paper, we have ignored purely logical and computational aspects of SRL. SRL has a sound and complete logic (see King 1989), and it is decidable whether an arbitrary description is satisfiable, i.e., whether there is some object in some interpretation at which the description is true (see Kepser 1994). For further work on the logical and computational aspects of SRL see Gerdemann and King 1994, Aldag 1997, King and Simov to appear, and King et al. to appear.

## 18.4 Formal and Informal Grammars

According to Pollard and Sag 1994, a HPSG grammar

"consists of a *sort hierarchy* and a set of *principles*. The sort hierarchy is presented as a taxonomic tree, with the root labelled *object* (the sort of all linguistic entities with which the grammar deals). For each local tree in the hierarchy, the sorts $\sigma_1, \ldots, \sigma_n$, which label the daughters, partition the sort $\sigma$, which labels the mother; that is, they are necessarily disjoint subsorts of $\sigma$ that exhaust $\sigma$. For two sorts $\sigma$ and $\tau$, $\tau$ is a *subsort* of $\sigma$ if and only if it is dominated by $\sigma$; sorts that label terminal nodes are called *maximal* (in the sense of maximally informative or maximally specific). A *feature declaration* of the form

$$\sigma: \begin{bmatrix} F_1\ \tau_1 \\ \ldots \\ F_n\ \tau_n \end{bmatrix}$$

where $\sigma, \tau_1, \ldots, \tau_n$ are sorts and $F_1, \ldots, F_n$ are feature labels, signifies that for each $i = 1, \ldots, n$, (1) the feature $F_i$ is appropriate for all objects of sort $\sigma$, and (2) for any such object, the value of the $F_i$ feature must be an object of sort $\tau_i$.

If sorts $\sigma_1$ and $\sigma_2$ bear the declarations $[F\ \tau_1]$ and $[F\ \tau_2]$ for the same feature F and $\sigma_2$ is a subsort of $\sigma_1$, then $\tau_2$ must be a subsort of $\tau_1$. A sort inherits the feature declarations of its supersorts; hence any feature that is defined for a given sort is defined for all of that sort's subsorts. By convention, the features that are declared for a maximal sort (including those inherited from its supersorts) are the only features defined for that sort. A special case is that of *atomic* sorts or simply *atoms*, maximal sorts for which no features are defined."                    (pages 395 and 396)

Moreover,

"The (finite) set of all sort symbols is assumed to be partially ordered, with sort symbols corresponding to more inclusive types lower in the ordering. For example, the sort *sign* is ordered below the sort *phrase* or *word* because signs include both phrases and words; we say, for example, that *word* is a *subsort* of *sign* and *accusative* is a subsort of *case*."                    (page 17)

Notice two points. First, the sort hierarchy is a finite partial order, sort *object* is a supersort of all other sorts, *object* denotes all linguistic objects, and the denotations of the immediate subsorts of a nonmaximal sort partition the denotation of the sort; therefore the maximal sorts are like species in that each linguistic object is in the denotation of one and only one maximal sort. Secondly, whereas for each nonmaximal sort and feature, the denotation of the feature can be defined on all objects in the denotation of the sort (as with feature PHONOLOGY and sort *sign*), on some but not all objects in the denotation of the sort (as with feature D(AUGH)T(E)RS and sort *sign*), or on no objects in the denotation of the sort (as with feature PERSON and sort *sign*), the maximal sorts are like species in that for each maximal sort and feature, the denotation of the feature can be defined only on all objects in the denotation of the sort (as with feature DTRS and sort *phrase*), or on no objects in the denotation of the sort (as with feature PERSON and sort *phrase*). In fact, each maximal HPSG sort is an SRL species, and each nonmaximal HPSG sort is the disjunction of its maximal subsorts. For example, maximal HPSG sorts *phrase* and *word* are SRL species, and nonmaximal HPSG sort *sign* is the disjunction of *phrase* and *word*. Each HPSG feature is an SRL feature, and an SRL appropriateness function A can express the HPSG feature declarations for the maximal sorts: for each maximal sort $\sigma$, for each feature $\varphi$, if $\sigma$ bears feature declaration $[\varphi \, \varsigma]$ then $A(\sigma, \varphi)$ is the set of maximal subsorts of $\varsigma$ else $A(\sigma, \varphi) = \emptyset$. The HPSG feature declarations for the nonmaximal sorts are inferable from A.[6] Thus, the signature component of an SRL grammar can express the sort hierarchy component of a HPSG grammar. Moreover, the theory component of an SRL grammar can express the set of principles that constitute the other component of a HPSG grammar. For example, since the SRL expression of nonmaximal HPSG sort *headed-structure* is the disjunction of the SRL species *head-complement-structure*, *head-marker-structure*, *head-adjunct-structure* and *head-filler-structure*, the SRL expression of the Pollard and Sag 1994 head feature principle "In a headed phrase, the values of SYNSEM | LOCAL | CATEGORY | HEAD and DTRS | HEAD-DTR | SYNSEM | LOCAL | CATEGORY | HEAD are token-identical" (page 399) is the SRL description

$$
\begin{bmatrix}
\begin{bmatrix}
: \sim phrase \ \wedge & 
\begin{bmatrix}
:\text{DTRS} \sim head\text{-}complement\text{-}structure \\
\vee :\text{DTRS} \sim head\text{-}marker\text{-}structure \\
\vee :\text{DTRS} \sim head\text{-}adjunct\text{-}structure \\
\vee :\text{DTRS} \sim head\text{-}filler\text{-}structure
\end{bmatrix}
\end{bmatrix} \\
\rightarrow :\text{SYNSEM LOCAL CATEGORY HEAD} \approx \\
\quad :\text{DTRS HEAD-DTR SYNSEM LOCAL CATEGORY HEAD}
\end{bmatrix} .
$$

Though perhaps not obvious, it is true that SRL as it stands can encode recursively defined relations (e.g., append), by using the reification technique pioneered by Aït-Kaci (1984) (also known by its detractors

---

[6] As pointed out to us by an anonymous referee, Pollard and Sag (1994) failed to make this point explicit. This rules out, for example, the possibility of a sort $\sigma$ partitioned by two subsorts $\tau_1$ and $\tau_2$, where some feature is declared for both $\tau_1$ and $\tau_2$ but not for $\sigma$.

as the 'junk slot' method); however this necessitates the introduction of features which do not correspond to the linguist's conception of a part of a linguistic entity.[7] Likewise, SRL as it stands is sufficiently expressive to encode some of the familiar ways of conceptualizing lexical rules in HPSG, such as the 'description-level' lexical rules of Meurers and Minnen 1998, and the closely related lexical-rules-as-sorts approach of Bouma 1997 and Abeillé et al. 1998,[8] and the same thing is true of linear precedence rules (see Richter and Sailer 1995).[9]

## 18.5    From Models to SGC: An Informal Synopsis

In Section 18.3, we suggested, as a first approximation, that the SGC of a grammar could be identified with the objects in a model of the grammar. On the other hand, in HPSG practice, the linguistic entities (words, phases, and their various kinds of parts) are usually represented by feature structures. But how do we get from objects in a model to feature structures? In fact, almost effortlessly. Temporarily postponing the technicalities, we can explicate the relationship as follows. A model of a grammar is an interpretation of the grammar's signature, and an interpretation is a unary partial algebra. And, given an object of the interpretation, we can look at the singly generated subalgebra generated in the interpretation by that object (using the denotations of the features as operations). But it is intuitively clear that a singly generated algebra determines a unique feature structure in a natural way: just take the generating object itself to be the root of the feature structure, the objects in the subalgebra to be its nodes, and use the operations to define the feature structure's labelled transitions in the obvious way.[10] Thus, every interpretation determines a unique set of feature structures in a simple and natural way. As far as SGC is concerned, it is these feature structures, not the model itself, that is of interest.

But more needs to be said. Notice that there is nothing to prevent

---

[7]Alternatively, SRL can be extended to allow for (bounded) quantification and relations; see Richter in prep..

[8]However, 'meta-level' lexical rules along the lines of Calcagno 1995, which require taking the closure of a set of relations on descriptions, are beyond the expressive power of SRL.

[9]SRL is not able to express the notion of 'set values' along the lines of Pollard and Moshier 1990. For an extension of SRL which is, see Alt 1996.

[10]To make the connection between objects and feature structures even more direct, we will simply *define* feature structures algebraically (instead of as graphs or as automata, as is usually done). In the terminology of the present paper, this works as follows: for a fixed signature $\Sigma = \langle S, F, A \rangle$, we define a ($\Sigma$-)**feature structure** to be an ordered pair $\langle v, I \rangle$ where $I$ is a $\Sigma$-interpretation and $v$ is an object which generates the universe of $\Sigma$ in the sense that every object in that universe can be obtained by applying to $v$ a function which is the denotation of a term.

two objects in a model of a grammar (or, more generally, in an interpretation of a signature) from determining isomorphic feature structures. On the other hand, as linguists, we are only interested in the feature structures in the set determined by the model *up to isomorphism*. As Pollard and Sag (1994) put it:

"One thing that [language] certainly does not consist of is individual linguistic events or utterance tokens, for knowledge of these is not what is shared among the members of a linguistic community. Instead, what is known in common, that makes communication possible, is the system of linguistic types. For example, the type of the sentence *I'm sleepy* is part of that system, but no individual token of it is."                                                  (page 14)

The (abstract) feature structures

"are intended to stand in a one-to-one relation with types of natural language expressions and their subparts. The role of the linguistic theory is to give a precise specification of which feature structures are to be considered admissible; the types of linguistic entities that correspond to the admissible feature structures constitute the predictions of the theory."                                          (page 8)

Here Pollard and Sag are adopting an (unnecessary!) ontological commitment to types; the point of view of this paper is more adequately reflected by replacing 'type' with 'isomorphism class' in these passages. It follows from this that we should really only be interested in the isomorphism classes represented by the set of feature structures associated with the model. In fact, there is a well-known means of associating a unique feature structure—called an *abstract* feature structure—with each isomorphism class of feature structures, and moreover distinct abstract feature structures are associated with distinct isomorphism classes. (As throughout this section, we postpone the mathematical technicalities to the following section.) This means that we can associate with each object $v$ in an interpretation $I$ a unique abstract feature structure $Abst_I(v)$, namely the abstract feature structure associated with the (isomorphism class) of the feature structure determined by $v$. In this way, each interpretation determines a unique set of abstract feature structures. In case the interpretation happens to be a model of a given grammar, we can thus think of the set of abstract feature structures determined by the model as the SGC of the grammar.

But wait: not all models of a given grammar determine the same set of abstract feature structures! For example, it is not hard to see that, given any model of a grammar, any subalgebra of that model—even a singly generated one— will also be a model; but clearly the subalgebra might determine a smaller set of abstract feature structures. And what if the model we have chosen as our touchstone of SGC is 'too small', in the sense that there is some object in some other model whose associated abstract feature structure is not among those determined by our chosen model?

There are a number of ways out of this fix, all of which lead to the same result. The first way is to forget about trying to chose a particular model to be be our touchstone for SGC. Instead, we form the set consisting of all those abstract feature structures which are $Abst_I(v)$ for some object $v$ in some model of the grammar. This set, finally, is what we have been after: it is our way of capturing the traditional notion of strong generative capacity. In fact, we might as well *define* the **SGC** of a grammar to be the set of abstract feature structures which are $Abst_I(v)$ for some object $v$ in some interpretation $I$ which is a model of the grammar.

Now consider the following question: among all the models of our grammar, can we find one which is 'so big' that the set of abstract feature structures determined by its objects includes the whole SGC of the grammar? As it happens, we can; in fact, as long as the grammar has any models at all, it will have a proper class of models with this property. We call such a model an **exhaustive** model. That is, a model is exhaustive just in case it contains, for any object $v$ in any model, an object $v'$ which determines the same abstract feature structure. This gives us a second route to SGC: we identify the SGC of a grammar with the set of abstract feature structures determined by some (any) exhaustive model.

A third way to obtain the SGC of a grammar (and the last we will consider here) is simpler than the others. We begin by limiting our attention to the set of ($\Sigma$-)abstract feature structures. We then select from it the subset of abstract feature structures which are models! What makes this so simple is the fact that we never need to construct exhaustive models, or consider proper classes of models. We only have to look at singly generated models, and, of those, only one from each isomorphism class.

To summarize, the SGC of an HPSG grammar is the set of its models which are abstract feature structures.

## 18.6 Technicalities

As before, we assume a fixed signature $\Sigma = \langle S, F, A \rangle$. An interpretation of $\Sigma$ is called **singly generated** if its universe contains an object $v$

such that every object in the universe is **accessible** from $v$; here $v'$ is defined to be **accessible** from $v$ just in case it is the value at $v$ of a function which is the denotation of a term. Now let $I = \langle U, S, F \rangle$ be an interpretation and $v$ one of its objects. We define the interpretation **generated by** $v$ in $I$, $I_v$, to be $\langle U_v, S_v, F_v \rangle$, where

$U_v$ is the set of objects accessible from $v$,

$S_v$ is the restriction of $S$ to $U_v$, and

$F_v$ is the total function from terms to partial functions from $U_v$ to $U_v$ whose value at each term $\tau$ is $F(\tau) \cap (U_v \times U_v)$.

Obviously, $I_v$ is a singly generated interpretation.

We define a **feature structure** to be an ordered pair $\langle v, I \rangle$ where $I$ is an interpretation and $v$ is an object of $I$ such that $I = I_v$. The objects of $I$ are called the **nodes** of the feature structure, and $v$, its **root**. For an arbitrary object $v$ in an interpretation $I$, we call $\langle v, I_v \rangle$ the feature structure **determined** by $v$ in $I$.

An **isomorphism** between two feature structures is just an algebraic isomorphism between their underlying interpretations which preserves the root. It is not hard to show that two feature structures are isomorphic just in case their respective roots have the same theory relative to their respective interpretations.[11]

We now single out a set of feature structures, called the **abstract** ones, which will serve as canonical representatives of isomorphism classes of feature structures. A couple of preliminary definitions are required. First, we define a set of terms $\beta$ to be **prefix-closed** just in case

$: \in \beta$,

for each term $\tau$ and each feature $\varphi$, if $\tau\varphi \in \beta$ then $\tau \in \beta$.

Second, an equivalence relation $\rho$ on $\beta$ is called a **right congruence** just in case

for any two $\rho$-equivalent terms $\tau_1$ and $\tau_2$, for each feature $\varphi$,

if $\tau_1\varphi \in \beta$ then $\tau_1\varphi$ and $\tau_2\varphi$ are $\rho$-equivalent.

We now define a feature structure $\langle v, I \rangle$ to be **abstract** just in case the following conditions are satisfied:

There is a prefix-closed set of terms $\beta$ and a right congruence $\rho$ on $\beta$ such that the nodes of the feature structure are the $\rho$-equivalence classes of $\beta$;

the root of the feature structure is the $\rho$-equivalence class of $:$;

---

[11]Two objects (not necessarily in the same interpretation) are called **indiscernible** if they have the same theory relative to their respective interpretations. Thus two objects are indiscernible iff they determine isomorphic feature structures.

for any two nodes $v$, $v'$ and any feature $\varphi$, the function denoted by $\varphi$ maps $v$ to $v'$ just in case there is a term $\tau$ in $\beta$ such that

$v$ is the $\rho$-equivalence class of $\tau$ and

$v'$ is the $\rho$-equivalence class of $\tau\varphi$.

The utility of abstract feature structures is just that every feature structure is isomorphic to precisely one abstract feature structure. In fact, given an arbitrary feature structure $\langle v, I \rangle$, it is easy to see that there is a natural bijection from the objects of $I$ to the set of $\rho$-equivalence classes of $\beta$, where $\beta$ is the set of terms which denote functions defined at $v$, and where two terms in $\beta$ are $\rho$-equivalent just in case the functions they denote (are defined at and) have the same value at $v$; the bijection in question maps each object to the equivalence class of all terms whose denotations map the root to that object. We then take these equivalence classes to be the nodes of an abstract feature structure, using the bijection to transfer the denotations of species and features from the original node set to the new node set in the obvious way. It is not hard to see that this construction reduces to the identity if the original feature structure is itself abstract; and two feature structures are associated in this way with the same abstract feature structure just in case they are isomorphic.

Now let $I$ be an interpretation. We define a function $Abst_I$ from the objects of $I$ to abstract feature structures in the obvious way: $Abst_I(v)$ is the abstract feature structure isomorphic to the feature structure determined by $v$ in $I$. In addition, we define the **abstract** of the interpretation, $A(I)$, to be the set whose members are the abstract feature structures $Abst_I(v)$ for $v$ an object of $I$.

Finally, let $\langle \Sigma, \theta \rangle$ be a fixed grammar. We say the grammar **generates** an abstract feature structure $\langle v, I \rangle$ just in case $I$ is a model of the grammar; and the **SGC** of the grammar is defined as the set of abstract feature structures that the grammar generates.

Obviously $\langle v, I \rangle$ is generated by the grammar just in case there is a model $I'$ of the grammar such that $\langle v, I \rangle$ is in $A(I')$: in fact we can choose $I'$ to be $I$ itself, since $Abst_I(v) = \langle v, I \rangle$! It can also be shown that the grammar has an **exhaustive** model, namely a model $I$ such that $A(I)$ is the SGC of the grammar. One such model can be constructed as follows: we take as its objects the set of pairs $\langle v', \langle v, I \rangle \rangle$ where $\langle v, I \rangle$ is generated by the grammar and $v'$ is one of its nodes. We leave it as an exercise for the reader to guess what the denotations of the species and features should be in this model.

# References

Abeillé, Anne, Danièle Godard, and Ivan A. Sag. 1998. Two Kinds of Composition in French Complex Predicates. In Erhard Hinrichs, Andreas Kathol, and Tsuneko Nakazawa, eds., *Complex Predicates in Nonderivational Syntax*. Syntax and Semantics, vol. 30. New York: Academic Press.

Aït-Kaci, Hassan. 1984. *A Lattice-Theoretic Approach to Computation Based on a Calculus of Partially Ordered Type Structures*. Ph.D. thesis, University of Pennsylvania.

Aldag, Bjørn. 1997 *A Proof Theoretic Investigation of Prediction in HPSG*. Master's thesis, Eberhard-Karls-Universität, Tübingen.

Alt, Natali. 1996. *A Typed Feature Logic with Set-Valued Attributes as a Foundation for LP Rules*. Master's thesis, Eberhard-Karls-Universität, Tübingen.

Bouma, Gosse. 1997. Monotonic Lexical Rules. Unpublished manuscript, Rijksuniversiteit Groningen.

Calcagno, Mike. 1995. Interpreting Lexical Rules. Paper presented at the Conference on Formal Grammar, Barcelona, July 1995.

Carpenter, Bob. 1992. *The Logic of Typed Feature Structures*. Cambridge Tracts in Theoretical Computer Science, No. 32. Cambridge: Cambridge University Press.

Gerdemann, Dale, and Paul J. King. 1994 The Correct and Efficient Implementation of Appropriateness Specifications for Typed Feature Structures. In *Proceedings of COLING 1994*, 956-960.

Johnson, Mark. 1988. *Attribute-Value Logic and the Theory of Grammar*. CSLI Lecture Notes, No. 14. Stanford: CSLI Publications.

Johnstone, Peter T. 1982. *Stone Spaces*. Cambridge Studies in Advanced Mathematics, No. 3. Cambridge: Cambridge University Press.

Kasper, Robert T., and William C. Rounds. 1986. A Logical Semantics for Feature Structures. In *Proceedings of the 24th Annual Conference of the ACM*, 235-242. New York.

Kepser, Stephan. 1994. A Satisfiability Algorithm for a Typed Feature Logic. Bericht Nr. 60, Arbeitspapiere des Sonderforschungsbereichs 340, Sprachtheoretische Grundlagen für die Computerlinguistik. Eberhard-Karls Universität, Tübingen.

King, Paul J. 1989. *A Logical Formalism for Head-Driven Phrase Structure Grammar*. Doctoral dissertation, University of Manchester, Manchester.

King, Paul J. In preparation. *Truth and Prediction in Head-Driven Phrase Structure Grammar*.

King, Paul J., and Kiril I. Simov. To appear. The Automatic Deduction of Classificatory Systems from Linguistic Theories. In *Grammars*.

King, Paul J., Kiril I. Simov, and Bjørn Aldag. To appear. The Complexity of Modellability in Finite and Computable Signatures of a Constraint Logic for Head-Driven Phrase Structure Grammar. In *Journal of Language, Logic, and Information*.

Meurers, W. Detmar, and Guido Minnen. 1998. A Computational Treatment of Lexical Rules in HPSG as Covariation in Lexical Entries. *Computational Linguistics.*

Moshier, M. Drew. 1988. *Extensions to Unification Grammars for the Description of Programming Languages.* Doctoral dissertation, University of Michigan, Ann Arbor.

Moshier, M. Drew, and William C. Rounds. 1987. A Logic for Partially Specified Data Structures. In *Proceedings of the 14th ACM Symposium on Principles of Programming Languages*, 156–167. Munich.

Pereira, Fernando, and Stuart Shieber. 1984. The Semantics of Grammar Formalisms Seen as Computer Languages. In *Proceedings of COLING 1984*, 123-129.

Pollard, Carl J. To appear. Sorts in Unification-Based Grammar and What they Mean. In Carl J. Pollard, *Lectures on Constraint-Based Grammar* Stanford: CSLI Publications.

Pollard, Carl J., and M. Drew Moshier. 1990. Unifying Partial Descriptions of Sets. In Philip P. Hanson, ed., *Information, Language, and Cognition.* Vancouver Studies in Cognitive Science, No. 1. Vancouver: University of British Columbia Press, 285-322.

Pollard, Carl J., and Ivan A. Sag. 1987. *Information-Based Syntax and Semantics.* CSLI Lecture Notes, No. 13. Stanford: CSLI Publications.

Pollard, Carl J., and Ivan A. Sag. 1994. *Head-Driven Phrase Structure Grammar.* Chicago: University of Chicago Press.

Richter, Frank, and Manfred Sailer. 1995. *Remarks on Linearization: Reflections on the Treatment of LP-rules in HPSG in a Typed Feature Logic.* Master's thesis, Eberhard-Karls-Universität, Tübingen.

Richter, Frank. In preparation. *Eine formale Sprache für HPSG und ihre Anwendung in einem Syntaxfragment des Deutschen.* Ph.D. thesis, Eberhard-Karls-Universität, Tübingen.

Smolka, Gert. 1988. A Feature Logic with Subsorts. LILOG Report 33. Stuttgart: IBM Deutschland GmbH.

# 19

# Off-line Constraint Propagation for Efficient HPSG Processing

WALT DETMAR MEURERS AND GUIDO MINNEN

## 19.1 Introduction

A major goal of a linguist writing HPSG theories is to express very general constraints to capture linguistic phenomena, leaving as much as possible underspecified. When such an HPSG theory is implemented faithfully, either processing is inefficient because only little information is available to guide the constraint resolution process, or the linguistic theory is annotated with information to guide processing. Usually such annotations are provided manually—a very time consuming and error-prone process which can change the original linguistic theory. In this paper we show that it is possible to automatically make a theory more specific at those places where linguistically motivated underspecification would lead to inefficient processing.

An off-line compilation technique called *constraint propagation* is used to improve processing efficiency by means of propagating constraints already expressed in the theory. Programs do not necessarily profit from constraint propagation. For processing grammars, constraint propagation can be very useful, since it makes it possible to process the general constraints expressing linguistic generalizations specified by the linguist, without falling prey to massive nondeterminism. The relevant observation here is that even though certain places in a grammar are underspecified, the grammar does contain enough constraining information—it just needs to be moved to guide processing. Constraint propagation also makes it possible to advance automatically generated

---

The authors are listed alphabetically.

*Lexical and Constructional Aspects of Linguistic Explanation.*
Gert Webelhuth, Jean-Pierre Koenig, and Andreas Kathol.
Copyright © 1998, Stanford University.

encodings, such as, for example, the definite clause encoding of HPSG grammars introduced by Götz and Meurers (1995, 1997b).

Constraint propagation can be performed on-line (le Provost and Wallace 1993) or it can be used to make programs more specific through off-line compilation (Marriott et al. 1988). In this paper we will focus on the off-line application of constraint propagation. While on-line constraint propagation is more space efficient since information in the code does not need to be duplicated, the off-line process can relieve the run-time from significant overhead.[1] We conjecture that the time-space tradeoff can be exploited by doing off-line constraint propagation *selectively*, i.e., only on those underspecified parts of the grammar which cause processing efficiency to suffer from massive nondeterminism. As such we presuppose that the places in a grammar which will profit from constraint propagation can be located automatically by either exploiting specific properties of the encoding of the grammar or abstract interpretation. The determination of where to perform constraint propagation is also of importance because underspecification can also be used to improve HPSG processing efficiency—see, for example, Kathol 1994, Krieger and Nerbonne 1992, Riehemann 1993 and Frank 1994. Unfortunately, a detailed discussion of this issue is beyond the scope of this paper.

Other techniques to prune the search space that are used in practical natural language processing are *dynamic coroutining*, also referred to as (goal) freezing or delaying, and *static coroutining* by means of Unfold/Fold transformation (Tamaki and Sato 1984). It is important to differentiate between coroutining and constraint propagation: Coroutining changes the way in which the search space is investigated by moving goals through a grammar either on- or off-line. Constraint propagation as conceived in this paper reduces the search space by making the arguments of calls to goals more specific. As we will discuss in Section 19.3, a combination of both techniques can be very useful as constraint propagation can be used to extract restricting information from the definition of goals also in cases where freezing of the call to these goals would hide this information.

This paper is organized as follows: We start with a discussion of two concrete HPSG examples showing how constraint propagation helps improve processing efficiency (Sections 19.2 and 19.3). In Section 19.4 sev-

---

[1]In case an operation for "subtraction" is available for the data structure used, it may be possible to reduce the space cost of the off-line process by eliminating the propagated constraints from their original specification site.

eral implementations of constraint propagation algorithms are discussed. Finally, in Section 19.5 we provide some implementation results.

## 19.2 Efficient processing of ID Schemata

In lexically oriented grammar formalisms like HPSG, the ID schemata specified by the linguist are very schematic since much syntactic information is specified in the lexicon. In faithful implementations this leads to inefficiency in top-down processing because it often is no longer possible to detect locally whether an ID schema applies or not. Consider, for example, the head-adjunct schema and the head-specifier schema of HPSG in Figures 1 and 2.[2]

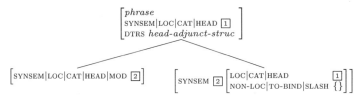

FIGURE 1  The Head-Adjunct ID Schema from Pollard and Sag 1994

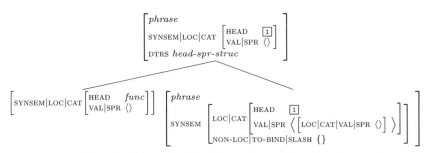

FIGURE 2  The Head-Specifier ID Schema from Pollard and Sag 1994

Due to underspecification, it cannot be determined locally whether the head-adjunct schema can expand specifiers or not. Only upon lexical lookup is it revealed that the head-adjunct schema does not have to be considered for specifiers: The lexicon contains only lexical entries like the one sketched in Figure 3, which specify the category they modify to have a *substantive* head, in this case a *noun*. This specification will

---

[2]The figures show the head-adjunct schema as expressed in the appendix of Pollard and Sag 1994 and the head-specifier schema from Chapter 9 of the same book - both including the effect of the Head Feature Principle.

therefore always clash with the specification in the head-specifier schema which demands a *functional* head value for the specifier daughter.

$$
\begin{bmatrix}
word \\
\text{PHON} < kleine> \\
\text{SYNSEM|LOC|CAT|HEAD}
\begin{bmatrix}
adj \\
\text{MOD|LOC|CAT|HEAD } noun
\end{bmatrix}
\end{bmatrix}
$$

FIGURE 3  The lexical entry for the adjective *kleine*

The sketched efficiency problem seems to suggest that top-down processing is not the right processing strategy to adopt for processing of lexically oriented grammar formalisms. This, however, is not necessarily the case. Strict bottom-up processing means that no filtering information resulting from the start category is made available. To have some guiding information in the case of parsing an extra-logical treatment of the input string can be used, for example, a link relation. However, it is unclear what such a treatment should look like for theories using more elaborate linearization operations. Furthermore, refraining from taking into account information provided by the start category is virtually impossible in the case of generation, and it is not generally clear what an extra-logical treatment of the logical form in a similar fashion as in parsing could look like. There exists an off-line compilation technique called *magic* that allows for filtering given a strict bottom-up processing strategy.[3] However, processing of magic compiled grammars suffers from linguistically motivated underspecification as discussed above just the same.

Returning to the above example, the insight behind constraint propagation is that lifting the common restricting information contained in the lexical entries up into the head-adjunct schema makes it possible to determine locally that there are no modified specifiers in the grammar. In other words, applying constraint propagation to the head-adjunct schema of Figure 1 in a grammar with a lexicon in which the only modifying entries select *substantive* heads, propagates the constraint [SYNSEM|LOC|CAT|HEAD *subst*] into the mother of the head-adjunct schema. The resulting head-adjunct schema shown in Figure 4 is now specific enough to convey immediately that it cannot be used when specifiers need to be licensed.

Note that this way of making grammars more specific is an off-line

---

[3]See among others, Ramakrishnan 1988. In Minnen 1996 applications of these techniques to natural language processing are discussed.

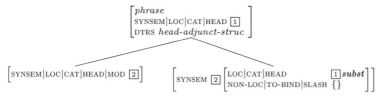

FIGURE 4   The Head-Adjunct ID Schema after constraint propagation

process performed completely automatically. It allows the grammar writer to specify theories in a lexically oriented fashion without any additional procedural specifications.

## 19.3   Efficient processing of the lexicon

Constraint propagation can also be applied to optimize automatically generated lexicons. In Meurers and Minnen 1997 a compiler is described which translates a set of HPSG lexical rules and their interaction into definite relations used to constrain lexical entries. This, so-called, *co-variation approach* uses the generalizations captured by lexical rules for processing and makes it possible to deal with the infinite lexicon proposed in many recent HPSG theories. Most of the current HPSG analyses of Dutch, German, Italian, and French fall into this category. This is, for example, the case for all proposals working with verbal lexical entries which raise the arguments of a verbal complement (Hinrichs and Nakazawa 1989) that also use lexical rules such as the Complement Extraction Lexical Rule (Pollard and Sag 1994) to operate on those raised elements. Also an analysis treating adjunct extraction via lexical rules (van Noord and Bouma 1994) results in an infinite lexicon.

The linguist inputs the lexical rules used in his/her theory. On the basis of this specification and the signature of the proposed grammar, the covariation compiler automatically deduces the transfer of properties which were left unspecified in the lexical rule provided by the linguist. The compiler then uses the lexical rules and lexical entries to produce a definite clause encoding of lexical rules and their possible interaction. The resulting lexicon consists of extended lexical entries calling an interaction predicate encoding the entries which can be derived by lexical rule applications. Figure 5 shows an example for an extended lexical entry: a simplified entry for a German auxiliary using argument raising in the style of Hinrichs and Nakazawa (1989).

The call to the interaction predicate encodes the possible sequences of lexical rule applications. For a simple theory with a Complement Extraction Lexical Rule (CELR) and a Finitivization Lexical Rule (FINLR)

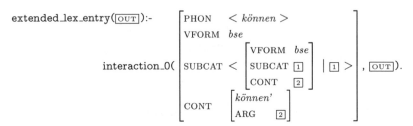

FIGURE 5   The extended lexical entry for the modal auxiliary *können* ('can')

the slightly simplified interaction predicate looks as shown in Figure 6 on page 305.[4] The encoding in Figure 6 already contains the deduced transfer information in the call to the lexical rule predicates; for example, the PHON, VFORM, and CONT values are transferred to the CELR by adding the corresponding structure sharings to the IN tag and to the AUX tag appearing in the call to the celr/2 predicate. Regarding the notation in the figure, a variable tag and a feature specification in the same argument slot are intended to be unified.

The automatically obtained encoding of lexical rule application in lexical entries shown in the above figures is not very efficient since before execution of the call to the interaction predicate it is unknown which information of the base lexical entry ends up in a derived lexical entry. One is therefore forced to execute the call to the interaction predicate directly when the lexical entry is used during processing, independent of the processing strategy used. Otherwise there is no information available to restrict the search space of a generation or parsing process.

Off-line constraint propagation can be used to avoid this by factoring out the information which is common to all solutions for the called interaction predicate. This is accomplished by computing the most specific generalization of these solutions and lifting this common information into the extended lexical entries. Let c be the common information, and $D_1, \ldots, D_k$ the solutions for the interaction predicate called. Then by distributivity we factor out c in $(c \wedge D_1) \vee \ldots \vee (c \wedge D_k)$ to obtain $c \wedge (D_1 \vee \ldots \vee D_k)$, where the D are assumed to contain no further common factors. The result of performing constraint propagation on the extended lexical entry for *können* is given in Figure 7 on page 306. In the next section we investigate in more detail how this result is achieved. Delaying the call to an interaction predicate as in van Noord and Bouma 1994 by freezing the recursive application of a lexical rule on the basis of

---

[4]The lexical rules in Figure 6 are simplified versions of the CELR (Pollard and Sag 1994, 378) and the Third-Singular Inflectional Rule (Pollard and Sag 1987, 210).

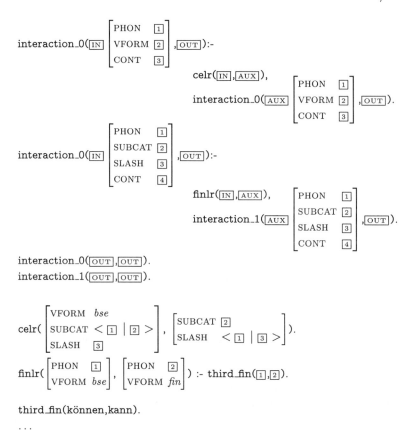

FIGURE 6 Encoding sequences of lexical rule application in definite relations

user-specified delay information, can hide important restricting information because it is specified in the definition of the frozen goal. Therefore constraint propagation can be useful, also when corouting techniques are used.

As discussed in Griffith 1996 an extension of the constraint language with *contexted constraints*, also referred to as dependent or named disjunctions, in certain cases makes it possible to circumvent constraint propagation. Encoding the disjunctive possibilities for lexical rule application using contexted constraints instead of definite clause attachments makes all relevant linguistic information available at lexical look-up. In case of infinite lexica, though, a definite clause encoding of disjunctive possibilities is still necessary and constraint propagation is indispensable for efficient processing (see Section 19.5).

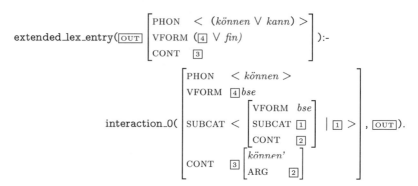

FIGURE 7   The extended lexical entry for *können* after specialized constraint propagation

## 19.4   Implementing Constraint Propagation

In this section we discuss implementations of some constraint propagation algorithms (in Prolog). We first present constraint propagation using a simple top-down interpreter and point out the problems of this basic algorithm. Subsequently, possible extensions of this interpreter with a, so-called, *branch-and-bound* optimization (le Provost and Wallace 1993) and a depth-bound are discussed. Finally, we show that it is possible to use knowledge about the specific structure of certain encodings to obtain specialized constraint propagation algorithms. In our case, we can exploit our knowledge of the encoding of the lexicon produced by the lexical rule compiler to define a specialized top-down interpreter that relieves us from termination problems related to the covariation encoding of infinite lexicons.

For reasons of exposition, in the remainder of this section, we assume a definite clause representation of an HPSG theory (Götz and Meurers 1995, 1997b) and do not make typed feature structure unification explicit.

### 19.4.1   Top-down constraint propagation

Consider the predicate constraint_propagation_on_goal/0 in Figure 8. The predicate get_goal/0 gets a particular goal on which we want to perform constraint propagation.[5] Subsequently, generalized_solutions_for_goal/2 is called to produce a possibly more specific instance of this goal. The call to write_goal/1 replaces the original goal with the possibly more specific

---

[5] If some kind of abstract interpretation is used to determine the places in a program where underspecification leads to massive nondeterminism, this information can be used to automatically make get_goal/1 select the relevant goals.

```
constraint_propagation_on_goal:-
    get_goal(Goal),
    generalized_solutions_for_goal(Goal,MoreSpecificGoal),
    write_goal(MoreSpecificGoal).
```

FIGURE 8  A predicate defining simple off-line constraint propagation
on a goal

goal obtained. As shown in Figure 9 generalized_solutions_for_goal/2 computes an instance GeneralizedSolutionsForGoal of Goal by finding all its solutions with a call to top_down_interpret/1 and subsequently generalizing over all the solutions.[6]

```
generalized_solutions_for_goal(Goal,GeneralizedSolutionsForGoal):-
    findall(Goal, top_down_interpret(Goal), SolutionList),
    generalize_all_solutions(SolutionList,GeneralizedSolutionsForGoal).
```

FIGURE 9  Generalizing all solutions for goal

Figure 10 provides the definition of top_down_interpret/1, a top-down interpreter provided by Pereira and Shieber (1987, 160ff).[7]

```
top_down_interpret(true).
top_down_interpret(Goal):-
    clause((Goal :- Body)),
    top_down_interpret(Body).
top_down_interpret((Body1, Body2)):-
    top_down_interpret(Body1),
    top_down_interpret(Body2).
```

FIGURE 10  A simple top-down interpreter

This interpreter falls prey to nontermination. For example, in the case of the recursive CELR of Figure 6 it is possible to remove elements from a

---

[6]Notice that in case there exists only one solution to a goal, the effect of performing constraint propagation on that goal is similar to its *partial evaluation*, see, for example, Pereira and Shieber 1987.

[7]The predicate is renamed here for expository reasons. The nonunit and unit clauses representing an HPSG theory are represented as clause(( Head :- Body )). and clause(( Head :- true )). , respectively.

(subcategorization) list that is underspecified as in the extended lexical entry of Figure 5 over and over again.

Motivated by efficiency considerations, le Provost and Wallace (1993) propose the *branch-and-bound* optimization. This optimization also improves termination behavior. However, there exist linguistically motivated types of recursion for which branch-and-bound does not terminate either. Minnen et al. (1996) introduce the notion of a *building series*. Intuitively understood, a building series "builds up" a structure recursively until it matches a "base" case.[8] This type of recursion is problematic for top-down processing as this building can go on forever. Branch-and-bound does not ensure termination in the light of this type of recursion.

These termination problems necessitate an alternative implementation that avoids infinite loops. One possibility is to extend the interpreter in Figure 10 with a depth-bound as shown in Figure 11.[9]

```
db_top_down_interpret(true, Depth, Max):-
    Depth < Max.
db_top_down_interpret(Goal, Depth, Max):-
    Depth < Max,
    clause((Goal :- Body)),
    NewDepth is Depth + 1,
    db_top_down_interpret(Body, NewDepth, Max).
db_top_down_interpret((Body1, Body2), Depth, Max):-
    Depth < Max,
    db_top_down_interpret(Body1, Depth, Max),
    db_top_down_interpret(Body2, Depth, Max).
db_top_down_interpret(_Goal, Depth, Max):-
    Depth >= Max.
```

FIGURE 11  A depth-bounded top-down interpreter

Notice that the use of this highly incomplete interpreter for constraint propagation can only lead to a common factor that is too general. Intuitively understood, the depth-bound can only cut off branches of the search space which will eventually fail or lead to a solution more specific than the partial solution that has been computed. When the depth-

---

[8]An example of a lexical rule that exhibits this type of recursion on structural information is the Add Adjuncts Lexical Rule proposed in van Noord and Bouma 1994.

[9]The call to **top_down_interpret/3** in **generalize_solutions_for_goal/2** shown in Figure 9 has to be changed accordingly.

bound hits clause 4 of db_top_down_interpret/3 in Figure 11, the result returned in the first argument does not become further instantiated. As a result the MoreSpecificGoal computed can never become too specific and correctness is guaranteed.

While the depth-bounded interpreter can be employed in general, it is far from optimal to use it for constraint propagation of the covariation encoding of the lexicon. This is due to the fact that lexical rule application is encoded as forward chaining using *accumulator passing* (O'Keefe 1990): The $\boxed{\text{OUT}}$ argument of an interaction predicate gets instantiated upon hitting a base case, i.e., a unit interaction clause. It serves only to "return" the lexical entry eventually derived. When the depth-bound cuts off a particular branch of the search space that corresponds to a recursively defined interaction predicate, the $\boxed{\text{OUT}}$ argument remains completely uninstantiated. Consequently, generalizing over all possible (partial) solutions does not lead to a common factor that is more specific than the original goal selected by get_goal/1. In the next section, we show that it is possible to overcome this problem with a specialized interpreter.

## 19.4.2 Specialized Constraint Propagation

We employ a specialized top-down interpreter that allows us to extract an informative common factor using constraint propagation even in cases of a covariation encoding of an infinite lexicon. The specialized interpreter makes the use of a depth-bound to ensure termination of the interpretation of the interaction predicates superfluous.[10] Intuitively understood, the specialized interpreter exploits the fact that automatic property transfer is not influenced by recursion. I.e., the specifications that are left unchanged by a recursive lexical rule are independent of the number of times the rule is applied. This is a general, i.e., theory independent, property of the covariation encoding of lexical rule application and interaction, and therefore the improvement of the covariation encoding using specialized constraint propagation can be accomplished completely automatically.

We discuss a possible extension of the simple top-down interpreter given in Figure 10. For expository reasons the interpreter given in Figure 12 is simplified in the sense that it deals only with directly recursive interaction predicates such as the one given in Figure 6. Indirectly recursive interaction predicates necessitate a further extension of the interpreter with a tabulation technique as indirect recursion can not be

---

[10]As nontermination can not only result from recursive interaction predicates, a depth-bound might still be needed for the other predicates. We ignore this complication in the remainder of this section for expository reasons.

identified locally, i.e., as a property of the interaction clause under consideration. The original top-down interpreter is extended with an extra clause, i.e., the second clause of spec_top_down_interpret/1, which is specialized to deal with recursive interaction predicates which are identified by means of a call to recursive_interaction_clause/1. By eliminating the call to the lexical rule predicate (corresponding to the application of the recursive lexical rule) the interpreter abstracts over the information that is changed by the recursive lexical rule. As a result, only unchanged information remains. Subsequently, spec_top_down_interpret/2 is called to ensure that the same recursive interaction predicate is not called (over and over) again.[11]

```
spec_top_down_interpret(true).
spec_top_down_interpret(Goal):-
    clause((Goal :- Body)),
    recursive_interaction_clause((Goal :- Body)),
            % True if the retrieved clause is a directly recursive
            % interaction clause.
    make_body_more_general(Body, AdaptedBody),
            % Removes the call to the recursive lexical rule predicate from
            % Body in order to abstract over changed information.
    spec_top_down_interpret(AdaptedBody,(Goal :- Body)).
spec_top_down_interpret(Goal):-
    clause((Goal :- Body)),
    \+ recursive_interaction_clause((Goal :- Body)),
    spec_top_down_interpret(Body).
spec_top_down_interpret((Body1, Body2)):-
    spec_top_down_interpret(Body1),
    spec_top_down_interpret(Body2).

spec_top_down_interpret(Goal, RecursiveInteractionClause):-
    clause((Goal :- Body)),
    \+ (Goal :- Body) = RecursiveInteractionClause,
            % Avoid repeated application of RecursiveInteractionClause.
    spec_top_down_interpret(Body).
```

FIGURE 12  A top-down interpreter specialized for constraint propagation on (calls to) interaction predicates in a covariation lexicon

---

[11]We exploit the fact that two interaction clauses can never stand in the subsumption relation. Otherwise, a more elaborate equality test is needed in spec_top_down_interpret/2 to avoid repeated application.

Since we abstract over the information changed by a recursive lexical rule, the common factor that is extracted by means of performing constraint propagation with the specialized top-down interpreter might be too general: In case we are dealing with an infinite lexicon not all (possible infinite) applications of a recursive lexical rules are performed and there might be cases in which the application of a lexical rule after the n-th cycle is impossible even though we are taking it into account during constraint propagation. It is important to note though that such a situation can only lead to a common factor that is too general since generalizing over too large a set of solutions can only lead to a less specific generalization, not a more specific one. Therefore constraint propagation does not influence the soundness and completeness of the encoding. At run-time the additional lexical rule applications not ruled out by constraint propagation will simply fail.

Reconsider the definite clause encoding in Figure 6. As a result of the fact that repeated recursive application of interaction_0/2 is avoided, much relevant information can be lifted into the extended lexical entry. Figure 7 given in the previous section shows the result of performing specialized constraint propagation to the lexical entry for *können* (Figure 5).

### 19.4.3 Constant time lexical lookup

As Figure 7 shows, optimizing the extended lexical entries by means of specialized constraint propagation can also lift up phonological information in case of infinite lexicons.[12] In the case of parsing, this information can be used to index the lexicon so that constant time lexical lookup can be achieved. For this purpose, the extended lexical entry is split up as shown in Figure 13.

ind_lex_entry(können, $\boxed{\text{OUT}}\left[\text{PHON} < \text{können} >\right]$):- extended_lex_entry($\boxed{\text{OUT}}$).

ind_lex_entry(kann, $\boxed{\text{OUT}}\left[\text{PHON} < \text{kann} >\right]$):- extended_lex_entry($\boxed{\text{OUT}}$).

. . .

FIGURE 13  The result of splitting up the optimized lexical entry in Figure 7

On the basis of the input string it is now possible to access the lexicon in constant time. Without specialized constraint propagation this is impossible as the possible values of the phonology feature are hidden

---

[12]If there are recursive phonology changing rules the phonological information cannot be lifted by the constraint propagation using the specialized interpreter presented.

away deep in the covariation encoding of the lexical entries that can be derived from the base lexical entry.

## 19.5 Implementation Results

The depth-bounded constraint propagation method was implemented for the ConTroll system (Gerdemann and King 1994, Götz and Meurers 1997a) under Prolog. Test results on a complex grammar implementing an analysis of partial VP topicalization in German (Hinrichs et al. 1994) show that constraint propagation significantly improves parsing with a covariation encoding of lexical rules. For the lexicons produced by the covariation compiler, the implementation revealed that the most specific generalization which is propagated contains much valuable information. This is the case because usually the lexical entries resulting from lexical rule application only differ in few specifications compared to the number of specifications in a base lexical entry. The relation[13] between parsing times with the expanded (EXP), the covariation (COV) and the constraint propagated covariation (OPT) lexicon for the above grammar can be represented as OPT : EXP : COV = 1 : 1.3 : 14.

## Acknowledgments

The research reported here was supported by Teilprojekt B4 'From Constraints to Rules: Efficient Compilation of HPSG Grammars' of SFB 340 'Sprachtheoretische Grundlagen für die Computerlinguistik' of the Deutsche Forschungsgemeinschaft. The authors wish to thank Thilo Götz, Dale Gerdemann and the anonymous reviewers for comments and discussion.

## References

Frank, Anette. 1994. Verb Second by Underspecification. In *KONVENS '94*, ed. Harald Trost, 121–130. Berlin. Springer-Verlag.

Gerdemann, Dale, and Paul King. 1994. The Correct and Efficient Implementation of Appropriateness Specifications for Typed Feature Structures. In *Proceedings of the 15th Conference on Computational Linguistics*. Kyoto, Japan.

Götz, Thilo, and Detmar Meurers. 1995. Compiling HPSG Type Constraints into Definite Clause Programs. In *Proceedings of the 33rd Annual Meeting of the Association for Computational Linguistics*. Boston, USA.

Götz, Thilo, and Detmar Meurers. 1997a. The ConTroll System as Large Grammar Development Platform. In *Proceedings of the ACL/EACL post-*

---

[13]The comparison was done without indexing the lexicon by the word form, since such indexing is not possible for the covariation lexicon without constraint propagation.

*conference workshop on Computational Environments for Grammar Development and Linguistic Engineering*. Madrid, Spain.

Götz, Thilo, and Detmar Meurers. 1997b. Interleaving Universal Principles and Relational Constraints over Typed Feature Logic. In *Proceedings of the 35th Annual Meeting of the ACL and the 8th Conference of the EACL*. Madrid, Spain.

Griffith, John. 1996. Modularizing Contexted Constraints. In *Proceedings of the 16th Conference on Computational Linguistics*. Copenhagen, Denmark.

Hinrichs, Erhard, Detmar Meurers, and Tsuneko Nakazawa. 1994. Partial-VP and Split-NP Topicalization in German—An HPSG Analysis and its Implementation. Arbeitspapiere des SFB 340 no. 58. University of Tübingen, Germany.

Hinrichs, Erhard, and Tsuneko Nakazawa. 1989. Flipped Out: AUX in German. In *Papers from the 25th Regional Meeting of the Chicago Linguistic Society*. Chicago, Illinois. Chicago Linguistic Society.

Kathol, Andreas. 1994. Passives without Lexical Rules. In *German in Head-Driven Phrase Structure Grammar*, ed. John Nerbonne, Klaus Netter, and Carl Pollard. 237–272. Lecture Notes 46. CSLI Publications.

Krieger, Hans-Ulrich, and John Nerbonne. 1992. Feature-Based Inheritance Networks for Computational Lexicons. In *Default Inheritance Within Unification-Based Approaches to the Lexicon*, ed. Ted Briscoe, Ann Copestake, and V. de Paiva. Cambridge: Cambridge University Press.

le Provost, Thierry, and Mark Wallace. 1993. Generalised Constraint Propagation over the CLP Scheme. *Journal of Logic Programming 10*.

Marriott, Kim, Lee Naish, and Jean-Louis Lassez. 1988. Most Specific Logic Programs. In *Proceedings of 5th Int. Conference and Symposium on Logic Programming*.

Meurers, Detmar, and Guido Minnen. 1997. A Computational Treatment of Lexical Rules in HPSG as Covariation in Lexical Entries. *Computational Linguistics 23(4)*.

Minnen, Guido. 1996. Magic for Filter Optimization in Dynamic Bottom-up Processing. In *Proceedings of the 34th Annual Meeting of the Association for Computational Linguistics*. Santa Cruz, USA.

Minnen, Guido, Dale Gerdemann, and Erhard Hinrichs. 1996. Direct Automated Inversion of Logic Grammars. *New Generation Computing 14(2)*.

O'Keefe, Richard. 1990. *The Craft of Prolog*. Cambridge, USA: MIT Press.

Pereira, Fernando, and Stuart Shieber. 1987. *Prolog and Natural Language Analysis*. CSLI Lecture Notes, No. 10. Chicago, USA: Chicago University Press.

Pollard, Carl, and Ivan A. Sag. 1987. *An Information-based Approach to Syntax and Semantics: Volume 1 Fundamentals*. CSLI Lecture Notes, No., No. no. 13. Stanford, USA: Center for the Study of Language and Information.

Pollard, Carl, and Ivan Sag. 1994. *Head-driven Phrase Structure Grammar.* Chicago, USA: University of Chicago Press.

Ramakrishnan, Raghu. 1988. Magic Templates: A Spellbinding Approach to Logic Programs. In *Proceedings of the 5th Int. Conference and Symposium on Logic Programming.*

Riehemann, Susanne. 1993. Word Formation in Lexical Type Hierarchies: A Case Study of *bar*-Adjectives in German. Master's thesis, University of Tübingen.

Tamaki, Hisao, and Taisuke Sato. 1984. Unfold/Fold Transformation of Logic Programs. In *Proceedings of the 2nd Int. Conference on Logic Programming.* Uppsala, Sweden.

van Noord, Gertjan, and Gosse Bouma. 1994. The Scope of Adjuncts and the Processing of Lexical Rules. In *Proceedings of the 15th Conference on Computational Linguistics.* Kyoto, Japan.

# Part VI

## Semantics and Pragmatics

# Conjunctive Semantics for Semantically Transparent Adverbials

DAVID P. BAXTER

## 20.1 Introduction and Background

This paper argues for the use of event indices and conjoined logical clauses in HPSG semantic representations of verbal constituents, based on evidence from intersective adverbial modifiers. This style of representation has been used in some recent HPSG works, including the HPSG-based syntax textbook currently under development by Ivan A. Sag and Thomas Wasow at Stanford University (Sag and Wasow 1997), as well as works based on the Minimal Recursion Semantics system (Copestake et al. 1997). These works represent a departure from the semantic representation system used in Pollard and Sag 1994, which used indices only for nouns, noun phrases, and their modifiers. Thus, this paper presents further evidence that these recent works are on the right track.

The argument laid out in this paper relies on the fact that some adverbials, such as those in (1) (those commonly referred to as intersective), have a property that may be described as SEMANTIC TRANSPARENCY.[1]

---

A preliminary version of this paper was presented at the HPSG workshop at Cornell University in July 1997. Thanks are due to the participants there, to Georgia Green and Peter Lasersohn, to my graduate student colleagues at the University of Illinois, and to Adam Przepiórkowski for helpful comments. All errors are my own responsibility.

[1]This property is distinct from the more commonly discussed property of referential transparency.

*Lexical and Constructional Aspects of Linguistic Explanation.*
Gert Webelhuth, Jean-Pierre Koenig, and Andreas Kathol.
Copyright © 1998, Stanford University.

(1)   Semantically Transparent Adverbials
    a.   Jack went to the market *slowly*.
    b.   Jack went to the market *on Wednesday*.
    c.   Jack went to the market *with Jill*.

These adverbials are transparent in the sense that a phrase modified by this type of adverbial still contributes its meaning to the sentence just as if the adverbial were not there at all. For example, if the VP modified by a semantically transparent adverbial is the VP of the main clause of the sentence, as is the case in (1), then the claim represented by that VP is entailed by the sentence despite the modification. The adverbial simply contributes a further restriction on the meaning of the sentence. For example, each sentence in (1) still represents a claim that Jack went to the market, in addition to a further claim about how or when he went to the market.

Semantically transparent adverbials contrast with SEMANTICALLY OPAQUE adverbials (corresponding to the class of adverbials that are semantic operators), such as those in (2).

(2)   Semantically Opaque Adverbials
    a.   Jack *apparently* went to the market.
    b.   Jack *allegedly* went to the market.
    c.   Jack *probably* went to the market.

The essential semantic difference between (1) and (2) is that the sentences in (1) all entail that Jack went to the market, while those in (2) do not. A verb phrase modified by a semantically opaque adverbial does not contribute its meaning directly to the sentence. Rather, the meaning of the verb phrase is contributed to the sentence indirectly, through the mediation of the adverbial.

The difference in entailments between transparent and opaque adverbials is related to the fact that they describe properties of different kinds of things. Intersective adverbials, like those in (1), describe properties of the EVENT of Jack going to the market: that it was slow, that it occurred on Wednesday, or that it occurred in the company of Jill.[2] Opaque adverbial operators, like those in (2), on the other hand, describe properties of the PROPOSITION that Jack went to the market—that it is either apparently, allegedly, or probably true.

In the system of semantic representation used in Pollard and Sag 1994 and similar works, no distinction is made between events and proposi-

---

[2]Note that Jack's going to the market, Jill's going to the market, and Jack and Jill's going to the market are distinct events in the terminology of this paper, even if Jack and Jill each went to the market only once. Events are defined by their participants and by the relation they instantiate.

tions. They are both represented with *parameterized states of affairs* (*psoas*). The use of event indices allows this distinction to be made. Adverbials that describe properties of events can take event indices as arguments, while those that describe properties of propositions can take *psoa* arguments.

This paper assumes a broad definition of EVENT, encompassing not only actions such as trips to the market, but also occurrences such as Jack falling down and static states of affairs such as a cow being brown or even a cow not being brown. In fact, the semantics of any predicative word or phrase describes an event in this sense.

## 20.2  Semantic Representations

The fact that a VP modified by a transparent adverbial contributes its meaning directly, while the meaning of a VP modified by an opaque adverbial is mediated by the adverbial, can be formalized by including in the semantics of the phrase consisting of a transparent adverbial and the VP it modifies a logical clause representing the semantics of the modified phrase, as in (3a),[3] and not including such a clause for semantically opaque adjuncts, such as *appear* in (3b).[4] This is the kind of semantic representation that will be argued for in this paper.[5]

---

[3]For the purposes of this paper, the relation represented by the verb *go* is assumed to relate an event, an entity that goes someplace (GOER), and a destination (DEST). The relation represented by the temporal *on* is assumed to relate an event with a time.

[4]The adverb *apparently* is assumed to represent a property of a proposition, namely that the proposition appears to be true.

[5]This treatment of semantically transparent modifiers as logical conjuncts to the propositions they modify is similar to the treatment of some adjuncts in Davidsonian and neo-Davidsonian semantics. Davidson (1967) analyzes prepositional phrases such as *to the Morning Star* in (ia) as predicates of events that introduce a proposition of their own, logically conjoined to the proposition represented by the main clause. He introduces the logical representation in (ic), in which the entailment of (ib) by (ia) follows from the rules of first-order logic.

(i)  a.  I flew my spaceship to the Morning Star.
     b.  I flew my spaceship.
     c.  $\exists x (\text{Flew}(\text{I}, \text{my spaceship}, x) \,\&\, \text{To}(\text{the Morning Star}, x))$

Davidson's representation is essentially the same as the representation in (3a) for the sentence *Jack went to the market on Wednesday*. The crucial feature in both representations is that the proposition described by the modified phrase is represented as logically conjoined to the proposition described by the adjunct phrase, which takes that event as an argument.

(3)   a.   Semantics of *Jack went to the market on Wednesday.* (transparent)

$$
\begin{bmatrix}
\text{INDEX} & e \\[4pt]
\text{RESTR} &
\begin{bmatrix}
go \\
\text{EVENT} & e \\
\text{GOER} & Jack \\
\text{DEST} & market
\end{bmatrix}
\ \& \
\begin{bmatrix}
on \\
\text{EVENT} & e \\
\text{TIME} & Wednesday
\end{bmatrix}
\end{bmatrix}
$$

b.   Semantics of *Jack apparently went to the market.* (opaque)

$$
\begin{bmatrix}
\text{INDEX} & e \\[4pt]
\text{RESTR} &
\begin{bmatrix}
appear \\
\text{ARG} &
\begin{bmatrix}
go \\
\text{EVENT} & e \\
\text{GOER} & Jack \\
\text{DEST} & market
\end{bmatrix}
\end{bmatrix}
\end{bmatrix}
$$

The representation in (3a) has two conjoined restrictions[6] on the event index $e$. The first conjunct is a constraint that the event to which the index is anchored is an event of Jack going to the market.[7] The second restriction constrains the event to be one occurring on Wednesday. The fact that the event index is shared between the two restrictions represents the fact that they are restrictions on the same event.

The representation in (3b) has a single constraint on the event index $e$. The restriction constrains the event to which $e$ is anchored to be an apparent event of Jack going to the market.

An alternative to this method of representation is to represent the meaning of *Jack went to the market on Wednesday* with a non-conjunctive formula such as that in (4a) and stipulate separately that the time relation encoded by *on Wednesday* (and all similar relations) entails its argument. This could be done with a lexical meaning postulate such as that in (4b).[8]

---

[6]The *psoas* in RESTR values in this paper are shown joined with ampersands to emphasize their conjunctive nature. The representation is equivalent to one in which the *psoas* are items in a set and the *restricted-index* represents the claim that the proposition represented by each *psoa* in the set is true.

[7]Matters of tense and the temporal ordering of events are ignored in this paper.

[8]Such a mechanism may be independently necessary for such entailments as squares having four sides ($square[\text{INST } x] \rightarrow_{four\text{-}sides}[\text{INST } x]$) or someone murdered being dead ($_{murder}[\text{MURDERED } y] \rightarrow_{dead}[\text{INST } y]$). This paper argues against the use of such a meaning postulate to account for semantic transparency, but leaves open the possibility that meaning postulates may be necessary elsewhere in the grammar.

(4) a.
$$\begin{bmatrix} on & \\ \text{EVENT} & \begin{bmatrix} go & \\ \text{GOER} & Jack \\ \text{DEST} & market \end{bmatrix} \\ \text{TIME} & Wednesday \end{bmatrix}$$

b.
$$\begin{bmatrix} on & \\ \text{EVENT} & psoa \end{bmatrix} \rightarrow psoa$$

An analysis such as that in (4) treats the entailment by a semantically transparent modifier of the proposition represented by the phrase it modifies the same as other kinds of lexical entailments. A meaning postulate analysis depends, however, on the semantically transparent adverbial taking that proposition as an argument. In other words, semantically transparent adverbials must be treated as semantic operators in this kind of analysis. In the case of the temporal *on* relation in (4a), for instance, it is crucial that the EVENT argument be the proposition that Jack went to the market, rather than an event index. This proposition is the consequent part (on the right side of the arrow) of the meaning postulate in (4b), which must be a function of the formula on the left side of the arrow for the postulate to be general.

It is assumed in this paper, however, that the EVENT argument of the temporal *on* relation is in fact not a proposition, but rather an event (in the broad sense including states of affairs, etc.), and if a non-conjunctive representation of the temporal *on* relation takes an event variable as its argument, then a meaning postulate such as (4b) cannot be formulated, as the entailed proposition (i.e. the right-hand side of the meaning postulate) is not a function of the *on* formula. It will also be shown (in Section 20.3) that a non-conjunctive formula such as (4b) makes incorrect predictions when an adverbial such as *on Wednesday* is itself modified.

The rest of this paper will present data supporting the conjunctive analysis and show how it can be derived compositionally using semantic innovations in an HPSG grammar described in Kasper 1997. It will also show that using restricted indices in the semantics of verbal phrases allows a uniform analysis of adnominal and adverbial modifiers and show how the restrictions on different types of modifiers can be efficiently represented in a hierarchical lexicon.

## 20.3 Recursive Modification

Further support for a conjunctive representation of semantically transparent adjunct sentences comes from the fact that it is possible to modify or deny the proposition contributed by the adjunct, as in (5), without modifying or denying the proposition contributed by the modified phrase.

(5)  a.  Jack went to the market, apparently on Wednesday.
     b.  Jack went to the market, not on Wednesday, but on Friday.

The sentences in (5) still entail that Jack went to the market, even though they no longer entail that he did so on Wednesday. This is unexpected if the only representation of the proposition represented by the modified phrase is inside the scope of the operator contributed by the adverbial, as it is in the non-conjunctive representation in (4a). If the formula in (4a) were the argument to an *appear* relation, the resulting formula would be as shown in (6):

$$
(6) \quad
\begin{bmatrix}
appear \\
\\
ARG \quad
\begin{bmatrix}
on \\
\\
EVENT \quad
\begin{bmatrix}
go \\
GOER \quad Jack \\
DEST \quad market
\end{bmatrix} \\
\\
TIME \quad Wednesday
\end{bmatrix}
\end{bmatrix}
$$

This formula represents a situation in which both the proposition that Jack went to the market and that he did so on Wednesday appear to be true, rather than one in which he definitely went to the market, and what is merely apparent is that he did so on Wednesday. The meaning postulate in (4b) does not predict that the formula in (6) entails that Jack went to the market, because (6) does not match the left-hand side of (4b).

Note that (7), in which *appear* takes the *go* relation as its argument, is no better. This represents a situation in which it appeared that Jack went to the market, and the time when it appeared that way was on Wednesday.

$$
(7) \quad
\begin{bmatrix}
on \\
\\
EVENT \quad
\begin{bmatrix}
appear \\
\\
ARG \quad
\begin{bmatrix}
go \\
GOER \quad Jack \\
DEST \quad market
\end{bmatrix}
\end{bmatrix} \\
\\
TIME \quad Wednesday
\end{bmatrix}
$$

The problem with both (6) and (7) is that the *go psoa* appears inside the scope of *appear*. The kind of semantic representation that is required for sentences like (5) is conjunctive: the logical clause contributed by the modified phrase must be separated from the inherent content of the modifier, which alone is modified by *apparently* or *not*. The necessary kind of RESTR value for (5a) is shown in (8).

(8)    Conjunctive representation of the CONT | RESTR value of
       *Jack went to the market, apparently on Wednesday.*

$$
\begin{bmatrix} go \\ \text{EVENT} \quad e \\ \text{GOER} \quad Jack \\ \text{DEST} \quad market \end{bmatrix}
\&
\begin{bmatrix} appear \\ \text{ARG} \begin{bmatrix} on \\ \text{EVENT} \quad e \\ \text{TIME} \quad Wednesday \end{bmatrix} \end{bmatrix}
$$

This formula accurately represents the restrictions on the kind of situation that can be described by (5a), i.e., one in which Jack definitely went to the market and it appears that his going to the market occurred on Wednesday. *Apparently* and *not* in (5) modify only the inherent content—the time information—of the phrase *on Wednesday*. The proposition expressed by the main clause—which is entailed equally by *apparently on Wednesday* as by *on Wednesday*—is not modified.

Given that (8) is the kind of representation that is required for the sentence as a whole, the question becomes how to generate this kind of semantics compositionally from the meanings of the words and phrases that constitute the sentence. Kasper (1997) provides one way[9] to do this for recursively modified modifiers.

### 20.3.1   Kasper's (1997) Solution for Recursive Modification

In order to achieve a result like (8) for adjectives, Robert Kasper (1997) posits three semantic attributes for adjuncts; in addition to the standard CONTENT attribute, he adds I(NTERNAL)-CONT(ENT) and E(XTERNAL)-CONT(ENT) attributes to an adjunct's HEAD | MOD value. The SYNSEM value of the modified phrase, which is the MOD value in previous HPSG analyses (e.g. Pollard and Sag 1994), is the value of a HEAD | MOD attribute labeled ARG in Kasper's (1997) theory. The MOD value therefore has three attributes: ICONT, ECONT, and ARG.

Whereas in previous HPSG treatments of adjuncts (e.g. the Semantics Principle in Pollard and Sag 1994) an adjunct's CONT value is shared with the CONT value of its mother, in Kasper 1997, an adjunct's CONT value is only the meaning inherent in the adjunct itself. In addition to its benefits for a treatment of recursive modification, this move allows predicative adjectives and attributive adjectives to have the same type of CONT value; in either case its CONT value is a *psoa*.

---

[9]For an alternative, see Copestake et al. 1997.

In previous HPSG grammars (e.g. Pollard and Sag 1994), because the CONT value of the adjunct daughter in a head-adjunct phrase is shared with its mother, predicative adjectives have *psoa* CONT values, and attributive adjectives have *nominal-object* (*nom-obj*) CONT values, and furthermore adverbs modifying different types of adjectives have correspondingly different types of CONT values.

Kasper (1997) gives a new version of the Semantics Principle as in (9):

(9)  Semantics Principle (not including quantification) inKasper 1997

    a.  For a head-adjunct phrase, the semantic content (CONT) is token-identical with the MOD | ECONT value of the adjunct daughter, and the MOD | ICONT value of the adjunct daughter is token-identical with the adjunct daughter's CONT.

    b.  For all other types of headed phrase the CONT is token-identical with the CONT of the head daughter.

The constraints stated in (9a) can be shown graphically as in (10):

(10)  Clause (a) of Kasper's (1997) Semantics Principle

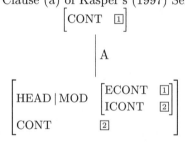

This clause ensures that a modifier word's ICONT value is the CONT value of the maximal phrase headed by the modifier word (which is distinct from its own CONT value just in case it is itself modified). If the word is used by itself as an adjunct daughter, then the Semantics Principle constrains its ICONT value to be shared with its CONT value. If the modifier word heads a larger phrase, then its ICONT value is passed up according to the Head Feature Principle to the maximal phrase headed by the word. The clause further ensures that the ECONT value of any modifier word is shared with the CONT value of the phrase consisting of the maximal phrase headed by the adjective and the phrase it modifies.

### 20.3.2  Adverbials in Kasper's (1997) System

This system can also account for the semantics of adverbials, including recursively modified adverbials such as *on Wednesday* in *went to the market, apparently on Wednesday*. It is only possible, however, if the inherent content of the adverbial (*on Wednesday*) is separated from the logical clause contributed by the modified VP (*went to the market*), as in the conjunctive representation argued for in this paper. The internally specified HEAD | MOD and CONT | RESTR values of *on Wednesday* (i.e., not including those attributable to its position in a particular phrase or sentence) are shown in (11).

(11)  HEAD | MOD and CONTENT | RESTRICTIONS values of *on Wednesday*

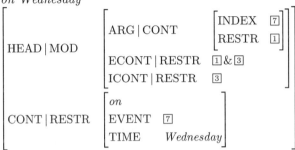

The CONT | RESTR value for *on Wednesday* is its inherent semantic content, i.e. the time information represented by the temporal *on psoa*. Following Kasper 1997, the ICONT | RESTR value is the CONT | RESTR value of the maximal phrase headed by *on Wednesday,* including any modifiers. The ECONT | RESTR value consists of the ICONT | RESTR value conjoined with the proposition contributed by the modified VP, e.g. that Jack went to the market. It is the CONT | RESTR value of *on Wednesday* (i.e. the temporal information represented by the *on psoa*) that gets modified by *apparently* in (5a). The HEAD | MOD and CONT | RESTR values of *apparently* are shown in (12).

(12)  HEAD | MOD and CONT | RESTRICTIONS values of *apparently*

$$\begin{bmatrix} \text{HEAD} \,|\, \text{MOD} & \begin{bmatrix} \text{ARG} \,|\, \text{CONT} \,|\, \text{RESTR} & ②\\ \text{ECONT} \,|\, \text{RESTR} & ③\\ \text{ICONT} \,|\, \text{RESTR} & ③ \end{bmatrix} \\ \text{CONT} \,|\, \text{RESTR} & \begin{bmatrix} appear \\ \text{ARG} & ② \end{bmatrix} \end{bmatrix}$$

Because *apparently* is an opaque adverbial, its ECONT | RESTR value is shared with its ICONT | RESTR value, rather than including the RESTR value of the phrase it modifies (tagged with ②) as a logical conjunct. Instead, the proposition contributed by the modified phrase shows up as the semantic argument of the *appear* relation: it is the proposition that appears to be true.

Using Kasper's (1997) Semantics Principle as in (9), the representations for *on Wednesday* in (11) and *apparently* in (12) yield the tree given in (13) for the phrase *went to the market, apparently on Wednesday*.

(13)    CONT and MOD values for constituents in
         *went to the market, apparently on Wednesday*

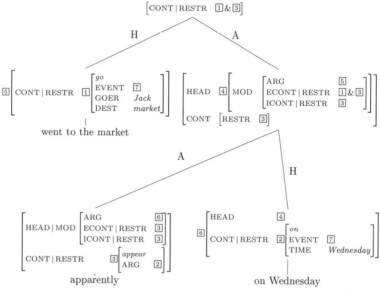

The adverb *apparently* selects the phrase it modifies via the MOD | ARG feature, as in Kasper's (1997) system. This value has the tag ⑥, which is shared with the SYNSEM value of *on Wednesday*. The CONT | RESTR value of *apparently* is an *appear* relation taking the CONT | RESTR value of *on Wednesday* as its argument. It represents a situation in which it appears that the event whose index is tagged with ⑦ occurred on Wednesday. Because *apparently* is not itself modified, its CONT | RESTR value is shared with its ICONT | RESTR value, and because it is an opaque adverbial, its ECONT | RESTR value is also shared with its ICONT | RESTR value. The CONT | RESTR, ICONT | RESTR, and ECONT | RESTR values of *apparently* all have tag ③ in (13).

The head-adjunct phrase *apparently on Wednesday* shares its HEAD value (tagged with ④) with its syntactic head, *on Wednesday*. The HEAD value includes the MOD feature, which both selects the phrase to be modified by *apparently on Wednesday* and specifies, via the ECONT feature, the CONT value of the resulting phrase.

Since *on Wednesday* is a transparent adverbial, its ECONT | RESTR value (and thus the ECONT | RESTR value of the phrase it heads, i.e., *apparently on Wednesday*) includes the CONT | RESTR value of the modified phrase as a logical conjunct. This value (marked with tag ①) is conjoined to the ICONT | RESTR value of *on Wednesday*, which is the CONT | RESTR value of the maximal phrase headed by *on Wednesday*, i.e. the CONT | RESTR value of *apparently on Wednesday* (marked with tag ③). Thus the CONT | RESTR value of the whole phrase *went to the market, apparently on Wednesday* is ① & ③, equivalent to the conjunctive RESTR value in (8).

It is the conjunctive nature of the ECONT value of the transparent adverbial *on Wednesday* that allows the correct semantic result. The conjunct that represents the inherent content of *on Wednesday* is modified by *apparently,* and the conjunct that represents the content of *went to the market* is not.

### 20.3.3  Semantic Generalizations

The semantic generalizations that can be made about semantically transparent and opaque adverbials as exemplified in (13) are shown in (14):

(14)  a.  Constraints on opaque adverbials (e.g., *apparently*)

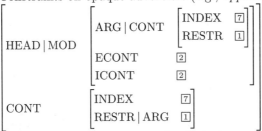

  b.  Constraints on transparent adverbials (e.g. *on Wednesday*)

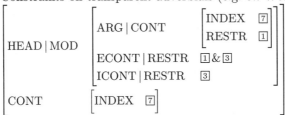

For both types of adverbial, the CONT | INDEX value (tagged here with ⑦) is shared with the CONT | INDEX value of the syntactic argument, representing the fact that adverbials, like all modifiers, describe a property of whatever the phrase they modify describes a property of.[10]

For an opaque adverbial, such as *apparently* in (14a), the ECONT value is shared with the ICONT value, as the internal content of the phrase it heads is all that it passes up to the head-adjunct phrase of which it is the adjunct daughter. If an opaque adverbial is not itself recursively modified, then its CONT value will be shared with its ICONT value (as stipulated by Kasper's (1997) Semantics Principle, in (9)). The restriction in an opaque adverbial's CONT value takes the CONT | RESTR value of the modified phrase (tagged here with ⒈) as an argument, because an opaque adverbial, being a semantic operator, always represents a claim about the proposition described by the phrase it modifies.

A transparent adverbial, such as *on Wednesday* in (14b), differs from an opaque one in that its ECONT | RESTR value includes the CONT | RESTR value of the modified phrase, conjoined with the CONT | RESTR of the maximal phrase headed by the adverbial. This ECONT value is passed all the way up to the CONT value of the head-adjunct phrase, resulting in conjunctive semantics for the phrase as a whole.

### 20.3.4 Type Hierarchy for Modifiers: Modeling the Generalizations

This system of representation for verbal semantics, incorporating restrictions on referential indices, parallels the standard representation for nominal semantics in HPSG, allowing a unified treatment of semantic transparency in both adverbial and adnominal modifiers. Except for the restricted-index representation of verbal semantics, the tree in (13) is exactly parallel to Kasper's (1997, 15) tree for the $\overline{\text{N}}$ *potentially controversial plan,* in which *potentially* is opaque and *controversial* is transparent. Incorporating the restricted-index representation for verbal semantics, this phrase has the structure shown in (15). Only the internal semantics of relations and the linear order in the top subtree differ from the tree in (13).

---

[10]This is true even in the case of a relative clause. Although a clause ordinarily represents a restriction on an event variable, a relative clause modifies an $\overline{\text{N}}$, and imposes a restriction on the index of that $\overline{\text{N}}$. The verb that heads a relative clause differs from its main-clause counterpart in syntax and morphology (in a language such as Korean this difference is overt), and wherever these differences are defined, either in a phrase type definition or a lexical rule, the semantic difference as well can be defined. In a verb that heads a relative clause, the INDEX value will be shared with the value of one of its semantic arguments, rather than with its INST(ANTIATED) value.

(15)    CONT and MOD values for constituents in
        *potentially controversial plan*

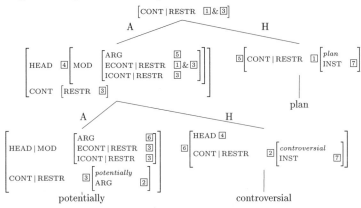

This means that the constraints given in (14) for opaque and transparent adverbials can actually apply to all modifiers. In an HPSG lexicon, which is organized as a multiple-inheritance hierarchy, the constraints in (14) can be stated as constraints on types *opaque-modifier* and *transparent-modifier,* with the syntactic heads of all adnominal and adverbial modifiers belonging lexically to one or the other type.

One dimension of the proposed hierarchy for modifiers is shown in (16).

(16)    Constraints on modifier types in hierarchical lexicon

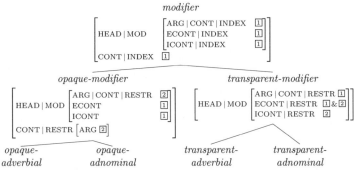

All lexical signs with non-empty MOD values will inherit the constraints associated with the type *modifier,* which specifies that all IN-DEX values are token-identical. This has the effect of ensuring that a modifier describes the same event, object, etc., that the word or phrase it modifies does. Further, each modifier inherits the constraints associated with either the type *opaque-modifier,* or the type *transparent-*

*modifier*. These types impose the semantic constraints in (14), corresponding to the difference between semantic opacity and transparency. Finally, words constrained to modify a particular part of speech will belong to more specific types, such as *opaque-adverbial* or *transparent-adnominal*. These types will inherit syntactic constraints from types in another dimension, specifying what category of word or phrase they can modify.

Some prepositional phrases in English can modify either verbal or nominal phrases, as demonstrated by the ambiguity in (17):

(17)   Jack chopped down the beanstalk behind the house.

In this sentence, *behind the house* can modify either the VP *chopped down the beanstalk* or the $\overline{\text{N}}$ *beanstalk*. The syntactic head of this PP—*behind*—would inherit the constraints associated with the type *transparent-modifier,* but would be a subtype of neither *transparent-adverbial* nor *transparent-adnominal*. It would be lexically underspecified as to the category of the phrase it modified.

## 20.4   Conclusion

This paper has shown that a conjunctive analysis using Davidsonian-style event indices is motivated for sentences containing semantically transparent adverbials. Including the semantic content of the head daughter as a logical conjunct in the semantics of a head-adjunct phrase where the adjunct daughter is semantically transparent is consistent with the truth conditions for sentences containing such phrases.

The separation of the internal and external content of modifiers as suggested in Kasper 1997 was extended to adverbials, and it was shown that adopting a restricted-index analysis of the semantics of verbal constituents allows the constraints on opaque and transparent modifier words to be stated more generally than in Kasper 1997.

## References

Copestake, Ann, Dan Flickinger, Ivan A. Sag. 1997. Minimal Recursion Semantics: An Introduction. Unpublished manuscript, Stanford University.

Davidson, Donald. 1967. The logical form of action sentences. In *The Logic of Decision and Action,* ed. by Nicholas Rescher. University of Pittsburgh Press.

Kasper, Robert. 1997. Semantics of recursive modification. Unpublished manuscript, Ohio State University.

Pollard, Carl and Ivan A. Sag. 1994. *Head-Driven Phrase Structure Grammar.* Chicago: University of Chicago Press.

Sag, Ivan A. and Thomas Wasow. 1997. *Syntactic Theory: A Formal Introduction.* Unpublished manuscript, Stanford University.

# 21

# Antecedent Contained Ellipsis in HPSG

HOWARD GREGORY AND SHALOM LAPPIN

## 21.1  Introduction

The sentences in (1) are examples of antecedent contained ellipsis (ACE), where an elided VP in a relative clause occurs within the matrix VP that provides the antecedent for interpreting the ellipsis site.

(1)  a.  John liked the girls who Mary did.
     b.  John threw flowers at the girls who Bill did.

May (1985) and Fiengo and May (1994) (F&M) observe that if the elided VP in an ACE structure like (1a) is an empty category at Logical Form (LF), as in (2), and reconstruction consists in copying the containing VP into the empty VP, then an interpretative regress results.

(2)  John [$_{VP}$ liked the girls who Mary did [$_{VP}$ ]].

The re-constructed VP will itself contain an elided VP that must be resolved through reconstruction.

In general, analyses of ACE adopt one of two approaches. On the first, and most common, a structure containing the ellipsis site is removed from a position within the antecedent VP to permit interpreta-

Earlier versions of this paper were presented to the University of York Linguistics Colloquium in February, 1997, the HPSG Conference at Cornell University in July, 1997, and The Ohio State University Linguistics Colloquium in January, 1998. We are grateful to the participants of these events for their comments and criticisms. We would also like to thank David Adger, Chris Kennedy, Carl Pollard, Ivan Sag, Stuart Shieber, and Adam Wyner for helpful discussion of some of the ideas presented here. We are grateful to Gregor Erbach and Suresh Manandhar for useful advice on implementational issues involving ProFIT. The research described in this paper was supported by grant GR/K59576 from the Engineering and Physical Science Research Council of the UK.

*Lexical and Constructional Aspects of Linguistic Explanation.*
Gert Webelhuth, Jean-Pierre Koenig, and Andreas Kathol.
Copyright © 1998, Stanford University.

tion of the elided VP without a regress. We will refer to this approach as the *extraction* view of ACE. The second approach, the *in situ* view, reconstructs the elided VP within the matrix VP that serves as its antecedent. It avoids the regress by either (i) enriching the structure of the elided VP, or (ii) adding operations to the reconstruction procedure.

The distinction between these two approaches cuts across the difference between syntactic and semantic accounts of ellipsis resolution. May 1985, F&M, Baltin 1987, Lasnik 1993, and Hornstein 1994, 1995 are examples of syntactic extraction treatments of ACE. Dalrymple et al. 1991 and Shieber et al. 1996, on the other hand, offer a semantically based extraction analysis. Recent *in situ* accounts (Lappin 1992, 1996; and Brody 1995) invoke syntactic reconstruction, but nothing in principle excludes the possibility of an *in situ* analysis relying on a purely semantic procedure for ellipsis resolution.

In Section 21.2 we present an *in situ* account of ACE resolution within an HPSG framework. Our analysis relies crucially upon the HPSG treatment of unbounded dependencies, and specifically on the NONLOCAL Feature Principle (NLFP), and the Complement Extraction Lexical Rule for introducing SLASH features on heads. In Section 21.3 we compare our HPSG account with (i) syntactic and semantic versions of the extraction approach, and (ii) with two other *in situ* treatments which have recently been suggested. We argue that the proposed account has significant advantages over these alternative analyses. Finally, in Section 21.4 we present an implementation of our account which we have developed within a ProFIT/HPSG grammar running in Prolog.

Pollard and Sag (1994) (P&S) posit three types of NONLOCAL features, (i) SLASH, (ii) QUE, and (iii) REL corresponding to a displaced constituent, a wh-question feature, and a wh-relative feature, respectively. INHERITED feature values are lexically introduced and passed up from daughters to mothers until the point at which a TO-BIND feature appears, and, in the case of SLASH, a filler phrase P whose local features match those of the INHERITED feature F is present. The TO-BIND feature is introduced either (i) by a lexical head, or (ii) by an immediate dominance schema, which licenses its presence on a phrasal head in certain configurational structures. This feature binds NONLOCAL features. It forces the unification of the value of SLASH and the LOCAL value of the filler P, and so effectively discharges SLASH. The NLFP governs the inheritance of NONLOCAL features from daughter to mother nodes in a feature structure.

(3) **The NONLOCAL Feature Principle**

For each NONLOCAL feature F, the INHERITED value of F on a mother M is the union of the INHERITED values of F on the daughters of M minus the value of TO-BIND F on the head daughter.

The topicalization structure in (4) (from P&S) illustrates how SLASH encodes an extraction relation.

(4)  S[INH|SL{ }]

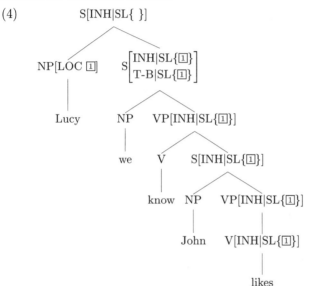

INHER|SLASH {⒈} is introduced in the object position of the SUBCAT feature of *likes* by the CELR, given in (5).

(5) **The Complement Extraction Lexical Rule**

$$\begin{bmatrix} \text{SUBCAT} & \langle \ldots, \boxed{3}, \ldots \rangle \\ \text{COMPS} & \langle \ldots, \boxed{3}[\text{LOC}\ \boxed{1}], \ldots \rangle \\ \text{INHER | SLASH} & \boxed{2} \end{bmatrix} \Rightarrow$$

$$\begin{bmatrix} \text{SUBCAT} & \langle \ldots, \boxed{4}[\text{LOC}\ \boxed{1}, \text{INHER | SLASH } \{\boxed{1}\}], \ldots \rangle \\ \text{COMPS} \ \langle \ldots \ldots \rangle \\ \text{INHER | SLASH} & \{\boxed{1}\} \cup \boxed{2} \end{bmatrix}$$

SLASH is passed up the immediate dominance hierarchy until TO-BIND {1} on the matrix S in (4) discharges it by unifying its value with the LOCAL value of the topicalized NP *Lucy*.

## 21.2  An HPSG Analysis of ACE

### 21.2.1  Relative Clauses

We will assume a treatment of relative clauses which is based on Johnson and Lappin's (1997) analysis of wh-questions. The main components of this analysis are as follows.

A. A relative clause RC is headed by a phonologically null complementizer with three alternative feature specifications.

(i) Wh-phrase RC's:

$$
\begin{bmatrix}
\text{SUBCAT} \left\langle \begin{bmatrix} \text{LOC } \boxed{2} \\ \text{INHER} \,|\, \text{REL } \{\boxed{1}\} \end{bmatrix}, \text{S} \begin{bmatrix} \textit{fin} \\ \text{INHER} \,|\, \text{SLASH } \{\boxed{2}\} \end{bmatrix} \right\rangle \\
\text{NONLOCAL} \,|\, \text{TO-BIND} \,|\, \text{SLASH } \{\boxed{2}\}
\end{bmatrix}
$$

(ii) That-RC's:

$$
\begin{bmatrix}
\text{SUBCAT} \left\langle \begin{bmatrix} \text{LOC } \boxed{2}[\text{CONTENT } \textit{relpron}] \end{bmatrix}, \text{S} \begin{bmatrix} \textit{fin} \\ \text{INHER} \,|\, \text{SLASH } \{\boxed{2}\} \end{bmatrix} \right\rangle \\
\text{NONLOCAL} \,|\, \text{TO-BIND} \,|\, \text{SLASH } \{\boxed{2}\} \\
\text{INHER} \,|\, \text{REL } \{\boxed{1}\}
\end{bmatrix}
$$

(iii) Bare-RC's:

$$
\begin{bmatrix}
\text{SUBCAT} \left\langle \text{S} \begin{bmatrix} \textit{fin} \\ \text{INHER} \,|\, \text{SLASH } \{\boxed{2}\} \end{bmatrix} \right\rangle \\
\text{NONLOCAL} \,|\, \text{TO-BIND} \,|\, \text{SLASH } \{\boxed{2}\} \\
\text{INHER} \,|\, \text{REL } \{\boxed{1}\}
\end{bmatrix}
$$

B. The CONTENT|INDEX feature value of the head N of an N′ is unified with (i) the INHER|REL feature value of its RC adjunct, and with (ii) the CONTENT|INDEX value of the SLASH feature inherited from the elided VP in the RC adjunct. Structure sharing of the CONTENT|INDEX connects the head N directly with the SLASH, and allows the SLASH's INDEX value to be interpreted effectively as a variable whose range is restricted by the head N's CONTENT value.

C. Nouns have a TO-BIND|REL feature, induced by a relative clause modifier, as proposed in P&S.

This account of relative clauses diverges from those of P&S and Sag 1997. It has the advantages that (i) it permits a unified treatment of subject and object extraction in *that* RC's, and (ii) it captures the fact that while *that* relatives behave like wh-relatives in permitting subject extraction, they operate like bare RC's in not exhibiting pied piping. However, our reconstruction procedure for ACE could be recast in terms of the analysis of relative clauses given in either P&S or in Sag 1997.

Therefore, our account of ACE does not depend crucially on the details of this treatment of relatives.

The relevant feature structure which this analysis assigns to the NP *every girl who John liked* is given in (6).

(6)

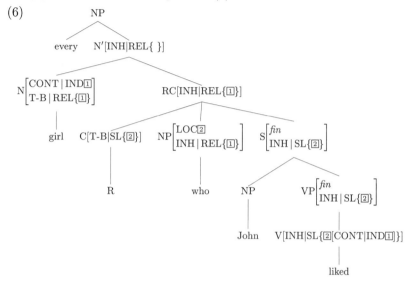

### 21.2.2 An *In Situ* Ellipsis Resolution Procedure

Lappin and Shih (1996) propose a generalized ellipsis resolution algorithm which consists in the specification of a relation of a (possibly partial) correspondence between the lexically unrealized head of an elided clause and its arguments and adjuncts as one term of the relation, and the realized head of the antecedent clause and its arguments and adjuncts as the second term. This algorithm is a generalization of the VP ellipsis resolution algorithm presented in Lappin and McCord 1990. When the generalized procedure is applied to VP ellipsis, it specifies the following strategy.

(i) Take the head verb A′ of the elided VP to be identical to the head verb A of an antecedent clause.

(ii) Inherit the non-subject complements of A to fill the corresponding complement positions in the SUBCAT list of A′.

(iii) Inherit any adjuncts modifying A (the VP headed by A) as modifiers of the VP which A′ heads.

Although we have formulated the generalized ellipsis resolution algorithm procedurally, it is not difficult to specify its main components declaratively. So, for example, (i)–(iii) can be re-stated as (i′)–(iii′).

(i′)  The head verb A′ of the elided VP is identical to the head verb A of an antecedent clause.

(ii′)  Let LA be the list of A′s non-subject complements, and LA′ SUB-CAT list of A′. Each element of LA fills the corresponding position in LA′.

(iii′)  If LAdj is the list of adjuncts modifying A (the VP headed by A), then the elements of LAdj are adjuncts of the VP which A′ heads.

The Prolog implementation of the algorithm consists almost entirely of such declarative clauses.

There are two main cases to consider: I. ACE in complement NPs, and II. ACE in PP adjuncts.

I. The elided VP occurs within an RC that modifies the complement of the matrix verb. The relevant feature structure of (1a) prior to ellipsis resolution is (7).

(1a)  John liked the girls who Mary did.

(7)

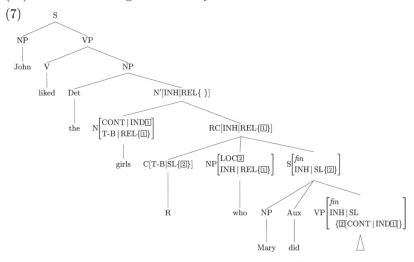

*liked* is identified as the head of the antecedent VP and substituted for the head of the elided VP. If the full feature structure value of the matrix object NP *the girls who Mary did* is unified with the object position in the SUBCAT list of the elided VP head verb and inserted as a COMP-DTR of this VP, then the feature structure of the elided VP will reappear in the reconstructed VP. This will generate a version of the interpretive regress. However, if a SLASH feature is substituted for the object argument in the reconstructed verb's SUBCAT list by the CELR, then reconstruction yields (8), which is a well formed feature structure and the desired representation for (1a).

(8)

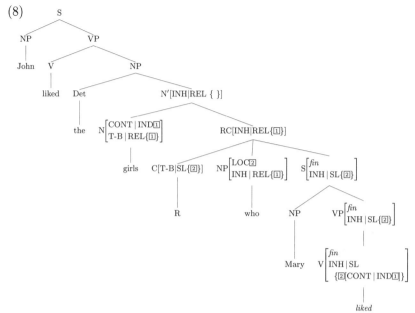

In fact, substitution of a slashed verb V as head of the empty VP, where the SLASH feature of V corresponds to the object NP of the antecedent VP, is necessary in order to map (7) into a well formed feature structure. If this substitution does not apply, then the SLASH feature which the empty complementizer R heading the RC in (7) binds (and which R requires in its complement RC) is not lexically anchored.[1]

II. The analysis applies directly to ACE structures in adjunct PPs. After the feature structures of the matrix verb, its complements (if any) and the P head of its PP ADJ-DTR are reconstructed in the elided VP, the CELR is applied to substitute a SLASH feature for the appropri-

---

[1] An anonymous reviewer asks about an ACE case like *Mary wanted the girls to leave who John didn't*, where the SLASH feature of the reconstructed empty verb *wanted* in the ellipsis site controls the unrealized subject of the reconstructed infinitival VP complement *to leave*. In fact, this is not a problem for the proposed account. Assuming that control is expressed through structure sharing of the INDEX value between an element in a matrix verb's SUBCAT list and the unexpressed subject element in the SUBCAT of its infinitival VP complement, the INDEX value of the object element in the SUBCAT list for *wanted* is unified with that of the unexpressed subject in the SUBCAT list of *to leave*. When *wanted* is reconstructed, a SLASH is substituted for the object *the girls who John didn't* in its SUBCAT, and its INDEX value will be unified with that of the unexpressed subject element in the SUBCAT list of the reconstructed AVM for *to leave*. This unification is forced by the constraints of the lexical specification for *want*, which are sustained under reconstruction.

ate argument of the reconstructed P's SUBCAT list. This procedure yields (9) as the reconstructed feature structure for (1b).

(1b)   John threw flowers at the girls who Bill did.

(9)

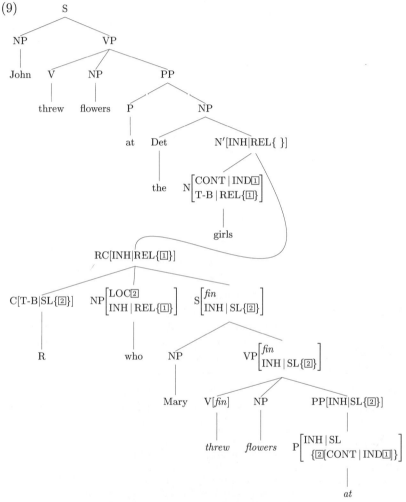

CELR is available in the grammar independently of its role in ellipsis resolution. Therefore, the proposed analysis does not stipulate any new rules or operations. It simply assumes that the verb heading an antecedent VP and the verb derived from it by the CELR are elements of an equivalence class for purposes of reconstruction (and similarly for the preposition heading an adjunct in the antecedent VP and the slashed P obtained from it by the CELR). Application of CELR to obtain a slashed verb or P in the reconstructed VP is forced by the requirement that the SLASH feature which R introduces originate in a slashed lexical head.

## 21.3 Alternative Approaches

### 21.3.1 Syntactic Extraction Accounts

#### 21.3.1.1 The QR Analysis

May (1985) and F&M avoid the regress in ACE by applying reconstruction to the output of a rule of quantifier raising, QR, which adjoins the quantified NP object of *liked* to the matrix IP, in order to derive the LF in (10a). The elided VP in (10a) is no longer antecedent contained, and so reconstruction yields (10b).

(10) a. $[_{IP'}$ [the girls who$_1$ Mary did $[_{VP}$ ]]$_1$ [John liked $t_1$ ]].
   b. $[_{IP'}$ [the girls who$_1$ Mary $[_{VP}$ *liked* $t_1$]]$_1$ [John liked $t_1$]].

There are at least three problems with the QR analysis of ACE. First, in at least some cases of ACE, the scope of ellipsis resolution is independent of quantifier scope assignment in a way which is problematic for the QR account. In (11) *every book that her supervisor did* takes narrow scope relative to *some professor*. However, the matrix VP headed by *made* is a possible antecedent for the elided VP.

(11) Some professor made a point of telling Mary to discuss every book that her supervisor did.

If the narrow scope reading of the embedded NP object is represented by adjunction of the NP to the complement clause (or the matrix VP) rather than to the matrix clause, then the post-QR structure will not provide the appropriate input for reconstruction with the matrix VP. The elided VP is still antecedent contained in this structure.

Kennedy (1997) observes that only a *de re* reading of the quantified NP *everyone Rosa does* is possible in (12).

(12) Max wants everyone Rosa does to answer these questions.

He takes this as evidence for a QR analysis of ACE. Application of QR to the quantified NP in (12) adjoins it to the matrix IP and so forces a *de re* reading. However, the *de dicto* reading of the quantified NP is also excluded (or is very difficult to obtain) in (13), where the relative clause has a fully realized VP.

(13) Max wants everyone Rosa wants to answer to these questions to answer these questions.

This suggests that the strong preference for a *de re* reading of the quantified NP in (12) is independent of ellipsis resolution.

Applying reconstruction to the output of QR requires that ellipsis resolution follow scope assignment. But if these procedures are independent of each other, then the QR analysis of ACE does not go through.

Lasnik (1994) raises the second problem. In the model of grammar developed in Chomsky 1995, covert movement affects only the formal features of an expression A. FF(A) does not include A's semantic features. Lasnik uses this restriction on covert movement to explain the fact that *many linguists* can only be understood as taking narrow scope relative to the negation in (14).

(14)  There aren't many linguists here.

Covert adjunction of FF(*many linguists*) to *there* cannot alter the scope relations between *many linguists* and the negation, as it does not affect the semantic features of the NP to which it applies. QR is a covert movement operation, and so the formal features which it adjoins to TP (or VP) cannot be the input to ellipsis reconstruction. In fact, given this view of covert movement, Lasnik's observation can be generalized to cast doubt on the possibility of sustaining any intepretationally motivated covert operation like QR within the Minimalist Program (MP).

The third problem is also a theory internal consequence of minimalist assumptions. According to Chomsky's (1995) copy theory of traces, a trace is a subset of the set of features that characterize the moved expression, where this subset excludes (at least) the phonetic features of the expression. But on this view, the trace left by QR in (10a) will contain the semantic features of the quantified NP to which QR has applied. Interpretable features are not deleted in the course of a derivation. It follows that the elided VP will reappear when the matrix VP is copied into the elided VP at LF, as in (10b). This will generate the interpretative regress which QR was intended to avoid.

The HPSG account of ACE does not render ellipsis resolution dependent on the same operation which (partially) determines quantifier scope. Moreover, it represents unbounded dependencies by means of inheritance of NONLOCAL features rather than syntactic chains containing empty categories. Therefore, these problems do not arise on the proposed *in situ* analysis.

Kennedy (1997) remarks that ACE structures can appear in NPs contained in adjuncts or complements of NP arguments of the antecedent VP, as in (15).

(15)  Mary read a review of every play which John did.

He takes this as evidence for a QR treatment of ACE. He claims that QR will extract *every play which John did* in (15) out of the indefinite NP object of *read,* while leaving the object NP *in situ,* as in (16a). Copying can then produce (16b), which is the intended interpretation of (15).

(16)  a.  $[_{IP'}$ $[_{NP}$ every play which John did $[_{VP}$ ]]$_1$
$[_{IP}$ Mary $[_{VP}$ read a review of $t_1$]]]

b.  $[_{IP'}$ $[_{NP}$ every play which John did $[_{VP}$ *read a review of $t_1$* ]]
$[_{IP}$ Mary $[_{VP}$ read a review of $t_1$]]]

However, contrary to Kennedy's claim, NP internal ACE structures also seem to be possible within definite and possessive matrix NPs, like the object NPs in (17a) and (17b), respectively.

(17)  a.  Max endorsed the evaluations for most courses that Rosa did.
b.  John supported Mary's application to every university which Bill did.

Given that overt extraction from definite and possessive NPs is, in general, excluded (18a,b), the fact that ACE structures are possible in this environment casts doubt on Kennedy's QR analysis of these cases.

(18)  a. ??What did Max endorse the evaluations for?
b.  *What did John support Mary's application to?

The HPSG account handles NP internal ACE straightforwardly. If the full feature structure of a COMP-DTR or ADJ-DTR for an argument NP of the verb heading the antecedent VP cannot be reconstructed without generating an interpretive regress, then the CELR can be applied to provide a SLASH feature in the SUBCAT list of the head of the COMP-DTR/ADJ-DTR. In the case of (15), the SLASH feature is substituted for the complement of the reconstructed preposition *of,* which heads the complement of *review,* the head of the containing NP. Reconstruction yields the feature structure in (19), which specifies the desired interpretation of (15).

### 21.3.1.2  Movement to SPEC of AgrO/SPEC$_2$ of $v$

Lasnik (1993), and Hornstein (1994, 1995) develop an extraction analysis which relies on the minimalist assumption that the quantified NP object of *read* in (1a) is moved to SPEC of AgrO for accusative Case checking. Recast in terms of the clause architecture proposed in Chapter 4 of Chomsky 1995, movement is to SPEC$_2$ of the higher light $v$ which takes the transitive VP as its complement. This yields (20), where *the girls who Mary did* is not antecedent contained.

(20)  John$_1$ [T $[_{AgrOP}$ [the girls who Mary did $[_{VP}$ ]]$_2$
[ AgrO $[_{VP}$ $t_1$ $[_{v'}$ liked $t_2$]]]]]]

For Hornstein, object movement for Case checking is covert. By contrast, Lasnik takes it to be overt, and so avoids the problem he

(19)

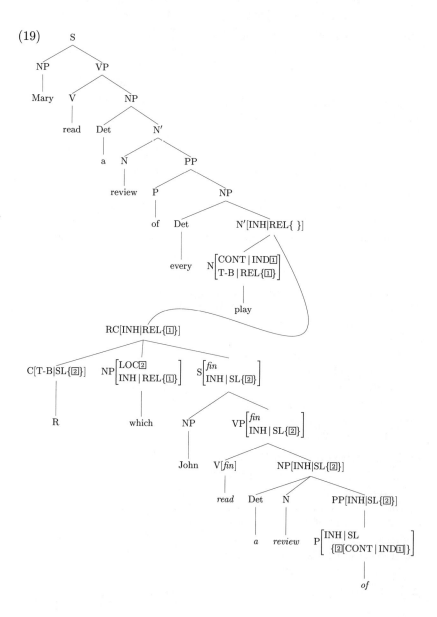

identifies with semantically vacuous covert movement. Hornstein takes ellipsis resolution to involve LF copying. Therefore it is not clear how his account avoids the problem which the copy theory of traces poses for the QR approach. Lasnik identifies VP ellipsis with PF deletion, and so he does not encounter this difficulty.

However, neither version of the analysis covers ACE structures in adjunct PPs.

(1b)  John threw flowers at the girls who Bill did.

(21)  Max performed in every city which Lucy expects to.

Lasnik (1993) attempts to accommodate these cases by claiming that in ACE structures within PP adjuncts the relative clause containing the elided VP is extraposed outside of the VP containing the PP adjunct. He takes this movement to be covert, as the relative pronoun in the relative clause can be null at PF in contrast to cases of overt extraposition.

(22)  a.  John stood beside [every painting [∅ Mary did]].
      b.  John stood beside [every painting] recently [which Mary did].
      c.  *John stood beside [every painting] recently [∅ Mary did].

There are at least three difficulties with Lasnik's treatment of ACE in PP adjuncts. First, it is unclear how Lasnik's covert extraposition analysis avoids the problem of semantically vacuous movement which he brings against the QR account.

Second, it is not obvious how a covert extraposition operation can be incorporated into the Minimalist Program. There are no obvious formal features which would force this movement.

Finally, it is reasonable to assume that extraposition is bounded, and so restricted to adjoining the relative clause to the first VP or clause in which it is contained. But then Lasnik's analysis incorrectly predicts that only the embedded VP is a possible antecedent for the elided VP in (23).

(23)  a.  John applied to study at every university that Bill did.
      b.  Mary intends to travel through every city that Lucy does.

In fact, the VPs headed by *applied* and *intends* are possible antecedents for the elided VPs in (23a) and (23b), respectively.

Hornstein (1994, 1995) takes adjuncts as generated in a position adjoined to the antecedent VP. This approach raises two problems. First, it makes the same prediction that Lasnik's extraposition analysis does with respect to the possibility of higher matrix VP antecedents. As the sentences in (23) indicate, this prediction is false.

Second, as Brody (1995) points out, Hornstein's treatment of adjunct ACE structures yields the wrong results by virtue of the fact that it does not generate a trace which can be reconstructed in the elided VP as the variable bound by the wh-phrase or relative operator. Moreover, as the PP occurs outside of the antecedent VP, it will not be copied. Therefore, the result of reconstruction through copying of VP1 for (1b) will be (24), which provides neither a well formed LF nor the intended interpretation of the elided VP.

(24) *John [$_{VP2}$ [$_{VP1}$ threw flowers] at
  [the girls [who$_1$ Mary did [$_{VP}$ *throw flowers*]]]].

In contrast to the Lasnik-Hornstein extraction approach, the proposed HPSG account provides a unified treatment of ACE in verb complements and adjunct PPs. It reconstructs a SLASH feature path *in situ* in the ellipsis site for both cases. Therefore, the problems which ACE in PP adjuncts create for Lasnik and Hornstein do not arise on this account.

### 21.3.1.3 A Semantic Extraction Analysis: ACE Resolution through Higher-Order Unification

Dalrymple et al. (1991) and Shieber et al. (1996) suggest that ellipsis is resolved by constructing an equation for the antecedent clause in which the source predicate is represented by a higher-order variable that takes a set of designated arguments (in the case of VP ellipsis, the subject). A solution to the equation will specify a lambda expression as the value for the predicate variable. This lambda expression is then applied to the parallel arguments in the elided clause. Taking *John* and *Mary* as parallel arguments in (25a), the equations in (25b,c) yield the interpretation of (25a) given in (25d).

(25) a. John knows Lucy, and Mary does too.
  b. $P(john) = knows(\mathbf{john}, lucy)$
  c. $P = \lambda x[x \text{ knows lucy}]$
  d. $knows(john, lucy)$ and $knows(mary, lucy)$

The higher-order unification treatment of ACE relies on the device of quantifier storage.[2] Applying storage to a quantified NP involves substituting a variable for it in the semantic representation of a sentence, and storing the NP as an assumption, which is an ordered triple containing the quantifier, a variable which it binds, and an open sentence that specifies the restriction on the variable. The scope of the quantified NP is determined by the point in semantic composition at which the assumption is discharged. (26b) corresponds to the representation of (26a) with a stored quantifier assumption, while in (26c) the assumption has been discharged.

---

[2]See Cooper 1983 and Pereira 1990 for discussions of quantifier storage.

(26) a. John read every book.
    b. $\langle$every x book(x)$\rangle$ ⊢ read(john,x)
    c. every(x, book(x), read(john,x))

The representation of (1a) prior to discharge of the quantifier assumption is (27).

(27) $\langle$the x girl(x) & P(mary)$\rangle$ ⊢ liked(john,x)

The variable P corresponds to the elided VP in the relative clause. If ellipsis resolution is applied before the discharge of the assumption in (27), then the value of P is specified by the equations in (28).

(28) a. P(john) = liked(john,x)
    b. P = $\lambda$z[z liked x]

Substituting the value of P given in (28b) for P in (27) and then discharging the assumption yields (29), which is the desired representation of (1a).

(29) the(x, girls(x) & liked(mary,x), liked(john,x))

However, if the assumption in (27) is discharged prior to ellipsis resolution, the result is (30a), and so the equation corresponding to (30a) is (30)b.

(30) a. the(x,girls(x) & P(mary), liked(john,x))
    b. P(john) = the(x, girls(x) & P(mary), liked(john,x))

The variable P occurs on both sides of the equation in (30b), and so it admits of no solutions. This is the formal semantic equivalent of the interpretive regress problem which the QR analysis is intended to solve.

The higher-order unification approach avoids the regress by applying storage to remove the representation of the quantified NP from containment within the representation of the antecedent predicate. It is the semantic counterpart of the QR analysis. However, it avoids the problems raised by covert movement and the copy view of traces by virtue of the fact that storage is an operation which applies to semantic representations. The variable which is substituted for a stored quantified NP and which is bound by discharge of the quantifier assumption is a genuine variable rather than a trace created by syntactic movement.

Haik (1987) observes that ACE structures exhibit syntactic locality effects, specifically sensitivity to subjacency, in the ellipsis site. This fact poses a serious problem for the higher-order unification analysis.

(31) a. John read everything which Mary believes that he did.
    b. *John read everything which Mary believes the claim that he did.
    c. *John read everything which Mary wonders why he did.

If ellipsis resolution consists in unifying a higher-order variable with the semantic object that constitutes the interpretation of both the antecedent and the elided VP, then syntactic constraints do not apply at this level of representation. Therefore, the higher-order unification analysis cannot account for locality effects in ACE structures.[3]

The fact that ACE structures are constrained by syntactic locality conditions is also a problem for the substitutional treatments of ellipsis proposed in Kempson and Gabbay 1993, Kempson 1996, and Crouch 1995.

The proposed HPSG account reconstructs the syntactic as well as the semantic feature structure of the elided VP. Specifically, it generates the full SLASH feature path in this VP. Therefore, it provides the syntactic structure required to capture the island effects exhibited in ACE cases like (31b) and (31c).

### 21.3.2 Two Alternative *In Situ* Theories

### 21.3.2.1 The Pseudo-Gapping Analysis

Lappin (1992, 1996) characterizes ACE as a case of partial VP ellipsis where only the head verb and, possibly, selected complements and adjuncts are elided, but a trace bound by the wh-phrase or relative clause operator is present in the ellipsis site. Therefore, the input to ellipsis resolution for (1a) is (32a), and reconstruction consists in copying only the head V in the ellipsis site, as in (32b).

(32) a. John $[_{VP}$ liked the girls who$_1$ Mary did $[_{VP} [_V ] t_1]]$.
     b. John $[_{VP}$ liked the girls who$_1$ Mary $[_{VP} [_V$ *liked*$] t_1]]$.

On this analysis, the elided VP in an ACE structure can be reconstructed *in situ* without generating an interpretive regress.

F&M raise a problem for the pseudo-gapping account when they note that pseudo-gapping is subject to a locality condition which requires that the realized arguments and adjuncts that appear in a pseudo-gapped structure be complements and modifiers of the elided verb. The elided material in (33) must be understood as *gave Lucy* rather than *claimed that he gave Lucy.*

(33) Max claimed that he gave Lucy flowers before John did chocolates.

This condition creates difficulties for the pseudo-gapping account of ACE. In (34) both the complement verb *read* and the matrix verb *promised* can be taken as the antecedent of the elided verb.

(34) John promised to read every book which Rosa did.

---

[3]See Lappin 1996, Forthcoming for more detailed discussion of syntactic effects in ACE structures.

If the trace of the wh-phrase is realized in the elided VP of the relative clause in (34), it can only be an argument of *read*. This incorrectly rules out the interpretation of the sentence on which *promised to read* is understood as the antecedent of the elided VP.[4]

Lappin (1992, 1996) responds to this argument by pointing out that there are cases of pseudo-gapping in which a matrix verb takes a non-tensed complement, and the elided verb can take either the matrix verb or the lexically realized complement verb as its antecedent. The matrix verbs in the sentences of 35), for example, are possible (and in (35b–d), the preferred) antecedents for the heads of the pseudo-gapped VPs.

(35)  a.  John will agree to complete his paper before Bill will his book.
      b.  Mary hoped to win the race more fervently than John did the baseball game.
      c.  Lucy wants to gain admission to Harvard as much as Sue does to MIT.
      d.  Max insists on visiting London more adamantly than Bill does Paris.

These cases are taken as instances of re-analysis, where the matrix verb and the complement verb are construed as components of a lexically complex verb. On this approach *promised to read* is taken as a single verb in (42).[5]

There are at least two problems with this proposal. First, the notion of re-analysis which generates complex verbs from verb-S complement structures is not specified, and so remains obscure.

Second, as Kennedy (1997) observes, matrix VPs can generally be taken as antecedents for ACE structures not separated from the matrix verb by a tensed clause, but this possibility is far more restricted and lexically conditioned in pseudo-gapping structures.

(36)  a.  John promised/expected/hoped/wanted to read every book which Mary did.
      b.  John promised/expected/hoped/wanted to complete his book before Bill did his paper.

The matrix VPs headed by *promised, expected, hoped,* and *wanted* can be taken as the antecedents of the elided VP in (36a). However, the embedded verb *complete* is the most natural antecedent for the elided verb in (36b). The fact that higher matrix VPs are freely available as

---

[4]Lasnik (1995, Forthcoming) raises additional objections to the pseudo-gapping treatment of ACE. However, it is not clear to what extent these objections really undermine the pseudo-gapping analysis. See Lappin Forthcoming for discussion of Lasnik's criticisms.

[5]Hornstein (1995) makes a similar suggestion.

antecedents for ACE constructions (subject to a tense barrier constraint) remains a significant problem for the pseudo-gapping analysis.

Cases like those in (36a) are not problematic for the proposed HPSG account. The ellipsis resolution algorithm reconstructs the feature structure of the verb which heads the higher antecedent matrix VP and the feature structure of its VP (or clausal) complement C until the point where the NP object of the embedded verb V heading C is encountered. Reconstruction of the full feature structure of this NP is blocked because of the interpretive regress, and so the CELR is applied to obtain a SLASH feature in the corresponding argument position of the SUB-CAT list of V's reconstructed counterpart. The reconstructed feature structure for (34) is (37).

(37)

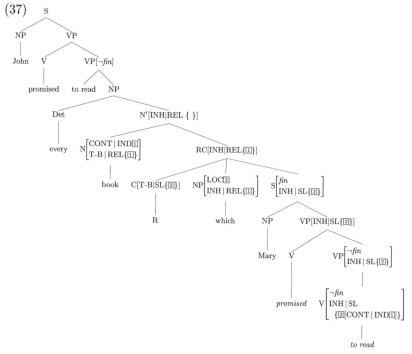

### 21.3.2.2 A Tense Constraint on ACE Antecedents

Baltin (1987), Lappin (1992, 1996), and Hornstein (1994, 1995) take tense as a barrier to the antecedence relation in an ACE structure. Either the embedded VP headed by *read* or the matrix VP headed by *expects* is a possible antecedent for the elided VP in (38a). By contrast, the embedded VP is the highly preferred antecedent in (38b).[6]

---

[6]F&M and Brody (1995) do not share this judgement, but it does seem widespread.

(38)  a.  John expected to see every play which Mary did.

     b.  John expected he would see every play which Mary did.

The tense constraint can be formulated as in (39).

(39)  In an ACE structure, the relative clause in which a reconstructed VP is contained cannot be separated from the V heading the antecedent VP by an S[*fin*].

Given (39), the contrast between (40a) and (40b) follows.

(40)  a.  Max believes everyone who Bill does to be competent.

     b.  *Max believes everyone who Bill does is competent.

In (40a) *everyone who Bill does* is either the raised object of *believes* or the subject of an infinitival complement clause. Under either analysis, the RC containing the elided VP is not separated from the matrix VP by an S[*fin*]. By contrast, in (40b) the quantified NP is the subject of a tensed complement clause, which intervenes between the RC and the head of the intended matrix VP antecedent.

### 21.3.2.3  The Vehicle Change Analysis

On Brody's (1995) view of ACE syntactic variables (A'-bound traces) can be substituted for quantified NPs in ellipsis resolution. This substitution is taken as an instance of vehicle change in the sense of F&M. The elided VP in (1a) is reconstructed *in situ*. Vehicle change applies to the reconstructed quantified NP object of *liked* to yield (41).

(41)  John $[_{\text{VP}}$ liked [the girls who$_1$ Mary did $[_{\text{VP}} [_{\text{V}}$ *like*$]$ $t_1^{var}]]]_1$.

In F&M's original formulation of vehicle change a pronoun is substituted for a referential NP. This relation of equivalence under reconstruction permits coreference between *John* and *he* in (42a), given the reconstruction of the elided VP indicated in (42b).

(42)  a.  Mary loves John$_1$, and he$_1$ wonders if Lucy does too.

     b.  Mary loves John$_1$, and he$_1$ wonders if Lucy does $[_{\text{VP}}$ *love him*$_1]$ too.

An independently referring NP ($\alpha$ expression) does not change its referential index when it is reconstructed as an $\alpha$ expression. Given F&M's assumption that A' traces are $\alpha$ terms, ACE structures with multiple elided VPs like (43a) poses a problem for Brody's analysis.

(43)  a.  Max trusts every person who Rosa does, but no one who Lucy does.

     b.  *Max trusts every person$_1$ who Rosa does $[_{\text{VP}}$ *trust* $t_1]$, but no one$_2$ who$_2$ Lucy does $[_{\text{VP}}$ *trust* $t_1]$.

If the matrix VP is the antecedent of the second elided VP in (43a), then the A'-bound trace which is substituted for *everyone who Rosa does* will retain the index of the matrix object. Therefore the reconstructed trace in the second elided VP will not be bound by the wh-phrase in its relative clause, as in (43b). Notice that this problem is not simply an artifact of the indexing procedure. If A′-bound traces are taken to be referential terms and the referential properties of an expression are preserved under reconstruction, then cases like (43a) are problematic for Brody's vehicle change analysis regardless of how the referential feature of the reconstructed trace is encoded. Given that this trace corresponds to the first quantified NP, its referential feature will not match that of the second quantified NP heading the relative clause containing the additional ACE site.

Multiple elided VPs in ACE structures are not a problem for the HPSG account. The value of a SLASH feature is unified with the LOCAL value of its filler only at the point where the filler discharges the SLASH value. Moreover, the CONT|IND value of the SLASH is unified with the CONT|IND value of the N heading the RC in which it appears. The CELR will introduce a distinct SLASH feature for each reconstructed verb heading one of the elided VPs in (43a). Each SLASH feature is discharged by the wh-phrase filler in its respective RC. Therefore the feature structure for (43a) under reconstruction is (44).

## 21.4   An Implementation of the HPSG Account

The implemented reconstruction procedure applies to the parse structures generated by an HPSG grammar developed in Erbach's (1995) ProFIT system, in which feature structure terms are compiled directly into Prolog. The grammar is used to parse sentences with a bottom up chart parser. It handles ACE structures in relative clauses modifying both verb complements and NP arguments of prepositions heading VP adjuncts.[7]

The reconstruction procedure for ACE consists of four main components.

**I.** The attribute-value matrix (AVM) of the sentence containing the ACE structure is mapped into a list of mother-daughter predicates (an mdr list), where each element of the list is of the form mdr(Mother_AVM, Relation, Dtr_AVM). The first argument of the predicate mdr is the AVM of a mother node, the third argument is the AVM of a dtr node of the first argument, and the second argument is the type of dtr relation which

---

[7]See Lappin and Gregory 1997 and Gregory 1996 for discussions of the implemented generalized ellipsis resolution algorithm of which the ACE procedure is a particular case.

(44)

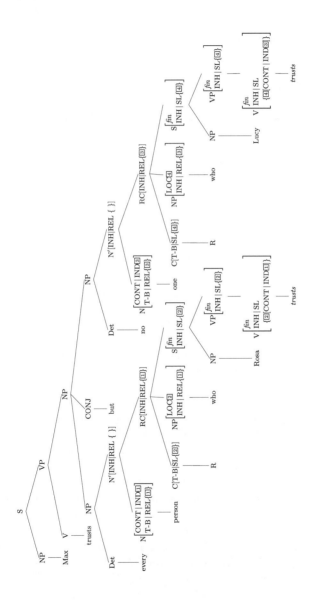

holds between them. So, for example, the rule for mdr for the case in which Relation = head_dtr is given in (45).

(45)    mdr(Mother,head_dtr,Dtr) :-
        head_dtr_of(Dtr,Mother & dtrs!head_dtr!Dtr).

The highest node of the sentence corresponds to the first argument of one (or more) members of the mdr list. This list represents the AVM of S as a transitive sequence of mother-daughter AVM's proceeding left to right to the lowest daughter AVM's of the feature structure tree. This sequence provides a convenient representation for searching the tree to identify the ellipsis site and the antecedent VP, and for reconstructing the structure containing the elided VP.

**II.** The elided VP EVP is identified as the AVM of an empty VP complement of an auxiliary verb, where EVP has a non-empty SLASH feature.

**III.** The head verb of the antecedent VP AV is identified by starting at the foot of the SLASH dependency in the EVP. The CONT|INDEX of this SLASH is shared with the CONT|INDEX of the head noun N which the relative clause containing EVP modifies. Two cases are tested. (i) If the NP which N heads is a complement of the matrix verb V, then AV is V. (ii) If the NP which N heads is the object of a preposition P heading a PP that modifies the matrix verb V', then AV is V'.

**IV.** For both case (i) and (ii) of III the RELATION feature of the CONTENT of AV is assigned to the elided head EV of EVP. In case (i) the SUBCAT feature of EV is specified as the list whose first element is identical with the subject value of the auxiliary's SUBCAT, and whose second element is unified with the SYNSEM value of an NP whose LOC value is identical to EVP's SLASH feature. EV's SLASH feature is also unified with that of EVP. In case (ii) the CONTENT features of the complements (if any) of AV and of the preposition P heading the PP adjunct of AVP are assigned to the AVM of EVP as COMP_DTRS and ADJ_DTRS, respectively. EV's SUBCAT feature is specified as including the subject value of the auxiliary, and any complements whose CONTENT values are reconstructed from AVP. The non-empty SLASH value of EVP is grounded in P, whose SUBCAT feature is defined as the list containing the SYNSEM value corresponding to this feature.

The reconstructed VP which is obtained by this procedure is substituted for EVP in the mdr list. The fully reconstructed AVM is generated by recursively replacing mother node AVM's to the left of EVP in the list until the entire list is reconstructed. The new mdr list provides the AVM of the reconstructed feature structure for the complete sentence.

(46) and (47) are (subsets of) the (truncated) reconstructed AVM's

which our procedure produces for a complement and a PP adjunct ACE structure, respectively. We have only included the (partial) AVM's for the elided VPs, where the reconstructed feature structure is highlighted in bold.

(46)   John liked the girls who Mary did.

syn!A5
   loc!cat!head!vform!<base&
   subcat![M4]&
   nloc!inher!slash![U2]&
   **dtrs!head_dtr!syn!loc!cat!subcat![M4, U2]&**
      **cont!N1&**
      **relation!<like&**
   **nloc!inher!slash![U2&**
      **loc!cat!head!case!<acc&cont!index!G1]**

(47)   John threw flowers at the girls who Bill did.

syn!S5&
   loc!cat!head!vform!<base&
   subcat![E5]&
   nloc!inher!slash![M3]&
dtrs!head_dtr!phon![]&
   syn!X7&
   **dtrs!head_dtr!syn!loc!cat!subcat![E5,V6]&**
comp_dtrs!phon![]&
   syn!V6&
   loc!cont!rest!B7&
      <flower_X ]&
adj_dtrs![phon![]&
   syn!loc!cat!head!mod!X7&
   loc!cont!A1&
      relation!<throw&
   **dtrs!head_dtr!syn!loc!cat!head!pform!Q1&**
      **<at&**
      **subcat![M3]&**
   **nloc!inher!slash![M3&**
               **case!<acc&index!Y1]**

In the AVM for (46), the HEAD-DTR of the reconstructed VP has the CONT | RELATION feature value *like*. The subject and object elements of the HEAD-DTR's SUBCAT list, M4 and U2, unify with the SYNSEM values of *Mary* and the SLASH feature value of the HEAD-DTR, respectively. The CONT|INDEX value G1 of this SLASH feature unifies with both the CONT|INDEX value of *the girls,* and the REL feature value introduced by *who* and discharged by the TO-BIND feature on *girls*.

The HEAD-DTR of the reconstructed VP in the AVM for (47) has the CONT|RELATION value *throw*, which shows up on the ADJ-DTR headed by *at*. This is due to the fact that the MOD value of the ADJ-DTR unifies with the SYNSEM value of the HEAD-DTR of the VP which the ADJ-DTR modifies. The COMP-DTR of the reconstructed VP has the CONT|RELATION value *flowers*, and the COMP-DTR's SYNSEM value V6 is unified with that of the the object element of the reconstucted HEAD-DTR's SUBCAT list. The SYNSEM value E5 of *Bill* unifies with the subject value of this list. The element of *at*'s SUBCAT list, M3, is unified with *at*'s SLASH feature value, whose CONT|INDEX Y1 is identified with the CONT|INDEX value of *the girls* and the REL value of *who*, where the latter feature value is bound off by the TO-BIND feature on *girls*.

## 21.5    Conclusion

Unlike the extraction approach, the proposed HPSG account resolves ellipsis in ACE structures through syntactic reconstruction *in situ*. Therefore, it avoids the problems of semantically vacuous covert movement, and of the copy view of traces encountered by syntactic extraction analyses.

The HPSG account captures the fact that ACE structures exhibit syntactic locality effects by virtue of the fact that reconstruction introduces a SLASH feature into the ellipsis site. These locality effects pose a difficulty for purely semantic treatments of ACE. The SLASH feature is subject to the constraints that govern NONLOCAL features, which represent unbounded dependency relations.

The proposed account provides a unified treatment of ACE in NP complements and PP adjuncts. In contrast to the pseudo-gapping theory, it allows for higher matrix VP antecedents. It covers reconstruction in multiple elided VPs within ACE constructions, which are problematic for the vehicle change approach. Finally, it applies straightforwardly to NP contained ACE structures.

The HPSG account of ACE resolution has been implemented as a reconstruction procedure that applies to the parse structures of an HPSG grammar developed in ProFIT. This procedure is a specific case of a generalized ellipsis reconstruction algorithm that applies to a variety of ellipsis structures. The algorithm has also been implemented for these ellipsis structures.

# References

Baltin, Mark R. 1987. Do Antecedent Contained Deletions Exist, *Linguistic Inquiry* 18, 579-595.

Brody, Michael. 1995. *Lexico-Logical Form: A Radically Minimalist Theory*, MIT Press, Cambridge, MA.

Chomsky, Noam. 1995. *The Minimalist Program*, MIT Press, Cambridge, MA.

Cooper, Robin. 1983. *Quantification and Syntactic Theory*, Reidel, Dordrecht.

Crouch, Richard. 1995. Ellipsis and Quantification: A Substitutional Approach, *Proceedings of the 7th Conference of the European Chapter of the Association for Computational Linguistics*, University College, Dublin, 229–336.

Dalrymple, Mary, Stuart Shieber, and Fernando Pereira. 1991. Ellipsis and Higher-Order Unification, *Linguistics and Philosophy* 14, 399–452.

Erbach, Gregor. 1995. ProFIT: Prolog with Features, Inheritance and Templates, *Proceedings of the Seventh Conference of the European Association for Computational Linguistics*, 180–187.

Fiengo, Robert, and Robert May. 1994. *Indices and Identity*, MIT Press, Cambridge, MA.

Gregory, Howard. 1996. *A ProFIT Grammar and Reconstruction Procedure for Ellipsis*, unpublished ms., School of Oriental and African Studies, University of London.

Haik, Isabelle. 1987. Bound Variables that Need to Be, *Linguistics and Philosophy* 11, 503–530.

Hornstein, Norbert. 1994. An Argument for Minimalism: The Case of Antecedent-Contained Deletion, *Linguistic Inquiry* 25, 455–480.

Hornstein, Norbert. 1995. *Logical Form*, Blackwell, Oxford.

Johnson, David E., and Shalom Lappin. 1997. A Critique of the Minimalist Program, *Linguistics and Philosophy* 20, 273–333.

Kempson, Ruth. 1996. Semantics, Pragmatics, and Natural Language Interpretation in S. Lappin, ed., 561–598.

Kempson, Ruth, and Dov Gabbay. 1993. How We Understand Sentences. And Fragments Too? in M. Cobb, ed.,*SOAS Working Papers in Linguistics and Phonetics* 3, 259–336.

Kennedy, Chris. 1997. Antecedent Contained Deletion and the Syntax of Quantification, *Linguistic Inquiry*.

Lappin, Shalom. 1992. The Syntactic Basis of Ellipsis Resolution in S. Berman and A. Hestvik, eds., *Proceedings of the Stuttgart Ellipsis Workshop*, Arbeitspapiere des Sonderforschungsbereichs 340, Bericht Nr. 29-1992, University of Stuttgart, Stuttgart.

Lappin, Shalom. 1996. The Interpretation of Ellipsis in S. Lappin (ed.), 145–175.

Lappin, Shalom, ed., 1996. *The Handbook of Contemporary Semantic Theory*, Blackwell, Oxford, 145–175.

Lappin, Shalom. Forthcoming. An HPSG Account of Antecedent Contained Ellipsis in S. Lappin and E. Benmamoun eds.

Lappin, Shalom, and Elabbas Benmamoun, eds., Forthcoming. *Fragments: Studies in Ellipsis and Gapping,* Oxford University Press, Oxford and New York.

Lappin, Shalom, and Howard Gregory. 1997. A Computational Model of Ellipsis in *Proceedings of the Conference on Formal Grammar,* ESSLLI'97, Aix-en-Provence.

Lappin, Shalom, and Michael McCord. 1990. Anaphora Resolution in Slot Grammar, *Computational Linguistics* 16, 197–212.

Lappin, Shalom, and Hsue-Hueh Shih. 1996. A Generalized Reconstruction Algorithm for Ellipsis Resolution, *Proceedings of COLING-96,* University of Copenhagen, 687–692.

Lasnik, Howard. 1993. Lectures on Minimalist Syntax, *University of Connecticut Working Papers in Linguistics,* Storrs, CT.

Lasnik, Howard. 1994. *Last Resort,* ms., University of Connecticut, Storrs, CT.

Lasnik, Howard. 1995, *A Note on Pseudo-Gapping,* ms., University of Connecticut, Storrs, CT.

Lasnik, Howard. Forthcoming. Some Puzzles about Pseudo-Gapping in S. Lappin and E. Benmamoun, eds.

May, Robert. 1985. *Logical Form: Its Structure and Derivation,* MIT Press, Cambridge, MA.

Pereira, Fernando. 1990. Categorial Semantics and Scoping, *Computational Linguistics* 16, 1–10.

Pollard, Carl, and Ivan A. Sag. 1994. *Head-Driven Phrase Structure Grammar,* University of Chicago Press, Chicago.

Sag, Ivan A. 1997. English Relative Clause Constructions, *Journal of Linguistics.*

Shieber, Stuart, Fernando Pereira, and Mary Dalrymple. 1996. Interactions of Scope and Ellipsis, *Linguistics and Philosophy* 19, pp 527–552.

# 22

# The Scope-Marking Construction in German

ANDREAS KATHOL

## 22.1 Introduction

Extractions out of embedded clauses, while more constrained than in English, are possible in many dialects of German, in particular with nonnominal fillers, such as the extracted PP *mit wem* in the matrix question in (1a) and the embedded question in (1b):

(1)  a.  **Mit wem** glaubst du [daß Jakob geredet hat]?
         with who believe you that Jakob talked has
         'Who do you believe Jakob talked with?'

     b.  Karl will    wissen
         Karl wants know

         [**mit wem** du  glaubst [daß Jakob geredet hat]].
         with who  you believe that Jakob talked has

         'Karl wants to know who you think Jakob talked with.'

Such constructions lend themselves rather straightforwardly to a treatment in terms of the analytical tools developed for parallel long-distance extraction phenomena in English, for instance by means of passing information about a "missing" constituent via the SLASH feature.

The prominent role of the English pattern in syntactic theory has for a long time obscured the fact that strong preference is given by virtually all speakers[1] to constructions in which the *wh*-phrase is only fronted within the embedded clause with a concomitant occurrence of the inter-

---

I would like to thank Paul Kay and an anonymous reviewer for helpful discussion and comments.

[1]See for instance Reis 1996, 278,n.2.

rogative pronoun *was* in an immediately superordinate clause. As with the genuine filler-gap construction in (1), both matrix and embedded construals are possible, as demonstrated in (2):

(2)  a.  **Was**  glaubst du  [**mit wem** Jakob geredet hat]?
          WHAT  believe  you  with who  Jakob  talked  has
          'Who do you think Jakob talked with?'

      b.  Karl  will     wissen
          Karl  wants  know

          [**was**   du  glaubst  [**mit wem** Jakob geredet hat]].
          WHAT  you  believe  with who  Jakob  talked  has

          'Karl wants to know who you think Jakob talked with.'

Constructions of this sort have only recently attracted serious theoretical attention (see for instance McDaniel 1989, Dayal 1994, Bayer 1996, and the papers contained in Lutz and Müller 1996.). While often referred to as *partial* Wh-*movement* in the transformational literature, they will be called (*wh*) *scope-marking* constructions here. This terminology suggests that the (highest) occurrence of the *was*-element should be viewed as a scope marker by indicating the syntactic domain that receives a question interpretation in the semantics: in (2a) the matrix sentence and in (2b) the clausal complement of *wissen*.

Except for the semantics-based approach by Dayal (1994) (also known as "indirect dependency"), theoretical accounts of this phenomenon have relied on some syntactic mechanism to establish a link between the lower *wh*-phrase and the scope marker *was* ("direct dependency"). One popular proposal (von Stechow and Sternefeld 1988, Beck and Berman 1996) has been to assume that *was* acts as an expletive and at Logical Form is replaced by a supercoindexed "real" *wh*-phrase.[2] As a result of this substitution operation, the long distance extraction cases in (1a) and the scope marking constructions in (2a) are associated with the same LF, sketched in (3):

(3)  **mit wem**$^i$ [glaubst du  [$t^i$ (daß) Jakob geredet hat]]?
     with who    believe you       that Jakob talked  has

In this paper, I will propose an analysis of the scope marking construction which, in the tradition of constraint-based grammar, rejects any syntactic level of LF and consequently does not permit the kind of syntactic manipulations underlying expletive replacement operations.[3]

---

[2] "The scope-marking element is an expletive which is replaced, in the syntactic representation that serves as input to semantic interpretation, by the wh-phrase(s) whose scope it indicates." (Beck and Berman 1996, 59)

[3] See also Höhle 1996, 50–51 for additional reasons arguing against LF movement in the analysis of this construction.

It thus follows recent work in HPSG (cf. Pollard and Yoo Forthcoming and Ginzburg and Sag 1997) that analyzes the syntax and semantics of interrogative constructions using purely constraint-based means.

I will first develop an analysis implementing a nonderivational and construction-based version of the direct dependency approach that improves in an number of ways on an earlier lexically-based proposal made in Kathol 1996. Upon discussing the shortcomings of the revised analysis, an alternative will be developed that shares some of the insights of Dayal's indirect dependency approach, albeit from a construction-based perspective.

## 22.2 A Constructional Approach to Scope Marking

For reasons of concreteness, we will adopt the version of HPSG proposed in Sag 1997 in the following, even though the gist of the analysis should carry over to other versions of the theory.

The basic idea to be pursued here is that SLASH chains need to be distinguished in terms of whether the SLASH dependency involves a (possibly) *operator-introducing* element or merely serves to *extend* the scope of a scope-bearing constituent. English-style UDC phenomena instantiate the first, whereas the linkage between scope marker and the lower *wh*-phrase in German is an example of the second. This distinction can be given content in the grammar by postulating the subtypes *s(cope)-intro* and *s(cope)-chain* for the values of the attribute LOCAL. All lexically introduced SLASH values belong to the first type. Accordingly, Sag's Complement Extraction Lexical Rule needs to be slightly adjusted as in (4b), with the subtypes of *local* listed in (4a):

(4)  a.

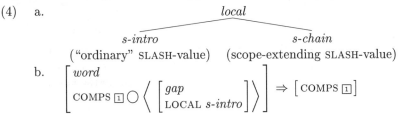

b.
$$\begin{bmatrix} word \\ \text{COMPS } \boxed{1} \bigcirc \left\langle \begin{bmatrix} gap \\ \text{LOCAL } s\text{-}intro \end{bmatrix} \right\rangle \end{bmatrix} \Rightarrow \begin{bmatrix} \text{COMPS } \boxed{1} \end{bmatrix}$$

SLASH dependencies of either kind are terminated in familiar constructions of type *filler-head-struc*, stated in (5):

(5)

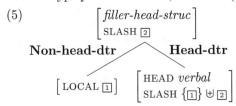

As was proposed in Sag 1997, the filler-head construction overrides the Slash Inheritance Principle, which normally requires identity in SLASH values between mother and head daughter. I suggest that German has an additional, closely related construction also overrides the Slash Inheritance Principle. While terminating one SLASH dependency, this new construction at the same time starts a new dependency. As a result, the cardinality of SLASH sets is not altered by constructions of type *scope-chain-intro-struc*.

(6)

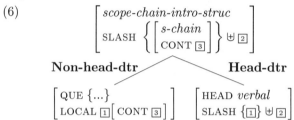

The new SLASH element bears the type specification *s(cope)-chain*. Thus, this type information directly reflects the fact that the linkage with the scope marker *was* is constructionally licensed.[4]

I postulate that the SLASH element is structure-shared with the lower filler in its CONTENT value. This has the effect that the *wh*-phrase is not interpreted at the site of its syntactic occurrence as a filler, but instead at the place where the scope marker occurs. In other words, the scope marker serves as a conduit for indicating the syntactic scope of the lower *wh*-phrase that it shares the CONTENT value with. For this to work, we need to assume that in addition to regular *was* there also exists a scope-marking variant, as outlined in (7). What distinguishes that entry from the ordinary version is, first, that it is completely underspecified in its semantic contribution, hence it unifies with whatever CONTENT value the lower *wh*-phrase provides. Second, with a LOCAL value typed as *s-chain* it can bind off a constructionally licensed SLASH dependency—in fact it is the only element in the language with that property.

(7)
$$\left[ \text{LOCAL} \begin{bmatrix} \textit{s-chain} \\ \text{CONT } \textit{nom-obj} \end{bmatrix} \right]$$

This "delayed" scope-taking of the lower *wh*-phrase is precisely what is required, for observe that none of the embedding predicates (*glauben* ('believe'), *denken* ('think'), *meinen* ('be of the opinion')) actually allows

---

[4]There is a certain conceptual similarity here with McDaniel's (1989) notion of "wh-chain"; however, while the latter is a relational concept involving traces and moved element, the type *s-chain* by necessity only applies to single *local* objects.

interrogative complements, as can be seen by the badness of examples such as the following:

(8)  *Du  glaubst  [**mit wem**  Jakob  geredet  hat].
     you  believe   with who    Jakob  talked   has

Such data strongly suggest that scope-marking predicates never take semantic questions as their complements. A number of facts follow from this. First, the unitary behavior in terms of semantic selection should ideally be correlated with a single lexical description for the predicates in question. This can be achieved by assuming that such predicates have the following lexical description for all syntactic environments.[5]

$$
(9) \quad \left[ \ldots|\text{COMPS} \; \left\langle \text{S} \left[ \begin{array}{l} \text{SLASH} \; set(local) \\ \ldots|\text{QUANTS} \; list(\neg wh\text{-}expression) \end{array} \right] \right\rangle \right]
$$

Note that the QUANTS value of the sentential complement is restricted to a (possibly empty) list of elements, none of which is a *wh*-expression. This is one way of ensuring that the complement has *propositional* semantics.[6]

Second, it is necessary that syntactic and semantic interrogativity be dissociated from each other. This point becomes relevant once we consider the constraints on the syntax-semantics interface. In particular let us consider the constraints on *wh*-quantifier retrieval, as for instance formulated by Pollard and Yoo (Forthcoming) for "'English-like' syntactic *wh*-movement languages":

(10)  A.  At any node, retrieval, if any, of *wh*-operators must include the member of the left peripheral daughter's QUE value.

      B.  At any filler-head node, if the filler has a nonempty QUE value, then its member must belong to the node's RETRIEVED value.

Clearly the second part cannot hold for German, as it would obligatorily require the lower syntactic *wh*-clause to give rise to a semantic question, hence violating the selectional restriction stated in (9). Therefore, being a syntactic interrogative is a necessary, albeit not a sufficient condition for having interrogative semantics in German.

Given these assumptions, we get the structural analysis outlined in (11) for the sentence in (2a).

---

[5] This is one of the crucial differences with the proposal made in Kathol 1996, where special lexical variants were posited for those variants of these predicates that occur in scope marking environments.

[6] An alternative is to employ type distinctions of the kind proposed by Ginzburg and Sag (1997).

(11)

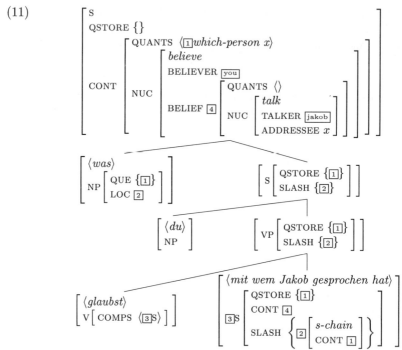

Let us now briefly consider some of the consequences of the analysis presented so far. First note that, as von Stechow and Sternefeld (1988, 355) observe, scope marking constructions obligatorily span multiple clauses. Hence the scope marker *was* cannot cooccur as a clausemate of the *wh*-expression whose scope it is supposed to indicate:

(12) ***Was** ist **wer** gekommen?
     WHAT is   who  come

This follows straightforwardly because the only way that a SLASH dependency is bound off by the scope marker (i.e., a filler typed *s-chain*) is if the structure contains an instance of (6). Since that schema crucially involves a left-peripheral filler-daughter, it also becomes immediately clear why no scope marking construal is possible in examples such as the following in which the *wh*-phrase appears in situ (from von Stechow and Sternefeld 1988, 355).

(13) ***Was** glaubst du [daß Fritz **wen** besucht hat]?
     WHAT believe you that Fritz who  visited  has

Next, consider the fact that for many speakers, no scope marker can be extracted out of a *daß*-clause, as demonstrated in (14):

(14) %**Was**   glaubst  du,
    WHAT  believe  you

    [**daß**  Karl  meint,  [**mit wem**   Jakob  gesprochen  hat]]?
    that  Karl  thinks   with whom  Jakob  talked      has

This follows if the lexical specification of *daß* is made sensitive to the origin of the SLASH dependency. In particular, *daß* only allows a (possibly empty) set of elements of type *s-intro* in its clausal complement's SLASH value, as is outlined in (15).

(15) *daß*
    $\left[\ldots|\text{COMPS}\ \langle S\left[\text{SLASH}\ set(\textit{s-intro})\right]\rangle\right]$

Only SLASH elements introduced lexically—that is in terms of the lexical rule in (4)—bear the type required by the complementizer. By contrast, any constructional introduction of the scope marker via the schema in (6) automatically results in the typing of the *local* object as *s-chain*, which is incompatible with the requirement in (15).

At the same time, however, Höhle (1996, 40), among others, reports that constructions of the type listed in (14) are indeed possible for some speakers. On our analysis such judgments can be accommodated by assuming that the typing constraint on the clause's SLASH elements does not hold for those dialects.

Besides ruling out illicit examples of long extractions of the scope marker for the majority of speakers, as in (14), our analysis also correctly predicts iterated occurrences of constructions of type *scope-chain-intro-struc*, leading to examples like (16), in which the lower occurrence of *was* terminates one SLASH dependency and initiates another:

(16) **Was**   glaubst  du,
    WHAT  believe  you

    [**was**   Karl  meint,  [**mit wem**    Jakob  gesprochen  hat]]?
    WHAT  Karl  thinks   with whom  Jakob  talked      has

    'Who do you believe that Karl thinks Jakob talked with?'

Both occurrences of *was* are licensed by the partial lexical description in (7), in which the scope marker is given a totally underspecified CONTENT. In the standard variety of German, only *was* has a LOCAL value of this type; therefore it is the only element that can terminate a constructionally induced SLASH dependency. As a result, the example in (16) gives rise to the interconnected chain of SLASH dependencies outlined in (17):

(17)

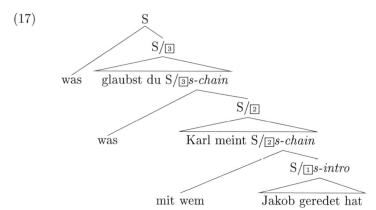

Another nontrivial consequence of our analysis is that it correctly predicts that the scope marker may occur in multiple question constructions. On the constraint-based approach taken here, multiple questions simply involve QUANTS lists with more than one *wh*-quantifier, cf. (18):

(18) a. Wer hat was gesehen?
 who has what seen
 'Who saw what?'

b. $$\begin{bmatrix} \text{QUANTS} & \langle \textit{which-person } x, \textit{ which } y \rangle \\ \text{NUC} & \begin{bmatrix} \textit{see} \\ \text{SEER } x \\ \text{SEEN } y \end{bmatrix} \end{bmatrix}$$

Importantly, there is nothing that requires that both *wh*-quantifiers are associated with a lexically sponsored SLASH element. Hence, the scope of one of the quantifiers may very well be mediated by the scope marker. This is demonstrated by the following example from Kathol 1996, 113:

(19) Was glaubst Du [**wem** Lisa **was** gegeben hat]?
 what believe you who-DAT Lisa what given has
 'Who do you think Lisa gave what?'
 which-person x which y [believe(you, gave-to(Lisa, y, x))]

Here, the initial occurrence of *was* brings about matrix scope for *wem*, occurring in the subordinate clause. At the same time, the quantifier associated with the lower interrogative pronoun *was* is passed up to the matrix level where it is retrieved.

Incidentally, while it may be tempting prima facie to think of matrix *was* as "binding" off two *wh*-chains in examples like (19), this would clearly be a misleading way of thinking about such examples. Instead, the scope marker is only connected to one *wh*-quantifier (viz. *wem*). The only way in which *was* interacts with the lower occurrence of *was* is that the first creates the *syntactic* environment—as required by (10A)—for the other quantifier to be retrieved from Q-STORE.

For many speakers (although apparently not for all, cf. Höhle 1996, 49, Beck and Berman 1996, 66), the scope marker can also act as the licensor of a multiple question whose second quantifier originates within the matrix clause. This is correctly predicted by the present account.[7]

(20)  Was  glaubt  **wer**  [**wem**   Lisa die Bücher gegeben hat]?
      what believes who   who-DAT Lisa what       given    has
      'Who thinks that Lisa gave the books to who?'
      which-person x which-person y
      [believe(y, gave-to(Lisa, the-books, x))]

One construction type that is universally rejected by all German speakers is a scope marking construction whose interrogative complement clause is an embedded yes-no question, as in (21):[8]

(21) *Was     glaubst du  [**ob**     Maria mit H. gesprochen hat]?
      WHAT believe you whether Maria with H. talked      has

This fact is again correctly predicted since the polar complementizer *ob* does not give rise to a *wh*-operator which is put in storage and which could take scope at a node higher than its overt syntactic occurrence.[9]

## 22.3   Indirect Dependency Reconsidered

The analysis presented so far requires no assumption of a syntactic level of Logical Form to account for scope-marking constructions. It is also an example of the Direct Dependency approach in that it creates a direct linkage between the scope marker and the lower "real" *wh*-phrase.

---

[7]It appears that less tolerant speakers require that interrogative environments for multiple questions be created by ordinary *wh*-phrases, i.e., those typed as *s-intro*, as opposed to *s-chain*, as in the case of the scope marker *was*.

[8]Beck and Berman (1996, 61) claim that embedded questions with initial *wieso* ('why') and *inwiefern* ('to what extent') also give rise to ungrammaticality. However, I simply disagree with the first claim and moreover would argue that cases with *inwiefern* are significantly improved by using a scalable predicate as opposed to Beck and Berman's *tanzen* ('dance'):

(i)    a.  Was    glaubst du  [wieso Maria getanzt hat]?
           WHAT believe you why    Maria danced has
           'Why do you think Maria danced?'
       b.  Was    glaubst du  [inwiefern      sie  recht hat]?
           WHAT believe you to what extent she right has
           'To what extent do you think she is right?'

[9]In order for this to work, it is necessary to assume that the complementizer is the semantic, albeit not necessarily the syntactic, head of the clause, as proposed in Kathol 1996, 109.

These two assumptions give rise to an explanatory impasse in light of the following contrast, first noted by Rizzi (1992):

(22)  a. *Was      glaubst  du   **nicht**  [mit wem   J.  gesprochen hat]?
          WHAT    believe  you  not       with who  J.  talked       has

      b.  Mit wem  glaubst  du   **nicht**  [daß  J.  gesprochen hat]?
          with who  believe  you  not       that J.  talked       has
          'Who don't you believe that Jakob talked to?'

Such examples show that negative environments seem to allow long-distance extractions without problem while disallowing the correlated scope marking variant. The solution to this "negation asymmetry" offered by Beck and Berman (1996) is to assume that LF-movement, but not S-structure movement, is barred from crossing a "negation-induced barrier". Hence their account depends on the very distinction between overt and covert syntax that is rejected in the present approach. While it may in principle be possible to reconstruct LF- vs. S-structure movement in HPSG,[10] it seems more promising to pursue an alternative route. To that end, I will abandon the central claim of the Direct Dependency approach, namely that scope marking and long-distance dependency give rise to the *same* semantic representation. In fact, this is precisely what Dayal (1994) proposes, by analyzing examples like (2) as consisting of two questions, roughly as 'what is the proposition $p$ such that you believe/think $p$ with respect to the question 'who did Jakob talked to'?'.

As Dayal (1996, 120) argues, there is a strong connection between scope-marking constructions and what she calls "sequential questions",[11] exemplified in (23a).

(23)  a.  What do you think? Who will win the match?
      b.  *What don't you think? Who is coming?

Strikingly, as (23b) shows, if the introductory question is negated, the result is unacceptable just as in (22a). Reis (1996, 263) further notes that the same pattern can be observed with German "integrated parenthetical constructions", which are distinguished from scope marking constructions by exhibiting root word order in the dependent question:

(24)  a.  Was   glaubt  Karl  [mit wem    ist  sie  verheiratet]?
          what  believes Karl  with whom  is   she  married
          'What is Karl's belief as to who she is married to?'

      b.  *Was  glaubt  keiner  [mit wem    ist  sie  verheiratet]?
          what  believes no one  with whom  is   she  married

---

[10] For instance, one may compare the projection line of *wh*-operators in terms of their occurrence in SLASH vs. Q-STORE.

[11] Cf. also Roberts' (1996) closely related notion of "strategy of inquiry" for narrowing down a discourse topic by means of a sequence of congruent questions.

Dayal's explanation for the negation asymmetry does not rely on any syntactic distinctions, but instead tries to link the observed pattern to semantic properties of the extractee which in turn are sensitive to negative environments. In the algebraic approach of Szabolcsi and Zwarts 1997, the crucial distinction is whether the domain for the *wh*-interrogative is unordered or comes with a partial order. No weak island effect arises in the former case, for instance when the quantification ranges over individuals. Other domains, such as manners or cardinalities, do have a partial order and are sensitive to negated contexts. Specifically, "propositions are ordered by entailment" (Szabolcsi and Zwarts 1997, 239), hence the unacceptability of the examples in (24b) and (23b) is precisely as is to be expected—as is that of (22a), if indeed one part of the question ranges over propositions rather than individuals only. By contrast, it is not the least bit clear how Beck and Berman's (1996) LF-based explanation should extend to those cases where the syntactic link between the two questions is more tenuous, as in (24) or even nonexistent, as in (23).

As a first attempt to make this intuition formally precise, I propose to replace the constructional introduction of a scopal chain in (6) by the schema stated in (25). Like the earlier version, this schema also allows for the constructional introduction of a SLASH dependency, thus overriding the Slash Inheritance Principle. Moreover, the type distinction between different *local* values is important to regulate whether a given dialect tolerates long extractions of the scope marker.[12] However, unlike in the earlier version, the lower *wh*-operator actually takes scope at the level of embedded clause. Concomitantly, the semantic linkage to the scope marker cannot be one of token-identity, but is somewhat less direct. Specifically, I propose that *was* ranges over propositions that answer the question expressed by the lower *wh*-clause. As a result, the embedded interrogative in scope-marking contexts is interpreted as a *proposition*, rather than a *question*. In the semantic representation, this is made explicit by means of the *answerhood* relation that relates the embedded question to possible (propositional) answers.[13]

---

[12]The term "scope marker" for the *wh*-expression in the matrix clause is slightly misleading in this context as it has the connotation of a semantically empty indicator of scope, contrary to what is assumed on the alternative analysis. For ease of reference, I will continue using it.

[13]To be consistent with standard principles of semantic composition, the constructional content should probably be stated not in terms of CONTENT by rather as C-CONT (construction content), as for instance proposed by Kathol (1997) and Copestake et al. (1997, 15). Also, note that we need to ensure that the *wh*-operator of the left-peripheral element does not make it into the Q-STORE of the mother node. How exactly this is best achieved technically will not be resolved here.

(25)

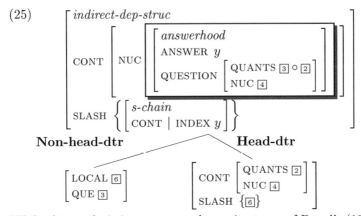

**Non-head-dtr**         **Head-dtr**

While this analysis incorporates the major tenet of Dayal's (1994) indirect dependency approach, it does not suffer from the drawbacks of the latter. In particular, as was observed earlier, Dayal's purely semantics-driven account cannot distinguish between embedded clauses that are constituent vs. polar questions, thus incorrectly predicting (21) above to be grammatical. By contrast, the present analysis rests on a strictly syntactic distinction, namely whether a SLASH dependency is licensed lexically or constructionally. That is to say, for *was* to occur in a scope-marking environment, there has to be an instance of the schema in (25) lower in the tree or else no SLASH element with the requisite type *s-chain* is present. Since subordinate polar questions are never involved in the cancellation of SLASH dependencies, the construction in (25) can never give them a propositional interpretation, hence they are semantically ineligible as complements of embedding predicates like *glauben*. Furthermore, I assume that the only way to form a question over propositions in German is by means of *was*.[14] This assumption is sufficient to ensure that the SLASH element can never be matched by expressions such as *welcher Glaube* ('which belief'), *welcher Gedanke* ('which thought'), etc.

Note further that the lexical description of the predicates in (9) carries over without any modification to the new analysis. As a result, long-distance extractions, as in (1a) will receive the same semantic representation as for the topmost node in (11) on the earlier analysis of scope marking. By contrast, the scope marking variant sentence in (2a) is now assigned the semantic representations in (26).

---

[14]See Dayal (1994, 162) for the argument that scope marking elements are universally drawn from interrogative expressions used to ask about propositions.

(26)

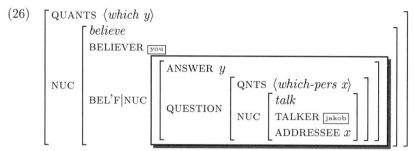

Finally, a brief comment is in order as to why in these two semantic representations appear to be equivalent in nonnegated environments. I would like to suggest that this has to do with the pragmatics of questions in general and of sequential questions in particular. So, even though the latter consist of more than one question, there nevertheless is only a single illocutionary act associated with their utterance. In particular, the introductory interrogative does not give rise to a separate question that is to be answered independently of the one following. Rather, as was noted independently by Dayal (1996, 119), only the most specific question, i.e., the one that narrows down the topic under discussion the most, is of pragmatic relevance. Consequently, it would be infelicitous to answer a question such as in (23a) in the following way:

(27) #I think that it's a little cold in here. Pete Sampras (will win the match).

However, because at the semantic level, scope marking constructions do involve a question over propositions, it is to be expected that negative contexts give rise to weak island effects.

## 22.4 Conclusion

The present proposal suggests that an adequate analysis of German scope marking constructions can only be achieved if some of the insights of the Indirect and Direct Dependency approaches are combined. From the first we take the idea that scope marking and long distance extraction result in different semantic representations. The second contributes the idea that not everything follows directly from semantics, but that syntax plays an irreducible role in this construction.

## References

Bayer, Joseph. 1996. *Directionality and Logical Form. On the Scope of Focusing Particles and Wh-in-Situ*. Vol. 34 of Studies in Natural Language and Linguistic Theory. Dordrecht: Kluwer.

Beck, Sigrid, and Stephen Berman. 1996. Wh-Scope Marking: Direct vs. Indirect Dependency. In *Papers on Wh-Scope Marking*, ed. U. Lutz and G. Müller, 59–83. No. 76 Arbeitsberichte des SFB 340. Tübingen/Stuttgart: SFB 340.

Copestake, Ann, Dan Flickinger, and Ivan A. Sag. 1997. Minimal Recursion Semantics: An Introduction. Unpubl. ms., Stanford University.

Dayal, Veneeta Srivastav. 1994. Scope Marking as Indirect *Wh*-Dependency. *Natural Language Semantics* 137–170.

Dayal, Veneeta Srivastav. 1996. Scope Marking: In Defence of Indirect Dependency. In *Papers on Wh-Scope Marking*, ed. U. Lutz and G. Müller, 105–130. No. 76 Arbeitsberichte des SFB 340. Tübingen/Stuttgart: SFB 340.

Ginzburg, Jonathan, and Ivan A. Sag. 1997. English Interrogative Constructions. Unpubl. ms., Stanford University and Hebrew University.

Höhle, Tilman. 1996. The W-...W-Construction: Appositive or Scope Indicating? In *Papers on Wh-Scope Marking*, ed. U. Lutz and G. Müller, 37–58. No. 76 Arbeitsberichte des SFB 340. Tübingen/Stuttgart: SFB 340.

Kathol, Andreas. 1996. The Syntax of *Wh*-Quantifier Retrieval. In *Language and Cognition*, ed. R. Jonkers, E. Kaan, and A. Wiegel, Vol. 5 of Yearbook of the Research Group for Theoretical and Experimental Linguistics, 101–114. Groningen: University of Groningen.

Kathol, Andreas. 1997. Concrete Minimalism of German. In *Zur Satzstruktur des Deutschen*, ed. F.-J. d'Avis and U. Lutz, 81–106. No. 90 Arbeitsberichte des SFB 340. Tübingen/Stuttgart: SFB 340.

Lutz, Uli, and Gereon Müller (ed.). 1996. *Papers on Wh-Scope Marking*. Vol. 76 of Arbeitspapieres des SFB 340. Tübingen/Stuttgart: SFB 340.

McDaniel, Dana. 1989. Partial Wh-Movement and Multiple Wh-Movement. *Natural Language and Linguistic Theory* 9.

Pollard, Carl J., and Eun Jung Yoo. Forthcoming. A Unified Theory of Scope for Quantifiers and *Wh*-Phrases. *Journal of Linguistics*.

Reis, Marga. 1996. On Was-Parentheticals and Was...W-Construction in German. In *Papers on Wh-Scope Marking*, ed. U. Lutz and G. Müller, 257–288. No. 76 Arbeitsberichte des SFB 340. Tübingen/Stuttgart: SFB 340.

Rizzi, Luigi. 1992. Argument/Adjunct (A)symmetries. In *Proceedings of the 22nd Annual Meeting of the Northeast Linguistic Society*, 365–381. Amherst: GLSA.

Roberts, Craige. 1996. Information Structure in Discourse: Towards an Integrated Formal Theory of Pragmatics. Unpublished ms., Ohio State University.

Sag, Ivan A. 1997. English Relative Clause Constructions. *Journal of Linguistics* 33(2):431–484.

von Stechow, Arnim, and Wolfgang Sternefeld. 1988. *Bausteine syntaktischen Wissens*. Opladen: Westdeutscher Verlag.

Szabolcsi, Anna, and Frans Zwarts. 1997. Weak Islands and an Algebraic Semantics for Scope Taking. In *Ways of Scope Taking*, ed. A. Szabolcsi, Vol. 65 of Studies in Linguistics and Philosophy, 217–262. Dordrecht: Kluwer.

# 23

# Lexicalization of Context

GRAHAM WILCOCK

## 23.1 Introduction

This paper proposes the lexicalization of context in HPSG. Instead of *phrasal* amalgamation of contextual information from a phrase's daughters, which is specified by the Principle of Contextual Consistency of Pollard and Sag 1994, we propose *lexical* amalgamation of context from a word's arguments by means of lexical constraints. The Principle of Contextual Consistency is replaced by a Contextual Head Inheritance Principle, in which a phrase's CONTEXT feature is token-identical to that of its contextual head daughter. We offer motivations for the proposal on theoretical, computational and linguistic levels.

The paper has three main parts. Section 23.2 shows that the proposal naturally follows other recent revisions in HPSG theory concerned with set-valued features, and brings the handling of context features into line on a theoretical level with the lexicalization of nonlocal features and of quantifier storage. Section 23.3 argues that the lexicalization of context, combined with the lexicalization of quantifier scoping, allows the idea of semantic heads to regain its original significance, which otherwise is lost when quantifier retrieval and background conditions are involved. Section 23.4 briefly sketches a linguistic analysis which combines the lexicalization of context with the lexicalization of nonlocal features, in an approach to register variation within Sag's analysis of English relative clauses.

A version of this paper was presented at the 4th International Conference on HPSG at Ithaca, NY in July 1997. The material included there on head-driven generation, which forms the main motivation on a computational level, has been transferred to another paper (Wilcock and Matsumoto To appear) which describes a computational implementation of the ideas presented here.

## 23.2 Set-Valued Features

We start by comparing two alternative approaches to the amalgamation of set-valued features: the phrasal approach of Pollard and Sag 1994 and the lexical approach of more recent proposals.

### 23.2.1 Phrasal Amalgamation

Three principles—the Nonlocal Feature Principle, the Quantifier Inheritance Principle, and the Principle of Contextual Consistency—specify constraints on certain set-valued features of a phrase and the equivalent set-valued features of the daughters. In Pollard and Sag 1994, these constraints are specified on *phrases*, that is, the values of the relevant features of all the daughters of a phrase are amalgamated by set union (possibly with subtraction of certain elements) to give the value of the relevant feature of the phrase. We therefore refer to this phrase-based amalgamation of set-valued features as *phrasal amalgamation*.

The Nonlocal Feature Principle requires each of the INHERITED features QUE, REL and SLASH of a phrase to be the set union of the equivalent feature of all the daughters, minus any elements of the equivalent TO-BIND sets of the head daughter. The Quantifier Inheritance Principle requires the QSTORE feature of a phrase to be the set union of the QSTOREs of all the daughters, minus any quantifiers in the phrase's RETRIEVED list. The Principle of Contextual Consistency simply requires the BACKGROUND feature of a phrase to be the set union of the BACKGROUND sets of all the daughters.

In recent revisions of HPSG theory, phrasal amalgamation has been divided into two distinct parts: the amalgamation part and the inheritance part. While the inheritance part is still specified by constraints on phrases, the set-valued feature amalgamation part is now specified by constraints on words.

### 23.2.2 Lexical Amalgamation

Following the proposals of Manning and Sag 1995, a word's arguments are lexically specified in its ARGUMENT-STRUCTURE (ARG-ST) list. A word's set-valued features can now be defined in terms of the amalgamation of the equivalent set-valued features of its arguments. This form of amalgamation, specified by lexical constraints, is referred to as *lexical amalgamation*.

Advantages of lexical amalgamation over phrasal amalgamation have already been proposed for nonlocal features and for quantifier storage. The lexicalization of nonlocal features is described by Sag (1997), who specifies lexical amalgamation of SLASH as in (1), where ⊎ designates disjoint set union and '−' designates contained set difference. (In these representations, the constraints specified on the right apply to the *type* specified on the left).

(1)    SLASH Amalgamation Constraint:

$$word \rightarrow \begin{bmatrix} \text{BIND} & \boxed{0} \\ \text{ARG-ST} & \left\langle \left[\text{SLASH } \boxed{1}\right], \ldots, \left[\text{SLASH } \boxed{n}\right] \right\rangle \\ \text{SLASH} & (\boxed{1} \uplus \ldots \uplus \boxed{n}) - \boxed{0} \end{bmatrix}$$

This allows a simplification of the mechanism for inheriting SLASH values. Sag states a new SLASH Inheritance Principle (SLIP) as phrasal constraint (2), where *hd-nexus-ph* is the head-nexus-phrase type from Sag's phrase type hierarchy and '/' indicates a default value. The combination of (1) and (2) means that a phrase inherits the SLASH values of its daughters indirectly, via the head daughter.

(2)    SLASH Inheritance Principle (SLIP):

$$hd\text{-}nexus\text{-}ph \rightarrow \begin{bmatrix} \text{SLASH} & / & \boxed{1} \\ \text{HD-DTR} & \left[\text{SLASH } \boxed{1}\right] \end{bmatrix}$$

Sag also introduces lexical amalgamation of QUE and REL, and a *Wh*-Inheritance Principle (WHIP) in which QUE and REL are inherited via a phrase's head daughter. The combination of SLIP and WHIP replaces the Nonlocal Feature Principle of Pollard and Sag 1994.

The lexicalization of quantifier scoping is very similar. Following the proposals of Pollard and Yoo 1995, QSTORE is a local feature which can be included in the features subcategorized for by a lexical head, and can therefore be lexically amalgamated in that head. These proposals have been extended to include lexicalization of quantifier retrieval by Manning et al. (To appear), who specify a Quantifier Amalgamation Constraint (actually a constraint on word stems) as in (3), where $\boxed{0}$ is the set of retrieved quantifiers.

(3)    Quantifier Amalgamation Constraint:

$$stem \rightarrow \begin{bmatrix} \text{ARG-ST} & \left\langle \left[\text{QSTORE } \boxed{1}\right], \ldots, \left[\text{QSTORE } \boxed{n}\right] \right\rangle \\ \text{QSTORE} & (\boxed{1} \uplus \ldots \uplus \boxed{n}) - \boxed{0} \\ \text{CONT} & \left[\text{QUANTS } \text{order}(\boxed{0})\right] \end{bmatrix}$$

Given the Quantifier Amalgamation Constraint, unscoped quantifiers are no longer inherited from all daughters but only from the semantic head daughter. This is stated in (4) as a revised Quantifier Inheritance Principle (QUIP).

(4)   Quantifier Inheritance Principle (QUIP):

$$hd\text{-}nexus\text{-}ph \rightarrow \begin{bmatrix} \text{QSTORE} & / & \boxed{1} \\ \text{HD-DTR} & \left[\text{QSTORE } \boxed{1}\right] \end{bmatrix}$$

$$hd\text{-}adjunct\text{-}ph \rightarrow \begin{bmatrix} \text{QSTORE} & / & \boxed{1} \\ \text{ADJ-DTR} & \left[\text{QSTORE } \boxed{1}\right] \end{bmatrix}$$

### 23.2.3   Lexicalization of CONTEXT

We now propose the lexicalization of contextual features, following the same approach as the lexicalization of nonlocal features and the lexicalization of quantifier scoping. For the set-valued feature BACKGROUND (BACKGR), we introduce the Background Amalgamation Constraint (5), in which a word's BACKGR set is the set union[1] of the BACKGR sets of its arguments.

(5)   Background Amalgamation Constraint:

$$\begin{bmatrix} \text{ARG-ST} & \left\langle \left[\text{BACKGR } \boxed{1}\right],\ldots,\left[\text{BACKGR } \boxed{m}\right] \right\rangle \\ \text{BACKGR} & \boxed{1} \cup \ldots \cup \boxed{m} \end{bmatrix}$$

Amalgamation of CONTEXTUAL-INDICES (C-INDICES) depends on how they are defined. As Pollard and Sag (1994) say, "each part of an utterance (at least each lexeme) has its own C-INDICES value." This suggests set-valued C-INDICES, amalgamated in phrases by set union. However, as Pollard and Sag also say, it is typical of discourse situations that the contextual indices are uniform throughout an utterance. In a coarse-grained analysis, a phrase's C-INDICES can be simply the *unification* of the C-INDICES of its daughters. The same simplification could be specified by the lexical constraint (6), in which a word's C-INDICES feature is the unification of the C-INDICES of its arguments.

(6)   Lexical Amalgamation of C-INDICES (simplified version):

$$word \rightarrow \begin{bmatrix} \text{ARG-ST} & \left\langle \left[\text{C-INDS } \boxed{1}\right],\ldots,\left[\text{C-INDS } \boxed{1}\right] \right\rangle \\ \text{C-INDS} & \boxed{1} \end{bmatrix}$$

If a more fine-grained analysis is required, the C-INDICES should be set-valued. For a single word the indices will usually be singleton sets, but for phrases these sets need to be amalgamated by set union. The

---

[1] Here, set union should not be disjoint. There may be duplicate conditions with the same index in examples such as *She saw herself.*

three standard indices of Pollard and Sag 1994 then need to be specified
by separate constraints, as in (7)

(7)  Lexical Amalgamation of C-INDICES (set-valued version):

$$word \rightarrow \begin{bmatrix} \text{ARG-ST} \left\langle \left[\text{SPEAKER } \boxed{1}\right], \ldots, \left[\text{SPEAKER } \boxed{m}\right] \right\rangle \\ \text{SPEAKER} \quad \boxed{1} \cup \ldots \cup \boxed{m} \end{bmatrix}$$

$$word \rightarrow \begin{bmatrix} \text{ARG-ST} \left\langle \left[\text{ADDRESSEE } \boxed{1}\right], \ldots, \left[\text{ADDRESSEE } \boxed{m}\right] \right\rangle \\ \text{ADDRESSEE} \quad \boxed{1} \cup \ldots \cup \boxed{m} \end{bmatrix}$$

$$word \rightarrow \begin{bmatrix} \text{ARG-ST} \left\langle \left[\text{U-LOC } \boxed{1}\right], \ldots, \left[\text{U-LOC } \boxed{m}\right] \right\rangle \\ \text{U-LOC} \quad \boxed{1} \cup \ldots \cup \boxed{m} \end{bmatrix}$$

Given the lexical amalgamation of BACKGR and C-INDICES, their
values can be passed up to higher levels by a new Contextual Head Inheritance Principle (CHIP), in which a phrase's CONTEXT is by default
token-identical to that of its *contextual head* daughter. We will assume
that contextual heads are defined in the same way as semantic heads: in
a head-adjunct-phrase the adjunct daughter is the contextual head, and
in a head-nexus-phrase the syntactic head is the contextual head. The
principle is stated in (8).

(8)  Contextual Head Inheritance Principle (CHIP):

$$hd\text{-}nexus\text{-}ph \rightarrow \begin{bmatrix} \text{CONTEXT} \quad / \quad \boxed{1} \\ \text{HD-DTR} \left[\text{CONTEXT } \boxed{1}\right] \end{bmatrix}$$

$$hd\text{-}adjunct\text{-}ph \rightarrow \begin{bmatrix} \text{CONTEXT} \quad / \quad \boxed{1} \\ \text{ADJ-DTR} \left[\text{CONTEXT } \boxed{1}\right] \end{bmatrix}$$

The combination of (5) and (8) ensures that a phrase inherits the
BACKGR values of its daughters, not directly but via the contextual
head daughter. This combination replaces the Principle of Contextual
Consistency of Pollard and Sag 1994.

## 23.3  Semantic Heads

We now link the lexicalization of context to the role of semantic heads in
head-driven grammar. Though HPSG is fundamentally head-driven by
*syntactic* heads, it is also to a secondary degree head-driven by *semantic*
heads. The definition of semantic head in Pollard and Sag 1994 is clear:
in head-adjunct phrases the adjunct is the semantic head, and in other

headed phrases the syntactic head is the semantic head. The definition is intended to work together with the Semantics Principle, so that the major semantic features of a phrase are inherited from the semantic head, while the major syntactic features are inherited from the syntactic head by the Head Feature Principle.

In Pollard and Sag 1994, when an NP is assigned as an argument of a verb, only the NP's index is directly assigned to the verb's content. Other semantic features from the NP are distributed to other features of the VP by phrasal amalgamation. If the NP is a quantificational NP, its unscoped quantifiers are added to the VP's QSTORE. If the NP is non-quantificational (a pronoun or proper noun), its background conditions are added to the VP's BACKGR. In both cases, which we will look at in turn, the VP includes major semantic features which it does *not* inherit from the verb which is its semantic head according to the definition. In effect, phrasal amalgamation "by-passes" the semantic head, which loses its intended significance.

### 23.3.1   Quantificational-Semantic Heads

The original form of the Semantics Principle in Pollard and Sag 1994, Chapter 1, equates semantic content with the CONTENT feature and simply says that a phrase has the same CONTENT as its semantic head. However, the principle is reformulated in Chapter 8 to cater for quantifier storage and retrieval, because only scoped quantifiers are included in the QUANTS list within CONTENT, while unscoped quantifiers are stored in the QSTORE set which is not part of CONTENT. In this approach to quantifier scoping, a quantifier may be retrieved from storage at any suitable syntactic node. A quantifier retrieved at a particular node is a member of the QSTORE set, but not the QUANTS list, of a daughter of that node, and due to the retrieval it is a member of the QUANTS list, but not the QSTORE set, of the mother node. As QUANTS is part of CONTENT, the effect of retrieval is that the phrase and the semantic head have different CONTENT values.

The reformulated Semantics Principle therefore makes a distinction between *quantificational* content and *nuclear* content, and requires only nuclear content (the NUCLEUS feature) to be shared between a VP and its head verb. This clearly reduces the significance of semantic heads. Though the verb is the semantic head according to the definition, it only passes one part of its semantic content up to the phrase.

In the lexicalized approach to quantifier scoping, with the Quantifier Amalgamation Constraint (3), this problem does not arise. Retrieval is located in the lexicon, inside the verb's lexical entry, and does not cause a difference in either QSTORE or QUANTS between a VP and its head verb. The phrase and the semantic head have identical QSTORE, identical QUANTS and identical NUCLEUS.

The identity of QUANTS and NUCLEUS between a phrase and its semantic head is full identity of CONTENT. We can therefore return to the original form of the Semantics Principle, in which a phrase inherits the full CONTENT of the semantic head. We restate this, renamed as the Semantic Head Inheritance Principle (SHIP) in the style of QUIP and CHIP in (9).

(9)    Semantic Head Inheritance Principle (SHIP):

$$hd\text{-}nexus\text{-}ph \rightarrow \begin{bmatrix} \text{CONTENT} & / & \boxed{1} \\ \text{HD-DTR} & \begin{bmatrix} \text{CONTENT} & \boxed{1} \end{bmatrix} \end{bmatrix}$$

$$hd\text{-}adjunct\text{-}ph \rightarrow \begin{bmatrix} \text{CONTENT} & / & \boxed{1} \\ \text{ADJ-DTR} & \begin{bmatrix} \text{CONTENT} & \boxed{1} \end{bmatrix} \end{bmatrix}$$

The identity of QSTORE between a phrase and its semantic head was stated earlier as a revised Quantifier Inheritance Principle (QUIP) in Section 23.2.2. The combination of SHIP and QUIP means that a phrase inherits all of its nuclear and quantificational content from the semantic head.

### 23.3.2    Contextual-Semantic Heads

Non-quantificational NPs such as pronouns or proper nouns generally have contextual background conditions. The way these are handled parallels the way a quantificational NP's unscoped quantifiers are handled. In both cases, only the NP's index is assigned to the verb's NUCLEUS. With phrasal amalgamation, a phrase inherits background conditions as well as unscoped quantifiers from all daughters. In general therefore, a phrase and its semantic head will have the same NUCLEUS feature but will have different BACKGR and QSTORE features.

Figure 1 shows the standard analysis of *She saw Kim* with phrasal amalgamation. *She* has a non-empty contextual BACKGR set (shown by tag $\boxed{4}$), stating a pragmatic requirement that the referent is female. This background condition is passed up from NP to S by the Principle of Contextual Consistency. Similarly, *Kim* has a background condition (shown by tag $\boxed{5}$) that the referent bears this name. This condition is also passed from NP to VP, and from VP to S.

As there are no quantifiers, V is the semantic head of VP and VP is the semantic head of S not merely by definition but also in the sense of the original Semantics Principle, since S, VP and V all share the same CONTENT (shown by tag $\boxed{1}$). However, VP includes the BACKGR con-

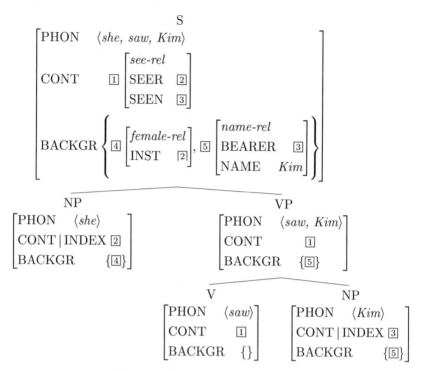

FIGURE 1 Contextual Background (Phrasal Amalgamation)

dition shown by tag ⑤ which it does not inherit from V, and S includes the BACKGR condition shown by tag ④ which it does not inherit from VP. If semantic features are understood in a wider sense, not restricted to the CONTENT feature, then in both cases the phrase includes a major semantic feature which is not inherited from its semantic head.

With lexical amalgamation, by contrast, the BACKGR sets of *she* and *Kim* are amalgamated in the verb's lexical entry by the Background Amalgamation Constraint (5). So the empty BACKGR set of *saw* in Figure 1 is changed from BACKGR {} to BACKGR {④, ⑤}. This set is inherited by VP from V and by S from VP by the Contextual Head Inheritance Principle (8). Since the contextual heads and the semantic heads are the same, all major semantic features (nuclear, quantifica- tional and contextual) are inherited via the semantic heads. In this way, semantic heads play a full role in the organization of the grammar.

### 23.3.3 Semantic Head-Driven Generation

The role of semantic heads is clear in semantic head-driven generation, which requires the identity of logical forms between phrases and their semantic heads. Though logical form is not a separate level in HPSG, we could use a logical form consisting of CONTENT, QSTORE and CONTEXT. These features are all needed to include sufficient information for generation. In order to achieve the required identity of logical forms between phrases and semantic heads, we need to combine lexicalization of quantifier scoping and lexicalization of context, so that SHIP ensures identity of CONTENT, QUIP ensures identity of QSTORE, and CHIP ensures identity of CONTEXT, as shown in (10).

(10)   SHIP + QUIP + CHIP:

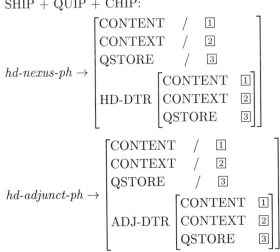

An alternative logical form with unscoped quantifiers and contextual factors is Minimal Recursion Semantics (MRS, Copestake et al. 1997). However, the reformulation of the Semantics Principle proposed by Copestake et al. greatly reduces the significance of semantic heads. MRS is therefore more suitable for non-head-driven generation. Head-driven generation would require lexical amalgamation of LISZT.[2]

## 23.4   Register Variation

To introduce the lexicalization of context in linguistic analysis, we now briefly sketch a simple approach to register variation. We combine the lexicalization of context with the lexicalization of nonlocal features.

---

[2]Different approaches to generation with HPSG are discussed by Wilcock (To appear). The need for lexicalization of context in semantic head-driven generation is described by Wilcock and Matsumoto (To appear).

To keep a representation for register variation as simple as possible, we assume that CONTEXT has an additional attribute REGISTER (REGSTR), with value of sort *register*, which has only two subsorts, *formal* and *informal*. To maintain the lexical amalgamation of context, we introduce a Register Amalgamation Constraint (11).

(11)  Register Amalgamation Constraint:

$$
word \rightarrow \begin{bmatrix} \text{ARG-ST} \ \left\langle \begin{bmatrix} \text{REGSTR} \ \boxed{1} \end{bmatrix}, \ldots, \begin{bmatrix} \text{REGSTR} \ \boxed{1} \end{bmatrix} \right\rangle \\ \text{REGSTR} \quad \boxed{1} \end{bmatrix}
$$

The combination of the Register Amalgamation Constraint and the Contextual Head Inheritance Principle (8) ensures that a phrase inherits the REGSTR values of its daughters via the contextual head daughter. In the same style as (6) for C-INDICES, this representation does not cater for register-switching, but assumes that register will typically be uniform throughout an utterance.

### 23.4.1  Relative Pronouns

In his revised analysis of English relative clauses (1997), Sag argues for treating relative *that* as a pronominal, rather than a complementizer, as the only real obstacle is that it disallows pied piping (12a), and this property is shared with relative *who* (12b) in many varieties of English.

(12)  a.  *The person [with that we were talking] ...
       b.  *The person [with who we were talking] ...
       c.  The person [with whom we were talking] ...

Observing that in such varieties the only pied-piped relative pronouns are *whose*, *which* and *whom* (12c), Sag comments that "the constraints on this variation have to do with case assignment, register restrictions, or both". We will look at two ways of specifying such constraints, first as clausal constraints, and then as lexical constraints.

We begin by noting that, while *whom* (13) is always accusative and formal, there appears to be systematic covariation of case assignment and register restrictions in *who* and *that*. Relative *who* is either nominative and unrestricted (REGSTR value *register*) as in (14) or accusative and informal as in (15). The same covariation seems to occur in relative *that*, and also in interrogative *who*.

(13)  *whom* (accusative):

$$\begin{bmatrix} \text{PHON} & \langle whom \rangle \\ \text{CAT} & \text{NP}[acc] \\ \text{REGSTR} & formal \end{bmatrix}$$

(14)  *who* (nominative):

$$\begin{bmatrix} \text{PHON} & \langle who \rangle \\ \text{CAT} & \text{NP}[nom] \\ \text{REGSTR} & register \end{bmatrix}$$

(15)  *who* (accusative):

$$\begin{bmatrix} \text{PHON} & \langle who \rangle \\ \text{CAT} & \text{NP}[acc] \\ \text{REGSTR} & informal \end{bmatrix}$$

### 23.4.2  Clausal Constraints

Nonsubject relative clauses such as *whose bagels I like* and *from whom I bought these bagels* are treated by Sag in terms of a single construction type *fin-wh-fill-rel-cl*. He hints that the constraints on this type have more work to do than the simplified formulation shown in (16), which states only that the filler daughter must be an NP or a PP.

(16)  $fin\text{-}wh\text{-}fill\text{-}rel\text{-}cl \rightarrow \begin{bmatrix} \text{FILLER-DTR} & \begin{bmatrix} \text{HEAD } noun \lor prep \end{bmatrix} \end{bmatrix}$

We can associate register restrictions with construction types. For example, a relative clause with a PP filler such as (12c) is formal. We could specify this by splitting the construction type (16) into two distinct subtypes *fin-wh-np-fill-rel-cl* (17) and *fin-wh-pp-fill-rel-cl* (18).

(17)  $fin\text{-}wh\text{-}np\text{-}fill\text{-}rel\text{-}cl \rightarrow \begin{bmatrix} \text{FILLER-DTR} & \begin{bmatrix} \text{HEAD } noun \end{bmatrix} \end{bmatrix}$

(18)

$$fin\text{-}wh\text{-}pp\text{-}fill\text{-}rel\text{-}cl \rightarrow \begin{bmatrix} \text{FILLER-DTR} & \begin{bmatrix} \text{HEAD } prep \\ \text{REGSTR } formal \end{bmatrix} \end{bmatrix}$$

Now we can describe the constraints in (12). In (12a) and (12b), *with* assigns accusative case to its arguments *who* and *that*. Given that accusative *who* is informal register in (15), the Register Amalgamation Constraint unifies its informal register with that of *with*. The value *informal* is then passed up to the PP by CHIP (8). The *formal* register restriction in (18) would then prevent the *informal* PP from being the filler of a relative clause. The clausal constraint would in this way block examples (12a) and (12b) but allow (12c) as required.

### 23.4.3 Lexical Constraints

It could be argued that the PP *with who* in (12b) is both formal and informal. That is, it violates some constraints on case and register consistency. These constraints should apply at the level of the PP, not only at the higher level of the relative clause in (18).

This could be done by specifying PP construction subtypes, putting the register restrictions on them instead of on relative clause subtypes. However, we will explore the lexicalization of context and the lexicalization of nonlocal features to show that the same result can be produced by lexical constraints. We specify systematic covariation between register and nonlocal features of prepositions. These covariations are stated in (19)–(21) as constraints on lexical subtypes.

(19)
$$\textit{rel-prep} \rightarrow \begin{bmatrix} \text{HEAD} & \textit{prep} \\ \text{QUE} & \{\} \\ \text{REL} & \{\boxed{1}\} \\ \text{SLASH} & \{\} \\ \text{REGSTR} & \textit{formal} \end{bmatrix}$$

(20)
$$\textit{que-prep} \rightarrow \begin{bmatrix} \text{HEAD} & \textit{prep} \\ \text{QUE} & \{\boxed{1}\} \\ \text{REL} & \{\} \\ \text{SLASH} & \{\} \\ \text{REGSTR} & \textit{formal} \end{bmatrix}$$

(21)
$$\textit{slash-prep} \rightarrow \begin{bmatrix} \text{HEAD} & \textit{prep} \\ \text{QUE} & \{\} \\ \text{REL} & \{\} \\ \text{SLASH} & \{\boxed{1}\} \\ \text{REGSTR} & \textit{informal} \end{bmatrix}$$

Lexical constraint (19) requires prepositions with non-empty REL to have formal register. Similarly, (20) requires prepositions with non-empty QUE to have formal register. By contrast, (21) requires prepositions with non-empty SLASH to have informal register. Prepositions whose nonlocal features are all empty have no register restriction.

The point of (19) is that it requires a *rel-prep* preposition to take as argument a relative pronoun which is formal. The non-empty REL requires the argument to be a relative pronoun, as its REL value is acquired by lexical amalgamation of nonlocal features. The *formal* register requires the argument also to be formal, as its REGSTR value is acquired by lexical amalgamation of context.

### 23.4.4 Interaction of Constraints

We can see in (22) and (23) how the lexical constraints, interacting with the lexicalization of nonlocal features and the lexicalization of context, provide an alternative way to block *with who* at PP level, while allowing *with whom*, as required.

(22)

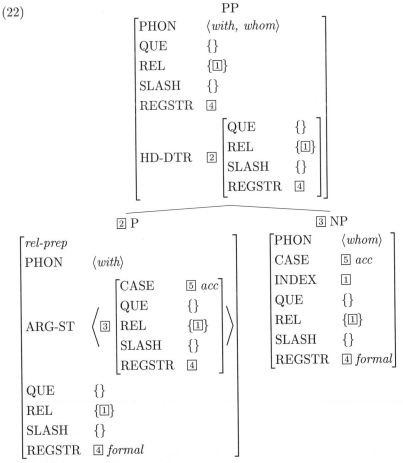

In (22), *with* assigns accusative case to its argument *whom*, which is lexically specified as accusative in (13) anyway. The SLASH Amalgamation Constraint requires *with* to amalgamate the non-empty REL of *whom* in its own REL. As the preposition has thereby a non-empty

REL, constraint (19) requires it to have formal register. As *whom* is lexically specified as formal register in (13), the Register Amalgamation Constraint simply requires the two formal registers to be unified.

(23)                                                    *PP

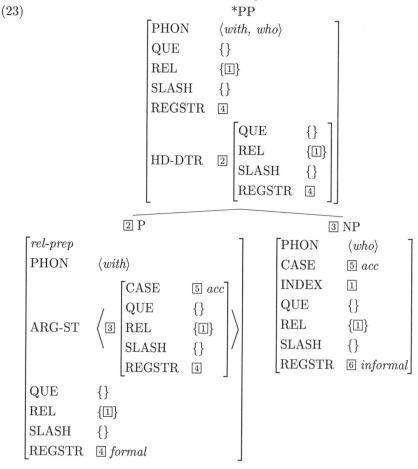

In (23), *with* also assigns accusative case to its argument *who*. Lexical constraint (15) thereby requires accusative *who* to have ⑥ *informal* register. As in (22), the SLASH Amalgamation Constraint requires *with* to amalgamate the non-empty REL of *who* in its own REL, and as the preposition has thereby a non-empty REL, constraint (19) requires it to have ④ formal register. The Register Amalgamation Constraint is therefore violated, as the informal register of accusative *who* cannot be unified with the formal register of *rel-prep with*.

## 23.5 Conclusion

We have proposed the lexicalization of context in HPSG, giving three motivations. On a theoretical level, it naturally follows other recent revisions in HPSG theory concerned with set-valued features, bringing contextual features into line with the lexicalization of nonlocal features and the lexicalization of quantifier scoping. Combining lexicalization of context and lexicalization of quantifier scoping restores and enhances the role of semantic heads in head-driven grammar (which is significant on a computational level for semantic head-driven generation). Finally, the lexicalization of context may be exploited in the development of constraint-based lexicalist approaches in linguistic analysis, as suggested in a brief sketch of lexical constraints on case assignment and register variation in English relative clauses.

## Acknowledgements

This paper was written as a visiting researcher of Sharp Corporation at UMIST, England and at NAIST, Japan. I am grateful to Mr Yoshikazu Nakagawa (Sharp), Prof Jun-ichi Tsujii (UMIST) and Prof Yuji Matsumoto (NAIST) for making this possible. I also thank the anonymous reviewers and Kristiina Jokinen for their comments on earlier drafts.

## References

Copestake, Ann, Dan Flickinger, and Ivan Sag. 1997. Minimal Recursion Semantics: An Introduction. Ms. Stanford University.

Manning, Christopher, and Ivan A. Sag. 1995. Dissociations between Argument Structure and Grammatical Relations. Paper presented at the Tübingen HPSG workshop.

Manning, Christopher, Ivan A. Sag, and Masayo Iida. To appear. The Lexical Integrity of Japanese Causatives. In *Readings in Modern Phrase Structure Grammar*, ed. R. Levine and G. Green. Cambridge University Press.

Pollard, Carl, and Ivan A. Sag. 1994. *Head-Driven Phrase Structure Grammar*. CSLI Publications and University of Chicago Press.

Pollard, Carl, and Eun Jung Yoo. 1995. Quantifiers, *Wh*-Phrases and a Theory of Argument Selection. Paper presented at the Tübingen HPSG workshop.

Sag, Ivan A. 1997. English Relative Clause Constructions. *Journal of Linguistics* 33(2):431–484.

Wilcock, Graham. To appear. Approaches to Surface Realization with HPSG. *9th International Workshop on Natural Language Generation*. Niagara-on-the-Lake, Ontario, August 1998.

Wilcock, Graham, and Yuji Matsumoto. To appear. Head-Driven Generation with HPSG. *17th International Conference on Computational Linguistics (COLING-98)*. Montreal, Quebec, August 1998.

# Name Index

# Subject Index